NEW LLANTHONY ABBEY

FRONTISPIECE

The abbey church, monastery and Plas Genevieve c1890. The barn in which the brothers spent their first six months at New Llanthony is the upper of the two stone buildings to the right of the monastery.

NEW LLANTHONY ABBEY

FATHER IGNATIUS'S MONASTERY AT CAPEL-Y-FFIN

HUGH ALLEN

Hugh Allen

PETERSCOURT PRESS

In memory of

WILFRED IDRIS DAVIES
1919-2011

and

HELEN ELIZABETH DAVIES
1931-2014

'. . . *Keeping house*
In a cloud of witnesses'

(Waldo Williams: *What is Man?*)

FRONT COVER PHOTO

The Llanthony community c1885, grouped in front of the unfinished abbey church. Picture by John Stabb of Torquay (1865-1917), chiefly remembered for his three volumes of *Some Old Devon Churches*. He was a keen Anglo-Catholic, and also produced photographs of London street scenes. Fr Ignatius stands second right holding what is perhaps a descendant of one of the Infant Oblate's famously flea-ridden cats; the dark-haired monk two away from him is his protégé Brother David (William Leycester Lyne, né Pritchard). To the right the edge of the corrugated iron convent is just visible behind the enclosed staircase by which the monks gained access to the church.

Contents

FOREWORD

To the traditional historian of the Welsh church, the fact that Joseph Leycester Lyne chose to settle his monastic community in the hills of south-east Wales presents a complete anomaly. We are used to thinking of Wales as a country dominated by protestant nonconformity. Our national identity is defined by the culture of the chapel, the preaching festival and the *gymanfa ganu*.

But this is to ignore much of the history of the church in Wales. The legend of an independent Celtic church in opposition to Rome was just that, a legend, invented by Elizabethan Protestant historians. Wales was a wholehearted member of the western Catholic communion for the best part of a millennium. After the Reformation, Catholicism was the Welsh nonconformity of choice for over a century: but more than that, Wales was marked by a combination of traditionalism and loyalism which made it a fruitful home for the ideas of men like William Laud (bishop of St David's before his elevation to Canterbury). Lyne may not have been aware of this long history of Anglican traditionalism when he chose Llanthony for the home of his religious community but he was certainly responding to the valley's long history of monastic seclusion.

The landscape of the Hoddni valley undoubtedly added to Father Ignatius's own charisma and for a short time made his little community a focus of Anglo-Catholic piety. Since they left, the buildings they erected there have attracted spiritual and artistic communities including the very idiosyncratic family of Eric Gill. The ruins of the monastic church are now on the local tourist circuit but there is much more to them, as Hugh Allen's work makes abundantly clear. He has for some years been a leading member of the Father Ignatius Memorial Trust and one of the leaders of the annual pilgrimage to the abbey church. He brings this personal involvement as well as detailed academic research and analysis to his study.

Madeleine Gray
Professor of Ecclesiastical History
University of South Wales

INTRODUCTION

'LLANTHONY TERTIA'

I N 1958 I WAS TEN YEARS OLD, and a pupil at a Catholic boarding school in rural Monmouthshire. At Parents' Weekend that summer term I was taken by a friend and his family for a drive to nearby places of interest. They were keen on antiquities, so we saw Raglan Castle and White Castle, Abbey Dore church amid the pastures of the Golden Valley, and Llanthony Priory in a valley with proper mountains on either side of it. Here at the hotel formed from the living quarters of the thirteenth century Austin Canons ('Llanthony Prima'; 'Secunda' was on the outskirts of Gloucester, where they took refuge from the marauding Celts) I think we stopped for tea. Our last port of call was four miles further on at Capel-y-ffin ('chapel at the end'). Here, perched on the side of the mountain, was a collection of run-down and slightly sinister-looking Victorian Gothic buildings beside the ruins of a church. The height of its surviving walls suggested it had been planned to be as imposing as the one at the Priory down the valley, although it had evidently been much smaller. It was in fact intended to be an exact replica, but in the event only the easternmost three bays were built.

The notice on the gate warned that the walls were still falling, but we picked our way among the saplings and mounds of rubble to a small clearing at the foot of where the altar steps had once been. Here, marked by a broken tiled cross, was the grave of the man who had built the church. According to the Latin inscription at the foot of his grave he was IGNATIUS OF JESUS, FOUNDER AND FIRST ABBOT OF THIS HOUSE and had died a few months short of fifty years before: the adjacent structure had evidently been intended to house a community of monks.

My school was run by Dominican friars, so I knew something about what is technically known as the Religious Life. My friend's parents, however, explained that 'Ignatius of Jesus' wasn't (in the generally accepted sense) a Catholic monk, but a clergyman who in the wake of the then burgeoning Anglo-Catholic revival had decided to found a Benedictine community in the nineteenth century Church of England.

In this attempt Fr Ignatius – born Joseph Leycester Lyne in the year of Victoria's accession – is generally held to have been unsuccessful: disastrously so, according to most commentators. If he had the inspiration to introduce monasticism into the Anglican Church he certainly didn't have what it took to preside over the day-to-day life of a monastic community. This was partly a matter of temperament. He had the vision to launch the project, but neither insight nor patience to make the best of the (not always particularly promising) human material that came his way. And if any of the people he recruited had been equipped mentally and spiritually for the office of Deputy Superior it is unlikely he would have made full use of them: the history of his relations with Mother Hilda at Feltham shows that delegation and the sharing of power were not characteristics that came to him naturally.

His failure was also the result of his own unavoidable ignorance and inexperience. At the age of twenty-four he clothed himself in the habit,[1] and as he later put it 'So I became a Benedictine'[2] – complete and ready-made, impatient to launch himself and his idea on to the world. And because of his semi-detached relationship with his own community he expected those who joined it to make their own way much as he had done, coming down on them like a ton of bricks when they got it wrong, but rarely at their side to direct or encourage them.

---

[1] The Benedictine habit, but with the addition of the Franciscan rosary, knotted cord and sandals (and no socks)

[2] *Autobiography of Rev. Father Ignatius OSB* (sixteen-page pamphlet published from Llanthony Abbey c1890), p8

The amount of time he spent away from 'New Llanthony' was a major handicap. For months at a time he would leave his monastic subjects with neither proper oversight nor sacramental ministrations while he raised money for his new foundation by doing the one thing he was really good at: travelling up and down the country preaching evangelistic missions. These almost always took place in hired halls, Ignatius having been banned from preaching in their churches by most Church of England bishops. Ticket sales, retiring collections and the bookstall of his tracts and reprinted sermons combined to bring in a tidy sum, as did the jewellery which lady congregants were in the habit of stripping from their persons and putting into the plate, although a number of these trinkets ended up decorating the tabernacle on the high altar of his abbey church. When not 'on the mission' he would be recovering from the resultant mental and physical exertion by taking little holidays or resting in his remote eyrie at the head of the staircase in the west wing of the monastery: at Llanthony he rarely attended more than a token amount of the daily choir office.

Ignatius was not, in any conventional sense, an Anglo-Catholic. Although he had a strong devotion to the eucharistic Presence and the Mother of God and a taste for ornate ceremonial he had an almost Calvinist obsession with the need for 'conversion', and tended to get on better with evangelical nonconformists than with members of his own church.

The story of Fr Ignatius's life has been told in three biographies. The first, by the Baroness de Bertouch (born Beatrice Caroline Elmslie), was the fruit of extensive collaboration between authoress and subject, its first edition appearing in 1904, four years before his death. Its central premise was that Ignatius's mission to restore (his version of) mediaeval monasticism and Catholic devotion within the nineteenth century Church of England having been given him by God, everything he did was Right and everyone who opposed him (for whatever reason) Wrong. On the basis of that simple but shaky principle she spun a fantastic web of myth and miracle, all 599 pages of it in the deepest purple of purple prose.

Donald Attwater's briefer and more sober biography, published in 1931, concentrated on Ignatius as monastic founder. He and his wife had spent some years living in the former monastery and at nearby Plas Genevieve, now The Grange Pony Trekking Centre. As an ecumenically-minded convert to Roman Catholicism he also developed an interest in the local Baptist community and its antecedents, which became the subject of several scholarly articles.

In *The Enthusiast* (1962) Arthur Calder-Marshall had no religious axe to grind: he wrote for the modern secular reader who finds religion and religious people puzzling if fascinating, especially from a psychological point of view. Unlike his predecessors he dwelt at some length on Ignatius's family background and the personalities of his parents, especially his father; he was also interested in the dynamics between the monk and the women in his life, and the tensions with his patrons and fellow-workers.

All three tell the story of the community as well as that of its founder, although they provide relatively little information about those who passed through it or what actually went on in the monastery from day to day. Individual monks and nuns appear from time to time in their pages, but for the most part they remain strangers, and we are given only occasional snippets of information about their observances. A little more is revealed in *Building up the Waste Places*, Peter Anson's typically tendentious study of Llanthony and the two later Anglican monastic foundations of Caldey and Alton. He was a junior monk at Caldey at the time of its conversion to Rome in 1913, and would have known some or all of the brothers from Llanthony who transferred there shortly before his arrival.

My first visit to Capel-y-ffin made a lasting impression. In my teenage years I went back several times, eventually becoming involved with the recently established Father Ignatius Memorial

Trust. I also had the good fortune to become friends with Wilf and Helen Davies and their family, then living at the monastery.

What follows is the story of the community from its foundation in the early 1860s to its demise shortly after that of its founder in 1908. I have tried to say something about each of the identifiable monks and nuns, as well as such tangential figures as the 'monastery boys' and 'abbey priests'. After monastic life at Capel-y-ffin finally came to an end (a difficult event to pinpoint, as will become clear in the narrative) it continues with the various uses to which the premises have been put over the succeeding hundred or so years, including the establishment of the Trust and the history (so far) of the site as a place of pilgrimage.

THANKS ARE DUE to many people. In a few cases my enquiries have led me to descendants or other connections of people who belonged to the community, and I am grateful for information thus received; in each case this is acknowledged *ad loc.* Otherwise my main sources have been two sets of archives, viz:

(a) those of the Father Ignatius Memorial Trust, conveyed to the Abergavenny Museum in 1993, and managed in proper conservation conditions by Rachael Rogers and her staff, for whose patience and ready help I owe a deep debt of gratitude. Much of the material had in fact passed through my hands twenty years before that, when in my summer holidays I helped catalogue the beginnings of this collection at the former monastery at Capel-y-ffin. In those days I lacked both the time and the experience to analyse the individual items and fully assess their significance, but at least I acquired sufficient familiarity with them to know what was there and what wasn't.

(b) those of Prinknash Abbey, Gloucestershire, which include a number of items from Llanthony, among them Fr Ignatius's Register of Professions and his one surviving diary fragment. In the main community archive are two other relevant diaries: that of Dom Wilfrid Upson who was acting Superior at Caldey Abbey when the survivors of Ignatius's community were settling (or failing to settle) there, and Dom Joseph Woodford's record of his daily doings when he lived at Capel-y-ffin in the 1920s. It also includes a complete run of the Caldey/Prinknash periodical *Pax*, and records of discussions within the community at the time of the sale of the former monastery to Mary Gill in 1931. The guardian of this documentary goldmine is Fr Aelred Baker: I am enormously grateful to him for allowing me access to it as well as for his advice and encouragement, and to the Abbot and community for numerous acts of hospitality.

Other significant sources of information have been the cache of material assembled by Arthur Calder-Marshall when he was writing *The Enthusiast* and later deposited at the Norfolk county record office, and the massive *Churchman's Family Bible* in whose margins Ignatius jotted various notes between its acquisition in 1895 and his death thirteen years later. This is preserved along with a relatively annotation-free Bible belonging to Dame Mary Cecilia at the parish church of Ss Julius & Aaron in Newport, home since 1932 of the monumental reredos which was once the focal point of Ignatius's abbey church, and I am grateful to the Reverend David Matthews and his Churchwardens for allowing me to browse in it at my leisure.

Since the advent of the internet two sources previously out of reach of the home researcher have become available with a few clicks of the mouse and the payment of a modest subscription: the census and registration records on www.Ancestry.co.uk, and the collection of historic newspapers at www.britishnewspaperarchive.co.uk. Basic information about individuals has come more or less equally from the Professions Register and the first of these websites; I am indebted to the second for the great majority of the newspaper citations.

As well as those acknowledged above or in the text I am grateful to the following for information or other assistance: the staffs of the county record offices of Devon, Gwent, Hereford, Powys and West Sussex; the staffs of the Lambeth Palace, Devon County, Devon &

Exeter Institution, Exeter Cathedral, Exeter University and Hereford libraries, and of the Parliamentary archives; my family; occupants both past and present of places associated with Ignatius and his community, and fellow-members of the Father Ignatius Memorial Trust. Lastly, I am indebted to those who have allowed me to use images in their possession to illustrate this work: a full list of picture credits will be found on page 481.

SOME PARTS OF THE STORY are better documented than others, and more detailed treatment of them has been possible. By dividing the narrative into sections and putting the less immediately relevant details into footnotes I hope I have made it easy for the reader to navigate his way through the mass of material, and to skate over the bits he finds unappealing. One individual whose family have been particularly generous in providing me with information about his later life is John Henry Docking, better known as the Infant Oblate. This would have occupied a disproportionate amount of the last chapter in which he figures, so has been placed in an appendix: the reader may care to jump to the back of the book at the appropriate point.

In recounting the 'Llanthony Apparitions' I have reproduced numerous extracts from contemporary press reports, a source of which so far as I know no-one writing about these events has previously made use. If the resultant narrative appears lengthy and occasionally repetitious I would ask the reader to persevere, in the hope that they will help him (as they have helped me) to understand a little more clearly exactly what was going on at the monastery in August and September 1880.

I BEGAN WORK on this project in 2008, a hundred years since Fr Ignatius's death and fifty since my first visit to his former monastic home. In the first decade of that fifty years the last survivors of the Llanthony community died, followed soon afterwards by the last of those with personal memories of visits to Ignatius and his monastery. Now as the next generation — those with direct knowledge of people who knew Llanthony in monastic days — is passing away, it seems important to get the story down in black and white before it is lost in obscurity, or before fantasy overtakes fact in how it is recounted.

Tiverton
21 March 2016
Feast of St Benedict

ABBREVIATIONS & REFERENCES

Attwater	Donald Attwater, *Father Ignatius of Llanthony* (Cassell 1931)
Barclay Album	Two volumes of photographs and press cuttings assembled by Miss E. Barclay in c1937, now lodged in the Norfolk Record Office; ref MC 2133/7 and MC 2133/8
Bertouch	The Baroness de Bertouch, *The Life of Father Ignatius OSB/The Monk of Llanthony* (Methuen 1904)
BAL	Peter F. Anson, *Bishops at Large* (Faber & Faber 1964)
BUWP	Peter F. Anson, *Building up the Waste Places* (Faith Press 1973)
Call	Peter F. Anson, *The Call of the Cloister* (Second edition SPCK 1964)
Enthusiast	Arthur Calder-Marshall, *The Enthusiast* (Faber & Faber 1962)
FIIA	Fr Michael OSB, *Father Ignatius in America* (John Hodges 1893)
FMTB	B.G.A. Cannell, *From Monk to Busman* (Skeffington 1935)
Kilvert	William Plomer (ed), *Kilvert's Diary: Selections from the Diary of the Rev. Francis Kilvert* (3 vols, Jonathan Cape 1938)
LMN	*Llanthony & Mission News.* Illustrated magazine published from Llanthony, of which there appear to have been only four issues, one for each quarter of the year 1894. Copies of the first and third in Abergavenny collection, refs A1993.139.3.7 and A1993.3.14

Molloy	J.F. Molloy, *The Faiths of the People* (2 vols, Ward & Downey 1892)
MSO	Fr Ignatius, *Mission Sermons & Orations* (William Ridgway, in conjunction with Hamilton, Adams & Co 1886)
MT	*Church of England Catholic Chronicle & Monastic Times.* Quarterly news-sheet published from Llanthony September 1883 to September 1885 inclusive. Bound volume (incomplete) in Abergavenny Museum, ref A1993.137.4
NL	Sister Mary Agnes OSB (J.M. Povey), *Nunnery Life in the Church of England, or Seventeen Years with Father Ignatius* (Hodder & Stoughton 1890)
Spence	John Spence/Brother Cuthbert's account of the twelve months he spent as a novice at Llanthony in 1871-2. Photocopy of typed version, ninety numbered pages of which three are missing. In Abergavenny collection, ref A1993.137.1
Walker	Charles Walker, *Three Months in an English Monastery* (Murray & Co 1864)

The place of publication of works cited here and in the body of the book is London unless otherwise stated.

CHAPTER 1

FIRST STEPS

ONASTIC LIFE AT 'New Llanthony' began on 22 July 1870, when
M an assortment of boys and young men arrived on the hillside
site at Capel-y-ffin from their most recent temporary home, at
Laleham-on-Thames in Middlesex. Their leader was 32-year-old
Joseph Leycester Lyne, deacon in the Church of England and first
to attempt to restore to it the religious life for men. The community
had then been in existence since early 1863, although the Superior
preferred to date its foundation to the autumn of 1861,[3] when a
preliminary (and abortive) attempt had been made during the first
of his two brief curacies.

Lyne, better known by his monastic name Ignatius, was born
in London on 23 November 1837, second of the seven children of
Francis Lyne (1801-1888) and his wife Louisa Genevieve Leycester
(1815-1877). Francis's forebears came from Cornwall, where many
of them had served as clergy; more recently the family had been
distinguished by an enterprising mercantile element. Francis himself
was born in Lisbon, where his father had been associated with another
Cornish family, the Stephenses, whose fortune had been made in the
manufacture of glass (and which had received a significant boost in
the reglazing of Lisbon after the 1755 earthquake). One of his first
cousins was Stephens Lyne Stephens (1802-1860), recognised as 'the
richest commoner in England',[4] and on his death the Lynes expected
to benefit handsomely from his enormous inherited wealth. In the

---

[3] On 24 October, according to Ignatius's account in LMN April-June 1894

[4] Jenifer Roberts, *Glass: the Strange History of the Lyne Stephens Fortune*
(Chippenham, Templeton Press 2003) p275. Calder-Marshall
understandably but incorrectly names him as *Stephen* Lyne Stephens.

event their share of Stephens's estate was adequate but not enormous: an annuity of £360 per annum for Francis, in Arthur Calder-Marshall's description 'a small London merchant',[5] and £1000 to be divided among his children. The major part went to his widow, the French ballerina Yolande Duvernay, whom he had married when well into middle age but who bore him no children. When Yolande died in 1894 the Abbot of Llanthony was disappointed that his long cherished hope of a substantial endowment for his monastery from her estate failed to materialise. Instead, the comparatively modest share due to him as one of a large company of residuary legatees would only be released several years after his death.[6]

The Leycesters were a minor branch of a family owning considerable estates in Cheshire and elsewhere, who lived at White Place in the parish of Cookham. After the death of Louisa's brother Augustus in 1892 the house would be sold to William Waldorf Astor, who had recently acquired the Cliveden estate on the opposite bank of the Thames; he demolished it and on the site built a farmhouse in the popular Arts and Crafts style.[7]

Joseph Leycester – usually known by his second name, and in his family by the diminutive 'Lessie' – was ordained deacon on 23 December 1860. After failing to survive the rough and tumble of St Paul's School he had emerged from a pious and delicate childhood by

---

[5] Enthusiast p27

[6] One tangible monument to the Lyne Stephens fortune is the cathedral-like Roman Catholic church of the English Martyrs in Cambridge, whose construction was funded by Yolande Lyne Stephens in the 1880s. The history of the Lyne and Lyne Stephens inheritance is outlined by Arthur Calder-Marshall in the opening chapter of The Enthusiast. A more recent and much fuller treatment of this fascinating story (though with only a passing mention of Ignatius) can be found in Roberts, op cit.

[7] G. Tyack, S. Bradley & N. Pevsner, The Buildings of England: Berkshire (Yale University Press 2010) p254. For some information about the White Place Leycesters see Robin & Valerie Bootle, The Story of Cookham (privately printed 1990) pp90ff.

way of private tutors and clerical crammers. At the age of nineteen he had been admitted to the theological college at Glenalmond in Perthshire, recently founded by W.E. Gladstone and others.

His clerical ambitions were encouraged more by his mother than by his father, who found his second son's intense piety and High Church leanings rather hard to take. Leycester owed his place at Glenalmond to Robert Eden, Bishop of Moray, Ross and Caithness and a kinsman of his mother's. After two years of academic preparation (at which he distinguished himself only moderately) he needed to occupy himself for a further year or more until attaining the canonical age for ordination, so Dr Eden licensed him as a catechist, allowing him to officiate at Mattins and Evensong: first at the mission chapel of Blinkbonnie on the outskirts of Inverness, then at the little 'English kirk' at Glenurquhart on the shores of Loch Meiklie. Here he lived with Mrs Cameron of Lakefield, a pious upper-class widow who was happy to receive spiritual direction from her juvenile protégé, including his ruling that she should have a bath on Saturday evenings in preparation for the next day's worship. He was also popular among the estate workers and their families, some of whom preferred his colourful and emotional services to the customary Presbyterian sobriety. Defections from Kirk to Church would have upset the delicate balance on which social stability depended, so Dr Eden solved the problem by revoking the young man's licence – the first of his many brushes with bishops.

At Glenalmond one evening a fellow student had lightheartedly likened the gown-wearing trainee clergymen crossing the quad to Evensong to mediaeval monks processing to Vespers. As a boy he had felt the call to become 'no ordinary clergyman'. From that moment he decided that his life's work would be to restore monastic life to the Church of England – a mission which could be carried out only by a clergyman very far from 'ordinary'.

PLYMOUTH

LEYCESTER'S FIRST CURACY was a junior post under George Rundle Prynne, Vicar of the recently founded parish of St Peter, Plymouth.[8] The Bishop of Exeter (Philpotts) decreed that as a non-graduate he should remain in deacon's orders for three years rather than the usual single year, and until advanced to the priesthood not be permitted to preach sermons in that diocese. The position was a supernumerary one, so no stipend was attached to it. His small legacy from the Lyne Stephens estate (£142 17s 1½d) and the proceeds of jewellery donated by Mrs Cameron should have been sufficient to keep him for the next three years, especially as he was billeted (probably free of charge) with Prynne and his family in the Vicarage at 25 Wyndham Square. In the following year's census (7/8 April) he was listed at this address, as was his 20-year-old brother Augustus Adolphus, who would have been in Plymouth in pursuit of his naval career, and whose occupation is given as 'Clerk's Assistant, R.N.'.

There were several reasons for Leycester to have accepted this particular curacy. The most compelling would have been Prynne's reputation as a pioneer in the Catholic revival, and his faithfulness to 'Church principles' in spite of powerful local resistance. What religion there was in Plymouth tended to be puritan in tone (St Peter's had at first occupied a former proprietary chapel named 'Eldad'), and the Vicar had had to contend with opposition from his fellow clergy as well as with prejudice and indifference among the population at large.

There were also family connections. Two decades earlier Prynne had served as curate to Charles Lyne, Vicar of Tywardreath, thirty miles or so across the Cornish border. Prebendary Lyne, a churchman of the old 'high and dry' school and a local magistrate, was a distant cousin, assisted in later years by his son Charles Richard Nunez Lyne,

---

[8] Prynne (born 1818) was instituted as the parish's first Vicar in 1848, and would remain there until his death fifty-five years later.

a slightly older contemporary of the new deacon. It was probably at his invitation (and despite the no-preaching stipulation) that Leycester's first sermon was delivered in one of the outlying churches of their scattered parish, St Samson's, Golant, where an alabaster carving of the head of Christ stands as a memorial to him and to this significant event.[9]

And living in Donegal Terrace near the new Devonport railway station were his mother's brother Captain Edmund Leycester with his wife and two children, sixteen-year-old Rafe Neville and thirteen-year-old Isabel. As small children they had been captivated (to their parents' dismay) by the teenage Joseph Leycester's dramatic retelling of the stories of early Christian martyrdoms,[10] but as the family moved to a new posting in Liverpool soon after their cousin's ordination they wouldn't have seen much of him in his new role. They had, however, got together when he came to Plymouth to fix up his curacy the preceding July, as Rafe recorded in his diary:

> Leycester Lyne has just come down here for a short time in order to make arrangements for being curate to a Mr Prynne a Puseyite clergyman of Plymouth. Leycester has brought with him a young Scotchman of the name of Buchan, an[d] who is dressed in Highland costume. The latter is rather a nice fellow and we have been to bathe &c several times. They have dined with us several times and the latter was one day sitting on one of our chairs which have horse-hair cushions, when he was obliged to get up and beg to have a softer cushion to sit upon.[11]

---

[9] Until the creation of the see of Truro in 1876 Cornwall was part of the diocese of Exeter. The memorial would have been installed by E.A.L. Clarke, Vicar of Golant (by then a separate parish) 1919-25. As a young man in the 1890s and 1900s he was one of Ignatius's disciples, and took part in his funeral.

[10] Bertouch pp44f; *Enthusiast* pp38f

[11] No other reference to Buchan has come to light. The quotation is from the entry for 26 July 1860 in 'Crawling through Life': *The Diaries of Rafe Neville*

As a young priest Prynne had come under the influence of Dr Pusey, who after Newman's conversion to Rome had become the acknowledged figurehead of the Catholicising tendency in the Church of England: 'Puseyite' was the usual – and usually derogatory – term to denote its adherents. Another of Pusey's disciples was Priscilla Lydia Sellon, who had responded to the Bishop of Exeter's appeal for assistance in making good the 'spiritual destitution' of neighbouring Devonport in the same year that Prynne began work at St Peter's. In their first year Miss Sellon and her little band of companions had organised themselves into the 'Church of England Sisterhood of Mercy' – very nearly the first community of women in post-Reformation Anglicanism – and started schools and an orphanage. The following year the sisters were to prove their worth as nurses and general relief workers in the cholera epidemic which swept through the 'Three Towns' of Plymouth, Devonport and Stonehouse: it was this emergency that brought Prynne and Miss Sellon together.[12]

The relationship soured, however, after the Prynnes made their infant daughter Lucy over to Mother Lydia as an 'infant oblate' – a precedent Leycester would himself follow, as we shall see – but later claimed her back. When the child protested at being parted from her 'Dearest [adopted] Mother' her real parents were understandably upset, and a certain coolness developed between Prynne and Sellon, and by extension between Prynne and Pusey; it also led to the sisterhood withdrawing from work in St Peter's parish.[13] However, Miss Sellon's younger half-sister Caroline

---

Leycester, 1859–1865, published on the internet at www.day-books.com; retrieved 2 March 2014.

[12] On the wider stage the sisters became known and valued when they joined Florence Nightingale as nurses in the Crimea. Sellon's life and achievements are narrated in T.J. Williams, *Priscilla Lydia Sellon* (SPCK 1950); the meeting between her and Prynne is described on pp68f.

[13] ibid p137

(who was Lucy's godmother) continued to live with the Prynnes as 'governess and friend', and also figures in the 1861 census as one of the Vicarage household.[14]

Never one to let grass grow under his feet, the 'boy deacon'[15] seems to have regarded even this first rung on the clerical ladder as an opportunity to start putting his monastic ambitions into effect, and the proximity of Miss Sellon's community would have been another factor influencing his choice of parish. Although he found time for some pastoral activities (including miraculous healings and exorcisms, if the Baroness de Bertouch is to be believed) his mind was obviously focused on other matters. 'One of his first steps' in Plymouth was to form 'a species of Guild for men and boys', to which he gave the name 'Society of the Love of Jesus'.[16] This organisation was said to 'have a monastic flavour about it', with its members adopting the style 'Brother' and their leader the title 'Superior'. Pious guilds of this sort were not uncommon in Anglo-Catholic circles at the time, but few of their founders envisaged their creations evolving into fully-fledged monastic communities – or if they did, they kept the idea to themselves. When the membership of Leycester's guild approached forty he decided the time had come to 'place the whole concern on a more serious footing', and ventured to call on the Lady Superior for help and advice.

Bertouch tells us that his approach to the Devonport sisters was 'not without many a misgiving'. One of these may have been that as

---

[14] ibid p134; she was still there in 1871. For two years (1852-54) she had been a 'Child' (roughly equivalent to a novice elsewhere) in her sister's community. In middle age she would become the second wife of a distinguished Indian Army officer named Lionel d'Arcy Dunsterville, and step-mother (although he was by then grown up) to the original of Kipling's Stalky.

[15] According to Ignatius's adopted son 'Brother David' this was how Mrs Prynne referred to her husband's junior curate.

[16] Bertouch p92; subsequent events are narrated on the following pages. The name may have been a compliment to Miss Sellon, whose 'Second Order' took the title 'Company of the Love of Jesus' at much the same time.

Prynne's curate he might be given the brush-off – the Vicar and his wife did their best to discourage him – but he was received graciously, and taken seriously. At some point Miss Sellon introduced him to Pusey, and between them they seem to have adopted 'Brother Joseph' and his planned foundation as a pet project. A house in Stoke Damerel belonging to the Devonport sisters was made available (possibly the building which had recently been used to house their Orphanage): by early autumn it had been equipped with basic essentials (including those necessary for furnishing an 'oratory'), and was ready for the fledgling brotherhood to take up residence.

In the event only two of its members felt able to leave their homes and throw in their lot with their young Superior. Their first night in the new establishment was interrupted by the appearance in the small hours of a seemingly self-ignited candle at the foot of the stairs, interpreted by Pusey (a little rashly, perhaps, in view of how things were to turn out) as a 'Heaven-sent sign of Divine approval' and 'emblem of the illuminating influence which monasticism was to shed upon the Church'.[17] He was, however, prudent enough to advise those concerned to 'treasure these marks of favour in the silence of their own spirits, and as things too sacred to be desecrated by the touch of public curiosity'.

No mention of this monastic experiment is made in Prynne's biography,[18] although his time in the parish is acknowledged. It would be interesting to know what the Vicar thought about his junior curate decamping to a house in a neighbouring parish, and whether Pusey and Sellon had advised the young deacon on the subject of clerical protocol as well as on the practicalities of setting up a religious house. Neither the curacy nor the community was to last much longer, however. After just two days the would-be Superior

---

[17] Or so the Baroness reports: ibid p97.

[18] A. Clifton Kelway: *George Rundle Prynne: a Chapter in the Early History of the Catholic Revival*, Longmans, Green & Co. 1905

fell victim to typhoid fever and congestion of the brain, and was carried off to be nursed back to health by a lady well-wisher. Arthur Calder-Marshall is surely correct in suggesting the possibility of a psychosomatic element in this collapse:[19] similar escapes into illness had caused his withdrawal from St Paul's and nearly brought his Glenalmond career to a premature end. The same would happen four years later in Norwich, and a continuing strain of hypochondria runs through his years at Llanthony.[20]

His share of the Lyne Stephens inheritance had enabled Francis Lyne to move upmarket from Hunter Street to Montagu Square, and to take his wife and daughters to Belgium for an extended holiday.[21] As soon as she could obtain a passage back to England Mrs Lyne rushed to her favourite son's bedside, although by the time she reached it he was over the worst. Mother and son left Plymouth together, the latter abandoning both his curacy and his first attempt to found a monastic institution. We learn that the two leaderless brothers were 'temporarily sheltered through the kind hospitality of Dr Pusey',[22]

---

[19] Enthusiast p66

[20] An anecdote from his time as Prynne's curate is related on pp79f of *A Rambler's Recollections* by the conjuror and drawing room entertainer Alfred Capper, published in 1915: 'Many years ago he was assisting my dear old friend the Rev. G. R. Prynne in Plymouth, where he lived with the Vicar and Mrs Prynne at the Vicarage. One winter night Ignatius, the Rev. Arthur [sic] Leycester Lyne as he then was, was returning from church when he met a perfectly filthy and deplorable creature, a regular music-hall or cinematograph tramp. The man stopped and begged alms for a night's lodging. "Oh, you poor fellow!" cried the youthful curate. "Here, you must have my bed." And forthwith he stole up the Vicarage staircase, thrust his tramp friend into the dainty bedroom and himself spent the night in the summer-house in the garden. Imagine the horror of Mr Prynne's smart housemaid when she took Mr Lyne's shaving-water into his bedroom next morning and found the foul and disgusting tramp snugly ensconced between those dainty sheets.'

[21] They were out of the country when the census was taken in April 1861, and daughter Harriet's diary locates the girls and their mother in Belgium for a good part of 1862.

[22] Bertouch p100. He would do the same for the survivors of the Norwich monastery.

though there is no record of how long this continued or of what happened to them subsequently. The only one of Leycester's followers from this period to surface as a monk at Llanthony – Thomas Bray, a choirboy at St Peter's and in the monastery one of several successive Brothers Dunstan – would at seven or eight have been a little young to have been a member of the resident brotherhood, though he might conceivably have been a very junior member of the guild.[23]

VISITS TO BELMONT AND LLANTHONY

By THE MIDDLE OF DECEMBER Leycester was back on his feet, and spent a few days with Henry Stillingfleet, a priest with whom he had become acquainted a few years earlier when boarding with a private tutor in Worcester. Stillingfleet, ten years his senior, had been at the time of their first meeting curate to the prominent Tractarian W.J. Butler at Wantage, where he shared lodgings with the up-and-coming ecclesiastical architect G.E. Street; since then he had married a French wife and settled in Herefordshire to the life of a country parson, initially as curate of Clehonger. On this holiday Leycester made two visits which helped to focus his vision for the future.

Across the fields from Stillingfleet's parsonage a group of Gothic revival buildings was just then nearing completion, the most prominent of them a great church designed by Edward Pugin. This was Belmont Priory, pro-cathedral of the new Roman Catholic diocese of Newport and Menevia, and joint house of studies for the Benedictine monasteries of the English Congregation. Calder-Marshall[24] quotes from the diary of the then Novice Master (Dom Alphonsus Morrall, later Prior of Downside), who observed that on 17 December a 'young Puseyite...remained for about an hour at prayer' in the church and then had some conversation with the Prior.

---

[23] See Chapter 6. When he arrived at Llanthony in 1872 he was eighteen.

[24] *Enthusiast* p77

It seems that he asked for a hair-shirt, but came away with a more practical souvenir: a copy of the Rule of St Benedict.[25]

The second visit made an even more powerful impression. It was to the ruined Augustinian priory at Llanthony, just across the Welsh border in the mountainous Vale of Ewyas.

Llanthony (Llanddewi Nant Hodni: Church of St David in the valley of the Honddu) was founded in the twelfth century, although the site was hallowed by a tradition that five hundred years earlier St David had lived there as a hermit. In his *Journey through Wales* (1188) Archdeacon Gerald de Barri ('Giraldus Cambrensis') singled it out as 'most suited to the practice of religion and better chosen for canonical discipline than any of the other monasteries in the Island of Britain'[26] – a pardonable instance of hyperbole on the part of this patriotic Welsh churchman.

At Llanthony the curving ridges between which the valley runs, Ffwddog and Hatterall, form a kind of natural amphitheatre, in which one has the impression of being surrounded by a mountain wall and cut off from the outside world. Its remoteness from the amenities of city life had proved too much for the mediaeval canons, whose daughter house in Gloucester quickly superseded Llanthony *prima* as their main residence; the downside of Llanthony's contemplative isolation was its vulnerability to attack by local tribesmen, whom another early chronicler described as 'savage, without religion, thieves, and vagabonds'.[27]

Similar sentiments had been expressed by its current owner, the poet Walter Savage Landor (1775-1864). Half a century before the young clergymen's visit he had tied up most of his inherited

---

[25] Bertouch p129. Ignatius's other biographers follow her by placing this visit in the next phase of his life, although Calder-Marshall (*Enthusiast* p77) correctly gives the date as 17 December 1861, less than two months after his collapse in Plymouth.

[26] Book 1 Chapter 3

[27] Quoted in Malcolm Elwin, *Savage Landor* (Macmillan 1941) p124

wealth in the Llanthony estate, making ambitious plans to build a great house on the hill above the Priory ruins, plant a million trees on the hillside and civilise the inhabitants by providing them with education and employment. But it was not long before he reported himself living among 'rascals [with] as great a hatred of a Saxon as their runaway forefathers had', and in consequence found himself wishing that 'Julius Caesar had utterly exterminated the whole race of Britons'.[28] He took refuge in Florence, where he received an income from the land rather smaller than his investment should have generated, and left its management to a resident bailiff and local lawyers.

It's easy to understand how Leycester fell in love with these ruins. His view of history was as romantic as the Llanthony scenery, and took no account of the fact that the former priory had been in secular hands for almost as long as it had been a religious house. To him it was quite simple: the ruined priory belonged to God, and it should be reclaimed for Him. Later he would come to regard its reclamation as his personal duty.

FAMILY INTERLUDE

WHILE LEYCESTER WAS IN PLYMOUTH supposedly preparing for ordination to the priesthood, his elder brother Francis Palmer ('Franky'), now aged 25, had followed their uncle Edmund Leycester into the Navy as an Assistant Paymaster. In the 1861 census he appears among the ship's company of HMS Gannet at Constantinople; the following year his family heard that he had been ordered to Corfu.[29] Augustus Adolphus ('Gus' or 'Gussie') had also, as we have seen, embarked on a naval career. While Leycester was trying and failing to establish his brotherhood in Plymouth Gussie was setting out on a three-month voyage to the Cape on HMS Pantaloon; a few months

---

[28] ibid p125

[29] Harriet's Diary (for which see below), 5 June 1862

later the ship struck a rock, from which the crew were rescued by a Portuguese vessel and taken to India, whence they were sent home via Alexandria.[30] In the following decade he would follow his brother into the ministry; he died (aged 59) in 1900 as Vicar of St Saviour, Westgate-on-Sea.

Franky and Gussie also appear in their cousin Rafe Leycester's diary, as do their sisters Louisa Jane ('Louey'), Elizabeth Gertrude ('Gert'), and Harriet Jemima. Franky was evidently keen on jokes and pranks, while like Rafe himself Gussie had an eye for a pretty girl. The following episode was recorded in the autumn of 1864, when Rafe was staying with the Lynes who were temporarily residing in Brighton:

> This morning went to church. Fashionable edifice, crowds of people, jolly looking girls, wonderful bonnets &c &c. Made Girt [sic] laugh during the service I am sorry to say.... After lunch Gus & I went to see Mary Anne Richardson who is staying with some Miss Oakes. Then on the parade where we picked up two girls, mine an awfully jolly one, with fair ruddy complexion, blue eyes & light hair. Walked with them. Gus had to abandon his precipitately, having met the Tuckers with Louey & Harriet. Promised to write to my girl, who said her name was Davis, 59 The Parade, & promised faithfully to answer it & say when she would return to Town. I shall write but wont get a reply, too good luck for me. When I returned to the house there was a little scene, the girls having rushed upstairs & told Mr Lyne that they had met Gus walking with a common girl, &c &c.[31]

---

[30] ibid 2 February and 21 June 1862. A few years later Augustus Adolphus would publish a prolix but entertaining account of a journey he had made in the Holy Land in the spring of 1871 with a group of fellow officers and midshipmen: *The Midshipmen's Trip to Jerusalem and Cruise in Syria; Or, The Adventures of a Cavalcade of British Naval Officers in the Holy Land* (Low, Marston & Searle 1872).

[31] R.N. Leycester op cit: entry for Sunday 2 October 1864

In January 1862 Leycester travelled to Belgium to complete his recuperation in the bosom of his family. At the time they were based in Brussels, where the three girls (then 21, 19 and 17) were taking lessons in music and German and enjoying an active social life with other members of the British colony; a popular winter pastime was skating at the Zoological Gardens. The youngest brother, Clavering Mordaunt, celebrated his thirteenth birthday on 14 February; he spent most of the year at boarding school in England, joining the others in Belgium for the holidays.[32] On Sundays and red-letter days they attended services at the English church, with whose chaplain and his wife they were on friendly terms. The building was shared with the Lutherans and Calvinists, so the Anglican service had to begin at the early hour of 9 o'clock.

Our main source of information for this period is the diary kept in the first half of 1862 by Harriet Jemima, of which two portions survive: one between 19 January and 8 February, and the other from 29 May to 1 July, by which time they had moved to an unidentified coastal resort, probably Ostend.[33] The diary ends abruptly after Gertrude is proposed to by a young man who two days later is found to have been concealing a shady past. In their father's absence Leycester subjects his sister's unsuitable suitor to an interview; the point at which the narrative breaks off is where they join the rest of the family in the drawing room, presumably for the denouement of the affair. The Baroness mentions Leycester's 'intervention and intercession in a pathetic family love affair', but provides no further details.[34] Eight years later she would marry Arthur Bloomfield, an unimpeachably respectable officer in the Volunteers.

---

[32] The 1861 census lists him as a pupil at Totteridge Park School, a preparatory school in Hertfordshire.

[33] The diary is in the Fr Ignatius collection at Abergavenny, Museum refs A2010.8613 and A2010.8614. A near-contemporary source mentions Leycester visiting his family in Ostend: Walker p27.

[34] Bertouch p108

After the restrained Tractarianism of early 1860s Plymouth this exposure to continental Catholicism at its most demonstrative came to Leycester as an amazing revelation, and one can identify some of the more exotic customs he adopted in years to come from his sister's descriptions of sights they witnessed. Colourful outdoor processions were a frequent occurrence, with flag-lined streets, banners, monks and nuns in a variety of habits, little girls in white dresses and little boys in sheepskin to represent John the Baptist in the wilderness. In the churches they visited (sometimes to hear sermons, or to listen to nuns singing at High Mass) they were impressed by the masses of candles. On one occasion (after a big funeral) there were said to have been four hundred and fifty of them around the catafalque; significantly it is Leycester who is credited with guessing the number, or perhaps actually counting them.[35]

One episode missing from Harriet's diary is the affair of her brother's first religious habit; the story is, however, told by the Baroness[36] and copied by Attwater and Calder-Marshall. After his departure from Plymouth a rough hooded frock had been made for him by Caroline Sellon and despatched to Montagu Square, but Francis Lyne had intercepted the parcel and confiscated the contents. A replacement was then sent to Leycester in Brussels, where at Solemn Benediction in the Redemptorists' church of St Joseph he clothed himself in this garment, 'belonging to no special monkish denomination'. It is unlikely that at this stage he wore it as his everyday costume, but we are told that 'having sealed an irrevocable promise' to live as a monk he now considered himself to be one 'in the eyes of God and His Church', and that he devoted much of his time in Belgium to studying the rules of various religious orders.

---

[35] Forty years later Belgian piety would have a similar effect on the sixteen-year-old Alfred Hope Patten, future restorer of the Marian shrine at Walsingham. See Colin Stephenson, *Walsingham Way* (Norwich: Canterbury Press, 2nd edn 2008) p92.

[36] Information in this paragraph from Bertouch pp104f

At the end of this process he would declare himself a Benedictine, although (as with the habit he eventually adopted) his version of the Benedictine life would always be eclectic, incorporating customs and observances borrowed from other orders or invented by himself.

What the Baroness describes as a 'chance introduction'[37] solved the problem of his immediate future. At some point – probably on a visit to Bruges, from which Harriet tells us he had returned to his family 'very tired and poorly' on 3 June – Leycester became acquainted with Bryan King, Rector of St George's-in-the-East in Stepney. On the following Saturday she notes that 'Mr Bryan King and Mr Lee the Rector of Stepney from London came from Bruges and had breakfast with us'.

King had been Rector of St George's since 1842. The population of the parish had increased enormously in recent decades, and it was characterised by poverty, overcrowding and every kind of vice. In 1856 the St George's Mission had been founded in Wellclose Square, with C.F. Lowder as priest-in-charge. Through overwork and stress consequent on the recent 'St George's Riots' King had taken leave of absence in 1860 and moved with his family to Bruges. The year after his breakfast with the Lynes he returned to England, exchanging livings with J.L. Ross, Vicar of the quiet Wiltshire village of Avebury: here he would spend the remaining twenty years of his life.

It is not clear what part 'Mr Lee' played in what followed, if any. This would have been F.G. Lee, who was not in fact Rector of Stepney, although he had officiated at St George's occasionally in 1859-60, at the time of the riots. After that he had a parish in Aberdeen, from which in 1867 he returned to the capital as Vicar of All Saints, Lambeth. For much of his 32-year incumbency there he combined his duties as a parochial clergyman with the exercise of a dubious species of episcopate as one of the three prelates in the Order of

---

[37] Information in this and the following paragraphs from ibid p109 unless otherwise noted.

Corporate Reunion, which came into being in 1877.[38] Rumour would later connect Joseph Leycester Lyne with this shadowy organisation,[39] almost certainly without foundation even if his paths would cross from time to time with those of Lee, who on this occasion may simply have been staying with King as a friend and former colleague.

Also visiting King at around this time was Charles Lowder, who just then had a vacancy on his staff at the Mission.[40] An introduction was effected, and the result was the offer of a job, to which Leycester moved shortly afterwards.

WELLCLOSE SQUARE

THE SIX MONTHS or so Leycester spent at St George's Mission are dealt with in some detail by Bertouch, as well as by Calder-Marshall. He began to make a name for himself as a preacher, and there were further miraculous healings – including the alleged resurrection of a girl named Lizzie Meek.[41]

At the same time he had not abandoned his plans to revive the monastic life. He tells us that while at the Mission he 'became acquainted with the rule of St Benedict and with some Benedictine monks',[42] and wrote a 'short but stirring' pamphlet – the first of many

---

[38] H.R.T. Brandreth, Dr Lee of Lambeth (SPCK 1951) ch 2 (pp10-45)

[39] BAL p75

[40] This was occasioned by the preferment of Fr Mackonochie to St Alban's, Holborn.

[41] A novel by David Thomas with the title The Raising of Lizzie Meek (Robert Hale 1993) is based loosely on this event and its aftermath. The author takes a number of historical liberties, and appears to derive most of his knowledge of Ignatius from the published biographies and Sister Mary Agnes' sensationalist exposé, Nunnery Life in the Church of England, published in 1890.

[42] Autobiography p7. There is no mention in Bertouch or elsewhere of him meeting any Benedictine monks while at Wellclose Square, so the reference is probably to his visit to Belmont in December 1861. The acquaintanceship appears to have been quite superficial, as he is said not even to have given his name. Of course he may also have met monks during his stay in Belgium.

from his pen – which he sent to 'the Anglican clergy, and those of the laity whose Catholic sympathies were likely to be aroused'. Early in 1863 he exchanged cassock and biretta for the monastic habit,[43] and started to set the wheels in motion.

---

[43] This may at first have consisted of no more than a scapular over his cassock. Bertouch (pp129ff) recounts an occasion when thus attired (with the addition of a clerical hat) Leycester took a party from the Mission on pilgrimage to St Edward's shrine in Westminster Abbey. They were not well received by the vergers, who were unused to the sight of visitors praying outside service times.

CHAPTER 2

BENEDICTINE BEGINNINGS

THE CHANGE OF DRESS posed a problem. Fr Lowder had engaged Leycester as curate, not as monk-in-residence, so when he started wearing his unconventional costume around the parish there were murmurings from the Mission's financial backers. It was, after all, only a couple of years since the riots, whose immediate cause had been the use of the surplice in the pulpit, at the time a controversial innovation.

Lowder tried to explain the difficulty to his assistant, and asked him to dress less provocatively. But once he began to regard himself as a Benedictine – even if for want of a monastic superior his 'clothing' consisted simply of vesting himself in his version of the Benedictine habit – Leycester could not compromise on his new identity. 'I felt called to come before the world as a Monk,' he told the Baroness de Bertouch, so he

> silently took up his scapular, and with both hands measured the space of an inch upon its hem. 'Tell your patrons,' he said slowly, 'that I will not yield that much of **this**,' and he reverently pointed to the sombre black serge and the measured modicum that lay between his thumbs. 'But I will do something else,' he added, suddenly cheering up, 'something that will help you out of your difficulty quite as well, and even better – I will leave!'[44]

---

[44] Bertouch p133. It is instructive to compare his dogmatism on this subject with near-contemporary practice in English Roman Catholic communities. According to Dom Hubert van Zeller in *Downside By and Large* (Sheed & Ward 1954), it was only seventeen years before Leycester's assumption of monastic costume that the Downside monks began to wear the habit in and around their monastery. Previously their

By this time – February 1863, barely six months since his arrival in Stepney – the newly-made monk had acquired patrons of his own. The first of these was a new patron saint. To mark his entrance into the monastic life Leycester took the name Ignatius, after Ignatius Loyola, sixteenth century founder of the Jesuits.

For a nineteenth century Anglican the choice of a Counter Reformation saint might seem strange, but it was not inappropriate. The spiritual diet on which he would feed himself and his monks owed more to post-Tridentine Catholicism than to classical Western monasticism. And if one had to choose one adjective to describe his attempt to reintroduce the monastic way of life in the Victorian Church of England one could scarcely improve on 'quixotic' – an epithet that has been applied with no less justification to the young Loyola.[45]

Leycester's knowledge of the Jesuit founder probably dated from his stay at Glenurquhart. In neighbouring Strathglass the Old Faith had (with the support of local landowning families such as the Frasers and the Chisholms) survived three centuries of repression and state persecution. Through the network of narrow mountain passes it was priests of the Society of Jesus who came to say Mass and minister to the needs of the flock, so the native Catholicism became influenced by Jesuit spirituality and devotion to Jesuit saints. A thriving parish was centred on Marydale, where the two glens met; a new church would be opened there a few years after his stay, and a structure named 'St Ignatius's Well' erected at Glassburn a couple

---

everyday dress had been the tailcoat with academic gown, although the monastery possessed one token habit which novices put on (and took off again) at their Clothing. Ignatius insisted on the full rig for every brother all the time, even in bed at night, claiming that this was stipulated in the Rule. (His assertion of this last point was contradicted by Dom Cyprian Alston, whose personal pilgrimage took him from Llanthony to Downside in the 1890s, and who pencilled a number of corrections and elucidations into the margins of that monastery's copy of Bertouch. This one is on p337.)

[45] Macdonald Hastings, *Jesuit Child* (Michael Joseph 1971) p103

of decades later.[46]

CLAYDON

THE OTHER PATRON was an earthly one, the Rector of Claydon, near Ipswich.[47] 'Firm Father George' Drury (1819-95) was one of that now extinct species, the long-serving rural incumbent of Anglo-Catholic views and 'advanced' liturgical behaviour. In the hundred years or so between the rise of what came to be known as Ritualism ('ceremonialism' would be a more accurate term) and the end of the 1950s the Anglican countryside was studded with a host of these often colourful characters, whose attempts to turn their parishes into islands of True Belief depended for their success on two crucial factors. The first was the security of tenure enjoyed by the incumbent as possessor of the Parson's Freehold; in this respect Drury's position was doubly secure, as he was patron of his own living. The second was sufficient money (either the clergyman's own or that of wealthy lay supporters) to re-equip the church in a way that would mark it out clearly and as near as possible irrevocably as a Catholic place of worship.[48] Drury was not only a man of means, but a skilled

---

[46] Information from a letter of Dom Edmund Fatt OSB of Pluscarden Priory to Douglas Lyne, 27 July 1969 in Abergavenny collection: ref A2010.86.227.59. For a glimpse of Catholic life in Strathglass in the 1930s the reader is referred to Peter F. Anson, *The Caravan Pilgrim* (Heath Cranton 1938) pp170-177.

[47] Information about Claydon and its incumbent from www.suffolkchurches.co.uk retrieved 2 March 2014. In the following decade Drury would become notorious for refusing to allow a nonconformist minister to officiate at the burial of a child in the churchyard at neighbouring Akenham. Newspaper reports of the ensuing court case (which led to the Burial Laws Amendment Act of 1880) are reproduced *in extenso* in Ronald Fletcher's *The Akenham Burial Case* (Wildwood House 1974).

[48] For some of these characters (though mostly from the latter part of this period) see Michael Yelton, *Outposts of the Faith: Ten Anglo-Catholic Portraits* (Norwich: Canterbury Press, 2009). Various factors would bring an end to the phenomenon, one of them being the tendency to combine formerly independent parishes in large groups served by a single priest. In the nature of the case it was always the churches holding to Catholic

amateur craftsman; much of his handiwork is still visible in the church at Claydon (ironically now out of use, though maintained by local volunteers).

Ignatius (as we must now call him; his mother dutifully began to refer to him as 'my son Ignatius') paid a preliminary visit to Claydon in November 1862 and preached in the parish church. At first the plan was for him to establish a monastery in Ipswich itself. Drury introduced him to two local solicitors with Tractarian sympathies, and there was talk of renting the former fish market as a chapel and school.[49]

He was, as we have seen, convinced that his vocation was to 'come before the world as a Monk', and could not envisage his foundation as being anything other than a very public act. Even before his community was an established fact Ignatius was referring to it as a 'mission', and from the outset the handful of brothers would be expected to engage in educational and social activity with the surrounding population. The same motive would lead him to 'throw open' (a favourite Ignatian expression) his successive chapels and churches to outside worshippers, and hardly let a day pass without one or other of the choir offices having a popular sermon or lecture attached to it – even (in the Norwich phase) Prime at 6.0am! And in his scheme of things his 'English Order of St Benedict' would only be complete when in addition to the 'first order' of monks it comprised a 'second order' of nuns and a 'third order' of lay supporters and sympathisers;[50] this last began to take shape during the first year.

---

traditions of worship which had to make the greatest concessions.

[49] There had in fact been a short-lived branch of J.M. Neale's East Grinstead community in Ipswich a year or two earlier (Call p350).

[50] The nomenclature is reminiscent of the Dominicans, although the idea was probably borrowed from Miss Sellon. Ignatius seems never to have fully understood that historically there was no such thing as a Benedictine 'order', whether first, second or third; just a network of self-governing monasteries (some of men, others of women) held together by their common acceptance of St Benedict's Rule.

Claydon Rectory was large – large enough for a family in which there would eventually be nine children, with the usual quota of servants. Ignatius had no money to fund premises in Ipswich or anywhere else, so Drury offered him the use of a then unoccupied wing of his house until his community found its feet. In return, the brothers – initially there were two, Anselm and Martin – would assist in the parish and their Superior act as unofficial curate. Neither Ignatius nor his host saw a need to refer this arrangement to the Bishop of Norwich: Drury perhaps hoped that the monks would be with him for only a few weeks, and Ignatius would always maintain that his monastery was *ipso facto* extra-diocesan.

In the event the brotherhood was at Claydon for just under a year, from 17 February 1863 (Shrove Tuesday) until the end of January 1864. A certain amount of information can be found in local newspapers, although this mostly deals with the associated 'goings on' in the parish church and their repercussions. Some of these – disturbances in Claydon itself and in Ipswich, including threats of violence from 'drunken mechanics' – also figure in the diary kept by the wife of a local gentleman farmer, Elizabeth Cotton of Amor Hall, Washbrook. Her first mention of Ignatius occurs on 12 April 1863, when she made this entry: 'Ada West spent the day here, and in the evening went with [Elizabeth's children and others] to Claydon Church. They heard a clergyman calling himself Brother Ignatius and drest in a monk's robes preach.' From then on she went there quite frequently, and she and her family became keen supporters of the Rector and his monastic lodger.[51]

CHARLES WALKER

THE MOST FREQUENTLY quoted source for this period is *Three Months in an English Monastery: a Personal Narrative*. This was rushed into print by

---

[51] Photocopies of the relevant ms pages (22 in all) are in the Fr Ignatius collection, ref A1997.22.2. Further extracts were published in Sheila Hardy, *The Diary of a Suffolk Farmer's Wife, 1854-69* (Macmillan 1992).

Charles Walker (otherwise Brother Anselm) soon after the brothers left Claydon, by which time its author had returned to secular life.

At Drury's suggestion Walker had been given the title Prior, with the idea that he might relieve the Superior of some of the day-to-day administrative concerns. He was much the same age as Ignatius, and like him (but unlike most of his monastic subjects, at that time or later) came from a relatively privileged background. He had attended a boarding school in then rural Tottenham run by the family of the postal reformer Rowland Hill, and although apparently not a university graduate could translate at sight from the Latin breviary and had a developed literary style, albeit a little grandiose.

The 'three months' of his title fell in two parts, one of five weeks in February and March, the other of ten between August and October. It was typical of Ignatius's quixotic approach that he regularly bit off more than he could chew, and expected his disciples to achieve even more unrealistic feats of endurance. Walker's failure to survive the full six weeks of that first Lent was scarcely surprising; neither (although he never led the life with the same rigour he expected of his subordinates) was Ignatius's need of an extended autumn holiday in Scotland.[52]

It was to manage the household in his absence that Walker returned for his second spell. How long he was planning to stay at Claydon after Ignatius's return and on what terms we cannot tell, as within days of Mr and Mrs Cotton's introduction to him on Sunday 18 October ('Evening Claydon Church.... Ignatius introduced us to Brother Anselm') he had taken his leave, this time for good.

This second departure was almost certainly a forced one. A few days after Walker's introduction to the Cottons (it was dated 20

---

[52] This was also to explore the possibility of establishing a female branch of his community north of the border. Elizabeth Cotton records attending a 'farewell' service on 13 August; Ignatius was still in Scotland on Holy Cross Day, 14 September (Bertouch p153; BUWP p53), and next appears in Mrs Cotton's record on 18 October, as noted in the text.

October) Ignatius received a letter from A.H. Mackonochie, his predecessor at the St George's Mission and newly-appointed Master of the Society of the Holy Cross (*Societas Sancti Crucis*, or SSC). This Anglo-Catholic priestly society had been brought into being eight years earlier by Lowder and others, and had in fact been responsible for the foundation of the Mission; at this time Ignatius was himself a member. 'It is said (under secrecy),' Mackonochie wrote,

> that one of your Brethren is a married man – that he had been in the habit of ill-using his wife, and has now left her to become a monk in your order. I should think you will quite agree with us that a person whose life could be so described is hardly the material with which one would try to reconstruct the great Monastic system. If it is to make its way its beginnings must surely be free from such a great and manifest offence.

On 24 October Ignatius wrote back:

> You ask me if one of our Members is not a married man who has treated his wife badly. We have a married man, a Brother of the Third Order, who comes backwards and forwards on a visit now and then from Brighton. He would gladly join our First Order as a Novice only, situated as he is of course he cannot. I do not blame him for what has happened half so much as those who advised him into it. Fancy a man of 23 marrying a woman of past 40! The woman ought to have been ashamed of herself, and those who advised the young man to such a step. He wanted to break it off but she and his advisers would not allow him to do so. He was married without his own consent and only out of obedience to his spiritual directors.[53]

---

[53] Walker's misguided marriage would have been the recent 'sharp personal trial' mentioned on p18 of *Three Months*. A copy of the correspondence was made available to the Father Ignatius Memorial Trust in 1974 by the Reverend A.H. Simmons, then Master of SSC (Museum ref A1993.139.113).

THE MONASTERY AND ITS OCCUPANTS

WALKER'S TWO PERIODS of residence spanned the greater part of the brotherhood's year at Claydon. In his book he gives us a good deal of information about its organisation and daily routine (doubtless subjected to a measure of 'spin'), and a few clues about its composition.

The monks' quarters consisted of four rooms opening off a narrow upstairs corridor. As befitting his dignity as Superior Ignatius had a bedroom to himself;[54] the other rooms were a 'parlour' for the reception of visitors; the refectory, where their simple meals were brought from the Rectory kitchen; and the brothers' dormitory. This probably held no more than three or four beds, as well as washstands for the occupants' ablutions.

The main meal was midday dinner, at which pious books were read aloud. The food

---

Mrs Walker had been born Mary Preedy in 1819, and the couple were married at St George's, Hanover Square, in late 1860. The following year's census listed them at an address in Brighton, in which town Charles's family also resided. In 1871 they were living apart (Charles with his parents at 4 Belgrave Place, Brighton, and Mary with her sister and their 89-year-old mother in St Albans), but by 1881 they were once more under the same roof, back in Brighton. Meanwhile Charles had served as Master of Ceremonies to the controversial Fr Purchas at the church of St James, in 1866 publishing a handy if somewhat fanciful guide to Anglo-Catholic ceremonial under the title The Ritual Reason Why. In 1878 he seceded to Rome (this and the connection with Purchas are noted by Peter Anson in BUWP); the Walkers' final marital home was within a few hundred yards of the newly-erected Roman Catholic church of St Mary Magdalen in North Street, where he would have attended Mass and may well have continued to share his ceremonial expertise. There is no record of him making further visits to Ignatius's community, although their paths may have continued to cross in Brighton and elsewhere. Some confusion may arise from the fact that a slightly younger Charles Walker who was curate of St Michael's, Brighton, 1863-67 and also a writer of Anglo-Catholic literature was admitted to the Brighton branch of Ignatius's Third Order (as 'Brother Ambrose') in 1863, and that the 'Three Months' Charles although said by Ignatius also to have belonged to the Third Order was not listed in its Register of members.

[54] In which he took his vows of poverty, chastity and obedience with Mr Drury as witness (Fletcher, op cit p127)

consisted ordinarily of a small portion of suet dumpling – the almost invariable commencement of a Suffolk dinner – seasoned, according to taste, with sugar, salt, or treacle – and a portion of plain boiled or roast meat or steak. On Wednesdays and Fridays, and on vigils, the meat was omitted, and a hard dumpling took the place of the suet pudding; and on Sundays some kind of sweet pudding was added.

In theory this was the first meal of the day, although on Sundays and feasts (and every day for those with delicate constitutions such as Ignatius and Walker himself) breakfast was served just before 9.0am. It is noteworthy that at this stage the diet included flesh meat; by the time they settled at Llanthony this would no longer be permitted, except for guests (and the ever-delicate Superior). The only other refreshment was a scratch tea just before the daily parish Evensong at 7.0pm.

According to his account there were (at least for a time) six brothers in residence, and although in some cases 'habits of obedience' were acquired more slowly than in others he tells us that the atmosphere was agreeably harmonious. This was surprising, considering the extremely close quarters at which they had to live, as well as their 'different characters and dispositions, and...different habits of life previous to joining the order', Walker's delicate way of alluding to social class. One of them – a 'lay brother of middle age, who occasionally accompanied me to Ipswich and elsewhere, and was frequently my companion in recreation time' – he would certainly have regarded as his social inferior:

> He was, of course, very imperfectly educated, and had been brought up in the focus of dissent and radicalism, the *atelier* of an east-end tailor.

Despite the social gulf Walker felt 'drawn' to this brother because 'he never seemed to have any interest for anything but religion', and used to amuse his leisure hours by composing sermons, which he generally read to me on their completion; and though, of course, they had grave defects both of style and grammar, I could not help thinking that a body of preachers taken from the lower ranks would be a great boon to the Church.

In Walker's opinion such working class 'monastic preachers' might have helped to stem the leakage to the dissenting bodies, whose appeal was mainly to 'the poor'. The fact that the ministers of these bodies were drawn from the same class as their ordinary members meant that they could 'understand them better than the gentry [could]', and explained why they were apparently so successful.

This brother had only once travelled outside his native city, and to Walker it was

quite charming to see his appreciation of rural scenes and incidents. An enormous flight of crows, who literally covered a large field on one of our walks, gave him the child-like pleasure that is rarely witnessed in its perfection except among a party of children at a pantomime or a raree-show.

Another brother, a 'not altogether satisfactory' one, 'had joined shortly before I came' (for his second visit). This individual 'committed an act of disobedience, with certain attendant circumstances'. The situation was considered serious enough for the brother to be placed on a regime of solitary penance, consisting of meditations and other religious exercises appointed by the Prior (i.e. Walker himself), then deputising for Ignatius in the latter's absence, and daily recitation of the entire Psalter as well as the hours of the divine office. The object was to 'test his vocation rather severely'. He is said to have survived this ordeal, although we aren't told how long he remained in the monastery after undergoing it.

Walker tells us that this young man had been 'disgusted with the Protestant aspect with which the Church of England came before him' and had gone over to Rome, hoping to join a Catholic community. 'On hearing of Brother Ignatius, however, he immediately begged to be admitted.' One wonders what other motives played a part in this decision, and where he went next. Another brother had found the Cistercian noviciate too tough, but having 're-studied the controversy, and convinced himself of the claims of the English Church' was happy to have a monastery of that communion in which to pursue his vocation. Yet another, who arrived after the author's departure and took part in the migration to Norwich, had also been thinking of joining a Roman Catholic community.

Throughout this time Ignatius kept in touch with Miss Sellon, whose community was now based at Ascot. Walker relates how one of the brothers was sent to her priory there 'to assist at the farm'; this was probably towards the end of the Claydon period, as the arrangement was only intended to last 'till larger premises were secured at Claydon, or elsewhere'. Potential overcrowding in the monastic dormitory doesn't seem to have been the only motive for the passing on of this particular human parcel; the young man was accompanied by a letter stating that 'though possessing many good qualities' he 'required a careful surveillance'. This was more than the invalid Abbess could provide, and he was promptly returned to sender.

Then there were the 'children of the community', who seem to have become a feature of the Ignatian establishment even before any monks were in a position to take first vows. They are mentioned – in passing – because one of the chores which devolved on the small number of adult brothers was that of providing them with tuition. We are also told that like the Abbot and the Prior these boys were given breakfast. Elsewhere in the book there is a passing reference to 'one of the boys, a novice of the Order', and another to young boys who would surround a brother (presumably Walker himself) when he took a turn in the Rectory grounds at Recreation: '...a boy hanging to each arm, another leaping about excitedly in front, and perhaps two more, each contesting with its possessor his right to the arm....' These may have been village children rather than occupants of the monastery, suggesting that in what would now be termed its 'outreach' the brotherhood was making more progress than in the difficult business of establishing a firmly based monastic life; this would always be its weakness.

'RIDICULOUS MIMICRIES'

IF A SURPLICE IN THE PULPIT had provoked riots in Stepney, how much more controversial was the exotic Ritualism being introduced at Claydon. Drury had already made a start (a comparatively cautious one, perhaps), but with the arrival of the fledgling Superior and his associates all discretion was thrown to the winds, and by and large the parishioners didn't like it. 'Parishioners' of course meant all the people of the parish, including those who worshipped in dissenting chapels or nowhere at all. Church played a greater part in people's lives then than now, even if only as one of the pillars supporting stable society, and church news was eagerly followed: not surprisingly, the ritual developments at Claydon featured in the local papers for much of the brotherhood's time there.

The publicity began with an account in the *Ipswich Journal* of the services for Ascension Day, whose observance or lack of it was for Ignatius always a touchstone of authentic churchmanship (he had asked the village shopkeepers to shut down for the day, with only partial success). The report was noticed by the leader writer of *The Times*, who on 27 May reproduced some of the highlights from the local paper's report:

> The ruling idea evidently was to outdo everything that has been done in the way of services, ceremonies, processions, ornamentations, and gesture.... Of course the walls and everything else were covered with flowers, ecclesiastical letters, gold and silver tinsel. There were about thirty candles at the altar, great and small, two of them ten feet high.

Brother Ignatius appears to be always in the church, in and out of service time, moving about in a quaint and novel dress, with a large black and gold crucifix hanging from his side, appearing and disappearing, and of course never reappearing but to make his due obeisance, and occasionally a prostration. He is assisted by youths dressed with equal taste, with the addition of short white surplices, and hempen cords knotted at intervals round their waists. The Rector also had a novel and elegant costume.... There were all kinds of mysterious significations in the movements of the assistants and choristers, in the candles that were lighted and that were not lighted, and that were put out and lighted again. A censer was brought in and made a good deal of, Brother Ignatius incensing the Rector, and the Rector incensing Brother Ignatius, the altar, every part of the church, the choristers, and the congregation.

All this was at the Vigil Service on Wednesday. On Thursday there was all this and a good deal more....

The point for *The Times* was whether these 'ridiculous mimicries' could be anything other than a diversion from the most serious issue facing the Church in the early 1860s: the 'awful question' of whether the Bible was or was not a record of historical facts, and if it wasn't whether the Christian faith could survive without it. It was only four years since Darwin had published his *Origin of Species*, and in this leader one can sense the discomfort felt by thinking people as old certainties melted away. The writer's unease was compounded by the facile way in which the 'simple villagers' of Claydon appeared to be being offered theatrical entertainment in place of solid religion:

As fast as religion has lost its hold on the heart and mind, a race of scene-painters, mechanists, property dealers, tailors and masters of ceremonies have come to its rescue with devices of their own.

Ignatius was untroubled by any such doubts, and the ensuing correspondence in the local press centred on questions of legality, historical precedent and Biblical and patristic exegesis: a far headier brew than would be accepted by the editor of a local weekly nowadays. Lengthy arguments both *pro* and *con* were printed in the *Ipswich Journal*, including some heavyweight contributions from 'An English Churchman' in Brighton; this of course was Charles Walker, at home with his parents between his two spells at Claydon.

On 30 May the *Norfolk News* gave an account of the Pentecost celebrations, which seem to have equalled those of Ascension Day in magnificence. J.F. Molloy, whose two-volume survey *The Faiths of the Peoples* includes some material on Ignatius not published elsewhere, gives the following account:

> Crowds came from far and near to witness the strange sights in Claydon Church; but no disturbance seems to have taken place, save on one occasion, when a carrier, sitting solitary in the building to await a service, watched Ignatius marching up and down before the altar, apparently rehearsing. The Brother on seeing the spectator, requested him to depart in peace; but the yokel refused, whereon the Brother called on the Father to eject him, which the Rev. George Drury did with the aid of a red-hot poker snatched from the stove, which he laid about the man's forehead and face; an assault for which he was fined five pounds and costs.[55]

This court appearance (in November) was the second that Mr Drury had had to make that year. Earlier the Bishop of Norwich had issued a directive that on account of the controversial innovations

---

[55] This two-volume collection of essays on various expressions of popular religion was published in 1892 and includes a not totally reliable history of Ignatius's monastic ventures under the title *Monasticism in the Church of England*. This and the following quotation from vol 2 p142.

in the parish none but the incumbent should preach in the churches
at Claydon and Akenham.

> But the Rev. George Drury being disinclined to obey, his lordship took
> proceedings against him in the Arches Court, which were eventually
> abandoned on the Rector agreeing to discontinue the processions,
> ceremonies, and observances complained of, and to submit to the
> Bishop's desires in the arrangements, ornamentation, and furniture
> of the church.

The 'carrier' ejected by Drury was a local labourer named
Abraham Watkins, whose voice Ignatius recognised from his part in
demonstrations against his activities, which continued for much of
his stay in Claydon. Watkins had come into the church through the
vestry door (the principal door being locked) while the monks were
at Vespers, claiming that he wished to attend the parish Evensong
an hour later. Among the witnesses to appear in the Rector's defence
was one of the three monks who had been present with Ignatius in
the church (Brother Patrick; he testified in the habit and was named
as 'Mr Matthews'); by the time the case came up three weeks after
the event the other two had left, one for St George's Mission and
the other for Worcester.[56]

As a result of the episcopal inhibition Ignatius began to preach
sermons (technically billed as 'lectures') in the Rectory barn, although
the community continued to recite their offices in the church and
to assist with the regular services.[57] Walker claimed that Ignatius's

---

[56] Report in *Ipswich Journal*, 28 November 1863. Matthews also left soon
afterwards. A fortnight after his court appearance several papers noted
that he had been received into the Roman Catholic Church at the
Brompton Oratory, although he later denied this.

[57] His last actual sermon – which he was careful to say wasn't a sermon,
although it was delivered at a service in the church (it was in fact an
explanation and justification of his position) – was on Whitsunday
evening. A summary was included in the *Journal* report of 30 May 1863.

influence had increased church attendance and the number of communicants, but this did nothing to lessen opposition among certain sections of the parish. Quite early on he mentions a group of boys who had formerly served as choristers in Claydon church, but whose schoolmistress had 'in a fit of anti-monastic zeal' moved them to another parish. Their loyalty having been 'easily swayed' against the brothers they now made a nuisance of themselves by taunting them with such unpleasantnesses as 'a disgusting parody of the "Venite", interlarded with imprecations that made the blood boil, coming from such young boys'.

More serious was the mob organised by some of the local farmers (payment being 'had out in beer') to disrupt the sermons in the barn –

Their work was to hoot and insult the ladies, women, and children, many of whom came from a distance, and who were, of course, very much frightened, and to 'annoy' the Brothers in every conceivable way short of actionable violence. This latter object was accomplished by discordant yells, rude jests, oaths, maniacal shrieks, pushing each other against them, slamming gates upon them, &c., occasionally diversified by dung-throwing and...rotten-egg throwing.

Another source of annoyance was

the old woman who swept out the Baptist chapel, and who, in spite of some sixty years or so, used to dance before the Brothers when they went to visit any sick person, or had any occasion to pass through the village, clapping her hands, tinkling a small bell, or beating a watering-pot with a stick.

Walker tells us that the 'chief sufferer' on these occasions was the watering-pot. Later the rabble took to throwing stones through the windows of the church and Rectory, the brothers and their

supporters – including on one occasion the Rector himself – narrowly escaping serious harm.

LEAVING CLAYDON

BEFORE ANY SERIOUS OPPOSITION had come his way – on St Benedict's Day (21 March) – the young Superior and a companion had awarded themselves an excursion to East Bergholt. This was to visit the community of Catholic Benedictine nuns which had established itself there six years earlier. Originally founded in Brussels in 1598, they had had to abandon their property there at the Revolution and take refuge in Winchester.[58] After a rather sticky start (the sisters' teenage boy servant said 'in a somewhat disagreeable tone, that the sisters were in chapel, and that no-one was admitted on any pretext', but relented when Ignatius threatened to report his insolence to the Abbess) they were admitted to the parlour and regaled with a collation of bread, wine and oranges. The two nuns who received them (the Abbess was unable to do so as she was confined to bed by an attack of gout) told them something of their community's history, including their absolute poverty when they arrived in Winchester. When the two brothers confided that they were in the same state at Claydon they were told 'very emphatically, "Then you'll succeed."'[59]

---

[58] In 1939 the sisters had to move from East Bergholt to temporary quarters outside the danger zone. After the war the convent relocated to Haslemere, where it survived until 1987. Their former home was occupied by Franciscan brothers for some years; it now houses a secular commune (see http://oldhall.org.uk).

[59] Walker is quite emphatic that he wasn't Ignatius's companion on this occasion, which is why he places this account in his Introduction rather than the body of his book. As the visit took place a couple of days short of the 'five weeks' the author tells us his first stay lasted it is likely that he had in fact just left, and that the Superior and his one remaining subordinate were consoling themselves with the luxury of a day out. Anson (BUWP p53) erroneously states that 'no record' exists of Ignatius visiting this community. The visitors were surprised that the nuns bent their timetable to the exigencies of their communal life by reciting Vespers at 2.0pm and Compline an hour later. Their hosts asked after Miss Sellon, and members of Dr Neale's sisterhood

The East Bergholt nuns had survived sixty years in protestant England by shunning the limelight and getting on quietly with the Benedictine business of *laborare* and *orare*. Ignatius's vocation, by contrast, was defined by its visibility – 'to come *before the world* as a Monk'. The presence of his monastic enterprise at Claydon may have brought some positive gains to the life of the village, but at the cost of disturbance to its normally quiet routine; and in spite of the *maigre* diet it must also have inflated the Rectory household expenses. When Mr Drury suggested that a financial contribution might be in order (something Ignatius himself would later insist on from intending aspirants) the monastic kitty was empty and with no immediate prospect of being replenished, and it was clear that the community would have to find a new home.[60]

At this point Ignatius seems nearly to have given up the struggle. His father tried to lure him back into a conventional ecclesiastical career by offering him another foreign holiday (in Italy, this time), and assistance in finding a suitable curacy. He asked God for a sign, and received it one morning at Mass in the parish church. When Mr Drury elevated the Host he perceived it as momentarily transformed into a 'living ball of light' from which 'a single ray of glory' seemed to 'leap out', flashing 'like a meteor across the silent sanctuary' and

---

who had briefly operated a branch house in Ipswich. The rudeness of the boy servant was explained by his being 'a convert'; happily this problem seems to have been overcome by June of the following year, when Elizabeth Cotton paid the first of many visits to the convent (she also became very friendly with the Roman Catholic priests in Ipswich and members of their congregation).

[60] Two years after Ignatius's departure Drury was instrumental in setting up another neo-Benedictine community in his parish, this time of nuns, which seems to have lasted at least until the early 1880s. It was presided over by a Miss Mary Ware, who bought a house in the main street with the intention of running a school for the village children. This sisterhood, dubbed by Drury's enemies as his 'harem', does not figure in *The Call of the Cloister*, Peter Anson's more or less comprehensive catalogue of Anglican religious communities, but is mentioned in the diary of Elizabeth Cotton, who with her eldest daughter Alice was a frequent visitor; see Hardy op cit pp187ff.

burying itself 'in his own troubled heart'.[61] This may have been no more than a sudden burst of sunshine coming through the east window and lighting up the Host and the surrounding area, but to the ever-suggestible Superior it was sufficient to resolve his indecision.

IGNATIUS THE EVANGELIST

A NEW HOME for his monastery would cost money. The Baroness says Ignatius needed £300 to secure suitable premises, and that within a few weeks he did indeed manage to get this sum together.[62] Calder-Marshall suggests that this consisted of 'five-sixths promise',[63] which explains why when he had to come up with a £50 deposit his resources were once again exhausted.

His new source of income was the preaching of missions in towns and cities up and down the country, an enterprise suggested to him by Drury. It was to become the main support for his monastery for the rest of his (and its) life, and began with a tour of the Westcountry.

Press reports indicate that the main thrust of this campaign was propaganda for the restoration of the monastic life. He took what for most of his hearers was the novel line that although not explicitly mentioned in the Bible something very like monasticism was evident both in the Old Testament and the New. The call of Jesus to leave one's family for his sake and the Gospel's was nothing if not a call to the monastic life, and Our Lord himself was the perfect example of 'a preaching monk'. This suggestion (made at a meeting in Exeter in December) was received unfavourably by the correspondent of *Trewman's Exeter Flying Post*,[64] although his opposite

---

[61] Bertouch p159

[62] ibid p160. Perhaps £20,000 in today's money?

[63] *Enthusiast* p109

[64] Issue of 16 December 1863

number on the *Western Times*[65] seems to have been a little more sympathetic. The latter report notes that this event (in the Clarence Hotel, just opposite the Cathedral) was rather thinly attended (by about forty people, which number had 'towards the close of the lecture...considerably diminished'), and provides a revealing picture of the early Ignatius at work:

> The personal appearance of Ignatius is rather interesting. He has regular, intelligent, features, which, however, are very feminine, and from his adopting the monkish habit of shaving [the face: luxuriant side-whiskers were then the usual fashion], you would hardly know whether you were listening to a 'sainted brother' or a holy sister, if it were not for his masculine voice. His manner is very impressive, and he has a continual habit of shutting his eyes, as if invoking the help above....

Soon after this meeting his cousin Rafe Leycester came across Ignatius at the house of some mutual friends in Ealing:

> This afternoon went to the Fentons where I saw Leycester Lyne who is got up as a monk[,] cowl cape sandals &c &c is looking very ill & no wonder. He has just succeeded in getting subscriptions & is endowing £300 per anm on a monastery which is to be taken & filled with these monks.[66]

A similar address to the one he had given in Exeter was delivered at the Victoria Rooms in Bristol on 22 January:

> The rev. lecturer concluded by asking the meeting to aid them, by joining their third order, an association for prayer for the restoration

---

[65] Date unverifiable; report copied in *Birmingham Daily Post* of 21 December 1863.

[66] Rafe Leycester's diary, entry for Sunday 3 January 1864. He seems to have misunderstood the significance of the figure £300, and it is not clear to whom the word 'these' refers.

of their religious homes, by annual subscriptions, and by contributions of the very commonest furniture for their first home, one of the old monasteries which they entered upon next week, and which they were going into without any beds.[67]

---

[67] Bristol Mercury, 23 January 1864

Picture 2: The former monastery at Elm Hill, Norwich

CHAPTER 3

NORWICH

THIS 'FIRST HOME' was in Norwich, where Ignatius had obtained
a run-down collection of buildings in Elm Hill, containing
altogether some forty rooms. Today this historic thoroughfare is
regarded as 'the most picturesque street' in the city,[68] and its ancient
and characterful buildings are cherished accordingly. When the
'English Order of St Benedict' moved into the ramshackle dwellings
now comprising numbers 12, 14 and 16 the area would certainly
have been classed as a slum. Running back from number 12 was a
disused rag and bone warehouse, distinguished by a lack of glass in
its windows; contemporary photographs such as the one on page 59
show that the rear of number 16 was even more dilapidated.

To describe it as 'one of the old monasteries' was rather an
exaggeration, although the land it occupied may at one time have
belonged to the adjacent Dominican priory. Across the alleyway to
the side of the property was the east end of the former conventual
church, which unusually for such a building had neither been
taken over for parish use (central Norwich is still particularly well
provided with parish churches, some of them of considerable size)
nor demolished piecemeal to provide materials for other projects.
Instead – as it still does – it served the city as a central public hall.

The particular vocation of the Dominicans was preaching, and a
large church had been necessary to accommodate those who came
to hear. For Ignatius the proximity of this secularised House of
God may have been a thorn in the flesh – at one point he thought

---

[68] Pevsner, *The Buildings of England: North-East Norfolk and Norwich* (Penguin
1962) p270

seriously of buying it[69] – but it was also an incentive to develop his own version of the Dominican speciality. If the Black Friars had 'thrown open' their church to those who came to hear their sermons in pre-Reformation Norwich, he would 'throw open' his monastery chapel for the same purpose to their nineteenth century descendants.

The Superior and 'one or two others' moved into the new monastery on 30 January, to be joined within the next few days by a further seven or eight, for the time being making ten altogether.[70] The Baroness identifies the 'one or two others' as a brother – named by Calder-Marshall as Dunstan, who for a time was Walker's successor as Prior – and a 'huge and magnificent' dog; in default of adequate bedding this animal kept Ignatius and Dunstan warm at night.

Elm Hill was not a prosperous part of the city, but the neighbours – many of them workers in the building and allied trades – rallied round to stop up the gaps. Some of them also brought what small gifts they could afford – a few potatoes or dried herrings, or perhaps a sack of coal. On one occasion the brothers were brought a parcel containing what at first they thought might be some obscure ecclesiastical vestment, but which turned out to be a frilled flannel nightgown sent by an elderly lady concerned at their lack of heating. The Baroness tells us that the resultant 'hilarity...was in itself a consummation of the donor's intention, inasmuch as...they laughed until they were thoroughly warm, all round'. [71]

Ignatius promoted himself from 'Brother' to 'Father' and assumed the title Abbot, expecting to be accorded appropriate signs of reverence. He is said to have 'introduced a most slavish kind of

---

[69] This 'ambition' was mentioned in the *Manchester Times* report (9 April 1864) of a lecture Ignatius delivered at the Free Trade Hall.

[70] The figures and dates are from Walker, who was writing as events unfolded. The Baroness misdates the arrival in Norwich to January 1863, and is consistently a year in advance for the period dealt with in this and the preceding chapter.

[71] Bertouch p180

homage, enjoining his associates of the order never to speak to him unless they went down on their knees, and never to pass him without making a prostration'[72] – the same signs of reverence John Spence would complain about having to observe a few years later. He also introduced the full monastic tonsure for himself and his brethren: when a few months later Elizabeth Cotton attended a lecture delivered by Ignatius in Ipswich she was shocked to find that he now wore 'his hair almost quite shaved off'; he was also looking 'ill and very altered'.[73]

Within a few days of their arrival the brothers had furnished a temporary chapel and opened it to the public. At first it was in an upstairs room, which at a pinch could hold sixty people,[74] but by Ash Wednesday (10 February) it had been relocated to the ground floor of the rag warehouse, where three rooms were joined together. The *Norfolk Chronicle* sent a reporter to attend the morning service the following Sunday (Morning Prayer and Ante-Communion, followed by an '"incantation" to the Virgin Mary', and a 'Meditation upon the Temptation of Christ' delivered by the Superior 'in a slow and measured tone'). The new chapel was 'about fourteen yards long, and five or six wide', and pervaded by an atmosphere of 'mouldy dampness...which was not at all inviting'. The altar was set on a triple footpace, and 'gaudy' in appearance, with 'bright and glittering' hangings and numerous candles on the three gradines rising up behind it, as well as a crucifix and vases of artificial flowers.

The opening procession was led by Ignatius himself, 'bearing a crucified figure on a brass wand', and followed immediately by a small boy carrying an 'incensory'. After him came four monks, each wearing a 'white surplice, with a black stripe down the back, and a grotesque, black, sharp-pointed cowl'. The juvenile thurifer wore a

---

[72] Norfolk News, 1 July 1865

[73] Hardy op cit pp183f

[74] Bertouch p173

'white gown, tied with pink ribbon', and the correspondent noted that he took a 'prominent part' in the service and had a 'beautiful voice', as indeed had the Superior. There were four other choristers, arrayed like the incense-bearing one in 'white gowns'. Towards the end of the service the monastery dog (a 'large mastiff') found its way into the chapel, causing 'much anxiety' to those present.

A few weeks later the monastery received a visit from the priest-poet Gerald Moultrie, who wrote an enthusiastic account for the *Church Times*.[75] He arrived a little before 8 o'clock on the evening of Saturday 2 April, and as he was led by the 'old porter' (a volunteer from the neighbourhood) through the courtyard at the rear of the building he could hear 'the clear voice of the Superior preaching' through the open windows of the chapel. Having been shown to his room he 'slipped in' to the chapel to join the congregation, which he estimates at around three hundred, with many standing and an overflow outside. (This was the age of the crinoline, and a special cloakroom had to be instituted with a Third Order sister in attendance to assist with the removal and reinstating of the hidden

---

[75] What now serves as 'trade journal' for Church of England clergy had been founded to promote the Anglo-Catholic cause in the same month that Ignatius arrived in Claydon; the report was reproduced as an appendix to Walker's *Three Months* (pp 293ff). Moultrie (1829-86) is assumed by Calder-Marshall and others to have acted as chaplain to the community, but this was probably his only visit. He is said by Bertouch (p176) to have been Headmaster of Reading Grammar School (a fact not mentioned in his *Crockford* entry, nor known at the school itself, now known as Reading School: reply to email enquiry, 8 January 2013). He was, however, living in that town at the time, and in the census three years earlier had been listed as curate of Binfield, another (?) omission from his *curriculum vitæ* in *Crockford*. This gives his first post after graduating as an assistant mastership at Shrewsbury School (1852-55; he was made deacon by the Bishop of Lichfield in his second year there), followed by nine years (1855-1864) as Chaplain to the Dowager Marchioness of Londonderry, during which period (in 1858) he was priested by the Bishop of Durham. Later in 1864 he moved to the parish of Barrow Gurney in Somerset, and from there in 1869 to that of South Leigh, Oxfordshire, where he remained until his death. He is perhaps best remembered nowadays for his translation (*Let all mortal flesh keep silence*) of the hymn sung at the Great Entrance in the Liturgy of St James.

framework so that the ladies who came thus attired took up no more than their fair share of space.)

Moultrie rated the chapel

> very pretty...so far as interior decoration makes beauty. The cross-beams of the ceiling supported on iron pillars clad in red cloth, three down each side; thus giving an appearance of central nave with side aisles. A conventional chancel is made by a high screen, rendered impervious to the eye by coloured hangings, except where the richly vested altar with crucifix and candles, flowers, &c., is seen through the central arch. Within the chancel sate the Brothers, seven or eight in number, surpliced and cowled, together with two or three choristers and acolytes.

On his visit the altar crucifix acquired a special significance. As a visiting priest Moultrie was naturally invited to celebrate Mass for the community, at which Ignatius played the organ. At the Crucifixus in the Creed, Moultrie 'distinctly saw the Figure on the Cross move':

> First the upturned Eyes closed and then re-opened, then the Head, which was originally raised, fell forward as in contemplation, and finally the Face turned right round and fixed Its gaze on the Monk Ignatius. The look, said Mr Moultrie, was one of ineffable sweetness, and it was bestowed so slowly that he was able to grasp its full intensity, but that was all. After a moment's space, the Head gradually regained Its former pose, the Lids lifted once more, and the Crucifix became what it had been before — an inanimate image.[76]

---

[76] Bertouch pp182f. The cross was later used at Llanthony for the Veneration on Good Friday. It reappeared when the Father Ignatius Memorial Trust began to assemble its collection of monastic archives and artefacts, but has since gone missing. Moultrie made no mention of this incident in his *Church Times* account.

From time to time Fr Drury also said Mass in the monastery chapel, but by 'administering the Holy Communion on unauthorised premises' he found himself once again in trouble with his Bishop.[77] On another occasion the visiting celebrant was Ignatius's cousin Charles Lyne, in whose Cornish cure he had preached his first sermon.[78]

Soon Ignatius made a convert of the Vicar of St Lawrence's, Mr Hillyard, who up to that time had identified himself as an evangelical. At Easter he started celebrating the Holy Communion in a chasuble at an altar embellished with crucifix, candles and flowers, and for the rest of that year the brethren went in procession every morning to Mass in his imposing Perpendicular church.[79] Calder-Marshall tells us that 'after his "first Catholic Mass" in St Laurence's, Mr Hillyard was afraid of being stoned alive' by his enraged parishioners,[80] and that on Ignatius's orders his Third Order members entered the church by night and destroyed their privately rented pews. Numerous complaints about the ritualistic activities at St Lawrence's were reported the Norwich papers that year, but how the pews were removed seems to have gone unmentioned. (However, the fact that they had been taken out and replaced with 'rush-bottomed chairs' was noted at the end of the following year.[81])

---

[77] *Ipswich Journal*, 11 March and 15 April 1865

[78] In a letter to *The Times* (11 April 1878) Charles Lyne would publicise his apology to his own Bishop and the Bishop of Norwich for having 'thoughtlessly and foolishly, celebrated the Holy Communion in vestments' in the Elm Hill chapel. The letter was doubtless prompted by the passing four years earlier of the Public Worship Regulation Act, which attempted to control by the heavy hand of the secular power the use of such tokens of Ritualism as vestments, candles and incense, and was responsible for not a few 'political' disavowals. But he made no apology for having on a later occasion preached at a service connected with the dedication of a new Masonic lodge in Barnstaple, part of which event included among other ritualistic features the ceremonial carrying of incense in front of the Provincial Grand Master (*North Devon Journal*, 24 August 1871).

[79] Now 'St Lawrence Textile Centre'

[80] *Enthusiast* p97, following Bertouch pp224f

[81] *Norfolk News*, 30 December 1865

Readers of the *Ipswich Journal* were still kept up to date with news of the community after its removal to Norwich. When they had been there three months it reported that on emerging from St Lawrence's one morning the brothers were subjected to pushing and shoving by 'roughs', in the course of which Brother Augustine (whom we shall encounter shortly) 'was trodden on to such a degree, that he is reported to have fainted, and was obliged to have assistance to the monastery'.[82]

The same report carried details of a 'mutiny' at the community, although strictly speaking not so much a mutiny as an escape. On this occasion the rebellion was confined to 'two of the "brethren" [running] off...with the habiliments of the Order', soon after which 'two others followed their example..., escaping by the back window'. No record survives of the identity of the four escapees, nor of where they went; their break-out occurred too late for them to have been the same individuals against whom the Abbot had issued a warning at the beginning of the month by a letter to the Church press, copied by other papers:

> Two persons pretending to be emissaries from our convent are going about the country raising money under false pretences. They have already deceived several charitable persons.... As these persons wear our habit, we feel that the trick is likely to succeed unless timely warning is given....[83]

The relationship with St Lawrence's came to an abrupt end in January 1865, when Ignatius 'excommunicated' its incumbent, as well as several other members of the Third Order. Having strict views on the impropriety of dancing (as well as of smoking and the

---

[82] Issue of 30 April 1864

[83] *Manchester Times*, 9 April 1864.

theatre, although not of the consumption of alcohol[84]) he had issued an edict forbidding their attendance at a ball in St Andrew's Hall, the former Dominican church. The young Abbot (he turned 26 in November 1864) expected the same obedience from his tertiaries as from members of his 'First Order', but Fr Hillyard and his family and friends had no intention of subjecting their social life to his dictation. In that first April (1864) Hillyard's association with 'certain people calling themselves monks, whom he [had] allowed to participate in the services of his church' had contributed to the loss of his post as chaplain of the local workhouse; in June it also cost him his honorary position with the district schools committee.[85]

Meanwhile the monastery had acquired a resident chaplain, the Reverend Gideon Ouseley, a clerical 'rolling stone' who came to rest in Norwich for just a year, having decided to move there to 'help the Catholic cause'.[86] Ouseley had been born in Portugal and baptised into the Roman Catholic Church, to which he would return in old age as a layman. He was brought up (in Ireland) as an Anglican, married, and ordained by the Bishop of Down and Connor. After a brief curacy in that diocese he came to England, where a few years after his association with the Elm Hill brotherhood he was reordained

---

[84] The subject of another pencilled correction by Dom Cyprian Alston, this time in the margin of p52 of the Downside copy of the former Brother Gildas (B.G.A. Cannell)'s memoir of life at Llanthony in the 1890s, From Monk to Busman.

[85] There is an oblique reference to the parting of the ways between the Abbot and Fr Hillyard in the Bury and Norwich Post of 31 January 1865. The penances imposed on those who would accept them included lying in ashes on the chapel floor (for females) and public flogging by Ignatius (for the younger males); see Enthusiast pp98f. An enquiry into Hillyard's shortcomings as Workhouse chaplain was fully reported in the Norfolk News of 29 October 1864; among other complaints was that he had on occasion employed Gideon Ouseley (see below) to do duty for him.

[86] From his reported evidence at the Hillyard enquiry. Gideon Jasper Richard Ouseley (1835-1906) was the son of General Sir Ralph Ouseley, whose brother (another Gideon) was celebrated in Ireland as a Methodist preacher. The first mention of him in the surviving records of the Elm Hill monastery is as officiant at a baptism on 24 June (see Appendix 1).

as a priest in the Catholic Apostolic (Irvingite) Church, serving at its place of worship in Maida Avenue, Paddington.[87] Glimpses of Ouseley in his Norwich days are provided in various newspaper reports. One, of a meeting to discuss plans for the forthcoming Church Congress, noted that 'the Rev. G.J. Ouseley, who assists Brother Ignatius in the ministrations established at the monastery of the English Order of St Benedict, was present in his peculiar garb'[88] – probably the Roman-style cassock and biretta which he wore for our photograph. Another, entitled 'Christmas Day with Brother Ignatius',[89] included these observations:

Picture 3: The Reverend Gideon Ouseley, Chaplain at Elm Hill

[87] Ouseley's esoteric beliefs would eventually cause his separation from the Irvingites. In line with his enthusiasm for fruitarianism and animal welfare he propagated an eccentric version of the Gospel at whose Last Supper there was no Paschal Lamb, causing Judas Iscariot to ask why there was no meat to eat. For further details see http://www.tektonics. org/lp/ouseley01.html.

[88] Ipswich Journal, 14 January 1865

[89] Norfolk Chronicle, 31 December 1864

The Communion prayers and commandments, in which part of the Litany was oddly mixed up, were read, sung, or mumbled in a most remarkable fashion. Mr Ouseley cannot be complimented upon his style of chanting. His voice is weak, and, as compared with Brother Ignatius, his musical and general powers are of a secondary order. Thus the manner in which he gave, for instance, the word 'grace' – which he rendered 'gra-a-a-a-ace' – was wearisome in the extreme, while portions of the service, which he mumbled over with startling rapidity, were utterly unintelligible.

Ouseley also officiated at the liturgy on the following Good Friday, which was attended by 'a numerous and closely-packed congregation, principally of the poorer class'. As the opening procession 'advanced at a snail's pace through the gloom' of the darkened chapel '[t]he voice of Brother Ignatius could...be detected in the hymn which the procession was singing', and it could be observed that he was carrying 'what appeared to be a small coffin draped with black, and surmounted by a crown of thorns' – evidently not too small to contain a large and life-like crucifix. The service included two anthems sung solo (with 'much pathos') by the Abbot, who also chanted the Passion Gospel:

> ...At the words 'It is finished, and he bowed his head and gave up the ghost,' an attempt was made to portray the lightning and thunder which the Scripture narratives record to have attended the real event. The thunder was more successful than the lightning, which may be said, indeed, to have been a mere flash in the pan; some of the kitchen utensils would seem, from the nature of the sound evolved, to have been concerned behind the scenes in the production of the thunder. At this extraordinary scene – or rather attempt at a scene – Brother Ignatius, Mr Ouseley, all the monks, and most of the congregation prostrated themselves for a few seconds. The children present appeared to be particularly impressed with the mimic thunderings and lightnings....[90]

---

[90] Bristol Mercury, 22 April 1865

THE FIRST BROTHERS

IN THE COURSE of its two and a half years' existence numerous aspirants passed through the Elm Hill monastery. The first to stay for any length of time was William Pointer, whose age was given as 22 years and three months when he arrived on 1 May 1864, and whose 'life' profession took place on the same day four years later. Like the Abbot himself he would then be elevated from 'Brother' to 'Father', his name in religion being recorded as 'Fr Philip of the H— R—' ('Holy Rosary', perhaps). One of the customs Ignatius had picked up from his researches into various forms of the religious life was that of tagging extra dedications on to the names of his monks, although there was no Benedictine precedent for this; he himself was 'Ignatius of JESUS'.

Pointer was a local boy, brought up by his grandparents at a pub called the Three Jolly Dyers around the corner in Wensum Street. A few years later John Spence remembered him as 'a short sunburnt man', 'dark and evil-looking' with the mixed blessing of a 'handsome face like Mephistopheles'. Being 'naturally idle' he had been unable to survive in the secular world after his grandfather's death; Spence relates that since his admission

> he had run away seven times but failing to keep himself had always returned, and had now taken life vows, not, as he once confided to me from conviction but at the persuasion of the Reverend Father.

He 'could read and write decently', but was a 'hardhearted selfish, misanthropic man' and would 'rarely do a kindness for anybody'.

Brother Augustine, whose surname was Green, and whose ill-usage by the 'roughs' outside St Lawrence's was noted earlier, had arrived before Philip but did not stay so long. Ignatius made him his secretary, in which capacity he published a leaflet entitled The Benedictine Brothers at Norwich soon after Easter. This was partly a prospectus setting out their actual and intended activities, and partly an appeal for funds.

An unnamed brother, 'similarly apparelled' to but 'healthier looking' than Ignatius is mentioned in the report of a lecture he delivered in Manchester that April.[91] He was 'a lad of about eighteen years of age', who sat beneath the platform and kept his eyes 'fixed upon the Superior with an expression of reverence', but he may have been a Third Order member rather than an actual monk. Another teenage brother, 'Brother Oswald, a rosy-cheeked, merry-eyed lad of fifteen', is singled out by the author of a description of the procession of monks (six of them, on the occasion in question) to daily Mass at St Lawrence's for his 'evident enjoyment of the sensation he was helping to create'. This regular outing was said to have been

> invariably accompanied by hundreds who laughed and jested, hissed and groaned, and hustled each other into the church, where they stood on the seats to see the black-garbed figures prostrate themselves at full length in front of the altar, their foreheads on the ground, before receiving the sacrament.[92]

The names of various youths who joined the community crop up from time to time in local press reports. One of them, William Henry Claxton, was called to give evidence at the enquiry into Hillyard's performance as chaplain to the workhouse; he had 'formerly been an inmate of the monastery', but 'was not a monk now, having left three months'.[93] He was twenty, and had earlier been a Third Order brother with the name Alban.[94] Another was 17-year-old Walter Bell,[95]

---

[91] *Manchester Times*, 9 April 1864

[92] Untraceable newspaper extract quoted in Molloy vol 2 p145

[93] *Norfolk News*, 29 October 1864

[94] By 1871 he had married and was listed in the census at an address in Elm Hill, giving his occupation as tailor; later he would go into business elsewhere in his native city as a herbalist and chiropodist.

[95] Probably Walter Taylor Bell, listed in 1861 as a page and errand boy but apparently missing from later censuses.

who had spent four and a half months as (the second?) Brother Martin until he absconded in October 1864. On All Saints' Day he returned and was readmitted, but left again a couple of weeks later, allegedly taking with him a bundle of clothes and some loose change. Ignatius's reaction was to announce that in future he would not admit any more 'Norwich monks'.[96]

The name of Brother Brannock often figures in reports. This was Harry Fane Incledon Webber, 'a tall, gentlemanly-looking young man, with well-chiselled features, characterised, however, by a certain settled sadness'.[97] His family were prominent in the north Devon village of Braunton, where St Brannock is the local saint,[98] and he would have been 23 when he joined the community in early 1864; he stayed, as we shall see, until the Norwich venture came to an end in the summer of 1866. As with Charles Walker at Claydon his genteel origins would in Ignatius's view have made him the obvious person to act as his deputy in his frequent absences, and he was appointed 'senior brother' after the defection (or expulsion, perhaps) of Brother Dunstan.

BOYS

THE NORWICH MONASTERY (like the Ipswich one that never got off the ground) was conceived as a 'mission', and from the beginning Ignatius began to collect disciples. Boys, especially, were drawn into its orbit; when Charles Walker's book appeared at the end of April 1864 it included this report:

---

[96] *Norwich News*, 26 November 1864

[97] *Morning Post*, 31 March 1866; from a description of that year's Good Friday observance at Elm Hill.

[98] Usually nowadays spelt without a final 'k'. The name 'Brannock' easily became confused with the surname 'Bannock': when Ignatius's authority was challenged in the June 1865 rebellion (see below) it was reported that a monk named 'Thomas Bannock' had been installed in his place.

At Norwich, where the Brothers are now settled, they have a Sunday afternoon service, specially for boys, which is working with happy results. 'Yesterday afternoon,' Brother Ignatius wrote to a lady who took a deep interest in the work, 'there were more than a hundred boys at my boys' class. When it was over they were so interested, that some volunteered to come and sing in our choir, &c., and all seemed to wish to shake hands with me before they left. There was no noise, although they had evidently come in for "a lark". Before they left, I got them down on their knees on the bare stones, and they joined heartily in the "Litany of the Holy Name". It was a beautiful sight – boys of all ages and classes, who had come for a game, being brought to think seriously, as they evidently proved by their extraordinary devotion. It seemed something like a miracle.'

Later he wrote, 'How I wish I could describe last Sunday to you! ...I should think, at least, a thousand boys of all ages and classes beset our doors, waiting to attend our boys' service. Between three and four hundred, I should think, crowded our chapel and court-yard. Several want to join our third order already.'

Ignatius lost no time in starting a guild for them under the patronage of St William, a 12th century Norwich boy whose alleged martyrdom by the Jews had been celebrated in a popular mediaeval cult. Half a century later an elderly Norwich journalist recalled the 'picturesque garb of red and white' its members wore, and their visits 'over Mousehold [Heath] to what was alleged to be the site of the chapel of St William-in-the-Wood'. Here the 'cross of large stones' they laid on the site was said to have outlasted the guild by several years.[99]

---

[99] Report of Mr J.T. Varden's boyhood memories in the *Eastern Daily Press* of 10 January 1933. For Mousehold Heath and the site of the chapel see http://www.edp24.co.uk/norfolk-life/norfolk-history/46_mousehold_heath_1_214282

There were, of course, worries on the part of some parents that their sons would be enticed into leaving home altogether and becoming monks – as we have seen, some of those Ignatius accepted as postulants were very young indeed. Their fears were scarcely relieved when one wing of the monastery was made over to the St William's boys, complete with a dormitory where they could spend the night. From time to time the local press would report on the alleged 'abduction' of some adolescent adherent, usually accompanying it with comment on the perceived 'unnaturalness' of the monastic state, and the implied (and not always unjustified) suggestion that their association with the monks could place these youths in moral danger.[100]

One of these young disciples was a fifteen-year-old printer's apprentice named Samuel Hase. On 'Feast Sancti Crucis' 1864 (14 September), Brother Augustine was unwise enough to write a letter declaring passionate love for him (unrequited, as he himself realised). The declaration was accompanied by a request that the boy would go to a local photographer's studio and have his portrait taken in cassock and cotta.

The missive was intercepted by Samuel's stepmother, and passed by her to the Norfolk News. A few days later – while Ignatius was in Newcastle conducting a mission – the paper reproduced it with comments, including the suggestion that the Superior himself was 'sweet on' the boy, and had encouraged him to come to the monastery against her wishes.[101] In the following week's issue Ignatius replied. He had told the boy in her presence that without his stepmother's

---

[100] The information about the dormitory was given in a letter from Ignatius to the Norfolk News of 29 April 1865, replying to accusations that a youth named George Mills had been abducted by the community. He argued that Mills did not (as had been alleged) 'sleep at the monastery, but in the easternmost wing of the building set apart for the St William's boys and into which only the monk in charge can enter'. It would not have strengthened his case that at the time this individual was Brother Stanislaus, whom we shall encounter shortly.

[101] Norfolk News, 17 September 1864

permission he would not be allowed 'inside the monastery gate', but on the following Sunday he had turned up again, assuring him that the necessary permission had been given, and had therefore been allowed to sing in the choir and have dinner with the monks and other choirboys. Ignatius was quite clear in his mind that monastic life was inherently superior to that 'in the world', and would never willingly discourage his young followers from considering it if they showed the slightest interest (as young Hase evidently had).[102]

However, on this occasion he was able to say that boy novices were not being received at Elm Hill itself just then, as he was too busy with other concerns. Instead they were being passed on to 'a convent of Sisters of Mercy, the Superior of which has kindly consented to receive my young novices and give them all the attention they require' – Miss Sellon's community, presumably. As we have seen, one young man had been despatched to Ascot Priory from Claydon (and speedily returned), and two boys had apparently been sent there under this new arrangement, although what happened to them then or later is not recorded.

The erring brother was of course dismissed:

> I have seen the absurd and ridiculous letter which Brother Augustine wrote. I can only account for it by really believing that it was penned during a temporary fit of insanity. Nevertheless, our rules compel his expulsion, for his having infringed the orders of the house, firstly by writing a letter secretly, secondly by attempting to procure a photograph, or anything else, without leave....

In fact he hadn't waited to be expelled; according to the same newspaper's comment column he 'ran away, fearing the Superior, or something superior to them both'.[103]

---

[102] Samuel Hase continued to work in the printing trade. He married in 1871, and died of consumption in 1888.

[103] Calder Marshall (*Enthusiast* p114n) says that Augustine was 'convicted of pederasty some years later'.

Another boy disciple was Francis George Widdows, otherwise known as George Nobbs. He was thirteen when the brotherhood took up residence in Elm Hill,[104] and quickly came into its orbit. He later claimed to have been baptised and given his first Communion in one or other of the two local Roman Catholic chapels, as well as to have served at its altar; there is, however, no record of his admission to the sacraments in the registers of either of them.

The boy's mother (Elizabeth Nobbs) had been made pregnant by a man named Widdows, but because he provided no support for the child much of his early life was spent in the local workhouse. In adult life he would become notorious as an anti-Catholic propagandist, signing himself 'F.G. Widdows (Frater Aloysius), Ex-Franciscan Monk', and assuming the title 'Reverend'. In fact neither of these claims could be substantiated any better than that of his Roman Catholic childhood; his knowledge of the religious life seems to have been derived partly from his teenage association with Ignatius's community, and partly from a period in his twenties employed in Catholic schools in Canada.[105]

It is quite probable that he was indeed (as he later claimed) 'the first boy to have served Mass at the Monastery on Elm Hill',[106] in which case he may well have been the bearer of the 'incensory' mentioned in the newspaper description at the beginning of this

---

[104] Born in Norwich 13 August 1850

[105] For Widdows see Seraphim Newman-Norton, *The Terrible Tale of Ex-Monk Widdows* (Seraphic Press, 2006); I am grateful to Abba Seraphim for the information given here. Widdows's notoriety stemmed not only from his activities as an anti-Catholic propagandist but for his repeated convictions for homosexual acts, usually with under-age boys. Between 1883 and 1927 he presided over a place of worship known as 'Martin Luther Church' in Speldhurst Road, Hackney, where protestant preaching was combined with a *sui generis* form of liturgical worship. This became more ornate towards the end, when even if the rumour that Widdows had obtained irregular episcopal orders was untrue he certainly shared his pulpit with a mysterious figure known as 'Bishop Clive' (see also BAL p226).

[106] *Dundee Advertiser* 6 June 1879, quoted Newman-Norton op cit p23

chapter; certainly by the end of the first year he was well and truly involved. In the *Norwich Argus* of 7 January 1865 it was reported that the observance of Holy Innocents' Day had included a 'lecture' by 'one of the boys', whom Ignatius some years later identified as Widdows. The talk seemed ill prepared, and therefore 'not very well connected':

> Once or twice he ran to the cloister door, where one of the monks seemed to be prompting him what to say. The boy spoke of the cruelty of Herod, and his violent attempt to kill Jesus, which was all in vain, and then began saying that the Protestants with all their cruel attempts to destroy the monks had not succeeded, as they were getting on better than ever. The monks certainly did not tell the boy to say this, but after a visit to the cloister door he came back and spoke of the happiness of suffering for Jesus as the babes of Bethlehem did, and that every one who really loved Jesus must suffer in this world.

THE INFANT OBLATE

A FEW MONTHS EARLIER the monastery had acquired a real live 'babe' (who also played a part in the Innocents' Day celebrations, vested as a 'miniature priest' and 'enthroned by the acolytes in front of the altar'). This was oblate Brother Ignatius, sometimes referred to as the 'Infant Samuel', but known throughout his time in the community and beyond as 'Baby'.

Like Widdows, this child – John Henry Docking, born in Ber Street, Norwich, on 1 January 1862 – had had a poor start in life. His mother (Emily, née Vincent) had come under Ignatius's influence and been enrolled in the Third Order, so it was to him that she turned when her husband Joel, a bricklayer, abandoned her and their three children. She would have had to go out to work to put food on the table, and while the elder two (six-year-old Richard Thomas Joel and nearly five-year-old Emily Sarah) would have needed less looking after, the youngest, John Henry, was at two and three-quarters too young to leave unattended. She therefore handed him over to the Abbot at a ceremony in the Elm Hill chapel.[107]

The event was recorded in the Monastic Register:

> The Infant oblate, was dedicated to GOD on the Altar at S. Mary & S. Dunstans Monastery Norwich [several illegible words], by his Godmothers [several illegible words]. He was dedicated in the octave of the Nativity of Our Ladye, September 1864, at the Mass said by the Rev. Gideon J. Ouseley at 9 o'clock. He was 2 years (two years) & 9 months old. Having been born on the Jan 1st 1862 & baptised in the Monastery Chapel August 20th 1864. Name of Dedication: Ignatius of Mary.

Picture 4: The Elm Hill community, c1865. The Infant Oblate is at Ignatius' knee; the boy on the right may be Francis George Widdows.

---

[107] Joel and Emily had married in a local Wesleyan chapel on 12 May 1857, in which year he was seventeen and she eighteen (although both gave false ages). Joel's family had converted to Methodism some years earlier, and his elder brother Thomas (1826-1902) was a Sunday School teacher; later he qualified as a doctor and became an enthusiastic promoter of Spiritualism, Theosophy, Rosicrucianism and other strange cults. I am indebted for these and other details of his family history to Colin Affleck of Edinburgh, a great-grandson of John Henry Docking by his first wife.

The two illegible sections (respectively two-thirds of a line and a line and two words) have been heavily crossed out; the first may refer to the 'deed of gift' mentioned by the Baroness,[108] and the second is probably a list of his Godmothers (the last word could be the surname 'Trinkett'). The various dates are also less than distinct through having been corrected, and the exact date of the hand-over is not given. 'On the octave' would mean the actual octave day (15 September), but 'in the octave' could mean any day between the feast and its octave day, i.e. between 9 and 15 September.

Picture 5: John Henry Docking in middle age

We learn that his mother (who must have been given a special dispensation to enter the monastic choir) placed him on the altar, from which he was picked up by Ignatius and wrapped in the white linen 'Communion cloth'. He was then carried into the enclosure and vested in a miniature white habit and sandals, in which he functioned as a kind of monastic mascot, attracting attention wherever he went.

---

[108] See Bertouch pp231f for an account of the ceremony.

The Superior's mother took one look at him and commented, 'Don't set your heart upon that boy, he will only disappoint you. He has a very curious disposition, and not a nice one.'[109] John Spence was told that his own mother continued to visit him until the monastery moved from Norwich, so his disappearance into the enclosure would not have given her what Peter Anson suggested was her 'last peep' of her son.[110]

MORE FESTIVALS

SOME HIGHLIGHTS from life at Elm Hill in 1865 are given in Molloy's *The Faiths of the People*:

On Good Friday Ignatius, having, as he remarked, 'the impoliteness to imagine people had eyes as well as ears', had a Passion Play performed in his chapel by way of change. Later on the feast of Corpus Christi in June he and his monks, as early as half-past three in the morning, went in procession through the town, carrying lighted candles and banners, and singing so loudly as to wake the inmates of the houses they passed; but as few were abroad at that hour they were unmolested....

In the March of this year he announced that 'a forty hours adoration of the Blessed Sacrament' would take place in his chapel, adding that any one who subscribed twenty shillings towards the new church would be prayed for during that time. But on the following May, at the feast of the Ascension, he gave fuller scope to his love of display. For some weeks previous to the festival the town of Norwich was placarded with showy bills headed 'The Coronation of the King', under which was a large black cross. Then followed the admonition, 'All faithful subjects begin to prepare for grand doings on Thursday, the 25th of the month. It is the coronation day of the King. He will

---

[109] ibid pp269f

[110] BUWP p64

expect you to keep it with great solemnity and rejoicing. Get up a public and general subscription for decorating your streets, and for a grand illumination in the evening. It is the most triumphant day in all the year. All shops must be closed, the bells rung all day, and the guns from the Castle fired. Our own dear Queen Victoria, whom we all so much love, will do homage to the King on that day'

At two o'clock on Ascension morning lauds and matins began in the priory, ending with a 'procession of the Host' at four o'clock through the empty streets, the route selected being strewn with flowers, whilst hymns were loudly sung.

The report goes on to describe what it rather unkindly calls the 'imitation of the mass', celebrated later that morning by Gideon Ouseley. In the entry procession the Abbot wore a cope of white brocade and 'a paper mitre' and carried a crozier, but laid aside these symbols of office in order to accompany the service at the organ.

In the evening Ignatius, carrying in his arms the Infant Samuel and accompanied by his monks, attended St. Peter's Hungate Church; he had quarrelled with the Rector of St. Lawrence's. They took their places in the chancel and behaved quietly until the Creed, which they intoned, much to the surprise of the clergyman Mr Titlow who in vain begged them to desist, and then waited until they had finished, when he began the Creed again. An immense crowd had during the service gathered outside the church to divert themselves with a sight which had not yet lost its novelty, and to accompany Ignatius back to his residence.

The report of this Ascension Day celebration concludes with the observation that 'a regular scene of jostling, bustling and crowding ensued, notwithstanding the vigorous efforts of the police to prevent a disturbance'. Outside the Priory 'one of the monks...appears to have lost his temper,' doing his best 'to give as good as he got'. Also at the gate 'a woman' was trying 'to prevent her boy entering the place, and as might be supposed, she got a large number of sympathizers'.[111]

Among those who assisted at the early morning procession that day (Anson[112] says he helped to carry the canopy over the Host) was a young American Episcopal priest named Charles Grafton who was visiting the community at the time, just possibly with the idea of joining it. Soon afterwards he became one of the founder members of R.M. Benson's Society of St John the Evangelist (the 'Cowley Fathers'); many years later he would play a tangential part in the Llanthony story as Bishop of Fond du Lac, Wisconsin.

THE THIRD ORDER...

MENTION HAS BEEN MADE of the 'Third Order' into which Ignatius began to enrol his supporters. During the Elm Hill period just under three hundred names were listed, a good half of them (50 brothers and 92 sisters) belonging to the Norwich branch. Other numerically significant branches were in Manchester (30 brothers and 20 sisters), London (20 brothers and 19 sisters) and Bristol (23 brothers and 18 sisters). Theoretically there were another seven branches, ranging from Cheltenham (three brothers and four sisters) down to Durham (one brother), but it is unlikely that the smaller ones experienced much in the way of corporate life, or that any of them endured for long.[113] Before the decade was out there would be a new organisation, the 'Associate Brothers of the Blessed Scapular', which as the name suggests was confined to males, with a separate (and apparently quite small) body of female associates.

---

[111] Vol 2 p145; pp148-151

[112] BUWP p70n

[113] At the time of the 'Rebellion' in June 1865 it emerged that Ignatius had disbanded the Norwich branch in late April, although those who had belonged to it still identified themselves as members (*Norfolk News*, 1 July 1865).

The Abbot's preaching tours enabled him to keep in touch with this scattered flock, and to provide his followers (many of them young men in their teens and twenties) with opportunities to participate in services more exotic than those at their parish churches. A report in *Reynolds's Newspaper*[114] describes how by hanging a curtain on the wall and placing a table with crucifix and candles in front of it the Manchester Corn Exchange had been transformed for a Sunday afternoon and evening into a ritualistic church, albeit a rather rudimentary one. A processional route had been marked out, and the proceedings opened with the solemn entrance of numerous vested participants, most of them Third Order members. At the front came 'a tall young man dressed in a black robe, over which was a short white muslin frock', carrying the processional cross. Behind him walked others in the same costume, in pairs, and behind them 'two small boys...in scarlet skull caps and robes', one of whom 'swung a burning censer'. The place of honour at the back was occupied by Ignatius, walking between 'two tall brethren habited in white and gold, and blue and scarlet vestments with crosses on their backs'. One of them carried 'a mahogany crook, something like a bishop's crozier'.

The leader of this branch was H.D. Nihill, curate of the St Alban's, Cheetwood, who went by the name of 'Fr Basil'. Later that year he would be inhibited by his Bishop for unauthorised ceremonial and move to London. As Vicar of St Michael's, Shoreditch, he became a leading light in the Anglo-Catholic movement, in the early 1880s serving as Master of the Society of the Holy Cross.

ITS BRISTOL OFFSHOOT...

THE MANCHESTER REPORTER observed that the brethren there 'appeared to be persons of good social position', a description which would certainly have fitted the young man Ignatius appointed Prior

---

[114] Issue of 6 August 1865; the service had taken place the previous Sunday (30 July).

of the Bristol branch. This was nineteen-year-old Charles Amesbury Whitley Deans Dundas, great-grandson of the first and last Baron Amesbury and heir to a considerable fortune, a large part of which he devoted to Ritualistic and other money-consuming projects. With a number of others of similar age he was admitted in January 1865, taking the name Cyprian.[115]

Picture 6: Brother Cyprian OSB iij (C.A.W.D. Dundas)

Dundas's name was often in the Bristol papers over the next few years, usually in connection with the part-time brotherhood which developed from the local manifestation of 'OSB iij', and

---

[115] The dates 17 and 25 January are given in the Register, but no year. Ignatius later claimed to have admitted the first Bristol tertiaries either in 1863 or in October 1864, when he was in that city for the Church Congress.

whose speciality seemed to consist of shocking the respectable protestants of that city with their elaborate ceremonies. Like its parent community in Norwich it had to endure a certain amount of ragging, the participants in which usually ended up in the local police court. Anson quotes a couple of examples,[116] as well as mentioning Dundas's excommunication of two of the members who had disturbed the devotions of their brethren by turning up drunk for Vespers. Their ejection was carried out in accordance with Ignatius's detailed directions, and took place in the Oratory they had opened in a former workshop in Trenchard Street. After the reading of a lengthy preamble all knelt and recited the Miserere, while the altar was draped in black and all lights extinguished, except for one standing 'in the midst of the great altar itself in front of the crucifix'. The two erring brothers (Benedict and Ethelred, young men like the Prior probably still in their teens) were then 'pronounce[d] separated from all the spiritual blessings of our order, from a share in the prayers and intercessions of the monks, from the private worship and congregation of our faithful sons and daughters', and being given 'over to Satan, that their souls may be saved in the day of the Lord'. They were also wished a number of lesser ills, including (perhaps appropriately, in view of the nature of their sin) that 'their food [might] be terror and their drink...grief'.[117]

The following summer the Superior relieved Dundas of his priorship and dismissed him and his associates from the Third Order. Much of what he had to say about his former collaborator is not so very different from what others were saying about Ignatius himself. Brother Cyprian was accused of having

publicly opened, and, in spite of repeated warnings,...refused to close, a conventicle in Trenchard-street, opening it to the general public, and

---

[116] BUWP p69

[117] Bristol Mercury, 20 May 1865

constituting himself (entirely unsuited for such office, and without any authority) a public preacher in the same conventicle, which has · been called 'The Benedictine Chapel'. Considering this to be an open act of schism on the part of a young and (at present) uneducated layman, professing to act under his authority, the Reverend Father Ignatius publicly pronounces Brother Cyprian as deposed....[118]

This was soon after the final collapse of the Elm Hill venture, when it seemed to all the world that the Ignatian version of Anglo-Benedictinism was as good as finished, so Dundas can scarcely be blamed for ignoring Ignatius's expostulations and reinventing his part-time community as 'The Confraternity of St Augustine', although they continued to be known familarly as the 'Bristol Benedictines'. By this time he had acquired a property in the suburb of Montpelier which would shortly be opened as a (never very successful) home for orphan boys, in whose grounds he erected a large and splendidly furnished corrugated iron chapel. Here he continued to officiate at daily services and sometimes to preach, vested in cassock and surplice and the Confraternity's special tippet.

On occasion Mass would be celebrated by visiting clergymen. One of them was Gideon Ouseley, who by the autumn of 1866 had fetched up in the Westcountry, although Dundas would eventually dismiss him for his refusal to stick to the authorised Prayer Book. (Ouseley also helped out in the then notoriously ritualistic chapel of ease at Northmoor Green near Bridgwater, where he is reported to have used the Communion service from the 1549 Prayer Book and to have omitted the *Filioque* from the Creed.[119])

A few days after the publication of Ignatius's letter, the opening of 'St Augustine's Home' was celebrated with a grand High Mass. Work on the iron church would not begin for another year, so it

---

[118] ibid, 21 July 1866
[119] ibid, 20 October 1866

took place in a temporary chapel (a marquee, perhaps?) on the front lawn. The celebrant was Fr Malet, Vicar of Ardley (Herts) and Rector of the 'Order of St Joseph'; he was assisted as Deacon by Ouseley, and as Subdeacon by Brother Brannock, who had also by that time left Elm Hill.[120]

A distinguished visitor to the orphanage chapel was the 'Bishop of Iona' (Jules Ferrete, 1828-1904), a former Dominican missionary in the Near East who had obtained episcopal orders from the Syrian Orthodox Church, but apparently felt equally at home ministering as a Presbyterian. On this occasion he celebrated the (eastern) Liturgy of St Basil clothed in western vestments, and was assisted by Ouseley acting as deacon.[121]

Ferrete had recently arrived in England, where his plan to assist the reunion of the churches by multiplying the number of 'validly' ordained clergy caught the attention of among other interested parties F.G. Lee and George Nugée, well-to-do Vicar of Wymering and founder the following year of a community of part-time Augustinians.[122] Later that autumn Ferrete would be the guest of Dr J.T. Seccombe of Terrington St Clement in Norfolk, on whom it is believed he bestowed the episcopate around this time; eleven years later Lee and Seccombe would become two of the three prelates at the head of the mysterious Order of Corporate Reunion.[123]

---

[120] ibid, 28 July 1866. The reporter noted that under his vestments Fr Malet wore the 'brown cassock of the Order of St Joseph'. The history of this short-lived brotherhood is given in Call pp90f; it ran an orphanage in Holloway, from which a number of boys were sent to the new establishment in Bristol.

[121] Ibid, 6 October 1866

[122] Call pp 91-103.

[123] Seccombe was 'of an excitable temper' and with 'an unusual interest in religious controversy'; as a young man he had for a while been a novice at the Cistercian abbey of Mount St Bernard, and would be the prime mover in the development of the OCR (Henry R.T Brandreth: Dr Lee of Lambeth SPCK 1951 p120). From Ferrete and his successors are derived the orders of numerous episcopi vagantes: see BAL, especially Chapters 1, 7 and 10; also Abba Seraphim (Newman-Norton), Flesh of Our Brethren (The British Orthodox Press, 2006).

In 1867 Dundas took a wife who would bear him three children, although in the 1871 census he was listed not with them at the marital home in then rural Oldland but at St Augustine's Home in Montpelier, of which he had appointed himself Warden. A couple of months earlier he had announced his imminent reception into the Church of Rome[124] and began to turn his attention to politics, standing unsuccessfully as a candidate for the local council; he also founded a newspaper to promote the Conservative cause. The orphanage was closed and the chapel dismantled and re-erected in Bedminster, where in 1873 it was inaugurated as a chapel of ease for the Ashton district.[125] Dundas died on 9 September 1874 at the age of 28, and his funeral at All Saints, Clifton, was as grandiose a function as any he had presided over at 'The Benedictine Chapel' in Trenchard Street or that of St Augustine's Home. The fact that it took place at this prominent Anglo-Catholic church suggests that he did not, in fact, become a Roman Catholic, or that if he did so he failed to persevere.

...AND AN ENTHUSIASTIC RECRUIT

IN JANUARY 1864 the future Poet Laureate Robert Bridges (then nineteen and in his first year at Oxford) received an excited letter from his sixteen-year-old fellow apprentice poet Digby Mackworth Dolben. 'I am to have an introduction to Brother Ignatius of Claydon!!! My S. Barnabas cousin [Euseby Cleaver, curate of St Barnabas, Pimlico] knows him well.'[126]

Between that first letter and Dolben's death by drowning three years later Bridges would receive many more reports of his association

---

[124] *Bristol Mercury*, 25 February 1871

[125] ibid, 29 March 1873

[126] This and subsequent quotations from the memoir prefaced by Bridges to the collection of Dolben's poems he brought out some fifty years later. The two were distantly related, and had become acquainted at Eton. At the time Bridges shared Dolben's enthusiasm for the Anglo-Catholic revival, though on his own admission with rather less passion than his younger kinsman.

with the 'English OSB'. On 'Maunday [sic] Thursday' of the same year Dolben informed Bridges that he had now become 'Br Dominic OSB iij' and took to signing himself thus, although he soon had to point out that only fellow-tertiaries were supposed to address him in this style. In July he obtained leave from his Eton housemaster for the Eton—Harrow match at Lords, but went instead to Ascot Priory, where he and Ignatius slept in an outhouse and were awoken by Dr Pusey 'thumping at the door' and crying 'Brothers Ignatius and Dominic, I am waiting for you to celebrate the Holy Communion.' Bridges observed that 'to be called in the morning by the great Dr Pusey himself "thumping at the door" must have been very satisfactory to the truant'.

At Christmas 1864 Dolben left Eton to cram for Oxford entrance. Perhaps because his mind was elsewhere progress was slow, and he was still not up to matriculation standard when he died. In the summer of 1866 he paid a visit to Birmingham, where he discovered that the choir of the new church of St Alban, Bordesley, consisted chiefly of young men belonging to the local 'OSB iij'. Their 'quiet earnestness' compared favourably with the 'noisiness' of their Bristol counterparts – perhaps the difference lay in their having the support of their parish priest, in this case the parish's first Vicar, James Pollock, said to be 'a true friend to our Order'. Dolben had recently taken to walking about in monastic habit and bare feet and this 'created some astonishment' at St Alban's, its ritualistic tradition notwithstanding.

THE FIRST NUNS

ON ST BENEDICT'S DAY (21 March) 1865 Miss Sellon, referred to in the press reports as the 'Mother Abbess', attended a service in the Elm Hill chapel. She wore 'the Benedictine frock, scapula [sic] and head-dress', and was attended by 'an acolyte bearing her handsome pastoral staff'. Her presence in Norwich was said to be 'to inaugurate a congregation of Benedictine nuns'.[127]

---

[127] *Bury and Norwich Post*, 18 April 1865

She took a lease on an imposing property near the Cathedral, Samson and Hercules House, where her original intention was to open a branch house of her own order. In fact she turned it over to a group of Ignatius's Third Order sisters who wished to lead a life in common (probably only on a part-time basis), remaining with them, according to her biographer, 'until they were established'.[128] One of them was a Mrs Taylor, who took the name 'Sister Louisa' – in tribute, it is said, to Ignatius's mother, who had spent some weeks staying at her house that Lent, keeping a watchful eye lest her son's austerities should damage his health.

Earlier it had been reported that 'the lady superior of the "Nunnery" in the Close' had 'several fresh noviciates [sic] under her charge'.[129] A member of the new community had caused a stir one Sunday afternoon at the Cathedral, when 'coming in some twenty minutes after the service had commenced', she

> prostrated herself before the altar, and, when the parties usually attending turned round to pray, she stood in an opposite position, thus evidently desiring to draw the attention of the audience [sic] to herself. As usual, she was dressed in a serge dress, and wore a brass cross on the left breast.

Few details have survived about this organisation, whose members were known as the Sisters of Mount Calvary. Calder-Marshall suggests[130] that it disbanded as a community when Ignatius fell ill later that summer, most of its members accompanying him to the seaside as his nurses and attendants. Exactly what happened at Samson and Hercules House over the next couple of years is not known, but in March 1867 it would be advertised as available for sale

---

[128] Williams, *Priscilla Lydia Sellon* p216

[129] *Bury and Norwich Post*, 14 March 1865

[130] *Enthusiast* p157

or rent from the following Michaelmas, being described as 'now in the occupation of Miss Sellon'.[131]

REBELLION

THE CHAPEL IN THE rag and bone warehouse was only a temporary expedient, until a more suitable building could be erected on land behind the monastery. The design for this was prepared by Brother Brannock, who in the 1861 census had been listed at home in Braunton as a civil engineer, and seems to have been a talented young man. The project would involve Ignatius in considerable fund-raising, and in June 1865 he was away in London with (a new) Brother Augustine, 'lecturing in St Martin's Hall on behalf of the funds for the erection of a new chapel in Norwich'.[132] Brannock was left in charge; under him were Brothers Philip, Clement, Maurus and Stanislaus, with Gideon Ouseley as chaplain, although later Ignatius would maintain the household had been twice that size – perhaps his reckoning included boys in the St William's Guild annexe.

In his absence rebellion broke out. The instigator was a newcomer, Brother Maurus, who had been admitted to the monastery just two days before Ignatius's departure for London. On the day after it (Sunday 18th) Maurus broke the rule of silence, and, as Charles Walker had done in a similar instance two years earlier, Brother Brannock reported the fact to the Superior and a penance arrived by return of post – letters travelled with amazing speed in those early railway days. The 'poor Monk who unfortunately happened to speak to his neighbour' (the culprit's own words) was ordered to kneel 'three hours on the damp cold ground in the early morning'

---

[131] Norfolk Chronicle, 2 March 1867

[132] Information and quotations in this section are unless otherwise stated from contemporary numbers of the Norfolk News and Norfolk Chronicle, and (re Brother Maurus) issues of the Worcestershire Chronicle in November and December 1872.

and 'lick up the dust in the form of a cross seven times on the dirty stone floors', as well as recite six hundred Our Fathers and the whole Psalter.

Maurus was short and slightly stout, with a pale face and close-cropped dark hair. He was said to have had 'the appearance of a monk' even after laying aside the habit, and had a 'scowling brow' as well a distinctive look in his eyes. He seemed older than the others (he was actually 26 or 27, though Ignatius thought him forty), and knew how to manipulate them to his own advantage. He claimed to be 'the Rev. Dr Morton', a former chaplain to the Chief Justice of Tasmania; in fact his name was Joseph James Crouch, born in or around 1839 to a village washerwoman and her husband in Sussex. She died when he was six or seven, so he and his younger sister ended up in the workhouse at Battle. Here he began to display a precocious literary talent and what the authorities classed as a 'morbid' interest in religion, allied to a devious disposition and an unpleasant temper. At the age of thirteen or fourteen he persuaded the Roman Catholic priest in St Leonard's-on-Sea to receive him into his Church and have him released into the care of well-wishers (it is said that he spent some time in a religious house in Hastings); after a few years he proceeded to a missionary college in Rome.

Rapidly falling foul of his superiors there, he spent the next few years honing his skills as a confidence trickster, using variations on the Morton alias and occasionally that of 'Dr Keatinge', flitting from Catholicism to protestantism and back again as the fancy took him, and making occasional forays on to the lecture platform with *exposés* of life in Catholic institutions. From time to time he succeeded in doing duty under one name or another as a clergyman, sailing to Australia early in 1862 as chaplain to an emigrant ship, the *Boanerges*. Dismissed on arrival for unclerical behaviour on the voyage, he got into further trouble which landed him in prison in Tasmania: hence the germ of truth in his claim to have been employed by the Chief Justice of that province. The return journey was made as tutor to the sons of a home-coming passenger, presumably earning him a free passage, landing him in London on 25 May 1865 (Ascension Day, the day of the great early morning procession). Three weeks later he had found his way to Norwich and added a fresh identity to his portfolio, that of the monk Maurus.

Stanislaus was also a recent entrant, who though 'deficient in looks, speech, wits and education' came recommended by the Vicar of St Mary's, Soho, J.G. Chambers, as a 'most holy man'. Ignatius's mother, however, judged him 'an unmitigated scamp', in whom her son would be most unwise to place any trust.[133] His real name was James Barrett Hughes and he was fond of boys, so the Abbot put him in charge of the Guild of St William. (One of the rebels' complaints against Ignatius was that he was 'constantly receiving visitors and cheerfully conversing in his own room with young people', but that the ordinary monks were denied such social opportunities – doubtless a deprivation Stanislaus felt deeply.) He seems to have been rather a weak character, but as events unfolded had his uses as Maurus' sidekick.

Not surprisingly Maurus refused to carry out his penance, and tried to get the others to side with him against Ignatius's 'tyrannical' regime. At first he was unsuccessful. 'Brother Brannock declared him "a liar" and "a rogue", and "an escaped convict"' – one wonders how much about the new novice's past life he knew, or guessed. Next Maurus tried to play the victim: 'When he threatened to go and drown himself, Brother Brannock shortly informed him in which direction the river lay.' Once again he changed his tune, and by the middle of the week had so worked on his fellows that they agreed to hold a Chapter meeting – quite likely the first in the community's history, and the last (other than the 'Chapter of Faults', a quite different affair) until after its Founder's death.

---

[133] *Enthusiast* p117

The meeting (on Thursday 22 June) was attended by all five brothers, together with Gideon Ouseley. Brannock's appointment as Deputy Superior was declared null and void on the grounds that none of his fellows had been consulted about it, but having given an undertaking to govern according to the 'constitutional rules of St Benedict' he was elected Superior, still with the title of Prior. A document was drawn up citing Ignatius to appear before the assembled brethren 'with all convenient speed': at this gathering (in the chapel, and before the Blessed Sacrament exposed) unspecified charges would be laid against him and his 'claim to the title of Superior' rejected, although they were prepared to have him back if he would submit to an election.

This document – in whose composition as in the whole affair the hand of Maurus is clearly discernible – was delivered to Ignatius in London, and treated by him as a 'huge joke'. A further Chapter was therefore held on the Saturday, at which 'the Rev. Joseph Leycester Lyne, formerly Brother Ignatius of our said order' was declared to be acting without the authority of the community in gathering funds (the fruits of his missions being allegedly used for 'his own purpose' rather than for the general benefit), and pronounced excommunicate. This time Philip did not sign the citation, and the Abbot's laughter when the cringing Stanislaus brought it to his London lodgings was tinged with menace: he would 'return on Monday, when he should put the refractory brethren to penance, and...if the doors were not open to him, he should enter by force with a body of policemen'.

On the Sunday the public morning service was attended as usual by Ignatius's loyal supporters (mostly members of the officially defunct Third Order), who 'continually interrupted by lewd and irreverent observations' and at the end turned to violence – so much so that 'the monks were advised by a lay friend' not to hold the customary evening service, at the normal hour for which further disturbances broke out. What particularly enraged the congregation was Maurus's sermon, in which he contrasted the motivation of the 'sham monk' Ignatius (who had started the monastery so as to 'rise to fame otherwise difficult of attainment') with that of those who had 'given up much for Christ, and for Christ alone', among whose number he included himself.

Further violence occurred the next day, when a boy trying to take letters from the rebel monks to the post was 'roughly handled' by the crowd and forced to surrender them; his supporters evidently knew that Ignatius had given orders for no written communication to be sent out in his absence. On Tuesday a fresh complication arose, when bailiffs arrived to 'distrain upon the furniture and effects' for arrears of rent amounting to some £60. They were sent by Stephen Balls, one of the local sympathisers who had advanced money for the purchase of the property, none of which Ignatius had succeeded in repaying. He feared that the 'English OSB' was on the verge of collapse, and that he would be the poorer for it.

Rather than allowing the bailiffs to do so, the rebel brothers dismantled the chapel, removing the Reserved Sacrament from the tabernacle and burying it in the garden. Bertouch[134] presents this as an act of sacrilege, but it may have been done to prevent the Sacrament getting into profane hands. By this time the monastery had lost its chaplain: disenchanted with Ignatius's 'unCatholic and unEnglish extravagances' as well as shaken by recent events, Gideon Ouseley left Norwich that same day. In a faux-emotional letter written that evening Maurus was able to add the fact that 'God's holy altar' had been 'desecrated' to the list of disasters for which he held Ignatius personally responsible, and tried to undermine him by suggesting that 'the people' were now supporting the rebel cause; failing, however, to mention Fr Ouseley's defection.

Thursday morning saw Maurus and Stanislaus for the second time that week at the magistrates' court in the Guildhall, pursuing their case against the man who had snatched their letters and applying

---

[134] pp282f

for police protection against the hostile crowd. While they were thus occupied Ignatius returned, neatly turning the key against them and refusing to let them back in, even to collect their personal possessions. The *Norfolk News* ended its account with this note:

> The last we heard of them on Thursday evening was that they were wandering about the city in their monastic garb, and applying at one hotel after another without finding one that would take them in. – At a still later hour, we learned that, after all their professions of abhorrence at Ignatius's tyranny, all except Brother Maurus were once more submissive, and were humbly doing penance for their offences!

In fact Stanislaus was also sent away. Calder-Marshall says Ignatius gave him and Maurus £5 each and told them to clear off, and that Stanislaus 'persuaded one of the boys from St William's Guild to follow him'.[135] The boy was young Widdows/Nobbs, otherwise 'Brother Osmund', with whom he set up house in London, putting it about that Ignatius had united them in a blasphemous parody of the marriage service. This unlikely fiction was included in the evidence given at a police court hearing in February 1869, when the now 19-year-old 'George Widdows Nobbs' was charged with stealing £15 from his partner (they ran a small shop together) and assaulting him (the case was dismissed).[136] Stanislaus had earlier made a much-publicised recantation of Romanism and Ritualism at an evangelical Anglican church in Islington, and took to appearing on protestant propaganda platforms clad in the religious habit in which he had taken his departure.[137]

In the melée at the monastery Maurus had ransacked Ignatius's room, pocketing his letters of orders. From Norwich he too went to

---

[135] *Enthusiast* p120

[136] Newman-Norton op cit pp12ff

[137] *Islington Gazette*, 4 February 1868

London, where he applied to a 'clerical agent' for a curacy. Somehow he succeeded in superimposing his own (assumed) name over that of Joseph Leycester Lyne and changing the other details (not very expertly, as it would turn out), on the strength of the forgery obtaining a post at St Martin's, Worcester. Here he impressed the Rector with his evidently 'considerable talent' and 'superior education', as well as his 'engaging' manners and ability in the pulpit.

After a couple of weeks he was rumbled, and left Worcester without stopping to pick up his dirty washing. The case would not be brought to trial until 1872, by which time he had committed a string of similar offences, including a few in America. He received sentences of eighteen months' hard labour for the forgery and five years' penal servitude for the false pretences, after which he would be under police supervision for a further seven years. In 1886 (as 'Theodore Oswald Keatinge') he would be imprisoned for further offences of the same kind perpetrated in Dublin,[138] and five years later news would reach these shores that he had died in Darlinghurst Gaol, Sydney, where he had recently begun a five-year sentence for criminal assault.[139]

THE NEW CHAPEL

IGNATIUS BARELY TOUCHED DOWN in Norwich. For most of July he was on the road, spending a week or more in Sheffield, where 'monks from Manchester' (Third Order variety) came over to assist at Sunday afternoon 'Benedictine Vespers' in the Theatre Royal, and the local Vicar served him with a notice from the Archbishop of York forbidding him to preach in the churches of his diocese.[140] He also visited Manchester, Birmingham, Bristol and Cheltenham, always concluding his addresses with an appeal for funds for the new chapel.

---

[138] *Gloucester Citizen*, 13 December 1886
[139] *Morning Post*, 9 April 1891
[140] *Sheffield Daily Telegraph*, 10 July 1865

Meanwhile the more businesslike of his supporters were clearly worried about the future prospects of the monastery, and the fact that the money he was collecting was being devoted to this ambitious new structure rather than to secure ownership of the premises themselves. On 14 July (with the aid of a £500 mortgage from a Miss Stone, and without Ignatius's knowledge) the freehold was conveyed to Fr Drury, who became in effect the community's landlord.[141]

At this stage the new chapel was only 'half built', although Ignatius hoped to have it finished before November, when at the Church Congress 'there would be a host of clergymen from all parts of the country' in the city, whom he was anxious to impress.[142] In fact the shell was only completed the following spring, when a descriptive article appeared in The Builder, of which an abridged version was printed in the Bury and Norwich Post.[143]

Unlike the intentionally more grandiose abbey church at Llanthony, the Norwich chapel has survived as a useable building; these days it houses the media department of the Norwich University of the Arts, whose main premises are in the cloisters of the former Dominican friary. It is in fact several feet longer and wider than what was actually built at Llanthony, and would have accommodated a much larger congregation, if not 'afford[ing] room for 1000' as Ignatius suggested.[144] However, Brannock had allowed for the eventual addition of side aisles, which would have effectively doubled the capacity – perhaps six hundred with aisles, or three without.

---

[141] BUWP p67

[142] Manchester Courier, 26 July 1865; Birmingham Gazette, 5 August 1865. In September Digby Dolben asked Bridges to try and raise money towards the completion of the chapel. Their mutual friend V.S.S. Coles (in later life Principal of Pusey House) had sent £1, but 'nobody else thinks they have anything which they could give'.

[143] Issue of 6 March 1866

[144] South London Chronicle, 8 July 1865

Picture 7: Brother Brannock's new chapel: recent external view, looking towards the (liturgical) north-west corner. The white-framed windows were let into the blind arches when the building was converted to secular use.

Picture 8: Brother Brannock's new chapel: contemporary internal view, looking from nave to sanctuary.

The main structure is of red brick, 78 feet by 30 internally and composed of five bays, with the roof rising to 40 feet at the apex. The style was said to be 'simple and solid, divided between the Norman and First Pointed'. The easternmost bay (liturgically speaking; the orientation is actually north-west/south-east) would have been separated from the nave by a substantial screen, incorporating baldachins for subsidiary altars either side of the central opening, and ambones approached by concealed stairs and passageways from the monks' choir. This last was not going to be in the conventional English position between the screen and the sanctuary, but beyond and a few feet above the high altar, with the vestry and sacristy underneath. It was to house these that what looks like a two-storey extension was built against the gable wall, in which traces can be discerned of the arrangement of arches through which the sound of monastic chanting would have wafted through to the body of the church; the organ was also going to be sited in this space. In the first bay of the nave would be the 'lay choir', separated by a low wall from the part occupied by the congregation.

It was hoped one day to raise a tower above the monks' choir, which is why it appears less permanent than the rest of the building. On the wall above the altar there were to have been frescoes of the 'annunciation, manifestation, and ascension'; the description also refers to a 'baldachin' which would have blocked the view through to the choir, and to a 'super-altar' and 'spire of stone on marble shafts' acting as a canopy to the tabernacle and exposition throne. The last-named feature sounds very like what was erected twenty years later at Llanthony, also from the designs of (by then ex-) Brother Brannock, and which may have been a recycling of his original plan.

COLLAPSE

ON THE WAY HOME from his fund-raising tour Ignatius spent a couple of nights with the Cistercian community at Mount St Bernard's, founded twenty years earlier on one of his Leicestershire estates by the Catholic convert Ambrose Phillipps de Lisle. As one of the founders of the Association for the Promotion of the Unity of Christendom he was keen to encourage the spread of Catholic practices in the Church of England, and hoped it might lead to the establishment of a uniate church in communion with Rome. At Mount St Bernard's Ignatius was flattered to be given a stall alongside the Abbot, although the novice deputed to look after him tried to fob him off with a seat in the strangers' tribune ('A convert, you know,' he was told by way of an excuse; 'they are often a little peculiar').[145] Several newspapers reported on the visit, on which he was accompanied by Brother Aloysius, an eighteen-year-old Third Order member from Norwich named Nicholson.

> Their monkish make up and the closely shaven head of Father Ignatius, who carried a large crozier, while his attendant had a massive Bible, caused much curiosity amongst the villagers.[146]

A week or two later Ignatius had a visit from a representative of the *Belfast News-Letter*, whose account appeared in the 22 August edition of that paper. The Irish journalist was given a guided tour of the half-built church, and noted that it promised 'to be of a somewhat imposing appearance', being constructed of 'red brick...in the Gothic style, with the utmost architectural effect which can be procured for the smallest possible expenditure of money'. He reported that the Abbot 'spoke in his usual cheerful tone,' but 'showed..., by his countenance, the great mental anxiety' which the recent rebellion had caused him. A few days later, while celebrating Ante-Communion for the feast of St Bartholomew – he had, of course, lost both his resident chaplain and since the break with Hillyard his only supporter among the Norwich clergy – Ignatius collapsed and took to his bed.

---

[145] BUWP pp67f

[146] *Norfolk News*, 5 August 1865

CHAPTER 4

NO FIXED ABODE

WHEN IGNATIUS HAD been out of action for two days, a letter from his medical attendant appeared in the local paper. He was too ill to undertake any work 'for some time to come', and all chapel services and 'other mission work' had been suspended.[147]

For a week or more he lay at Elm Hill, delirious and apparently at death's door. He was then removed to Margate, where it was hoped the sea air would aid his recovery. Meanwhile the other monks had been sent home 'on holiday',[148] although some if not all would soon return. One of the returnees was Brannock, although since his participation in the recent rebellion the office of Deputy Superior was now being exercised by 'Brother Placidus, a new accession',[149] if not one who can be identified by name. Mentioned in the same report was 'Brother Dunstan, who has been some time in the monastery and who is the son of a policeman in the West of England' – 17-year-old Samuel Thomas Garland (Dunstan of the Crown of Thorns), whose father was actually a Bristol bootmaker, and who had been received as a postulant that August (scarcely 'some time'), having previously been a member of Dundas's Third Order branch.[150]

---

[147] Dr Joseph Allen, one of the local supporters who had encouraged him to settle in Norwich but with whom later he would fall out (*Norfolk News*, 26 August 1865)

[148] *Reynolds's Newspaper*, 10 September 1865

[149] *Morning Post*, 11 September 1865

[150] His birth had been registered in Clifton in the second quarter of 1848, and he is listed with his parents and brothers in Bristol in the 1851 and 1861 censuses.

The brothers were doing their best to 'revive' the services in their chapel, although the absence of the 'master spirit' had caused some diminution in their impressiveness. The new chapel was still unfinished when the Church Congress met in Norwich that October, but the correspondent of the London Standard took time off from the sessions in St Andrew's Hall to attend a service in the existing one, which he found 'extremely small' as well as 'extremely poor' in appearance and arrangement. The service – an amalgam of Vespers and Compline – was conducted by Brother Placidus, who wore 'an ample cope' of 'rich green satin'; with him in choir were 'a young "postulant", and two small, very small, boys'. It was, however 'not only thronged, but thronged with worshippers who joined from first to last in every portion of the rapid and intricate service', and he was clearly moved by their unAnglican 'devotional earnestness', especially in the singing of Fr Faber's hymn 'Oh! Paradise; Oh! Paradise'.[151]

Ignatius, of course, missed the Congress. A year earlier he had taken its predecessor in Bristol by storm, telling a hall full of distinguished and experienced churchmen that the parish system had had its day, and that the unchurched masses could only be reached by 'colleges' of celibate missioners following the rule of St Benedict.[152] The Standard correspondent may have been impressed by the 'devotional earnestness' of those attending the makeshift chapel, but evidence that this had been engendered by a settled and stable Benedictine community was as elusive as ever.

CASTLES IN THE AIR

ENFORCED INACTIVITY gave Ignatius time perhaps to reflect, and certainly to exercise his imagination. It was not long before he was 'sufficiently recovered to use his pen'.[153] A long letter appeared over

---

[151] Issue of 5 October 1865

[152] Western Daily Press, 13 October 1864

[153] Norfolk News, 28 October 1865

his signature in the *Standard* of 24 October, in which he justified both his attempt to restore the monastic life and the use of colourful ceremonial and unfamiliar costume. These last might be found off-putting by conservative churchpeople, but in Ignatius's view such visible signs would be 'more likely to attract the dull-minded, cold-hearted, and ignorant heathen of our poor – yea, and even of our heathen upper classes' than the 'dingy, sombre, and dull' externals encountered in most Anglican churches at the time.

In line with this observation he reiterated the pastoral and missionary motive behind the venture, harking back to a time when 'the monk...was the unpaid hospitaller, schoolmaster, physician, and friend of the poor'. Of these functions perhaps the most significant was the last, the driving force behind all true monastic activities being Christian love, and 'a monk's only wages' being 'the promise of the eternal inheritance': Victorian 'charity' was often a cold and impersonal affair (think Dickens). Despite the much-publicised setbacks, the Norwich monastery had brought '[n]umbers to holy baptism and the knowledge of Christ'. He reported that 'the drunkard, the heathen, the fornicator, the adulterer' had 'learnt to bend the knee' before its altar, and there gained 'the grace to change their sinful life'.

He reported that the cost of finishing the new chapel was now fully subscribed, a 'friend to our order having just given [or perhaps promised; he was, as we saw earlier, all too ready to count financial chickens before they were hatched] 500l for the roofing of the building', which presumably had still to be carried out. Money was needed for furniture and equipment, but he hoped to have it open by Christmas.

However, the completion of the Norwich chapel was only the first step in a rather more ambitious scheme. He anticipated receiving (mistakenly, as we have noted) 'some few thousands of pounds' from the estate of Stephens Lyne Stephens; this sum, with help from other 'rich people', he would happily devote to rebuilding 'an old desecrated monastery', if only 'any gentleman who owns such a thing' would be kind enough to give it to him.

> I should very much like to have Bolton Abbey, or Fountains, or Kirkstall, in Yorkshire, to restore as missionary centres and retreats for the north, or Llantoney Abbey [sic] in Monmouthshire, Wales, to stir up the Church there to zeal and energy, and love.

He did not say how he intended to staff such an establishment. At the same time it was reported[154] that he was proposing (again) to 'get up an order of nuns', whose 'reverend mother' would be 'Sister Ambrosia OSB ii', to whom interested parties were invited to apply. This lady was a Mrs More, widow of a Sheffield manufacturer and quite comfortably off.

In November he felt well enough to pay a second visit to Llanthony. His presence there was reported in several papers, and according to the *Devizes & Wiltshire Gazette*[155] the party included four brethren (more likely Third Order members from Bristol than brothers from Elm Hill) and the 'infant novice'. Ignatius spent several days at Llanthony, staying at the 'Travellers' Rest' (by which name the hotel in the west wing of the former Augustinian monastery was then known), and conducting an open-air service in the ruins by the light of the moon. The congregation included 'Baptists, Independents, Wesleyans and Mormonites, as well as several members of the English Church'.[156] He also met a mysterious foreign-looking visitor who was introduced to him as the heir to the Landor estate, the poet having died since

---

[154] *Sheffield Daily Telegraph*, 30 December 1865

[155] Issue of 30 November 1865

[156] *London Standard*, 8 December 1865. Earlier that year when Digby Dolben was studying with the Reverend Harry de Winton at Boughrood he and a fellow-pupil 'took a holiday and rode sixteen miles over the Black Mountains to Llanthony Abbey, he dressed in the full habit of a Benedictine Monk, and I riding by his side in ordinary costume. You can imagine the sensation he created passing through the Welsh villages.'

his earlier visit, and who seemed happy to discuss the possibility of the property being returned to monastic ownership.[157] A few weeks later it was widely reported that he had actually acquired it,[158] after which the story appears to have gone cold; there seems to have been a misunderstanding.

IGNATIUS ABROAD

ALTHOUGH HE HOPED to be back at Elm Hill for Christmas, Ignatius did not in fact return until early January, and then only for a few days.[159] Meanwhile he crossed from South Wales to Bristol to stay with Dundas's mother at Devon Villa, Richmond Hill, and to preach at the Trenchard Street oratory, at that stage still accepting his authority. On his various public appearances he was attended by 'two younger brethren of the Benedictine order...and a couple of "Anglican nuns"' (again, all of them probably Third Order members), and 'bore in his arms the Infant Samuel, about whom so much as been heard'.[160]

From Bristol he went to his family at the Hampshire village of Hambledon, where some months earlier his father had taken a three-year tenancy on a house called The Lodge.[161] Meanwhile Brother Placidus (according to Ignatius 'the son of wealthy parents' who had 'left a comfortable home to come and work for Christ in our order'[162]) was reportedly discharging his duties as stand-in Superior with 'zeal and discretion', and although apparently not in Holy Orders

---

[157] Bury & Norwich Post, 12 December 1865

[158] e.g. in Western Daily Press, 30 March 1866

[159] Norfolk News, 13 January 1866

[160] Bristol Mercury, 9 December 1865

[161] In the event they only stayed for half this period, and Francis Lyne was sued for damage caused in part by Ignatius's pet magpies and owl, which with other birds were allowed to fly freely around the house. The hearing, conducted in an atmosphere of barely restrained mirth, was fully reported in the Norfolk News of 2 February 1867.

[162] Ipswich Journal of 23 December 1865, reprinting a letter from Ignatius in the Church Review

both presided and preached at a public service on Christmas Day.[163] Brothers Brannock, Dunstan and Philip also took part (all vested in copes), as well as an unspecified number of juveniles. Placidus's regime was noticeably less strict than Abbot Ignatius's (the brethren were 'allowing their hair to grow again on the crowns of their heads', and 'being allowed more hours of uninterrupted sleep than formerly'), and reports that the monks had been unable to afford to buy food were dismissed as inaccurate (they were able to distribute meat to needy neighbours as well as buy it for themselves).

By the end of January Placidus had returned to his 'comfortable home...for reasons in which Brother Ignatius concurs' – there seem to have been numerous financial and other irregularities during his tenure of office.[164] The only person competent to take charge was Brannock, who was said to have 'seven brothers, all postulants' under him, and a strict rule of life for their observance. Lack of further news about these new recruits suggests they melted away quite quickly, although on 31 January a certain William Wade took vows of poverty, chastity and obedience for a year's noviciate (Ignatius's

---

[163] London Standard, 26 December 1865

[164] Sheffield Independent, 29 January 1866. Two years later Nobbs/Widdows and two other former St William's boys appeared with ex-Brother Stanislaus at anti-monastic protest meetings in London. Most of their 'evidence' was mere innuendo, hinting at (but failing to substantiate) the prevalence of 'disgusting practices'. They did, however, give some information about the former Brother Placidus, who was said to be currently living in South Australia (the implication perhaps being that he was there as a convict, still just possible in the late 1860s). Before joining the monastery he had been a prize fighter, and one evening had smuggled into the enclosure a girl dressed in boy's clothes, the trousers being provided by Nobbs (Reynolds's Newspaper, 2 and 16 February 1868). In his letter to Bridges of 30 September 1865 Dolben throws more light on this character: 'The Monastery is governed by an Etonian: N-----, now Br Placidus, is all in all to them now. I do hope and think that his vocation will be a real one. In a few years perhaps the names of Monk and Etonian may not seem as far apart as they do now.' (The combination of prize fighter, philanderer, Etonian and Ignatian novice sounds improbable, if not quite impossible.)

standard procedure).[165] The absent Superior's assertion that the cost of the new chapel had been fully subscribed seems to have been a trifle over-optimistic, as this report put the remaining shortfall at between £200 and £300, with £40 still to pay for the new organ. The sum of £180 intended for its installation was said to have been 'misappropriated' by someone in whom Ignatius had mistakenly placed his trust – ex-Brother Placidus, one may assume.

These details accompanied the news that Ignatius was about to leave for 'some months' abroad, in search of full 'restoration to health'. He and his companions (the Infant Oblate, Brother Philip and Sister Ambrosia, who financed the expedition) left Dover for Calais towards the end of January, travelling overland to Marseilles and thence by sea to Civitavecchia. The arrival in Rome of this ill-assorted and bizarrely clad party of schismatics caused a minor sensation, although Ignatius succeeded in procuring an audience with Pius IX, who presented him with a rosary; meanwhile his companions waited outside in a cab. This was on the feast of St Scholastica (10 February), and was immediately reported in a letter to Brannock, who lost no time in passing the news to the press. A separate report carried a communication from 'a Roman correspondent', who observed that in his 'mixed garb of three different orders' the visitor awakened 'the smiles rather than the sympathy of the true believers', and that his attempt to claim spiritual kinship with the Benedictines at St Paul's without the Walls had been met on their part with no great show of enthusiasm.[166]

The intention had been for the Anglo-Benedictine party to link up with Dr Pusey and Miss Sellon who were travelling to the Holy Land,

---

[165] His is the earliest of the Profession Charts and related certificates preserved in the Prinknash archives, and the only one surviving from the Norwich period. It is not known how long Wade remained at Elm Hill. He could perhaps have been the otherwise unidentifiable Brother Alban; see below.

[166] Both accounts appeared in the *Sheffield Independent* of 26 February 1866.

but various difficulties had delayed their progress. On a visit to the Dominican priory of Santa Sabina (on Ash Wednesday, 14 February) Ignatius suffered a fainting fit; a few days later another one prevented him getting any nearer the shrine of St Benedict at Monte Cassino than the local railway station. When the party arrived in Naples Brother Philip disappeared: he had been so impressed by what he had seen of authentic religious life at Santa Sabina that he tried to find his way back there, only abandoning the attempt when his lack of both money and the local language forced him to turn back.[167] After sleepless nights in Sicily and seasickness on the onward voyage they reached Malta, where finding that their intended fellow-pilgrims had already left they decided to rest for a few weeks and then return home.

Picture 9: 'Monk and Midshipman':
Studio portrait of Lessie and Gussie, Malta 1866

---

[167] Bertouch pp324ff. John Spence had heard the story from Philip himself, and claims that it was to Monte Cassino (which he misnames 'Monte Christo' [sic]) that the errant brother was trying to find his way. When he returned to their hotel Ignatius 'so rejoiced to see him back again that he allowed him to sleep with him which Father Philip said was heavenly' (Spence p43). One shouldn't necessarily read anything sexual into this on Ignatius's part; about Philip one can't be so sure.

The memory of his sojourn on this British island was preserved in a studio photograph of Ignatius blessing his brother Augustus Adolphus, whose ship put in at Valetta while he was there. It also gave him the opportunity to make his Confession (to Walter Trower, Bishop formerly of Glasgow but now of Gibraltar) before receiving Communion; a practice he probably gave up when he stopped requiring it of those under his authority.[168]

THE END OF ELM HILL

CORRESPONDENCE WITH DRURY on the homeward leg of the journey[169] suggests that however much he still believed in his mission to introduce monastic life into the Church of England he was in no hurry to return to Elm Hill: apart from his brief visit in January he had now been away nearly nine months. Meanwhile the pathetic remnant − Brannock and Dunstan, and maybe one or two others − were keeping up the observances as well as they could, but the debt on the property was still outstanding, with mounting arrears of rent and no money coming in.

It was at this point that as its legal proprietor Fr Drury began to assert his authority over the monastery. At first he seems to have made an attempt to reorganise the community without involving Ignatius. In the Norfolk News of 26 May it was reported that he intended to 'complete the unfinished chapel and continue the monastic operation' − a course of action the paper likened scoffingly to 'Hamlet without the Prince', suggesting that the monastery without Ignatius would turn out to be a 'more ridiculous failure' than it had been with him at the helm. A key figure in Drury's plan was Brannock, whose appeal in a recent number of the Church Review was quoted by Francis Lyne in a letter published in the London Standard of 31 May:

---

[168] Bertouch pp331ff. The change of mind on this issue was one of the consequences of Ignatius's 'conversion' later that year; see below.

[169] Quoted by Calder-Marshall: Enthusiast pp133-137

Father Ignatius has forfeited his claim to this place [the Norwich monastery].... The help and support which have been denied us lately would be gratefully acknowledged by the Rev. George Drury, if forwarded to him at Claydon Rectory, Ipswich, for the order of St Benedict.

Mr Lyne had also heard from Brannock himself, using his secular name and writing from Peterborough. The language is rather pompous, and just a little obscure ('You may continue to rest assured that you are not far from right in the assertion that I consider your son has been sufficiently long the victim of those who deceive him...') – the latter maybe deliberately, as exchanges with Lyne *père* always ran the risk of provoking an argument. Their contention was that the Rector of Claydon was as much the community's founder as Ignatius himself, so had an equal right to determine its future. In Drury's own words:

Father Ignatius is not the sole founder of the order. When he was here [at Claydon] he used to say that I was the founder; but if he has founded the order, this does not give him the right to unfound it.... The house at Norwich belongs to me. Father Ignatius agreed formally that I should take possession of house and furniture, if he threw up the work or left without consent.

This was in a letter to Brother Cyprian (Dundas), when a couple of months later Ignatius was trying to oust him as Prior of the Bristol Third Order group; it was reproduced as part of Cyprian's response published in the *Bristol Mercury*. He himself put the matter more succinctly, if not altogether accurately:

The English Order of St Benedict was founded at Claydon, near Ipswich, by the Rev. G. Drury, and he appointed Mr Lyne to act as superior under the name of Ignatius.[170]

---

[170] *Bristol Mercury*, 21 July 1866

Drury's letter went on to deal with more recent events. Ignatius may have been considering moving his surviving brothers to Ascot, to share the premises with Miss Sellon's sisterhood:

> When he was coming to England, and talked of going to Miss Sellon, at Ascot, I urged him to return to Norwich. He went to his father's, and gave him my letter to answer through the newspapers. Then I took possession at Norwich, and now I will not let him return *unless he will guarantee to conduct the affairs of the order in a proper manner*. I am acting with the advice of the best friends and members of the order here and in Norwich and London.

The proposed refoundation at Elm Hill came to nothing, but Brannock may then have tried to form an alternative community in his native Devon. As noted in the previous chapter, that summer he assisted as Subdeacon at the High Mass celebrating the opening of Cyprian's new orphanage; this was soon after both he and the Bristol tertiaries had separated from Ignatius, and significantly he was named as Brother Brannock, not Mr Webber. When 'Mar Julius' (Ferrete) visited that institution a few months later the Bristol Mercury singled out for comment a certain 'Brother Basil', robed in a habit of 'coarse black serge' and said to be a member of 'an Anglican community in Devonshire'. The name could be a shorthand-writer's slip for 'Brannock', or perhaps that of one of his associates (but would not have been that of the 'Basil' we encountered leading the Manchester tertiaries, H.D. Nihill, who by this time had been appointed to a curacy in the East End of London: see below).[171] The lack of mention

---

[171] The event is reported in the issue of 6 October 1866. Harry Incledon-Webber returned to secular life and resumed his career as a civil engineer. Eventually he settled in Manchester, where he had a job in the City Surveyor's department and played a prominent part in the local organisation for exiled Devonians. Like many of Ignatius's former monastic subjects he kept in touch with his former Abbot, and on at least one occasion visited the monastery at Llanthony (coinciding with

of Dunstan (Garland) in accounts of the comings and goings of Ignatius's monks during this rather chaotic period suggests that he might also for a time have been involved in such an attempt. His temporary defection might account for the fact that he was only clothed as a novice eighteen months after his arrival as a postulant – an unusually long interval by Ignatian standards.

In June of the following year agents acting for Drury advertised for sale 'the Spacious CHAPEL known as "THE MONASTERY"...and the FOUR COTTAGES & PREMISES adjoining',[172] but by getting his solicitor to warn off intending purchasers Ignatius succeeded in having the advertisement withdrawn. Two months later it was reported that Drury had let out the domestic buildings as 'small tenements' and planned to convert the chapel into a 'model lodging house',[173] although by April 1868 Ignatius understood that it was being used as a cheese warehouse.[174]

Eventually this Gothic white elephant would find a new role as an upholstery workshop, but not before it had enjoyed a brief flowering as a place of worship rather different from the variety for which it had been designed. At the beginning of 1869 – surprisingly, considering his antipathy to 'Dissent' – Drury let it to a Miss Robinson, pastor of a Baptist congregation in Norwich, who renamed it 'Jehovah-Jireh Tabernacle'.[175] As soon as news of this reached Ignatius's ears he despatched Philip to Norwich to demand the keys from Robert Liddlelow, an elderly carpenter in the city who acted for Drury's Ipswich man of business,[176] but he refused to hand them over.

---

the last illness and death of Ignatius's friend Dr Hanson: MT September 1883).

[172] *Norfolk News*, 22 June 1867

[173] *Pall Mall Gazette*, 15 August 1867

[174] *Lloyd's Weekly Newspaper*, 12 April 1868

[175] 'The LORD will provide': see Genesis 22.14

[176] Liddlelow had been one of Ignatius's supporters and was baptised by him two years earlier at the age of 65, as was his granddaughter-in-

This was on 16 January, a Tuesday. On the following Monday night (22nd) Ignatius himself arrived, and with the assistance of various followers and his lawyers succeeded in gaining admission through the yard between the old chapel and the new.[177] Attempts were made to have him evicted, but neither the police that night nor the magistrates the following day were willing to be drawn into the controversy.

On Tuesday 23rd a handbill was hastily printed to publicise a service in the chapel that evening at which Ignatius would officiate and preach, and a fair crowd turned out. In his sermon he refused to criticise Miss Robinson and her congregation, whose occupation of his property he put down to a misunderstanding on their part. Although they disagreed on many points he had nothing but respect and love for her as a fellow-Christian who was trying like him to spread the Gospel – indeed, he had far more time for a 'real Christ-loving Dissenter' like Miss Robinson than 'lukewarm' Anglicans and Roman Catholics. He ended by announcing that the collection would be given to her 'to help her pay the debt she has incurred under a false representation in regard to this building', and that she would herself hold a service there the following evening.

This attracted a large crowd of both the devout and the curious. Towards its conclusion Ignatius entered the building and joined Miss Robinson on the platform in front of the choir screen (she had not presumed to enter the sanctuary). Each made a speech, Miss Robinson resigning the chapel to him as its rightful owner and Ignatius suggesting that their fraternal accord would astonish the devils and cause the angels to rejoice. He claimed that news of

---

law Augusta. In the Register she and her husband Henry are listed as members of the local Third Order branch.

[177] The saga was fully reported in the *Norfolk News* of 30 January 1869. A fortnight earlier the same paper had carried an official-looking notice placed by Ignatius and announcing that he had let the old chapel (i.e. the one in the rag warehouse) to a supporter named Charles Lamb for meetings of the local Third Order branch, now presumably resuscitated.

it would 'go forth to the world', and that 'the Pope at Rome, the Patriarch at Constantinople, and every crowned head of Europe' would 'hear of it before long' and be amazed by it.[178]

'JESUS ONLY'

THESE EVENTS HAVE TAKEN US some way beyond Ignatius's return from abroad. This was early in May, when he went to stay with his family at Hambledon, where at his father's request he laid aside the habit.[179] While their hospitality was extended for a time to the Infant Oblate and his minder Sister Ambrosia (as well as to Ignatius's avian menagerie) it stopped short of offering house-room to any other refugees from Elm Hill. Brother Dunstan was wherever he was; Brother Philip, with Brother Alban, apparently the only other survivor from the Norwich debacle (and in the Bertouch narrative appearing for the first time at this point), was taken in by Dr Pusey.

When the summer vacation began the two brothers accompanied their host to his holiday home on the Isle of Wight, Southlands, above Blackgang Chine, a noted beauty spot,[180] where Ignatius later

---

[178] Exactly what happened at Elm Hill in the weeks following this ecumenical encounter is hard to determine. According to press reports (*Morning Post* 23 February; *Norfolk News* 10 April; *Bury and Norwich Post* 1 June) Ignatius and his community had resumed occupation of the monastery and were conducting services in the new chapel, which he was said to have 'consecrated'. Any monastic activity there in this period would almost certainly have been occasional rather than continuous, and if it involved brethren other than the Abbot they would have been of the Third Order variety, except perhaps for a 'First Order' travelling companion. Ignatius made another attempt to repossess the property in the summer of 1876, by which time Mr Drury's later Benedictine protégée Mary Ware had become involved (*Enthusiast* pp179ff).

[179] *Norfolk News*, 12 May 1866

[180] I am grateful to Mrs Fay Brown of the Ventnor and District Local History Society for confirming that this impressive Victorian residence was owned by Pusey and not (as has been suggested) by the Ascot sisterhood, and that following his death in 1882 it was converted into a sanatorium. Collapses in the cliff face threatening its stability it was demolished in 1910 and the stone reused in local building projects.

joined them. There was a chapel in the house where the Sacrament was reserved, and where each morning when in residence Pusey celebrated Mass.

Francis Lyne may not have had much sympathy for his son's monastic activities, but as a businessman it would have gone against the grain for him to stand by while the Elm Hill property fell into alien hands: much money and energy would be expended over the years on ultimately fruitless efforts to win it back. At the beginning of August he organised a meeting in Norwich at which Ignatius argued his case (unsuccessfully).[181] From there the dispossessed Abbot returned to the Isle of Wight, to find that apart from the servants the house was deserted.

That summer cholera had struck again. The rest of the Southlands household (Pusey, Miss Sellon and another nun and the two brothers) migrated to London to help care for the victims. Pusey himself stayed in the East End until the Oxford term began in October, serving as unofficial curate to the Rector of Bethnal Green and devoting himself to the spiritual care of the sick and dying, while Miss Sellon and her sisters (as well as the two brothers) looked after their physical needs in the temporary hospital she opened in a vacant warehouse.[182]

Throughout his life Ignatius hated being left on his own, and the absence of sympathetic company plunged him deeper into depression. With the loss of Elm Hill and a run of more than ordinary bad luck with recruits (Augustine, Maurus and Stanislaus, Placidus and all the rest) the monastic experiment appeared to have failed completely. Once again his father was urging him to give it up and settle down to a conventional ecclesiastical career, and the temptation to compromise

---

[181] The Norfolk Chronicle of Saturday 11 August reported that he had 'returned to Norwich' for a few days earlier that week, 'not in monkish dress'.

[182] Information from T.J. Williams, op cit, as well as vol 4 ch 5 of H.P. Liddon's life of Pusey. Pusey suggested to the medical superintendent that his difficulty in communicating with Jewish patients might be lessened if he (Pusey) spoke to them in Hebrew: this was successful and much appreciated.

must have been strong. Added to these external factors was his morbid fear of hell, which he rather thought had been the motive force of his spiritual life up to that point.

Matters came to a head on the day after his return. According to his recollection this was the 10th Sunday after Trinity, which that year fell on 5 August. Mattins and Evensong at Chale church did nothing for him; neither did prayer before the tabernacle in the Southlands chapel. Idly leafing through an evangelical hymnbook he picked up from the chair in front of him he was confronted by these lines –

> 'Tis a point I long to know,
>> O, it causes anxious thought;
> Do I love the Lord or no?
>> Am I His – or am I not?

– to which he could only answer with a tortured negative. In deep distress he rushed out of the house and down to the beach. Remembering that at Elm Hill this had been the hour of Compline he began to recite that office from memory, reaching the final *Salve Regina* as the sun went down. It was when he came to the climax of the prayer ('*Et Jesum, benedictum fructum ventris tui, nobis post hoc exsilium ostende*'; 'And after this our exile show unto us the blessed fruit of thy womb, Jesus') that he experienced a 'strange and wonderful thing'. The twilit English beach gave place to the Temple courts in Jerusalem, and to a vision of the scene when Mary and Joseph brought the infant Jesus to present him to the Lord.[183] From an observer of the scene he became a participant, when in response to his cry 'Give Him to me, even to me also!' he had a sense of Mary placing the child in his own arms, with the words 'Jesus is for you, as much as for Simeon.'

---

[183] St Luke 2 : 22-40

To Ignatius this was both comfort and assurance. He would describe it as his 'conversion', but the Baroness's prefers the word 'transfiguration' – aptly, as it took place on the eve of that feast. From that hour, she tells us,

> the entire current of the Monk's life was abruptly changed, and his soul transfigured by a revelation, the transmission of which has brought countless converts to the feet of a Personal and All-sufficient Saviour.[184]

THE NEXT STEP

SOON AFTER THIS EXPERIENCE Ignatius went to London, where he joined the rest of the Southlands party at the temporary cholera hospital.[185] On 30 August he preached (wearing 'a simple surplice with plain black hood, that of Trinity-college, Glenalmond') at a crowded Evensong to celebrate the first anniversary of the consecration of St Michael's, Shoreditch, where Nihill was now senior curate. It was on this occasion that Ignatius seems first to have given public voice to the ecumenical sentiments expressed in his encounter with Miss Robinson at Elm Hill, and which seem to have been one of the results of his conversion:

---

[184] See Bertouch Chapter XXXII for a full description, largely in Ignatius's own words. It is difficult to be exact about his movements in this period, but the date of his 'conversion' is quite certain. It was recorded as the 10th Sunday after Trinity in the account he gave the Baroness, as well as in the note he pencilled into his copy of *Hawker's Daily Portion*. He remembered that the tide had been on the ebb, and that while he was on the beach an increasing area of wet sand was exposed. This fits in with tidal records: high water at nearby Ventnor was at 5.57 that evening, an hour before his arrival at around 7.0pm (information for which I am grateful to the UK Hydrographic Office). The Transfiguration story evidently had strong resonance for Ignatius, who following this experience adopted as his motto the phrase 'Jesus Only' from the Gospel account, although perhaps for that reason he made more of the celebration of the Name of Jesus on 7 August than that of the Transfiguration itself on the preceding day.

[185] Williams, op cit p229. His fellow workers are said to have included Fr Grafton and the Hon Charles Wood (later Lord Halifax).

In the course of his sermon Mr Lyne said that all who loved Christ were members of the Church — Independents, Roman Catholics, Baptists — for though he would not deny that differences existed the unity of all who loved Christ should be the prayer of all Christians.[186]

There remained the question of what to do next, and where. His father had approached Archbishop Longley of Canterbury on his behalf, and at his own request Ignatius was sent to see the Vicar of Margate, Canon Bateman. The intention was that he should take up the threads of the probationary diaconate interrupted on his departure from Plymouth five years earlier, and that if he acquitted himself satisfactorily he would in due course be raised to the priesthood. This may have been how the Archbishop understood the matter and presented it to Bateman, and even the direction of Ignatius's own thinking when the plan was first mooted, but by the time he went to visit the parish for the weekend 8/9 September it was not as an unattached deacon in search of a curacy, but as Father Superior of the English Benedictine Order, whose other members (including, no doubt, the now nearly five-year-old Infant Oblate) would have to move to Margate with him — and whose affairs (including oversight of all those Third Order branches and their members) would doubtless require as much attention as his parochial duties. Not surprisingly, Bateman refused to consider such an arrangement, which would have been unlikely to work even in a parish sympathetic to the monastic revival (which Margate certainly wasn't).[187]

Ignatius may have briefly considered putting his monastic project on ice, but any doubts he had about carrying on with it were laid to rest when around a hundred and fifty supporters attended a meeting at the Store Street Music Hall, near Bedford Square. He

---

[186] Bury & Norwich Post, 4 September 1866

[187] The date of Ignatius's visit was given in an explanatory letter from Canon Bateman to his parishioners reproduced in the Morning Post of 26 September.

reported that the Archbishop of Canterbury had given his approval of 'nearly the whole of' the Rule (the habit would be modified, and the brethren would have to give up wearing it outside their monastery, as well as abandoning use of the term 'Benedictine'), and that the Bishop of London had promised to advance him to the priesthood. The meeting took place either just before or just after his visit to Margate; when it was reported in the press it was unclear whether he would open a house in London (possibly in conjunction with an appointment in the 'poorer neighbourhoods of Shoreditch'), or take up the Margate post.[188]

Among those present at the meeting was Fr Nihill, who suggested sending a 'memorial' to the Archbishop protesting at his proposed modifications to the Rule. In late October Nihill was involved in another gathering at Store Street (billed as a 'Chapter'),[189] where a 'gorgeously decorated' altar had been set up, and as 'Prior' of the Order (not just of the Third Order, apparently) he opened proceedings by officiating at 'Benedictine Vespers'. In an address at the close of this service he expressed the hope that the brethren would soon have a chapel of their own rather than being forced to worship in

---

[188] The *Western Daily Press* of 17 September reprinted reports from the *Church and State Review* and the *Church Times*. The second of these (possibly slower to catch up with events) stated categorically that he was about to take up the Margate post; the first alleged that he had secured 'the promise of the Bishop of London for his admission to priest's orders, with the express object of founding and directing a Benedictine monastery in the London diocese'. Other papers (including the *Norfolk News* of 15 September, from which the relevant quotation is taken) stated that this was to be in Shoreditch.

[189] *London Daily News*, 26 October 1866. The preceding weekend Ignatius had visited Lincolnshire, where he preached on both the Friday and the Sunday for his friend T.W. Mossman, incumbent of Fillingham with Torrington, and later the third prelate with Lee and Seccombe in the Order of Corporate Reunion (*Lincolnshire Chronicle*, 4 January 1867). At this time Mossman was trying to establish a brotherhood of young men to help him convert his parish to Anglo-Catholicism (*Lincolnshire Chronicle*, 16 June 1866), but after less than two years it ran into debt and was closed (*Pall Mall Gazette*, 1 April 1868).

such an incongruous setting, although on account of the 'pressing necessities' of his parish work he could not himself remain in office much longer. He also advised his Superior to avoid trying to combine his monastic vocation with a parochial appointment, expressing the hope that he would 'soon find a way to live with his own monks all together in a monastery', and thereby 'encourage the religious life of the order'.[190]

Ignatius himself then took to the floor, and outlined his vision for the future development of the order – or rather that of three separate but related Benedictine 'orders'. The first would consist of 'persons who would devote themselves wholly to religion', for whom he hoped to open a monastery in the following month. He was realistic enough to recognise the need for 'proper persons to act with him' in this endeavour, to prevent a recurrence of the troubles which had dogged their footsteps in Norwich.

The second was envisaged as an opportunity for 'young men [who] could not give themselves up entirely, but who might be desirous of leading an active life of charity' to 'live in community and engage in spiritual works'. For some reason the cost of opening this house was estimated at a princely '500l' compared with the mere '300l' required for that of the first order – maybe the 'active life of charity' was expected to appeal to larger numbers.

He hoped, he said, to 'form in London that evening a chapter of the third order' – a 'relaunch', perhaps, as according to the Register there were already some forty members in the capital, a good half of them in their teens and twenties and divided equally between

---

[190] Not long afterwards Nihill was summoned to an interview with the Bishop of London. In a letter to the *Oswestry Advertiser* the future Bishop William Walsham How stated that his Diocesan's advice, 'most kindly and courteously given' had 'led to the severing by Mr Nihill of all connection with the Benedictine Order' (reprinted in the *Wrexham Advertiser* of 17 November 1866). The following summer Nihill was appointed Vicar of the Shoreditch parish, rendered vacant by the death of the priest under whom he had served as curate.

the sexes. People 'engaged in businesses and professions' would be particularly suitable, as 'teaching night schools' would be one of their main functions. Another of their responsibilities, of course, would be contributing 'to a great extent' to the cost of maintaining the first and second orders.

The 'second order' seems never to have materialised, but (following Dominican usage) Ignatius seems already to have adopted this term to designate the female section of his community, currently subsisting in the person of Sister Ambrosia, who was looking after the Infant Oblate at her home in Scarborough. That autumn the child was recalled to London when Ignatius moved the remnant of the Norwich household into a modest suburban house in Milton Road, Stoke Newington, and Ambrosia, doubtless unsettled in her Anglicanism by the experience of her recent continental travels, converted to the Roman Church.[191]

At Christmas the Stoke Newington monastery received a visit from the noted scholar and controversialist Dr Littledale, who came to give 'Baby' his first Communion. Early in the new year (1867) the now 19-year-old Samuel Garland (Brother Dunstan) vowed poverty, chastity and obedience for a noviciate of one year, as did Henry Luddington, a young grocer from Ealing who had also been a member of the Third Order.[192]

MISSIONER IN MOOR LANE

BY CHOOSING TO CONCENTRATE on his community Ignatius had ruled himself ineligible for a conventional curacy. There was, however, scope for him to combine monastic life with employment as a part-time 'lecturer' at some suitable London church, and this might still lead to priestly ordination in due course. Such a post would provide

---

[191] Information from John Spence's narrative (p6)

[192] Luddington's name occurs in the roll of Third Order members (with his age on admission thereto on 3 July 1865 as 23); the documents they signed on this occasion are in the Prinknash archives.

a steady income, and the monastic part of his life would occupy a quite separate compartment.

That autumn an opportunity arose at the City church of St Bartholomew, Moor Lane, whose Vicar, William Denton, had been impressed by the young clergyman's ability as a preacher. Every Friday the Reverend Mr Lyne changed out of his habit into conventional clerical attire and reported to Denton's vicarage in Finsbury Circus: his duties were to lead a Bible class on the evening of his arrival, and to preach at St Bartholomew's on Sunday evenings. The stipend was £120 a year – a generous figure for a two-and-a-half day week.

It wasn't long before the unused galleries at St Bartholomew's had to be reopened to accommodate the crowds who came to hear the new lecturer – or before Mr Denton began to suffer pangs of envy, which before it had lasted quite a year would bring the arrangement to an end, and with it Ignatius's hopes of advancement to the priesthood. In Lent that year he also preached at Friday lunchtime services at St Edmund the King, Lombard Street, where the church was filled to overflowing;[193] by midsummer these extra services had become a regular fixture.

The scene was described by a correspondent to the London City Press.[194] The church was crowded with 'merchants, bankers and clerks', among whom could be detected 'many a devoted ultra-ritualist', anxious to see one whose 'fantastic tricks and would-be monkish habits have gained for him no enviable notoriety'. Not that there was much to indicate ritualism or monkishness either in the service itself or in the appearance of the preacher. Ignatius's sermon was preceded by the recitation of the Prayer Book Litany, and 'he assume[d] no extraordinary dress, but [wore] the surplice

---

[193] London Standard, 18 April 1867. He apparently prepared for this task by spending most of February with his family in fashionable Southsea, where his name was listed with theirs in the social column of the Hampshire Telegraph (9, 16 and 23 February).

[194] London City Press, 13 July 1867

and stole' like any other clergyman, 'curly black hair' now covering his 'once partially shaven head'. The writer quoted from someone who had attended the previous Friday's service, and who had been disappointed to hear 'nothing of the efficacy of the sacraments and the unspeakable privilege of the means of grace', nor any suggestion of the 'loving Gospel...of Jesus Christ'. The preacher 'became angry with his hearers for slight inattention'; rather than exercising the gentle but difficult art of persuasion he 'sought by scolding, intimidation and threats' to 'frighten' them into a change of heart.

Not everyone was so critical. Someone else who heard Ignatius preach around this time (at St Peter's, Vauxhall, rather than at one of his regular stints in the City) reported 'expecting to hear a discourse on the proper pattern of a chasuble; we, heard, instead one of the most truly evangelical sermons it has ever been our privilege to listen to'.[195]

On leaving St Bartholomew's Ignatius took on a regular Friday evening engagement at St Paul's, Bunhill Row,[196] meanwhile continuing with the lunchtime services at St Edmund's, where he now also preached on Sunday evenings. The Lombard Street sermons seem to have been interrupted for some weeks in the spring of 1868 – their resumption following the preacher's 'long illness' (how long, one wonders) was reported on 31 May in Lloyd's Weekly Newspaper – but by the end of the year he had lost the grudging episcopal permission under which he occupied these various metropolitan pulpits, and began to conduct regular services at the Store Street hall.

Calder-Marshall judges that the years 1867-8 were 'the peak of Ignatius's career as a preacher', when he 'had London at his feet and he kicked it around, deservedly',[197] but it was a peak from which descent was inevitable. An unwise comparison between the money-kings of Lombard Street and devotees of the Golden Calf provoked

---

[195] South London Chronicle, 29 June 1867

[196] South London Press, 28 December 1867

[197] Enthusiast p156

violent demonstrations in September 1868, but his suspension by Bishop Tait (one of his last acts as Bishop of London before his preferment to Canterbury, which took effect that Christmas) was occasioned not by the troubles in Lombard Street, but by Ignatius's 'excommunication' of a rebellious disciple.

In March 1867 he had opened a 'mission house' at 51 Hunter Street, Bloomsbury, just up the road from his childhood home at number 6. This doubled as his weekend *pied à terre* and headquarters of the Third Order, whose members congregated there for Vespers on Saturday evenings. The *London City Press*[198] printed an account of one such service, where the temporary chapel (two rooms on the first floor 'thrown into one') was 'literally crammed with people, many of the men being dressed in a hybrid, monkish attire, and not a few of the women as Sisters of Mercy'; among the latter the correspondent noticed 'a little girl about eight years old', conjecturing that she might have 'taken the place of the "Infant Samuel"'.

The 'Prioress' of this establishment was Gertrude Robins, a woman whose evident piety was matched by influential connections and ample means: it was principally through her generosity that the rent was paid and the household expenses met. Her father was Sanderson Robins (1801-62), a noted Broad Church educationalist and divine who had ended his days as Vicar of St Peter's-in-Thanet, and her mother a granddaughter of the 8th Earl of Thanet, whose estates Gertrude would herself in due course inherit. The trouble seems to have stemmed from her dissatisfaction with her status as a mere 'Sister', when as Superior (under Ignatius) of the Third Order she felt she ought to have held the rank of 'Mother'.

She was not, as Calder-Marshall suggests,[199] a middle-aged spinster seeking consolation for her condition in religious one-upmanship, but a young woman not quite twenty-eight years of age. His refusal

---

[198] Issue of 3 October 1868

[199] *Enthusiast* pp167ff

to accede to her desire – and hers to accept his refusal like a dutiful daughter – led to a confrontation, and to her ejection from both Third Order and mission house. His use of the term 'excommunication' in this connection was unwise, even though St Benedict had regularly used it as a synonym for 'exclusion'.[200] When Miss Robins reported her grievance to the Bishop she accused Ignatius of excommunicating her from the Church of England, and no amount of explanation on his part could persuade Dr Tait that that had not been his intention.[201]

LALEHAM

THE STOKE NEWINGTON MONASTERY was a temporary arrangement, lasting no more than a few months. In the summer of 1867 Ignatius moved the brothers to the then rural Middlesex village of Laleham, between Chertsey and Staines. The house, which was taken for three years, stood on the edge of Greenfield Common a mile or so north of the village, which in those days had a population of a little over six hundred. It was a modest redbrick affair with six (main?) rooms, to which he added a bell-turret and various pieces of ecclesiastical decoration.[202] In the garden was a coach-house which became the chapel (it was said to compare in size with a 'London dining room'), and a 'hillock' designated 'Mount Calvary' – he may have got the idea from his visit to Mount St Bernard's, where a natural rocky outcrop had been given this name and a large crucifix erected on it.

---

[200] Rule of St Benedict Chapters XXIII to XXVIII

[201] Gertrude Robins then briefly joined a Scottish Episcopal sisterhood, the Community of St Mary and St John, whose Warden was the Provost of Perth Cathedral, Edward Fortescue, a widower some twenty years her senior. In 1871 they married, and the following year were received into the Roman Catholic Church. They produced three children, of whom the second was the priest and polymath Adrian Fortescue (1874–1923) (Information from Aidan Nichols, *The Latin Clerk: the Life, Work and Travels of Adrian Fortescue*; Cambridge: Lutterworth Press 2011).

[202] The house is still known as 'The Priory', and is located at 151 Ashford Road, Laleham TW18 1RS. See article by S.G.A. Luff in Newsletter no 16 (June 1988) of the Father Ignatius Memorial Trust.

These details are taken from accounts of visits published in the *Belfast Morning News* of 13 May 1868 and the *Manchester Times* of 8 May 1869. Associated with the monastery was an 'old men's home' in a nearby cottage. This was a source of some controversy, as although money was routinely collected for its upkeep at Ignatius's mission services it was alleged to be empty of both occupants and furniture; the one person to have been admitted had speedily left, complaining that the diet was inferior even to that of the monks. Or so a visitor described the situation at an anti-Ignatius meeting reported in the *London City Press* of 25 January 1868.

The rent for the new monastery was subsidised by the Reverend Douglas Boutflower ('Fr Bernard'), a naval chaplain whom Ignatius had met at the 1864 Church Congress[203] and whose help and support continued until his death in 1882; in his last illness he would contribute £1900 towards the cost of building the south cloister at Llanthony. Two other supporters who had come on the scene in this period were a middle-aged spinster named Ann Easley and her widowed sister Frances Lack, who when he was still preaching at St Bartholomew's followed Ignatius back to Mr Denton's vicarage and asked to be enrolled in the Third Order. Ann ('Sister Winifred') would in due course subscribe the purchase price of the site at Capel-y-ffin; Frances ('Sister Frances') stepped into Gertrude Robins's shoes as Prioress of the Third Order.

With the move to Laleham the community began to settle into something approaching stability. The Register (the systematic keeping of which seems to have started around this time) records the life professions of Brothers Philip (Pointer) and Dunstan (Garland) – the one on 1 May 1868, the other on 6 July 1869. Also in the summer of 1868 Ignatius had established his convent of 'second order' nuns at nearby Feltham,[204] so with regular visits there as

---

[203] BUWP p80n

[204] See below, Chapter 8.

well as weekends at Hunter Street he would now be stretched in three different directions, making it difficult for him to oversee his growing company of monastic aspirants. In the eighteen months immediately before the move to Llanthony there were seven of them, all either very young or inadequate or both:

- Placidus (William Henry Wicking), youngest of the three children of William and Elizabeth Wicking of Holly Street, Dalston, in east London, 'clothed' (this is what the Register says, but I think it means admitted as a postulant) at Laleham on 22 December 1868 at the age of twelve years and four months. The elder William earned his living as a 'pianoforte tuner', and played the organ at the Dutch Calvinist Church at Austin Friars in the City. In Ignatius's propaganda tracts *Brother Placidus* and *Leonard Morris* this boy-monk appears with a very thin disguise: as 'little Brother Angelus' in the former, and 'Sunbeam' in the latter; Kilvert[205] mentions a pretty young novice with this nickname who matches his description. *Leonard Morris* includes an account agreeing substantially with what Wicking told John Spence about how he had been allowed to join the community after hearing Ignatius preach when he was only eleven, together with the text of a letter he wrote to his mother about the simple joys of life in the monastery.[206]

- Cuthbert (Albert Edward Giddy), who 'made first vows' (as a postulant?) on 4 February 1869, aged 24 years and seven months. He survived just over a year: on 9 February 1870 'having promised stability before [the] Bl[essed] Sacrament left the Monastery in

---

[205] Kilvert vol 1 p224

[206] *Leonard Morris* p 141ff; cp Spence p 9f. Unfortunately we don't have a record of anything the real-life 'Sunbeam' wrote to his mother, but the Superior was not averse to dictating whole letters purportedly from his subjects to their parents.

my [Ignatius's] absence thereby perjuring himself & the Bl[essed] Sac[rament]. On whose soul may GOD have mercy. He was a good man but very weak minded.'[207]

- Pancras (Arthur Atholbury Devey Rymer), 'professed as Postulant' (no date given); 'professed as Novice' on 4 November 1869 when he was sixteen or seventeen. He was born in or around 1853 in Douglas, Isle of Man, where his father John Devey Rymer (MB Paris, MD London) may have been practising as a doctor.[208] On 18 June 1870 Pancras 'broke his vows and left the Convent [at] Laleham in my [Ignatius's] absence'. Three days later he wrote 'as if he had done no wrong at all, and more affectionately than ever'. Later he wrote again 'most penitently and said he w[oul]d return, his vocation was stronger than ever, because in the world people "laughed at the world to come"'.

- Dunstan Paul (Alfred Griffiths) was 'professed' as both postulant and novice, the latter alongside Pancras on 4 November 1869; his age was given as sixteen. As the recently life-professed Dunstan (Garland) must still have been in the community it is strange that this young man was given the same name, but they didn't

---

[207] His birth was registered in the second quarter of 1844 in Bethnal Green. In the censuses of 1851 (aged six) and 1861 (aged sixteen, employed as a clerk) he was listed at his family home in Lambeth; his father was a tailor. Later censuses (when he had changed the spelling of his name to 'Giddie') chart his progress from being a 'merchant clerk' (1881) to flour merchant (1891) and residing in Camberwell with his wife and son to his final occupation as a coal merchant in Brighton. His death was registered at Elham (Kent) in the fourth quarter of 1906.

[208] The 1861 census shows Dr Rymer and his wife as having seven children, born variously in Somerset, Cheshire and Surrey as well as this one on the Isle of Man. The Doctor himself was not at home when the census was taken as he was doing time in Lewes Prison, possibly as a result of pecuniary difficulties (see *Morning Post*, 22 November 1856 and *Sussex Advertiser*, 10 August 1858; also *Pall Mall Gazette*, 24 May 1873). After his release he resumed his medical practice in the East End of London.

coincide for long. His Register entry includes the following note: 'Wednesday April 6 1870 (Passion Week) broke his vows & left the Convent, Laleham, saying that he was doing so much harm he could not stay. His mother's visits he said had robbed him of his vocation. He went in the habit at 7 o'clock this morning leaving a very affect[ionate] letter for me. I think Our Lord will bring him back.' History fails to relate whether he did in fact return, and nothing is known of his origins or subsequent career.

• Serene (or Serenus) (James Roberts) was 'admitted a postulant' on 22 December 1868, receiving his first Communion on Christmas Day. His date of birth is given as 15 January 1844 and his age at the time of his admission as 25 years two months: a discrepancy of three months. Soon after the move to Llanthony Ignatius's sister Harriet told the diarist-curate Francis Kilvert that Serene had been 'a gardener and a very drunken man'; he had begged the Abbot 'to take him and reclaim him', as a result of which he was believed to be 'an altered man'.[209]

• Maurus (William Swan) was 'clothed at his First Com[munion]' on Ascension Day (26 May) 1870; like Placidus he was only twelve years of age.[210]

• Theodore (Leonard Charles Frederick Cawkill Barker) was 'professed [as a] postulant' (no date given) and as a novice on 2 July 1870, shortly before his 26th birthday (27 July). His name is missing from the list of those who went to Llanthony on

---

[209] Kilvert vol 1 p176f

[210] His father (another William) was a Londoner who worked as a carver and gilder; his mother came from Liverpool, where both young William and his much older sister had been born, although by the time the 1861 census was taken they had moved back to the capital (Mary Street, Hampstead Road).

the 22nd of that month, so he may have been sent to stay with the Feltham nuns as a temporary measure; for several years Ignatius used the unenclosed portion of their convent as a place to isolate problem brothers from the rest of the community, as well as a staging post between Llanthony and the outside world. He was expelled on 8 September ('for disobedience, deceit & hypocrisy') – probably from Llanthony itself, as the novices observed that day's feast of 'Our Ladye's Nativity' by receiving Holy Communion in the temporary chapel,[211] and joined up with

- John Douglas Barney, son of a Suffolk clergyman and formerly a Lieutenant in the 67th Regiment, who had been received as a 'penitent' at the age of 26 in the spring of 1868 after leaving the Army in unspecified disgrace; inadvisedly 'without any introduction'. In the Register a page-long appendix under the heading 'Account of Br John of Laleham' includes the following:

I found out from his conduct & from his own account of himself that he was not sound in his mind. At one time he was troubled with a mania for murder, which caused me considerable anxiety. At another time, he fancied he must commit some unmentionable crime. I bore with him until July 1870 [i.e. until just before the move to Llanthony]. At this time he wanted me to sanction his opening a brotherhood & school under my authority. I refused this, on account of his entire unfitness & dangerous temptations, but offered to allow him to teach if he would do so under my eye at Llanthony. He would not, and at my desire he ceased to be an associate. He then said he should never cease to feel the greatest gratitude & respect for me. After this he became most violent because I felt it necessary to make a public statement to the effect that I had nothing to do with his 'Order of

---

[211] The Chronicle notes on 3 September that the novices were 'being prepared to receive their Communion' on that day (quoted Attwater p63).

Brothers of Charity', which he commenced with a man whom I had been obliged to turn out of our Order for falsehood & deceit, Bro Theodore, named Barker in the world.

Their collaboration seems to have been quite short-lived, as in the 1871 census Barney was listed as the only occupant of a house on Laleham Common described as a 'Monastry' [sic]. The Register account goes on to say that Barney 'continued his violent conduct & has since received another low person whom I had to expel from our house, another, a servant, who had stolen £3 from me, also two novices who had run away from Llanthony, & a boy, who had been entrusted to my charge'.

The identity of the 'low person' and the boy is not known; the so-called 'servant' would have been Brother Serene (Roberts), demoted from his status as postulant after the move to Llanthony. One of the escapees or expellees was Brother Pancras (Rymer); the others were later entrants. Their histories, together with further developments in that of Brother Serene, will figure in the following chapter.

According to the Register 'all at once' Barney 'gave everything up' and 'became [a] Romanist' in 1873, although as one of his sons (another John, 1887-1960) served as a clergyman of the Church of England his affair with Rome may have been only a flirtation. In 1879 he married the daughter of a Portsmouth tailor, from whom he lived mostly apart but with whom he had several children. He had private means, leaving over £11,000 when he died in 1919.[212]

Meanwhile the former Brother Theodore seems to have emigrated to South Africa, and was either ordained or began to pose as a clergyman.[213] As 'the Reverend St Charles Cawkill Barker' he was

---

[212] Information from public records, local (Hampshire) newspapers and Crockford's Clerical Directory

[213] His name is not listed in Crockford.

next heard of in the goldfields of the Eastern Transvaal, where he set up a school and an Anglican church (at first in a tent, then in a shack) at a settlement named Pilgrims' Rest. Here he was a popular local character, doubtless on account of his hard drinking and other extra-curricular interests as much as his spiritual leadership.[214]

LALEHAM WAS WELL PLACED to attract visitors, among them young men of a class superior to that from which most of his novices were drawn. Digby Dolben drowned in the River Welland on 28 June so is unlikely to have visited the brethren in their new home,[215] but another Etonian visitor (and friend of Dolben's) was Alfred Wyatt-Edgell, later Lord Braye. While an undergraduate he once spent Christmas in the Laleham monastery, but his association with it ended when shortly afterwards he converted to Rome.

An anecdote in the journal Truth[216] connects Wyatt-Edgell's visit with that of a German-born clergyman named Mistiwitz, a former Lutheran minister who had been reordained in the American Episcopal Church.

> It was an Ember Day, and Ignatius presided at the 'High Table', at which were seated Brother Thomas [Wyatt-Edgell], a guest, and the chaplain [Mistiwitz]. By-and-bye, three mutton chops and a shrunken little boiled sole made their appearance. Ignatius *(loquitur)*: 'Now, I must explain the dinner. Brother Thomas and I are ordered meat by the doctors. Mr ---- must have meat too. You, Father (addressing the chaplain) can have the fish to yourself.' The chaplain lifted up a doleful voice, saying, 'But Father, I am not very well. I think I would

---

[214] For this information and a contemporary anecdote see http://www.mpumalangahappenings.co.za/pilgrimsrest_characters.htm (under 'Elizabeth Russell Cameron').

[215] http://www.oxforddnb.com/view/article/37365?docPos=2; retrieved 28 May 2014

[216] Date unknown; reprinted in the *Hereford Times* of 25 September 1880.

rather not fast today.' Ignatius (peremptorily): 'Impossible, Father; I couldn't allow it to be said that my chaplain ate meat on an Ember Day.' 'But, Father, I took some medicine yesterday....' No further answer was vouchsafed by the inexorable Superior.

Another clergyman – also of German origin – who for a while formed part of the Laleham ménage was a Roman Catholic priest named Lohrum. He is said to have stayed for some weeks in 1867, and to have been happy for the brethren to receive Communion at his daily Mass (under the form of Bread; it fell to the Superior to administer the Chalice). When the authorities of his Church tried to put an end to this irregular arrangement he took no notice.[217]

'BABY' LOSES HIS MOTHER (OR SO IT APPEARS)

IN ROME THE INFANT OBLATE was said to have been asked to name his mother and father, and had replied, 'I am the child of Jesus Christ and of the Blessed Virgin and of the holy St Benedict.' [218] As far as the identity of his earthly parents was concerned John Spence reports hearing from Brother Dunstan (Thomas Bray, the third to receive this name) that 'in the society of England "Baby" was said to be the Reverend Father's own child' – he thought this unlikely, as they resembled one another only in 'disposition' – and that according to what he had been told by the Abbot himself the child had 'no idea' who his mother was (or presumably his father).

He relates being told how when Baby was 'seven or eight' Ignatius took him aside and told him to 'kneel down and pray for the soul of one who is dead', though without telling him who that person was. Spence understood it to have been the boy's mother, and had no reason to believe that Emily Docking had not in fact died. Actually she was at the time in question very much alive, having on 18 October

---

[217] Bertouch p387f

[218] Enthusiast p129

1869 (when her younger son was seven and three-quarters) been through a form of marriage at St Mary's, Haggerston in east London with Robert Drake, a shoemaker seven or eight years her senior originally from Norwich but now living in Bethnal Green.[219] News of this irregular union had probably reached Ignatius from contacts in Norwich, and his reaction was predictable. Bigamy was a mortal sin, so to all intents and purposes Emily was indeed dead.

LLANTHONY AT LAST

ELEVEN DAYS before Emily Docking entered into her bigamous marriage, on 7 October, the South Wales regional daily the *Western Mail* carried the following brief news item:

> FATHER IGNATIUS – This celebrated preacher, and a brother of his order, have paid a visit to Llanthony Abbey recently. The quaint dress in which they appeared, excited the curiosity of the natives.

Over the next four decades the South Wales 'natives' would become quite used to seeing the 'quaint dress' of Ignatius and his entourage. Having failed to obtain the ruins at Llanthony itself or those of any other 'old desecrated monastery' he used a £1000 gift from Sister Winifred to secure a site for his new establishment four miles higher up the valley at Capel-y-ffin, a tiny hamlet just across the Brecknockshire border. Although the purchase would not be completed until the following February he sent an advance party to occupy it in November, consisting of the now life-professed Philip and the postulant Serene.[220]

---

[219] She described herself as Emily Docking, Widow, daughter of William Vincent, Butcher. She and Drake appear together in the 1871 census; in that of 1861 he had been listed in Norwich with an earlier wife named Ann. In 1881 (in Tonbridge) he had acquired yet another wife, an Irishwoman called Kate – perhaps by this time Emily really was dead.

[220] During the first few years at Llanthony Ignatius recorded significant events in a mock-mediaeval 'Chronicle', now at Prinknash Abbey; it is

reproduced in *extenso* by Attwater (pp48-67, *passim*). The first entry notes the payment between 21 and 28 February 1870 of amounts totalling £936 3s 1d 'thro' the Lawyer Page' of Hay to the owner and mortgagees of the property, and the fact that 'in the Month of November 1869' Philip and Serene 'did take up their abode' there, '[l]iving through a most inclement winter in a hut on the mountain'. One wonders why, if possession wasn't obtained until the following February.

CHAPTER 5

THE FIRST YEAR AT LLANTHONY

THE LLANTHONY VALLEY IS – or was – a land of small farms. In the narrow upper part, from old Llanthony to the head of the valley beyond Capel-y-ffin, each holding of perhaps twenty or thirty acres (some more and some less) was arranged in much the same way. The hayfields and home pastures occupied the valley floor and the gentle lower slopes, either side of the valley road. From this road – until the 1930s just a track, after Llanthony – lanes ran directly uphill between the fields, each to a farmhouse with its attendant barn and other outbuildings. As one drives up the valley today one can see these little groups of buildings strung out at intervals just where the serious slope begins and the fields give way to open mountainside, on which each farm has its right of sheepwalk.

The houses themselves are typically small and squat, almost all of them now extended and modernised. In their original state they would have consisted of little more than a couple of rooms and a 'beast house' downstairs, with the sleeping quarters for humans nestling under the roof of stone tiles. The few small windows admitted only a modicum of daylight, but on a working farm only the very young and very old spent the day indoors. At night the windows would be shuttered to protect the occupants from the keen winds and sharp frosts of the Black Mountain winter, although at that time of the year no-one sat up for long after the animals had been seen to and the family had eaten their simple evening meal. The warmest place then would be bed, which for the child or unattached adult would almost certainly be shared with one or more siblings, or other relatives of the same sex.

This landscape had never been completely static, and neither had the population. At any one time the majority of those living in the valley might have been born in the immediate locality, but the need on the one hand for fresh blood to prevent inbreeding and on the other for occupations for the young had prompted a certain amount of movement in and out, with consequent adjustments to the housing stock. And (in the one case to provide for a young couple starting out, and in the other to make one economically viable unit out of two uneconomic ones) farms were from time to time divided or amalgamated.

One such amalgamation was Ty Gwyn ('the white house'), whose thirty-two acres included those of the adjacent farm Trecae.[221] This was the land which Sister Winifred's contribution enabled Ignatius to buy in February 1870, and where almost immediately he began to translate his monastic dream into physical reality. On the deeds the new owner was named not as Joseph Leycester Lyne but as Harriet Emily Stewart, Mother Hilda of the Feltham convent. This was because just then there was some uneasiness about the legal status of monastic institutions and their right to own property, although why a female religious should be considered less at risk in this respect than a male one is difficult to determine.[222]

The farmhouse – evidently fairly dilapidated – was approached by the lane which now serves both the monastery and the nearby Grange Trekking Centre, and stood just above the stable yard belonging to the latter, on the left as one goes up the hill. It was occupied just then by a tenant named Ben Pritchard;[223] in the next decade it would

---

[221] The next farm up the valley on the left hand side, otherwise known as Boxbush or Upper House. Now like Ty Gwyn a century and a half ago it is itself semi-derelict.

[222] Ownership was transferred to Ignatius in April 1879, following the separation of the two communities recounted in Chapter 8.

[223] Not to be confused with David Pritchard of Ty'r-ywen, Llanthony, whose son William would play an important part in the later history of the monastery. According to Spence, this Pritchard let the farmland 'go to

finally be demolished, and the stone recycled. Some of it may have
been used in the construction of Plas Genevieve, original name of
the Grange, or in that of the lower of the two outhouses opposite
the turning to the monastery, now itself in ruins. The upper one,
with large double doors and narrow slits in lieu of windows, is much
older, and was the barn belonging to Ty Gwyn.

BEGINNINGS

THE 'HUT ON THE MOUNTAIN' claimed by the monastic chronicler as
the place where Philip and Serene spent the winter was unlikely to
have been an actual 'hut'. According to Francis Kilvert[224] they lodged
in the farmhouse itself, although it is unlikely that the Pritchards (Mr
and Mrs in their mid-thirties; children of seven, five and one) were
able to spare them more than one room. It may even have been a
lean-to, so somewhere in the grey area between inside the farmhouse
and outside in a shed. The diarist had received his information from
workmen engaged on the new building, and tells us in addition that
they were reputed to live 'a good deal on milk', did for themselves
what little washing they required and allowed 'no woman to come
near them' – so they can't have lived at very close quarters with
their hosts.[225]

    With them for a time was a boy named Sam, although John Spence
said he 'soon got tired and left them'; he would have been the 'servant'

---

ruin [and] was dismissed', after which he 'established himself not far
off and made depredations upon the hedges of the monastery and shot
the old tom cat'.

[224] Kilvert vol 1 p78

[225] The confusion doubtless originated through the use of the word 'hut'
to denote the old farmhouse; see Chapter 9 below. Bertouch (p441)
says Philip and Serene lived in 'a small hut (locally termed a cottage)',
which by the time she wrote had 'long been removed from the monastic
estate'. She also has the stone-laying Mass (see below) taking place in
'the old farmhouse' (p440). Likewise Ignatius, who looking back over
twenty years remembers it having been in 'the broken-down farmstead'
(LMN April-June 1894).

noticed by Kilvert on his first visit to Capel-y-ffin on 5 April, when all three were hard at work moving earth from the builders' excavations to create a kitchen garden, on the slope below where in due course the abbey church would be built.[226] On 2 September – by which time the Abbot and most of the brothers were in residence, of a sort – Kilvert would pay another visit to the monastic building site (his third), coinciding with Ignatius's parents and his youngest brother Clavering (now 21), and joining them for an alfresco luncheon in the dingle, at which monastery-grown potatoes and beans accompanied provisions brought by Mrs Lyne. He pronounced these vegetables 'very good',[227] so their labours (doubtless benefiting from Serene's horticultural expertise) proved worthwhile.

Work on the new monastery began as soon as the purchase was completed. The architect was Charles Buckeridge, a keen devotee of the Ritualist movement who had taken over the Ascot Priory commission from George Gilbert Scott.[228] For the time being only one of the four blocks which would eventually surround the central cloister garth was to be built – the 'west cloister', the one nearest the visitor as he approaches from the original farm lane. In March – after abandoning the Laleham brothers for a short holiday at Aberdaron on the Lleyn peninsula, where he wrote a lengthy poem in honour of the twenty thousand saints buried on the nearby 'holy isle' of Bardsey – Ignatius paid a flying visit to Capel-y-ffin to lay the foundation stone. The date given for this in the Chronicle was 17 March (St Patrick's Day), although some accounts put it on the 18th, and the builder thought it had been in February.

---

[226] Kilvert vol 1 pp177f. In his Chronicle Ignatius puts it thus: 'From this time...the Brothers did spend much toil & labour in laying out & planting with vegetables, the Abbey Garden. With a good & zealous will did they work, knowing that they were toiling for the Lord, & that He loveth "a cheerful giver"' (quoted Attwater p52).

[227] Kilvert vol 1 p221

[228] For Buckeridge's work at Capel-y-ffin see The Builder, vol 30 (1872) p710, and the Ecclesiastical Art Review of 1878 p148.

The ceremony took place after a frugal lunch. Earlier Mass had been celebrated 'in the Monks Hut' (i.e. the farmhouse) by Ignatius's friend Edward Husband, who had accompanied him on the trip to North Wales; he was said recently to have returned to the Church of England from 'the Schismatic Sect established in our Country twenty years ago by the Bishop of Rome'.[229] Under the stone Ignatius placed a medal of St Benedict which he tells us had been received from the Abbot of Monte Cassino seven years earlier, when the community was in its early infancy at Claydon Rectory.[230]

Also present at the stone-laying was the builder, Edwin Foster of Abergavenny, together with his workforce of around twenty men. Some months later Mr Foster was summoned to give evidence to the Parliamentary Select Committee on Conventual and Monastic

---

[229] Husband (1843-1908), the son of a Baptist minister, was curate of Atherstone (Leicestershire) from his ordination in 1866 until he resigned to become a Roman Catholic three years later, when according to the *Birmingham Daily Post* (27 August 1869) his parishioners presented him with a four-volume Breviary. His sojourn in the Roman Church was not long. On 4 December 1869 the *Leamington Spa Courier* reported that Burns & Oates had published a pamphlet giving his reasons for joining it, but in early March 1870 (while at Barmouth with Ignatius) he wrote a letter explaining his return to the Church of England (report in *Staffordshire Sentinel* of 16 April). In *Crockford* he is listed as having been at Atherstone until 1872, when he moved to a second curacy in Folkestone. He remained in that town for the rest of his life, in 1878 becoming Vicar of the new church of St Michael and All Angels (designed 1871 by Bodley & Garner; demolished 1953 following serious war damage). Here he officiated at daily choral services, installing (and regularly playing) a magnificent four-manual organ, complete with bells, drums and other interesting effects (*Nelson Evening Mail*, 28 December 1889; see also article by J.H.M. Jay in *The Musical Times* of 1 July 1921). Like Ignatius he combined his Anglo-Catholicism with a taste for 'mission hymns'; his compilation *The Mission Hymnal* (1874) included four from his own pen, described in Julian's Dictionary of Hymnology as 'very simple, earnest, and impassioned'. As '+Cuthbert OSB, Atherstone' he had assisted at one of Ignatius's services in the Store Street hall (*London City Press*, 3 October 1868); a few months later Ignatius addressed a meeting in the Atherstone Corn Exchange (*Leicester Journal*, 12 March 1869).

[230] Account in Chronicle, quoted Attwater pp49f

Institutions,[231] and his answers to the Committee's questions provide some interesting detail. He said that the ceremony had taken place at about three in the afternoon; that although there had been little publicity the function attracted about twenty 'strangers' (supporters from elsewhere? Or locals wondering what was going on?); that it had consisted of the reading of prayers, the chanting of 'something like hymns' and the inevitable address by Ignatius, and that both incense and lanterns containing lighted candles had been used. This last he supposed was 'emblematic' rather than functional, which was a neat way of putting it. The abbot and his two subordinates wore their habits, while 'Mr Husbands' had had 'a white gown on, ornamented' – a cope, perhaps.[232]

Before we leave the subject of their quarters that first winter we have John Spence's assertion that Philip and Serene 'lived in the barn for six months after the monastery was begun', adding the detail that the two brothers 'suffered horribly…having nothing often but turnips to live on and begging barefoot from door to door – they did not receive much kindness from the country people'. He may perhaps have confused the period when Philip and Serene were living at Ty Gwyn with the time when they and the others slept in the barn (see below).

---

[231] Appointed to enquire into the legality or otherwise of monastic communities, both Anglican and Roman Catholic, with particular reference to their financial affairs. As stated above, there was some uncertainty about whether following their dissolution by Henry VIII they were in fact illegal institutions.

[232] Another account of the stone-laying appeared in the London Standard of 26 March. The correspondent reported that the two monks 'together with a third, a kind of lay-brother (Sam, presumably), were then living in a rude hut on the mountain, just beside a clear little stream of delicious water'. Inside it they had fitted up a 'temporary altar…for their own private devotions'. Having no form of lighting they had to retire to their 'humble pallets' at sundown, after reciting Vespers and Compline. This does sound more like a hut than the house (which was nowhere near a stream), so it is possible they moved from one to the other – perhaps one of the builders' huts mentioned below.

Ignatius may have hoped that the two monks would keep an eye on the builders, but if they observed how the building was coming on (or failing to come on) they were probably unable to do anything about it. On Midsummer's Day Kilvert paid his second visit, when he and his brother Edward ('Perch') stopped off on their way home from a walk to Llanthony Priory.[233] He met 'a different set of masons' from those he had seen in April, reporting that '[t]hey had not progressed with the building so fast as they had expected to do. I believe the contractor had failed or quarrelled with his employers and the works had been at a deadlock for some time.' Philip and Serene were not visible, but the garden was now 'in beautiful order[,] down to a pretty bank of flowers that ran along the top of the garden wall or fence'.

This midsummer visit was only a couple of weeks before Edwin Foster's interview with the Select Committee, when among other matters he was asked about his slow progress on the new building. His questioners may have wanted to suggest that 'the Rev. Mr Lyne' was having difficulty finding the full contract sum of £674,[234] but although there was still some money outstanding the problem seems to have lain elsewhere. Kilvert suggests the delay was due partly to the Abbot's naivety in business matters and partly to a lack of supervision, both of which undoubtedly contributed to it, but Ignatius (who was on the spot for the second half the of relevant period) emphasises the practical difficulties the men were up against, especially when winter began to set in:

Workmen would not stay in this desolate wilderness. They built themselves wooden huts in the ravine hard by; but once there came a great flood, and everything belonging to them, beds and all, were

---

[233] A round trip of some 26 miles, including the double ascent of the 1700-foot Gospel Pass on unmade roads. This part of Kilvert's entry for that day was omitted from William Plomer's three-volume selection, but reproduced on p54 of Donald Attwater's life of Ignatius.

[234] In his account of this period in LMN June 1894 Ignatius said he 'had £887 in hand to pay for' the work, and 'never went into debt'.

soaked with water. One of them got rheumatic fever and nearly died; the others were so wretched they would not stay.... It seemed as if it were an impossibility, in such a solitude, to build at all.[235]

THE MONKS ARRIVE

IN JULY THE LEASE on the Laleham monastery fell in, so despite the incomplete state of the building Ignatius had to relocate his community to Capel-y-ffin. The brothers arrived by train at Llanfihangel on the 22nd, '[t]he young novices, Placidus, Maurus and Ignatius' being ferried up the valley with the Superior and the Reserved Sacrament by horse and dogcart. Placidus (then not quite fourteen) and Maurus (twelve) we have already encountered; 'Ignatius' here is the Infant Oblate, although he was not in fact a novice. (If for some purposes he was counted with the novices and/or postulants and the floating population of acolytes and choirboys he lived apart from them; even after the move into the competed west wing he normally slept with the Abbot in his cell.) He was now eight and a half, and could perhaps be excused for his pitiful grizzling on the slow journey up the valley, when darkness fell and the horse looked as if it wasn't going to make it.[236]

The rest of the party ('Father Dunstan[237] a professed monk of our Order, together with Frederick an acolyte & Henry Mower, a Christian man, who doth greatly assist our Order') had to make the eleven-mile journey on foot, not surprisingly losing their way in the unfamiliar terrain and only reaching the monastic building site early the following morning. A fourth member of this group, 'Brother John, who is but an associate brother & a secular', failed to arrive altogether, having like many a later visitor taken refuge in the inn at old Llanthony.

---

[235] ibid

[236] A considerable drama was made of this incident in later Llanthony folklore; see Bertouch pp443ff.

[237] Garland

A gimcrack shed was thrown up against the outer wall of the unfinished structure as a temporary lodging for the Abbot and the Oblate; this small lean-to (not much more than eleven or twelve feet square) also housed the altar, and the Blessed Sacrament in a 'handsome oak tabernacle'.[238] The others slept several hundred yards away, in the Ty Gwyn barn.

Ignatius wrote two accounts of the early days at 'New Llanthony', respectively fifteen and twenty-four years after the events described.[239] The more detailed is the second, from which we have already quoted. We learn that the leaky and windowless barn was divided into three areas, one containing the community's store of furniture, another serving as refectory and the third as kitchen and dormitory for the half dozen or so monks and novices. 'The fire [for cooking]...was on the earthen floor up in a corner.... The wet would accumulate, after rain, in a hollow which when full, was suggestive of piscatorial possibilities.' Every day the brethren would pack into the little lean-to for the offices, starting with Prime at 5.0am and ending with Matins and Lauds of the following day recited after Compline.

> While the Summer lasted our troubles were only amusing, and a very real touch of romance halo-ed our surroundings. We were beginning just as some of the great monastic foundations of bye-gone days commenced.... But now 'the harvest was past, the Summer was ended', and we were still in the old barn and new shed. At night, these were very cold now at the end of September. We tried to hollow out a cave in the ravine, but it kept falling in as we dug.... By the end of October severe frosts set in. I used to rise at five in the morning from my

---

[238] Article by Ignatius, MT June 1885. He tells us that the shed was 'now used as a store-pantry'; it was next to what became the monastery kitchen and survives as part of the lean-to against the outer wall of the west wing. In the 1960s it was weatherproofed and converted into a bedroom for one of the holiday flats occupying that part of the building.

[239] MT June 1885 and LMN June 1894

bed in the shed, my blankets streaming with damp, and the stone floor wet with rain, or slippery with ice....

VISITORS

THE NEW MONASTERY quickly became an object of curiosity in the neighbourhood, and a sight not to be missed by those with sufficient leisure and stamina to make the journey. It must have been of particular interest to local Roman Catholics, who would not hitherto have had many opportunities to examine for themselves the movement to catholicise the Church of England from within.

In late August a small group of upper-class Catholics paid a call. Its leader was the Prior of Belmont (Dom Roger Bede Vaughan, a member of the Catholic squirearchy family of Courtfield, near Ross-on-Wye); the others were the 22-year-old Marquess of Bute (a recent and ardent convert), Lady Herbert of Lea, and another of whose identity Ignatius was uncertain. In his memoir of Bute Abbot Sir David Hunter-Blair reports that Ignatius 'insisted on his visitors keeping strict silence when walking over a field in which his cloisters were one day to be built'.[240] Ignatius may have hoped that the fabulously wealthy Bute would contribute to the building fund, but their divergent understandings of the term 'Catholic' would have stood in the way of this; besides, he had expensive projects of his own just then starting in South Wales, at Cardiff Castle and Castell Coch.

THE ERRANT SERENE

WHEN KILVERT JOINED the Lynes for lunch on 2 September he may not have noticed that one of the monks he had seen on his first visit was missing. This was Serene, who had absconded the day before, but returned that evening:

---

[240] Hunter-Blair, John Patrick, Third Marquess of Bute K.T. p49. The visit is mentioned in Bertouch pp449f, but does not figure in Rosemary Hannah's more recent biography of Bute, The Grand Designer (Birlinn 2012).

On this day there did return to our Holy House, Brother Serene afore
named, a postulant in our Order. He had been troubled with a sore
illness [nature and degree of severity undisclosed], and could no longer
endure the many trials which Our Lord doth require us to suffer for His
Name's sake. But having arrived on his journey as far as Oxford, Our
Lord, Who is a Good Shepherd, met His wandering sheep & told him
plainly that he must go no further, but return to his Monastery and
serve Him. Br Serene was filled with loathing of the world by all that
he saw by the way; & the next day he did return to the Holy Enclosure
of the Monastery, i.e. on this 2nd day of September. He arrived past
Compline time. He was now not permitted to receive the Postulants
dress which he had laid aside, but was admitted to be only a secular or
extern brother associated with us, in our Holy Fathers Name.[241]

It may have been this summary demotion that prompted him to
abscond for a second time three weeks later, on Sunday 25 September
('having stolen £3 from the oratory where the B[lessed] Sacrament
was', i.e. the Abbot's shed), and as we have seen to take himself to
'Mr Barney at Laleham'. While there he 'committed most serious
sins' – perhaps just being there and not at Llanthony. He 'wrote
imploring my pardon. I again forgave him. He was allowed to take
the vows as a penitent for one year, on Thursday November 17 1870
at Feltham Priory.' Six days later – on 23 November, Ignatius's thirty-
third birthday – 'he again ran away & this time with broken vows
added to his guilt. Mr Barney made this person one of his brothers,
'Brother Jerome', when he was a runaway thief.'

THE 'DREAM ABBEY' BEGINS TO TAKE SHAPE
AFTER THEIR OUTDOOR LUNCHEON Kilvert and the Lynes were taken
on a tour of inspection. They saw the temporary oratory – a 'tiny
square room in the Cloister, fitted with a lace and silk-covered

---

[241] Chronicle, quoted Attwater p63

altar upon which stands a super altar or Tabernacle in which [Ignatius] informed us in a low awestruck voice was "the Blessed Sacrament'". Slightly incongruously '[t]here was a couch in the room on which he sleeps', as well as the 'miraculous crucifix', the reason why it was so named having been explained to the diarist. The visitors were invited to climb on to the scaffolding and lay commemorative stones. These were at upstairs windowsill level, so there was still some way to go before the roof could go on and the brothers move in.[242]

Picture 10: The newly built west cloister, as photographed in 1872

On his midsummer visit, when the walls had almost reached this height, Kilvert remarked that the new structure seemed 'very thin and shallow...with a long front'. He may not have realised that what he describes as an incipient 'house' was in fact only one side of the proposed quadrangle, around which it was planned to erect a considerable complex of buildings. According to a later source[243] these

---

[242] Chronicle, quoted Attwater pp58f; Kilvert vol 1 p222

[243] The document I have designated '1891 Pilgrimage': see Chapter 10.

would have extended some way beyond the limits of the existing four blocks, and would have provided more spacious replacements for the refectory, community room and other ground floor rooms, whose dividing walls would then have been removed to create proper 'cloisters', forming a continuous passageway round the central garth.

If it had been completed, the largest and most impressive of these additional buildings would have been the abbey church, intended as a replica of the priory church at 'old' Llanthony. A massive central tower would have stood immediately to the west of the present ruined structure, with transepts lying north and south, the one on the latter side incorporating a worthy entrance from the monastic enclosure. The remainder of what became known as the 'Monks' Level' (the area west of the church as completed, alongside the lower northern block) would have been occupied by the lengthy nave with aisles on either side, the whole magnificent edifice being completed by an imposing façade and twin west towers.[244]

There would always be a discrepancy between the actual monastery and its occupants and Ignatius's idealised version of it. This spectral entity existed by definition mostly in his head, although soon after his arrival at Capel-y-ffin he began to share it with a wider public. Before the end of 1870 he had published *Brother Placidus and why he became a Monk*, a propaganda novelette designed to entice young men into the cloister. The following year he brought out its more substantial (though no less fantastic) sequel, *Leonard Morris, or the Benedictine Novice*.[245] Both were written in a summer-house 'hermitage' he caused to be put up before work on the permanent building was far advanced.

---

[244] See BUWP p108 for contrasting drawings of the monastery as proposed and as in fact completed.

[245] Both were reviewed in the national press. *Brother Placidus* was treated to a full page review in the *Pall Mall Gazette* of 28 February 1871, but considered to have 'no more bone or muscle...than there is in a periwinkle'. In its 13 November issue the same paper was equally scathing about *Leonard Morris*.

As well as some sidelights on actual members of the community[246] we are given an insight into the Abbot's building plans. In his introductory note to Leonard Morris Ignatius explains that as well as the completion of the cloisters 'Chapter-House, Schools, Refectory and domestic offices' had yet to be built, not to mention the greater part of the church. Furthermore, intending visitors 'have to be sent away, because Churchmen have not yet enabled us to build our Guest-House, that very necessary supplement to all monasteries...' (he looked to Anglicans of all shades for support, and was continually disappointed not to receive it). Although in the portrayal of the 'dream abbey' (the phrase used by Peter Anson as the caption for his drawing of the complex as it might have been if completed) there are one or two concessions to its unfinished state,[247] we are led to believe that the monastery already contained separate quarters for the monks and nuns and some visitors, as well as the lofty 'shrine of monastic devotion'. The main activity here was not the traditional Benedictine business of reciting the Office (although this indeed took place, with sundry 'devotional' additions, and frequent sermons from Ignatius, who in the fantasy version is split into three separate characters), but adoration of the Blessed Sacrament, in his view 'the one work to which they [the monks and nuns] have dedicated their lives'.[248]

When Ignatius was writing Brother Placidus the west wing was still unfinished, although certain features of it are recognisable from the text. On his arrival the eponymous hero is led through a 'lofty but small hall' from which a 'flight of broad stairs' leads to

---

[246] 'Little Brother Angelus' is easily recognisable, as is 'Father Philip', whose description as 'never...a very polished diamond' and 'when he was put out...far from being a sweet specimen of monastic perfection' is obviously based on his real life namesake.

[247] e.g. the uncompleted abbey church Leonard Morris p23, and the 'temporary cloister' ibid p126

[248] Leonard Morris pp107f

the dormitories. 'Both windows and doorways in this part of the building were square and modern-looking, very unmonastic, and out of keeping with the rest of the Convent' – one wonders why with his insistence everywhere else on the Gothic style Ignatius allowed Buckeridge to include these two rectangular windows on the main staircase. They pass through a door into 'a large, handsome room, fitted up as a temporary Chapel'; here the new arrival is interviewed by the Superior, 'Father Cuthbert'. 'At the further end of this room stood a stately altar, raised on three steps,… a handsome crimson dossal, with a golden crown at the top, and palm leaves rising from it' on the wall behind. In front of this was a 'highly polished brass crucifix…standing upon a very beautiful tabernacle, with richly enamelled doors'; the 'crimson glow' of the sanctuary lamp shining

> solemnly on the enamelled tabernacle and brass crucifix, lighting up also, with a soft glow, the faces of the Benedictine saints painted on the panels of the altar…. The stalls of the monks – six in number, with six seats for the novices and acolyte boys – were ranged round the Choir; in the centre of which stood a large oak lectern, supporting a huge Bible, Breviary, Martyrology, and Graduale. At the end of the Chapel, and opposite the altar, was the organ, which appeared too large and powerful for so small a Chapel

(even if it was 'a large, handsome room').

The windows in this room were four 'early English lancets', arranged as two pairs facing into what would eventually be the cloister garth. Over them 'hung some thin crimson curtains, which toned down the morning sunshine into a soft, religious light', and 'produced a very devotional effect'. The temporary chapel also contained 'small shrines' in honour of the Blessed Virgin and St Benedict. 'At the foot of the altar steps, was a prie-Dieu, covered with a handsome cloth. Here the brother knelt, who kept the watch of intercession and praise before the most holy Sacrament....'[249]

Meanwhile in real life the little group of young men and boys were still camping in the barn and the lean-to, and doing their watching and praying in the latter. In the evenings they took to warming themselves by a fire in the unfinished refectory, for which in daylight hours they went on wood-gathering expeditions on the mountainside. Instead of 'thin crimson curtains' to produce a 'devotional effect' the as yet unglazed windows were hung with blankets in a feeble attempt to exclude the icy winds.[250] At last in December they were able to move in properly, and the oratory was transferred to the room in which the fictional Brother Placidus was interviewed by the Superior. According to the Chronicle[251] it extended 'for twenty-five feet from the north corner of this cloister southward', occupying two of the five bays of the ground floor of this new block, and as described in the novel connected directly with the staircase hall.

At the opposite end of the new building was the kitchen, at twelve feet square a little on the small side for an institution which would eventually have accommodation for some twenty monks and guests, but it, too, would have given way to something bigger in due course. Between the kitchen and the chapel was the refectory, like the latter also of two bays, and for the time being the only kind of common room available to the brothers. Spence tells us that its inglenook fireplace (since removed) was a favourite place to sit during evening Recreation, and that this room was 'the usual place for writing and teaching' as well as for the occupants' rather unsatisfying meals.

Upstairs the small room at the north end was the Superior's cell, some years later embellished with an oriel window looking over the valley and a private bathroom built out at one side. This lofty

---

[249] Brother Placidus pp56ff

[250] Bertouch pp450f

[251] Quoted Attwater p64

and elegant structure with its three-light lancet looks more like a chapel than a bathroom (perhaps Ignatius changed his mind about its purpose while it was being built?), and was accessed by a steep flight of steps leading down from the landing. (It was probably unheated; in his 1908 diary fragment – the only one to survive – Ignatius refers to it as 'the cold lavatory'.)[252] The remainder was divided into two rooms of two bays each, which Spence tells us were open dormitories. The one nearer the staircase was for visitors (and sometimes also for the acolytes), and part of it was curtained off to form a 'parlour'; the other was for the monks. This had room for only four beds, so for the time being that was as many as could be admitted.

For celebrations of the Eucharist the community depended on visiting clergy, who came at irregular intervals. One such was 'Father Cyril', whose arrival for the first Llanthony Christmas is recounted by the Baroness in characteristic style.[253] It was his first visit to the monastery, and after breaking his journey in Hereford to visit the shrine of St Thomas Cantelupe he set out to walk from Llanfihangel through heavy snow. Darkness was beginning to fall, and not surprisingly he overshot the turning and got lost on the mountainside. Here St Thomas appeared to him and led him to the

---

[252] There were washstands for the monks in their dormitory. Eventually lavatories were installed in the semi-basement under the north cloister; what facilities existed before then it is perhaps wisest not to speculate.

[253] Bertouch pp454-50; Calder-Marshall (Enthusiast p198) misnames him 'Cyprian'. His secular name is not given, and no Fr Cyril is listed in the Register among the Tertiaries or associates. I believe he was William Arderne Shoults (1839-1887), curate of St Paul, Bunhill Row at the time Ignatius was preaching there, and after a four-year gap (which might explain his availability that Christmas) curate successively to Fr Nihill at St Michael, Shoreditch, and at St Edmund, Lombard Street. In the *Manchester Evening News* of 9 February 1870 it was reported that he had officiated at a service in the Hunter Street mission house, and in the following year's census he was listed as a 'visitor' at the home of Ann Easley/Sister Winifred's sister Frances Lack (as was Miss Easley herself). He married in 1878, and spent the remaining nine years of his life in scholarly retirement in Camberwell Grove, where as a young man he had lived with his parents.

monastery door, which he reached with just half an hour to spare before officiating at Midnight Mass in the temporary chapel.

If those who read Ignatius's publicity material took it at face value it is no wonder that young men coming to try their vocations were likely to be disappointed when confronted by the reality. A year after Fr Cyril's miraculous deliverance John Spence arrived to begin his postulancy, travelling with the Abbot from the station at Llanfihangel, this time in a carriage. As they came in sight of the building Ignatius

> exclaimed with enthusiasm, 'There it is! There is the Abbey!' I could not conceal my astonishment and disappointment, or believe that the small, bare, mean-looking building before us was indeed the Llanthony Abbey of my dreams. Only one side of the projected quadrangle was finished, and no appearance of anything more being built.

MORE NOVICES ARRIVE – AND DEPART

SOON AFTER THE ARRIVAL at Llanthony Brother Placidus (Wicking) was elevated to the status of 'professed novice': he was now just fourteen. This important event – the first in the new monastery – took place on 10 August, the feast of the early Roman deacon and martyr St Laurence. A proper chapel not yet being available he had to take his vows in the 'shed at [the] S[outh] West End of [the] West Cloister, the then Oratory' and temporary abbatial bedroom. Twelve months later the boy would renew his novice's vows for a further year: a wise move on Ignatius's part, considering his tender age.

The first to find conditions on the mountainside too harsh for his delicate constitution was life-professed Fr Dunstan (Garland). A few days after Placidus's profession he was sent home to his family in Bristol, 'being very ill and unable to keep any rule'. The young man had been 'craving to go to his family for some months, having not seen them for 5 years', but at the expiry of his six weeks' leave of absence he failed to return:

He joined the Romish Church in Sept 1870, the priests at Clifton telling him that his vows were void, not being taken in the Romish Communion. He wrote to me a most insulting letter November 11 1870. So far & so deeply do deceit and falsehood plunge the soul. But [he] has lovingly apologized[,] since owing to catalepsy [he] is unfit for religious life.[254]

The boy-monk Maurus (William Swan) stayed at Llanthony for just under a year. On 10 July 1871 he 'left...with his sister...at his own desire'. I can find no information about his later life, his only appearance in censuses being for the years 1861 (in London, aged three) and 1871 (at Llanthony, aged thirteen). Perhaps he emigrated.

On Thursday 4 August Brother Pancras (Rymer) 'returned to his obedience'; according to the Register he was 'entirely pardoned & received no penance', which seems a little unfair when compared with the treatment meted out to Serene and other delinquent brethren. One is of course handicapped by ignorance of the precise circumstances, but it's tempting to guess that Pancras's unconditional pardon had something to do with his relatively genteel origins, and Ignatius's ever cherished but never fulfilled hope that young men with some education and the right kind of accent would develop a stable vocation to the community.

On 1 November this errant novice renewed his vows, staying at Llanthony long enough to be listed there in the census the following April. But before the end of that month he left again, this time finally: 'Thursday April 27 1871 Again broke his vows

---

[254] Fifteen years later Ignatius could view the loss of this disciple in a rosier light. In MT June 1885 he tells us that the former Fr Dunstan had revisited the monastery 'two or three times', and describes him as 'a good fellow in every sense of the word' and 'devout, sincere, and very dependable', which suggests that the 'Romish Church' failed to hold him for long. A 'Samuel Alfred A. Garland' is recorded as having married in Bristol towards the end of 1880 and other members of his family are listed there in the censuses of 1881 and 1891, but apart from the mention of his marriage I can find no trace of him in later records.

& left his Monastery in my absence. Mr Barney received him at Laleham. Aug[ust] 3 1871 Wrote saying he cared for nothing but Monastic Life, & sh[oul]d join the Ch[urch] of Rome if he c[oul]d not be a monk in the Ch[urch] of Eng[land].' One wonders why he could not be an Anglican monk (presumably by this time he was no longer making the attempt chez Barney).

However much he 'cared for nothing but Monastic Life' he eventually found fulfilment elsewhere. In 1877 he married a woman from Highgate who in the course of thirty years used three quite different Christian names, two of them fairly unusual: she is listed as Gaville M. Rymer in the censuses of 1881 and 1891, Jahullie M. in 1901 and Isabella in 1911.[255]

The 'acolyte Frederick' (Weller) had arrived at Llanthony with the others on 22 July. On St Bruno's Day (6 October, three months before his fifteenth birthday) he was 'professed as [a] Novice' and became Brother Bruno of the Holy Wilderness. Nine months later the Abbot recorded his departure: 'Was sent away by me as utterly unfit for the life July 3 1871 after more than a year's trial [since his arrival as an acolyte]. He was injuring others by his example & therefore was sent away before his year's vows were over.'[256]

---

[255] When they are recorded as having been married 34 years, so there was only one Mrs Arthur Rymer, not three in succession. In 1881 they were living in St Pancras where he worked as a tobacconist's assistant, and in 1891 and 1901 in West Ham, where he was in the first said to be living on his own means and in the second a commercial traveller. In 1911 we find them at a furniture warehouse in Walthamstow (Arthur's employment is given as Furniture Assistant), with two 15-year-old male servants described as Assistant Pawnbrokers. Among the numerous Rymer children was a little boy called Ignatius, who was born in 1888 but died in 1894. The former Brother Pancras's own death was registered in Edmonton in the first quarter of 1932, his age given as 80.

[256] This boy's age is given as 15 in the 1871 census, which agrees with the figure in the Register ('15 on Dec 12 1870'), and his birthplace as Brighton, where the birth of only one child of this name was registered in the relevant period, in the first quarter of 1855 (probably held over from December 1854); he was therefore a year older than he claimed to be. In two of the three following censuses his age is also given as lower than it actually was,

Seventeen-year-old Hector Macduff[257] (Brother Oswald) was 'professed as Novice' on 17 November 1870, at the Feltham convent. Some time that winter he was allowed to join the others at Llanthony, where he remained just long enough to be listed in the 1871 census. He left on 'April 27 1871 Thursday...after a course of wilful sin & deceit' and 'in the absence of his Superior. On Wed May 10, I sent him notice to return, threatening him with excommunication. Mr Barney Lieutenant 67th Regt received him at Laleham & encouraged him in his sin. Excomm[unicated] May 29 1871. He stole some valuable things from the Abbey.'

Macduff moved in with Barney at much the same time as Arthur Rymer, the former Brother Pancras. The following year he entered the (decidedly Low Church) London College of Divinity, and was ordained (deacon 1877, priest 1878) by the Bishop of Chester. In the first six years of his ministry he served four curacies, being listed at the second of them (Boothby Graffoe, Leics) in the 1881 census. He then spent eighteen years (1883-1901) as a chaplain in India, before retiring to Godstone in Surrey. He died in 1907 at the age of 53.

Meanwhile another teenage novice had come and gone: Richard Edgcumbe Chevallier, born 13 October 1852, who was 'Professed as Postulant' on 11 March 1871 and as a novice the following day, being given the name Wilfred. As the Register discloses, his monastic career was of a brevity consistent with his 24-hour postulancy:

On Thursday Morning the 29th of this same March, 1871, just as the community were making their meditation after Matins & Lauds in the Choir, at 3.30 this novice ran away from the Abbey & broke his vows, having only been professed as a novice 2 weeks & 4 days. Very

---

and that of his wife Emily (whom he married in 1880 and by whom had several children) also varies. In 1881 they were in Brighton where following his father he became a master bootmaker; later they moved to Eastbourne where he worked as an electro-silver plater, dying at the age of 52 in 1909.

[257] Born Chelsea 22 October 1853.

excited & devout for a week, then most insolent & rebellious; then a perjurer & a blasphemer. Excom[municated] May 29 1871. Lord have mercy upon him.

In Aug 1871 this novice's father wrote telling me, since his son's fearful sin, 3 members of his family had dropped down dead! Himself was ruined, & going to fly from England. He had sent his son to Africa altho' he wanted to return here. The father had been too ill to write before! July 1872 Writes from Africa begging our prayers for the 'Lost Sheep' that he may return here.

Richard's father was Edgcumbe Chevallier, at the time of the boy's birth an official at HM Dockyard, Pembroke Dock; five years after his flight from England he died in South Africa. The family were connected to the Earls of Mount Edgcumbe and the Chevalliers of Aspall Hall, Suffolk (where they still live, making Aspall Cyder and various flavoured vinegars). The former novice returned to his father's house (then in Watford) just in time to be included in the 1871 census, in which he is described as a 'scholar'; perhaps he had run away from school to join the monastery.

His place was taken by a young man whose name is given in the Register as Robert Kidney Stewart who became the next Brother Oswald, and whose time in the monastery was almost as short (I suspect his middle name was actually 'Gidney'). He was admitted as a postulant at Feltham on 23 May 1871 and promoted to the noviciate (also at Feltham) on 6 June, but having in the interim made the journey to Llanthony left after just a week: 'This Novice had to return home after being at Llanthony a few days, on account of a very dangerous illness. He was greatly grieved at going.' Three months later, on 8 September, Ignatius 'received a most insulting letter from this man, from Mr Barney's house, to my most utter amazement. The astonishment & grief nearly paralysed me. We thought he was now dead.' As far as we know he was the last of the Llanthony novices to go on to live with ex-Lt Barney.

CHAPTER 6

BROTHER CUTHBERT AND HIS CONTEMPORARIES

There is just one period in the Llanthony community's forty-year history for which we have a full picture of its daily life and the personalities who came and went: the twelve months between December 1871 and December 1872. This was the year when John Spence (Brother Cuthbert) was a novice, afterwards recording his memories in a slightly haphazard but highly revealing account.[258]

When he joined the community Spence was eighteen and a half.[259] He tells us that he had 'for some time desired to retire from the world and assist in the restoration of the monastic life in England', so he 'entered into correspondence with the Rev. Father Ignatius'. It was arranged that he would join Ignatius in Brighton, where he was conducting a mission. This included an overnight visit to St Leonards for the delivery of an 'oration'; here he was stationed at the door with Clavering Lyne to receive the offerings of the departing congregation.[260]

---

[258] Spence's narrative was preserved by his daughter, mother of the portrait painter Guy Worsdell (1908-78). The text of his account (whether the original or a copy is not known) was given before the 1939 war to Dom Basil Heath-Robinson of Prinknash Abbey by Worsdell, who was his friend and contemporary (information from article on Spence by Stanley Luff in the 1991 Newsletter of the Father Ignatius Memorial Trust). As stated in the Introduction, two incomplete photocopies of the typescript are preserved in the Fr Ignatius collection at Abergavenny.

[259] The Register gives his date of birth as 18 May 1853.

[260] Clavering was now a couple of months short of his twenty-third birthday. Spence tells us that he 'had small deceitful eyes, black hair, a large aquiline nose and a somewhat sallow unhealthy complexion, but was

On the way from Brighton to Llanthony a night was spent at Feltham, where Spence made the acquaintance of the Infant Oblate and was measured for the habit he would wear as a novice. On Christmas Eve he was baptised[261] by the Superior, who also stood as his godfather, and 'at the end of about a week...clad in an old postulate's [sic] hood, frock and belt'. Soon after this he succumbed to a bad attack of diarrhoea, which put him out of action for several days, during which he was nursed by Brother Ethelred, with whom he struck up a friendship. On 25 January 1872 (feast of the Conversion of St Paul) – following a fast of twenty-four hours 'as the Blessed Sacrament had to be taken at the same time as the vows of chastity, poverty and obedience' – he committed himself to the community for the twelve months of the noviciate and received the new name of Cuthbert Mary of St Paul, together with a 'wreath of everlastings' on his head. Afterwards in the Abbot's cell he was given the tonsure. Having initially slept in the visitors' room he occupied that night for the first time one of the four (sheetless) beds in the monastic dormitory, but could not sleep because of the cold draught on his newly shaven head and the prickliness of his new serge habit.

Cuthbert had scarcely settled into the noviciate when 'at the beginning of Lent'[262] he was ordered to accompany the Superior on an extended preaching tour. This took them to Bristol, Bath

---

rather handsome altogether'; nevertheless 'his appearance was that of a draper's assistant'. Although he would later be ordained he was at the time 'learning farming at Cap House, Pontrilas', near enough to Llanthony for him to keep in touch with both Ignatius and their eldest brother Francis Palmer in Abergavenny. Cap House was on the estate of the Scudamore family of nearby Kentchurch Court. There were links between them and the family of Priscilla Lydia Sellon, whose home was in the next parish (Grosmont); her elder brother William Edward was Rector of Kentchurch from 1846 until his death in 1885.

[261] The Baptism register notes that he was (formerly) a Quaker, and his home at Lendal, York. The Spence family had earlier been prominent in the Society of Friends in the north east of England.

[262] Ash Wednesday that year was 14 February.

and Torquay and lasted almost until Easter. He may have welcomed this as a break from the already 'monotonous' Llanthony routine, although the experience of living at close quarters for several weeks with his Superior proved something of a trial.

> We lodged during our stay in Clifton in a miserable little back room, I was expected to keep my eyes on the ground, an unpleasant child encouraged by the Reverend Father used to come in and climb about and tear at me, but I might not speak notice or play with it. I had nothing to do but to read the life of Ignatius Loyola. When visitors came I had to go to my very cold little bedroom and sit sometimes for hours. The small window in the roof I could not look out of and I sometimes thought I should go out of my mind....
>
> We had one full meal a day during Lent. The Rev. Father ate largely. At breakfast he had ham, eggs, fish, cocoa &c &c and the basin of boiled milk and bread allowed me felt like nothing.... [For dinner] I had dry vegetables and beer, that was in accordance with the rule, but generally he ordered me a small piece of cod or other fish, but the strangest thing was he always asked me for some of it in addition to his own ample provision.

In Bath they spent ten days at Caerbadon House, on a hill overlooking the city, where a well-to-do widow named Mrs Ellis lived with her three daughters.[263] Life at Caerbadon was much more comfortable than in Clifton, with good food (here again Ignatius benefited from a specially rich diet to keep his strength up, but Cuthbert had to make do with something more Lenten), books to read, excursions into the countryside and much kindness from the family – not that Cuthbert had 'any talk with [them], being supposed

---

[263] They had recently moved there from Royal Crescent, where they were listed in the 1871 census. At that time Mrs Ellis was aged 55; her daughters were Emily (29), Katherine (25) and Harriette (18). Harriette will reappear later in this history.

to maintain strict silence'. This was difficult in the face of some gentle teasing from the elder daughters, who did not share the advanced religious views of their mother and younger sister. He had to sleep in a little dressing room opening off the room assigned to Ignatius; before they retired for the night they would sing Compline in the library, with the ladies of the household in attendance.

When they reached Torquay they had to put up with lodgings that were 'poor and bare', although Ignatius managed to obtain pots of Devonshire cream for his (but not Cuthbert's) breakfast. The young novice incurred the Abbot's wrath by failing to 'kneel when speaking to him' and 'genuflect and kiss his garments if he passed near' him; it was considered important for the monks to show such outward signs of reverence to Ignatius as 'the representative of our Lord'. There was also the problem posed by their unusual appearance: 'At Torquay' – as they had found rather more alarmingly in Bath – 'we could never go out without getting an enormous crowd after us; laughing, shouting, hooting, and pressing upon us.' However, if there was no danger from their pursuers and he was in the right mood 'the Superior...seemed rather to enjoy it'.

Back at the monastery Cuthbert was put to work on the farm: he had to do everything in bare feet as his sandals quickly wore out. The expense and inconvenience of having to maintain those thirty-two acres would always outweigh any benefit to be derived from them, although postcard photographs of monks milking cows and making hay (most of them from rather later in Llanthony history) had a certain publicity value.

Meanwhile, events were proceeding behind his back. On several occasions he mentions his family and 'friends', who had evidently been in touch with Ignatius (or he with them), and the subject of financial support had arisen. They were 'assured that if they refused to pay for me [he] would soon discover that I had no vocation'; prompting him to reflect later that 'after he knew that I should not take the life vows [Ignatius] tried to make [life in the monastery] too hard for me to bear and...would not have been sorry if I had run away, but I was resolved not to break my vows'.

At the same time he wondered why no letters came for him. They did, of course, but were withheld by the Superior, who 'continually assured' him that his outside connections had 'become reconciled to the step [he] had taken', although he took the precaution of getting the novice to write to them ('every word being at the Superior's dictation') expressing his determination to stay.

During his lengthy absence that summer Ignatius wrote to Cuthbert warning him that his vocation was likely 'to be tried by a test' which might involve him being removed from the cloister against his will; if anyone came looking for him he should 'send out a written message declining to see anyone'. It was only after his return to secular life that Cuthbert learned of the missing letters, and of a visit his mother had paid to Ignatius at Feltham. Although she promised that no-one would come to the monastery in Ignatius's absence she tried unsuccessfully to persuade him to release her son until he came of age, offering to contribute £50 a year for his keep on his eventual return to the monastery – always assuming that when the time came he still wanted to become a monk.[264]

It was the custom for the brethren not only to accuse one another face to face of infractions of the Rule, but to spy on one another and report disloyal conversations or behaviour to the Superior, by letter if necessary. This could be a way for a brother to deflect attention from his own misdoings, and that may have been what happened when Serene wrote to Ignatius early in December 1872, and Ignatius replied by ordering Cuthbert to report to him at Feltham, bringing his secular clothes (in fact he wore them).

---

[264] Spence's parents followed this interview up with an unannounced visit to Llanthony, prompted by a report from the local station-master that their son was 'lame and otherwise in a sorry plight'. They were kept waiting 'about an hour' while Ignatius had a shave and the other monks washed and put on clean clothes.

It was just a year since he had first joined Ignatius at Brighton and there were still a few weeks of his noviciate to run, but the Superior readily dispensed him from this duty and sent him on his way with his blessing.[265]

ETHELRED

WHEN JOHN SPENCE arrived at Llanthony there were two other novices in residence: Placidus (Wicking) and twenty-year-old Ethelred, in the world John Jones.[266] He had been there since 31 July, St Ignatius's Day, which may have been taken by the Superior as a good omen – misguidedly, as it would turn out. This young man was due to inherit £9,000[267] when he came of age, which would have proved a highly acceptable dowry if he had still been in the monastery when that time came. Ignatius was always on the watch for aspirants who could bring money with them, and dismissive (as we have seen, and will see again) of those whose family or friends were capable of making a contribution to their maintenance but failed to do so.[268]

---

[265] Comment in Register: 'Sent away, for trying to ruin every single person in the Monastery.' Spence is known to have died young; the death of a 32-year-old John Spence was registered in Marylebone in the second quarter of 1886.

[266] His name was corrected (probably mistakenly) to 'Etheldred' in the Register. St Ethelred was a 7th century king of Mercia who abdicated and became a monk of Bardney; 'Etheldred' is occasionally encountered as a variant of 'Etheldreda' (as is 'Audrey'). Information about this novice is drawn mostly from Spence, with dates &c from the Register. His secular name, alas, is too common for one to be able to trace his movements before or after his time at Llanthony. The Register gives his nineteenth birthday as 18 September 1870, and says he 'came as a postulant first' on St Ignatius's Day, but that he 'entered' on 14 August and was 'professed as a postulant' on the 26th, then 'professed as a novice' on 7 September. Ignatius's version of the stages of monastic initiation was inconsistent as well as eccentric.

[267] Equivalent to over £400,000 at today's (2015) values.

[268] Ignatius's adopted son Brother David reported that aspirants who were able to afford it were expected to contribute £40 for their subsistence during their year in the noviciate.

Jones had run away from his guardian, a chemist in Abergavenny, but this would not have deterred the Superior from receiving him. He was 'dark, small, and physically weak', so occupied more with sacristy work and teaching the acolytes than with hard labour in the kitchen or out of doors. He and Cuthbert were thrown together by mutual distaste for the other brothers: 'I rarely spoke to anyone but Ethelred, it felt very hard to associate with any of the others they were so ignorant, so unclean, and so different from what I had expected.' Both of them felt the reality of life at Llanthony fell a long way short of what an Anglican monastery ought to be like:

> Brother Ethelred and I helped each other on with visions of a future structure much purer and higher than this that we hoped to raise on Ignatius's ruins, for his keeping on in this way we were sure was impossible.

In May (1872) Ethelred became worried that a swelling on his breast might be cancer, and asked permission to go and consult his own doctor. This request had to be made by letter, as Ignatius was away at Feltham from soon after Ascension Day until the middle of July. When the answer came it was negative, so he did a bunk:

> One morning he did not get up to Matins at 2.0am, but as this was very common with Philip and the other brothers it attracted no surprise. When I went back to bed at four o'clock I saw an appearance of him in his bed and left it, then when I got up again at six, but on going to wash at eight I was surprised to see the same object and began to think he was dead. Being against the rule I never thought of speaking to him, but I touched him and he yielded and I found he was but an effigy.... On opening the bible at breakfast Philip found a note explaining the sense of his departure.

A few weeks later a message from Ethelred came via Farmer Jenkins at Maes-y-ffin, the next farm but one down the valley. It had been sent from Church House, Ewyas Harold:[269]

> After my Benedictine vows are up I am going to live as an anchoretical friar of the Church of England under the rule of St Augustine. I want you please to tell Brother Cuthbert that I am having a nice cell built in a quiet spot here and a private chapel made and fitted up and whenever he may be out of the monastery to be sure and come and see me and if he can stay with me a bit.[270]

History fails to relate whether Ethelred pursued this ambition, in Ewyas Harold or elsewhere, but for the time being his main objective was to complete the twelve months of his vowed noviciate. This meant returning to Llanthony. Ignatius was back there for some weeks before his return to Feltham for the autumn, so when Ethelred returned on 6 September he was

> admitted into the Reverend Father's room. He came barefoot as a sort of penance. After some time Father Philip and I were sent for and bidden to take a bowl of water. The Superior then said, 'Now, dear children, pay particular attention. I wish to ask Brother Ethelred in your presence if he wishes to fulfil his vows. Brother Ethelred, do you intend to fulfil your vows?'
> 'Yes, dear Father, but – .'
> 'Don't interrupt me, dear child. I wish to know whether you intend to remain here and keep your vows.'
> 'I do, as soon as —.'
> 'I have asked you, dear child, if you intend to keep your vow.'

---

[269] No house at Ewyas Harold is listed by this name in the censuses of 1871 or 1881.

[270] The continuation of the letter is on one of the pages missing from the copies of Cuthbert's ms in the Abergavenny archives.

'And I, dear Father, have told you that I do, when I have returned and settled some important affairs.'

'That is enough!' cried the Abbot. 'I wash my hands of you – Father Philip and Brother Cuthbert, you are witnesses.'

Whereupon he washed his hands in the bowl of water and dried them on a towel. Then we all four went into the Chapel and I was sent for a great red book, I did not know what it was. Then the Superior ascended the altar steps, Ethelred stood at the further end of the Chapel, Father Philip and I at the side. The Reverend Father laid the red book on the altar, opened it and once more asked Brother Ethelred if he would stay and fulfil his vows, but he replied 'Not now, Father Ignatius,' upon which the Superior proceeded to curse him in the usual form which runs as follows....

Like the page containing the conclusion of Ethelred's letter to Mr Jenkins the one recording the text of the abbatial curse is missing, but the narrative continues:

He [Ignatius] then walked out leaving us standing. The porter came and Ethelred followed him to the gate. He looked very pale, and as he went out he kissed his hand to me and said 'Goodbye.'

This took place less than a fortnight before Ethelred would attain his majority; it is probably safe to assume that settling 'important affairs' included putting his inheritance out of Ignatius's reach. The following year he wrote to the (by now also former) Brother Cuthbert to report that Ignatius had been trying to tempt him back to Llanthony. This was being done through 'the priest here' (whether 'here' means Ewyas Harold or somewhere else is not made clear), and in spite of the solemn curse with which he had been sent away. There is no further mention of him either in Cuthbert's narrative or in the Register.

DUNSTAN/THOMAS

THE NEXT RECRUIT was a new Brother Dunstan, eighteen-year-old Thomas Bray from Plymouth, who arrived at the end of January. He had been a chorister at St Peter's when Ignatius was a curate in the parish, and after his father's death had been brought up by his grandmother, as his mother was 'in some [domestic] situation'.

Like Placidus he was a pretty boy, although Spence detected 'a false look' and a corresponding 'mean and treacherous' disposition: Dunstan made 'great mischief in the place [by] telling tales true and false to the Superior'. Ignatius had been keen to recruit him because he had a good singing voice, and not only wrote to him himself but enlisted Ethelred to reinforce his efforts. The Abbot was doubtless aware that his employers – a Major and Mrs Fowler, for whom he worked as a page – were strongly opposed to his monastic ambitions, and 'did all they could to dissuade him'.

Dunstan (sometimes confusingly referred to as 'Brother Thomas') quickly became a favourite of Ignatius. He and Placidus used to visit him in the evening to receive his blessing and indulge his fancy for hugs and kisses – 'the Reverend Father was like a woman, there was nothing he liked so much as to be mollied, hugged, and kissed' – and were often required to stay at his bedside until he fell asleep, holding his hands. For this they were rewarded with 'sweet biscuits and jam'.[271] Dunstan was singled out to accompany the Abbot on walks on the mountainside, and seems to have acted as his personal attendant, looking after his room and cooking the special meals to which his perpetual 'hard brain work' entitled him. After Ethelred's defection Dunstan was put in charge of Baby's schooling,[272] though having himself received 'very little education'

---

[271] The rule was that 'a kiss should be given on the cheek or forehead; never on the lips'. These activities may not have been consciously homoerotic; Ignatius's horror of 'perversion' led him to condemn Plato and his 'abominations' (Bertouch p432f).

[272] A job Cuthbert would have liked for himself, but on account of his

he 'could neither teach him nor the acolytes anything'. However, he was able to play the organ. An unattributable press cutting of 1878 reports that he accompanied the midnight Mass at Easter that year, which followed the Sarum Rite, and a volume of slightly ambitious Mass and Benediction settings in the Abergavenny collection has his name stamped in gold on the front cover.[273]

Quite early on Dunstan was tempted to leave (and confided his plans to Cuthbert, who dated the beginning of his decline from favour to having failed to reveal them to the Superior forthwith), but Ignatius succeeded for the time being in persuading him to stay. In May he tried again:

> Brother Thomas (Dunstan)...had been very much unsettled and talked openly of going. Philip had therefore informed the Superior who ordered him to send Dunstan to him at Feltham. Dunstan strongly objected but was finally persuaded....

Once out of the monastery, however, 'instead of going to Feltham he slipped away to some friends at Oxford, from them he went to some connections at Paddington and got a good situation with Mr Mundilla [sic], MP for —.[274] But before he went there he thought he would go to Feltham and take a last look at Ignatius who of course soon persuaded him to stay with him.'

With Dunstan/Thomas back in the fold, Ignatius observed in a letter to Cuthbert (dated 11 June, feast of St Barnabas) that whereas Brother Ethelred had certainly broken his vows, 'Brother Thomas has not.' Was this just the myopia born of favouritism, or had the errant novice failed to tell Ignatius of the unauthorised diversions

---

superior physical strength he couldn't be spared from the outdoor work.

[273] Press cutting in Barclay album; Crown of Jesus Music, ed. H.F. Hemy (ref A1993.136.20)

[274] Anthony John Mundella, prosperous hosiery manufacturer and Liberal politician, MP for Sheffield (1868-85), then Sheffield Brightside (1885-97).

on his journey? A week later he wrote again: 'Brother Thomas is very much improved [and] the nuns are very much pleased with him. He keeps the rule especially silence beautifully. He is so loving and good too. I hope he will make a good monk.'

A few days before his return to Llanthony in mid-July Ignatius sent Dunstan/Thomas on ahead of him (in his instructions for ridding the monastery bedding of fleas he directed 'Brother Thomas must see to mine'), and when he had gone back to Feltham at the end of the summer he sent for him to join him there. The ostensible reason was so that the nuns could give him further instruction in cooking ('he had made him [Ignatius] such bad dinners'), but doubtless there was more to it than that.

After this we hear no more of him from Cuthbert, and are dependent on Ignatius's sparse records for the rest of his monastic history. This will be continued in the next chapter.

THE DEPARTURE OF PLACIDUS

MEANWHILE, WHEN CUTHBERT first became acquainted with him, Brother Placidus (Wicking) was beginning to outgrow the romantic fervour that had brought him to the cloister. In August 1872 he turned sixteen, and although still possessed by a 'blind enthusiasm for the Reverend Father' he was starting to feel that life was passing him by. As he was 'an easy, sleepy, good-tempered fellow' the full implications of this came to him slowly, and for the time being he carried on with his duties. These were mostly in the kitchen, although he was 'very fond of out-door work', if not of the Latin lessons which also formed part of his routine.[275]

As we have seen, that summer Ignatius was away from the monastery between May and July. Placidus was now quite certain that he wanted to return to the world, and wrote frequent letters to the Superior to this

---

[275] Perhaps only when the Superior was in residence? It's unlikely that anyone else except possibly Cuthbert himself would have had sufficient education for the task.

effect. Ignatius expressed himself as 'sadly grieved' by them – 'poor child, his letters make my heart ache' – but was realistic enough to accept that 'the world' would 'be his destiny' when the vows he had renewed the previous year expired in August. At the same time difficulties between Placidus and Philip may have exacerbated the situation. The monastic hothouse was a fertile breeding-ground for extreme feelings, whether of love or of loathing. Included in Cuthbert's narrative are two letters he received from Philip, of which the end of the first and the beginning of the second coincide with the first of his missing pages: my guess from the surviving portions is that Philip was in love with Placidus but Placidus quite definitely not in love with him.

Eventually the boy-novice received the summons to report to Ignatius at Feltham. 'He left one morning in pouring rain [12 July, according to the Register], glad to go, but afraid of the journey as he had to go in his monk's clothes' – he had of course long outgrown the secular attire laid aside when he entered. Later he wrote to Cuthbert 'saying he wished he had left before' and 'regretting he had spent so much time at the Monastery instead of learning something; he was going to try engineering'.

Whether he tried this first of all we don't know, but by the time the 1881 census came round William Henry Wicking had settled back into the family home in Dalston, where his occupation was given as Manufacturer of Harmoniums. He was still there for the three following censuses. In 1891 he had followed his father into piano tuning (perhaps he took over his round), and three years after that at the age of 38 he married a slightly older spinster neighbour named Elizabeth Phipps. His death was registered in 1934 in South Western Surrey.

A BABY NO LONGER

WHAT OF THE INFANT OBLATE? When Cuthbert first encountered him he was within a couple of weeks of his tenth birthday, and – allowing for the unusual conditions in which he lived – a surprisingly normal child. He is introduced as a beautiful little boy...with a sweet voice, he was barefoot, dressed in a short white serge frock, scapular and cord, he had light bright short hair and large blue eyes, full red lips which promised in time to grow coarse.

In addition we are told that he 'was designed in the future to be the head of a Carthusian Monastery' (which would explain the white habit), and that 'the Reverend Father believed him to be an angelic child, but there was much evil in him. He was cunning, treacherous, and the most accomplished liar [Spence] ever met with,' and although 'kept carefully secluded from the gaze of seculars' he had 'a knowledge of the world one would have thought it impossible for him to have got'.

As well as avoiding 'seculars' he was supposed to live apart from both the brothers and the acolytes, in spite of sharing lessons with the latter. He had 'plenty of playthings', but would also spend part of his indoor leisure time making 'coloured texts'. When Ignatius was in residence he enjoyed walking with him on the mountain (usually accompanied by one or other of his three flea-ridden cats), and in winter 'never seemed to feel the cold and would plunge about in the snow up to his knees simply for his pleasure'.

In church 'he always made a beautiful picture kneeling in his white dress between the Superior and Father Philip'; Cuthbert felt that Ignatius valued him chiefly for 'the useful part he played in the religious displays'. Services in church – even very long ones – were no hardship to him, although in Ignatius's absence he only attended them on Sundays, as 'he behaved so badly'.

ASCENSION FESTIVITIES

ONE DISPLAY in which he was to have taken a prominent part had been planned for Ascension Day, which that year fell on 9 May. A lamb had been acquired from Farmer Jenkins, which Baby, representing John the Baptist as Forerunner of the Lamb of God, was to have led in an outdoor procession of the Blessed Sacrament. In the event – and in spite of having prayed every day for a month for fine weather – it rained, so this part of the proceedings was cancelled, and the Mass for which Cuthbert and Ethelred had erected an altar in the Abbot's Meadow was transferred to the little church at Capel-y-ffin.

The celebrant was William Gordon, Vicar of St Mary's, Bathwick, who had been enrolled as an associate when Ignatius and Cuthbert were staying at Caerbadon House; Spence remarks that Fr Gordon 'trembled all the time he said mass'. Mrs Ellis and her daughters were also there, but the guest of honour was an ecclesiastic whom Cuthbert describes as 'a very grand man...whom I think they called the Provincial'. Although he arrived in his own carriage and presented Ignatius with 'the medal of his Order' and a case of wine (but 'drank quantities of brandy himself'), this distinguished but unnamed visitor had to share the visitors' dormitory with Clavering Lyne and others. At the service he was vested in 'a green and gold cope and...a little velvet cap with gold lace' and 'carried a splendid little crozier of tortoiseshell and gold five or six feet high'; he also had 'a large gold medal with rays hung round his neck by a purple ribbon', and a train which was held through large white cotton gloves by Brother Ethelred. Cuthbert thought he might have been 'Head of the Guild of the Holy Cross'.[276]

---

[276] The title 'Provincial' was used by the Order of Corporate Reunion, and there was a 'Brotherhood of the Holy Cross' associated with it in later years (not to be confused with the priestly Society of the Holy Cross), although that highly secretive body would not be properly launched for a further five years. In the OCR there were three Provincials, all in bishop's orders: F.G. Lee (Dorchester), T.W. Mossman (Selby), and J.T. Seccombe (Caerleon). Seccombe was, as we have seen, raised to the episcopate by the 'independent' bishop Julius Ferrete as early as 1866. In 1872 he may still have been assisting Ferrete in his project to set up a 'Western Orthodox' jurisdiction, based on the episcopal orders the latter had received from the Syrian Orthodox Church, so might well have appeared at Llanthony that year in episcopal rig. See Brandreth, Dr Lee of Lambeth pp126,141f; David F. Abramtsov, The Western Rite and the Eastern Church: Dr. J. J. Overbeck and his Scheme for the Re-Establishment of the Orthodox Church in the West (University of Pittsburgh MA Dissertation 1961), pp33-35 (consulted at http://anglicanhistory.org/orthodoxy/abramtsov.pdf on 13 March 2013);

'Many country folks from miles around' had turned out for the planned spectacle, which Spence judged 'an utter failure'; in the event they went home 'madly disappointed, cross, tired, hungry and wet'.[277] At the end of the service

> the Reverend Father cried out in a loud voice 'Now my dear brothers and sisters, if any of you desire my blessing stay behind and receive it.' Not a single man remained and only about forty women, they walked up to the Reverend Father in single file and knelt before him, he made the sign of the cross on the head of each, saying, 'God bless you my dear daughter.'

Abba Seraphim, *Flesh of Our Brethren* (London, The British Orthodox Press 2006), pp 5ff, and BAL Chapter 3. Even the cap might fit: Syrian Orthodox clergy wear a soft cap or hood (the *escime* or *eskímo*) which could possibly be made of velvet, with edging and a pattern of crosses in gold braid or lace. Seccombe's father had been knighted for his services as an administrator in the Indian colonies, and he himself was a prominent figure in Norfolk society as well as in his own profession; even in everyday clothes he might have seemed a 'grand man' to the young novices. He was a couple of years older than Ignatius, and they may have met when the latter was in Norwich, even if (as Cuthbert tentatively suggests) he hadn't necessarily 'been a friend of the Reverend Father's in his youth'. Another possibility might be George Nugée, with whom Ignatius had frequent contact in the 1870s, and who that year transferred his 'Order of St Augustine' from rural Wymering to metropolitan Walworth. Nugée (born 1819) would have had the additional qualification of age: this would not only have added to his grandeur, but might explain why – in addition to the effects of excessive brandy-drinking – when he 'fell out of bed in the night...he had not been able to regain it'.

[277] There is a reference to the 1872 Ascension celebrations in *Kilvert*, when on 10 July of that year the diarist and a companion encountered a young inmate of the monastery on an errand in the lane between Llanthony and Capel-y-ffin. He told them that '[o]n Ascension Day they had a grand service and procession in the monastery and for quarter of an hour the country people were admitted to the Chapel'. At the time of their meeting '[t]here were seven people of all sorts living at the monastery..., monks, novices and lay brothers;' he himself was about to take his vows and become 'a full monk'. If he had passed this step 'he would not have been able to speak to us but must have passed by in silence with his cowl down over his face and his eyes bent on the ground.' This may have been Brother Dunstan (Thomas Bray), who would be 'professed as novice' on 31 July.

As the visitors were leaving the monks had to sing a hymn, 'holding up our hands in parting benediction'. In the *Little Manual of Devotions* compiled by Ignatius for the Ascension Day pilgrimage a few years later this had developed into a picturesque little ritual, in which the monks with uplifted hands chanted a form of blessing over the kneeling pilgrims, who then turned away 'slowly singing: And now again we wander / Out on Earth's stormy sea; / Oh Jesus, King, protect us, / We have no help but thee' and four further verses in a similar vein.

SISTER WINIFRED COMES TO STAY

WHEN THE PRITCHARDS left Tygwyn it was occupied for some time by Jane Price, a widow in her fifties whose rather more prosperous sister lived at Chapel House down by the bridge; Jane's daughter lived there as a servant to her aunt, and would have been the 'buxom comely wholesome girl' who on his first visit told Kilvert it was 'none just' to the site of the new monastery.[278] Jane (sometimes referred to by ex-Bro Cuthbert as Jenny, and described by him as 'a very ignorant foolish old woman; but kind') had previously lived on the edge of the open mountain at Waingoch, scarcely more than a shack and probably in an even worse state than the dilapidated farmhouse; nothing remains of it today except a small heap of stones. She did some washing for the monastery (when Cuthbert resumed lay attire for his journey home she starched his collar), and on at least one occasion had to share her billet with female guests.

This was when Sister Winifred came on a visit, accompanied on her arrival by another associate, Sister Maria. Maria left with the other pilgrims at the end of the Ascension celebrations, but Winifred stayed on for several weeks.

Cuthbert and Ethelred had the job of making the 'habitable rooms' of the old house fit for their reception. Cuthbert had already propped up its bulging walls with fir poles to make it safe for Jane/

---

[278] Kilvert p77

Jenny; now the two young novices attempted to keep the rain from pouring through holes in the masonry by hanging old carpets over them. Perhaps in recognition of her piety and financial interest in the house Winifred was accorded the privilege of cleaning the chapel; she also filled time not spent walking on the mountain with Ignatius and the Oblate doing what the former perhaps visualised as a little ladylike sewing. Here we have an example of Cuthbert's ability to convey the frequent lapses into absurdity of Llanthony life, as well as a marker on his downward path from the Abbot's favour:

> When I was house brother she [Winifred] used to complain of my sending her so much sewing over. The Superior told me to send everything over that wanted the least repair, so the first day I sent four mattresses, blankets and other things and was proceeding to send more when she made a desperate remonstrance through notes. The Reverend Father said I had done it for contradiction and was highly indignant when I reminded him that only the day before he had told me that my judgment was simply nothing and had commanded me not to use it in any way but to obey him in the minutest particular, which in this case I had done.

Notes also played a part in the following:

> Sister Winefred [sic] was not young by any means but she was desperately in love with the Superior.[279] She used to write to him several notes a day, they were flying all over the enclosure. Jenny kept running across with them – they were laid on the step or mat or anywhere – I dare say the Reverend Father read most of them, for I think he was a little in love with her too.
>
> She used to quarrel with him and say he was unkind and did not love her at all, and when he would not go over to see her, she

[279] She was then fifty, and Ignatius fifteen years her junior.

would have hysterics sometimes. Once I remember she had a worse paroxysm than usual. Jenny came running across to give the alarm and the Superior being neuralgic sent Father Philip who took Dunstan and some brandy with him. But Sister Winefred on hearing that the Reverend Father had not come, was taken worse and screamed and stiffened herself and beat with her heels on the floor and Jenny said 'the noise was such that she was driven out of t'house'.

Philip was much disgusted; he said 'he never could abide women and didn't understand 'em when they had got their complaints on', and that 'he hated the sight of 'em and that now he had had to touch one'. He left her in her fit and Jenny got her to bed.

Father Ignatius told us that these attacks were caused by her refusing to believe in election[280] – he had told her she could not be saved if she did not believe in it, but that the moment that she said she did believe her salvation was secure. He visited her next morning and she had another attack that evening and Father Philip was again sent but he only called through the key-hole.

She might not go into any part of the Monastery but the Chapel and used to get in before us. One day as we entered a gauze curtain caught fire, it was only by a stone wall but she sprang and shrieked and clutched at it, Father Ignatius holding her back. Then she nearly fainted and sobbed and made a row all the rest of the service. She and the Prioress of Feltham – Father Philip told me – were awfully jealous of each other being equally in love with the Reverend Father who was indeed surrounded and supported by women in this condition.

Winifred was still there when Ignatius returned from Feltham in July. Spence tells us that at about this time she 'slipped off' to attend the funeral of a nephew (her sister Frances's 12-year-old son

---

[280] The belief accompanying that in predestination, i.e. that salvation is restricted to a predetermined number of elect souls. See Article XVII (of the XXXIX Articles), Of *Predestination and Election*.

William), although the Superior had forbidden the trip. She returned from the station in Farmer Dodd's dogcart and was in residence for some time after that, perhaps for the rest of the summer.[281]

MEANWHILE THERE WAS ANOTHER visit from Ignatius's family. In September 1865 his sister Louisa Jane had married William Barker Drawbridge, a clergyman a few years older than herself whose first wife had died after a very brief marriage, and who was serving as a chaplain in India. Like many another colonial wife Louisa seems to have made several extended trips home. She was now on her way back from one of them, and her farewell visit was the occasion for a high-spirited tea party in the garden of the farmhouse. Baby was summoned to attend, but the other occupants of the monastery were excluded from the festivities.

Louisa probably came over from Abergavenny, where their elder brother Francis Palmer was living in a substantial house in Chapel Road which he had named 'Lynederry'. Like his brother-in-law he had lost his first wife after a brief marriage, and in the 1871 census was listed at that address with two small children of his own (the elder being four-year-old Louisa Jane, named for her aunt) and two teenage stepchildren as well as his late wife's sister; that summer he would marry for a second time.[282] It is possible that 'Franky' with

---

[281] In his article 'The Monastery' (LMN July-Sept 1894) Ignatius informed his supporters that 'the kind lady donor of the £1000 became Sister Winifred, and she is still alive and well, and spending half the year at Llanthony from April to November, and is deeply loved and regarded amongst us, having been a Sister in our Order for over a quarter of a century'. For the last ten of those twenty-five years she would have been able to stay in more comfortable accommodation than the broken-down farmhouse, the newly-built Plas Genevieve.

[282] The marriage between Francis Palmer Lyne and Sarah Elizabeth Peake took place in London on 22 July 1871. She was the daughter of the Reverend Henry Peake, who combined the curacy of Llangattock-nigh-Usk with the headmastership of Abergavenny Grammar School. As his two children had both been born locally Francis Palmer had evidently settled in Abergavenny at least two years before his brother acquired the monastery

his new wife and their children (as well as Louisa Jane's two little boys) was also at the party; this would have accounted for some of the jollity reported by Cuthbert. (He might not have been able to see clearly into the garden from the monastery, but the sounds of merriment would have been all too audible.)

ANOTHER STONE IS LAID, AND ANOTHER DISTINGUISHED VISITOR RECEIVED

ON 22 AUGUST (Octave of the Assumption) Ignatius laid the foundation stone of the planned abbey church,[283] with 'Fr Cyril' on hand to bless it. In one of the letters Cuthbert received from Ignatius earlier that summer he was told that the Abbot was 'longing' to return to Llanthony for the occasion, and that 'three builders [were] trying for the work', but there is no mention of the ceremony in his narrative. He does, however, tell us that by October 'the workmen had left off building the church', adding the significant observation that 'Buckeridge the Architect had stopped the builder as it was badly built'. Perhaps if Ignatius had accepted one of the other tenders it would still be standing today.[284]

There is a little more about the event in the monastic Chronicle, where Ignatius tells us that 'the Sweet Name of Our Lord Jesus was graven upon the face of the stone which did lie upon the ground', and that 'few secular persons were present, for we monks did keep private our intention'.[285] He did, however, admit a representative of the *Western*

---

site at Capel-y-ffin, but by 1881 the family had moved to Hammersmith.

[283] Bertouch p460.

[284] The slating of the roof was particularly badly done. An *Abergavenny Chronicle* report of 28 October 1932 quoted B.G.A. Cannell (Brother Gildas, 1892-94): 'If the weather was bad, we were marched off to Church, and he [Ignatius] used to pray fervently for the "Angels to sit on the roof" to stop the slates from coming off.' According to Brother David the roof was reslated shortly after this time.

[285] This and the following extracts from the abbey Chronicle, quoted Attwater pp65f.

Mail, whose report was printed two days later. This, together with a shorter notice from the Church Herald of 21 September, was pasted on to a vacant page of the book in which the Chronicle was kept.

As at the previous stone-laying this ceremony followed 'a service' (identified in the Church Herald as Nones), for which Ignatius presided at the organ; it was 'partly in Latin', although 'a portion of it was taken from the Book of Common Prayer' and presumably in English. Both papers describe the procession to the site of the new church; the Herald (doubtless from information given by the Abbot) gives the running order as

> a monk with the processional crucifix of brass, attended by two others with lighted tapers in tall candlesticks; a novice with incense; the Brethren in order; a Monk with a red silk banner, on which was a rich jewelled gold crown, with palm leaves rising from it, the words 'Jesus Rex' were above and beneath the crown; after the banner followed the officiating Priest in surplice and a most gorgeous cope, the Superior closing the Procession.

The Western Mail account adds the information that the ceremony was conducted 'almost entirely in Latin, the prayers being from the old mediaeval books'. When Ignatius had laid the three-foot square stone 'in the name of the Holy Trinity' he 'poured a small quantity of port wine over it' – left over, perhaps, from the supply brought by the 'Provincial' on his Ascensiontide visit.

The Herald added the information that 'two young novices pronounced their first vows on the same day'; these would have been Brothers Oswald and Pancras (Powell and Crews, for whom see below). The description of the procession follows a typically Ignatian pattern in giving the impression of a community more numerous than in fact it was. However, there may have been as many as six in residence at this time as well as the Abbot and the Infant Oblate,[286] so if the last-named was carrying a candle or what the *Western Mail* called the 'censor' the numbers more or less work out.

The following week the monastery received a visit from Lord Hereford,[287] owner of the adjacent mountainside. He was 'exceeding friendly & kind & did consent that we should open a quarry in these mountains, for the building of the Abbey Church', the encounter bringing out all Ignatius's social consciousness, even if the mode of expression was suitably pious: 'We do bless Thee Oh! Lord Jesu, because Thou hast sent hither, thy servant, this good Lord & Noble Person, & hast inclined his heart towards us Thine unworthy servants.' While he was exchanging theological and other pleasantries with the Abbot the noble visitor's horse 'slipped its bridle. Lord Hereford and myself did try to catch the horse, but in vain, until it was stopped by some men on the mountain, a mile from hence.'

In case he was under the impression that the stone was intended as a gift, a few weeks later the Chronicle recorded a follow-up visit from 'Master Griffiths', Steward to the afore-mentioned 'good Lord & Noble Person', who told him the price would be 2d a yard.

CHARLES (OR JOHN)

OVER THE NEXT COUPLE OF YEARS the supply of young men continued, though none seemed to stay long. Spence mentions a 'Brother Charles formerly Brother John whose real name was Redhalls', although he doesn't figure in the Register. He says this individual arrived in January of that year (1872), and that at the outdoor procession on Ascension Day he 'provoked the laughter of the people by falling on his back in the mud and assuming the form of a V[,] feet and head nearly meeting'. After Dunstan's departure to Feltham he was for a

---

[286] Philip (Pointer), Serene (Roberts), Cuthbert (Spence), Dunstan/Thomas (Bray) and the two new arrivals, who would at first have occupied beds in the visitors' room.

[287] Robert Charles Devereux (1843-1930), 16th Viscount

short time put in charge of Baby, although within a few days Ignatius wrote to suggest that if he wanted to leave he had another aspirant keen to take his place. The fleas in the abbatial bedding were the result of a lack of vigilance on his part: he 'let the child [who had a weakness for bringing cats to bed with him] and [the] Superior's room and bed get into such a state that in order to have the place purified Baby was removed into the visitors' room' – doubtless one of the 'divers misdeeds he had committed' which prompted him to run away 'as the time for the Superior's return drew near'.

Charles Jasper Redhalls was born in late 1851 in East London, where his father was in later censuses listed successively as 'House Porter', 'Butler Unemployed' and 'Messenger for Wine Merchant'. Charles himself seems to have escaped inclusion in most of them: in 1891 he was registered with his parents in Limehouse as 'House Porter Religious House' (it would be interesting to know which one), and in his fifties and sixties spent brief periods in various metropolitan workhouses.

Spence rounds off his brief account of Brother Charles or John with this comment: 'When on leaving Llanthony I passed through London I heard that he had repented this step and meant to return at the first opportunity. He had run away four times, in fact this eccentric individual spent his days in agitating from town to country life and was suited with neither.'[288] The 1911 census succeeded where others failed: he was then 59, and apparently living in the hayloft at Lower Stanton, Llanfihangel Crucorney, his occupation given as 'Tramping Labourer'. Three years earlier Ignatius had noted in his diary 'Redhalls arrived, walked from London,'[289] so he had evidently maintained some kind of relationship with the monastery, even four decades after his brief postulancy.

---

[288] Redhalls may have been the ex-novice referred to in MT March 1885 as having 'walked all the way three times from London to be received back' and 're-admitted seven times' although 'our doors are now closed to him for ever'.

[289] Diary entry, 15 February 1908

OSWALD

THE PERSON IGNATIUS had wanted to install in Redhalls's place was 19-year-old Francis Powell, who arrived with Dunstan when the latter returned from Feltham in July. He was admitted as a postulant on the 18th of that month and clothed as a novice (as we have seen) just over a month later, with the name Oswald of the Blessed Sacrament.

Spence describes him as 'plain looking and poor' – so no chance of a contribution from his family – 'and never a favourite', and tells us that his mother was a widow living in London. According to census records he was the youngest of three brothers whose father had been a machinist, later a trades union official; it may have been this latter appointment which explains why in spite of its London roots the family was living in Manchester when the 1861 census was taken.

Soon after his admission the young man fell ill, and there was some concern about him. Dr Pryce was sent for, and 'not wanting the boy to die in the Abbey' Ignatius 'sent for his brother to take him home'. A carpenter by trade but out of work on account of a strike, Oswald's elder brother Josiah Alexander had had to walk some of the way, and by the time he arrived the patient was much better. In consequence he was now 'inclined to stay and the Superior...inclined to keep him', and Cuthbert was given the job of pacifying and then comforting the 'handsome and powerful' Josiah, who after initially appearing 'dangerous, ...broke down and cried'. Their mother had been ill ever since young Francis had left, and like Joseph's brothers in Egypt he 'dare[d] not go back without the boy'.

After 'hours' of 'going backwards and forwards' between the Superior and the distraught elder brother Cuthbert 'shamed' the former into paying his train fare back to London, but he might have saved himself the trouble. 'On St Luke's Day' (18 October) Oswald 'bolted'. The others 'made no effort to find him' (Ignatius was back at Feltham), but 'after two days Dr Pryce's coachman came to the gate saying he was there [Longtown; fourteen miles by road] and they did not know what to do with him'.

It seems that Dr and Mrs Pryce lent him the money to get home, and perhaps some less conspicuous clothes. That winter the unhappy Powell family went to try their fortunes in America, whence the renegade novice wrote in March to the Doctor regretting that he was just then unable to repay the loan, and in May to Ignatius: 'Writes in agony of mind from America begging to be readmitted.' A year later he was back -- 'March 21 1874 Our H[oly] Father's Day: Received back as a penitent at Feltham' – but although his entry in the Register ends at this point he can't have stayed more than a couple of years, if that long. In the 1881 census he was listed in Liverpool as a ship's cook with his locally born wife Mary Jane (shopkeeper) and three sons, the eldest of whom had been born in January 1877. Ten years later he was away from home (presumably at sea), although Mary Jane (now manageress of a public house) and the two elder boys were at another address in her native city. Four years after that (in the second quarter of 1895) the death of 42-year-old Francis William Powell was registered in Bristol.

A 'GENTLEMAN' NOVICE: PANCRAS

AT THE END of his narrative John Spence alludes to Ignatius's continual optimism that 'young men of rank' were about to discover vocations to his monastery, and that in consequence its tone would be raised and financial security guaranteed. Sadly this only happened in the pages of his novels, although a few of those who came his way (including Spence himself, whom Ignatius once grudgingly acknowledged to be a 'gentleman') seem to have raised his hopes, if only temporarily. Another relatively well-born aspirant was Sidney Crews (Brother Pancras), who was three months short of his seventeenth birthday when he travelled down with Ignatius in July. He is described as

> a great pleasant fellow generally laughing but kept the rule well, we
> thought he was some relation of Gilby [sic] the wine merchant. He
> was a gentleman and spoke correctly, and read beautifully, but we

knew extremely little of him. It was sometimes made the rule that the year- and life-vowed monks should not speak with newcomers and postulants and I believe this was the order when Sidney Crews came.

This injunction (for which there is confirmation in *Brother Placidus*) seems to have been so well observed that Spence tells us nothing more about him except that at the end of the summer he returned to Feltham. Pancras travelled with the trusted Brother Dunstan: Ignatius 'dare[d] not leave' him at Llanthony to imbibe the rebellious spirit of the other occupants.

Perhaps he should never have brought him away from the nunnery in the first place. In the Register alongside the dates of his admission to postulancy (18 July) and noviciate (22 August) is Ignatius's comment: 'Sent away in Dec[embe]r 1872 after a course of deceit thro' another novice's bad influence.' Comparing this with Cuthbert's entry it is not hard to guess the identity of this 'other novice'.

Sidney Crews was born on 9 October 1855 in Stepney, where his father was a customs officer. Some time after leaving the monastery he entered his father's profession, and by 1891 had risen to be an Assistant Examining Officer. In 1881 he was living with his quaintly-named bride Puella Letitia in Tower Hamlets and in 1891 they were based in suburban Bristol; later he was transferred to Harwich.[290] His death was registered in Ipswich in the fourth quarter of 1907, when he was just 52.

FURTHER GOINGS & COMINGS

ON SHROVE TUESDAY (26 February) 1873 – by ecclesiastical reckoning the tenth anniversary of the foundation at Claydon – Fr Philip finally left the monastery. He had been a monk for nearly nine years, although according to Spence he had previously run away seven

---

[290] His name is missing from the 1901 census, but appears in Kelly's Directory of Essex for both 1899 and 1906.

times, and had often spoken of 'going into some Roman Catholic establishment and used to endeavour to persuade me [Spence] to do the same'. Ignatius's account of his departure tells us as much about himself as about Philip:

> He was with me eight years, but had not God mercifully helped me to be patient and forbearing, he would not have remained eight weeks. In fact, when I was compelled to drive him out from this place, by a very extraordinary method, he was only tolerated six weeks at the Roman Monastery to which he betook himself. For a long time previously to his exodus, he had been neglecting his religious duties, not having communicated for months. His example was very depressing to the Novices, and they too became neglectful of Communion. Lent was drawing near, and I gave notice in choir that all must prepare to make their next Communion on Ash Wednesday. Those who were not 'fit' to receive the blessed Sacrament were not 'fit' to remain in the Monastery. Without saying a word to anyone, on Shrove Tuesday, Father Philip disappeared.[291]

He went first to the Catholic church in Abergavenny, then as now staffed by Benedictine priest-monks, and from there to Belmont Priory.[292] Here he wrote to his erstwhile Superior exhorting him to follow his example and become a 'true' (i.e. Roman Catholic) Benedictine, even if this final phase of his own monastic career

---

[291] MT June 1885, article 'Llanthony Monastery – its past, present & future'.

[292] Since Ignatius's significant visit there in 1861 there had been at least two in the opposite direction. The first, in August 1870, was mentioned in the last chapter. A later one took place when John Spence was in the community: 'I remember two of the brothers from this place visiting the Superior. One was called Fr Cuthbert and he shewed me a good deal of attention and I since received an affectionate message from him through the Reverend Father. They and Ignatius had long discourses together in the ravine.' This would have been Cuthbert Doyle, the Novice Master, who perhaps saw in his young namesake a possible recruit for his own establishment.

turned out to be rather short. The account tells us that he returned to his native county, 'obtained a situation on the railway...married and was no more heard of'. In the 1881 census he was listed with a wife named Bessy at an address in White Horse Street, Fakenham, where his occupation was given as Railway Porter. She was ten years his junior, and they had married in Norwich about eighteen months after his departure from the monastery. There were three children: Gertrude Mary (aged 6; she would have been conceived at about the time of their marriage), Edith Emily (4) and Arthur William (1). Ten years later 'Bessie Poynter' was a widowed laundress living in Yarmouth with the same three children and one other, three-year-old Cecil Leo (who was to die as a teenager in 1902). Her death was registered (same spelling of the surname) at Yarmouth in 1929; that of the former Fr Philip seems to have eluded the authorities.[293]

At the same time Philip's fellow-pioneer Brother Serene performed yet another defection and return. We last heard of him in November 1870, when within days of taking vows as a 'penitent' (for the second time in two months) he had gone off again to join Brother Barney at Laleham. In January 1871 he wrote asking Ignatius to receive him once more under his 'fatherly protection', but from the numerous additional notes crammed into the spaces around his Register entry it is not clear what happened in the following eighteen months, except that on 5 March 1871 Ignatius 'sent him £1 to return'; there is, however, no record of him actually having done so at that point.

When he eventually came back to Llanthony in July 1872 Ignatius ordered Serene to 'beg his way as the poor palmers did of old', and Spence reports that he 'walked a great deal of the way and [went]

---

[293] Among the testimonials included in a 9 September 1882 *Cardiff Times* advertisement for an appliance called the 'Magnetaire Belt' was a recent letter from William Pointer of Bridge Street, Fakenham. He described how five years earlier he had been left in great pain after an accident at Norwich Goods Station, but that after wearing the belt for two or three months he had been fully restored to health.

without food a long time'. He describes him as 'a man of about twenty-nine with a handsome face, good teeth and sunken blue eyes, a little bald on the forehead which gave him the appearance of more brain than he really had'. He also notes that 'he was dressed nautically in blue, his brothers were sailors of some sort, and were now quite tired of helping him and had cast him off so there was nothing for him but coming back.'

Serene's penitential regime included sleeping in the kitchen and wearing 'a pointed hood with holes for the eyes'; in chapel this 'had to be pulled down over his face and he found it very hot work singing under it'. When Ignatius and his immediate entourage disappeared to Feltham in the autumn the resident community was reduced to Philip, Serene and Cuthbert, who tells us that the other two 'quarrelled incessantly'. On 14 February 1873 (by which time Cuthbert had been gone two months, so he wasn't in a position to tell us) the Register notes that Serene was 'excommunicated' but that he 'returned to take [the] discipline' the following day. As his entry shows, the cycle of expulsions and reconciliations appears to have gone on for another few years:

> 1875 sent away for making love to Miss Wallington the saddler's daughter in Abergavenny. Bro Serene returned March 1877. Sent away November 1877 for making love to Alice Frew, a Nurse in Hay.

EARLY IN 1873 Brother Dunstan (or Thomas) made a second attempt to return to the world. In the Register Ignatius noted: 'I caught this novice just as he was going to run from the monastery this evening – entirely under the dominion of Satan thro' temper & disobedience.'

Possibly. Another explanation might be that like Cuthbert, Ethelred and Philip he realised that the religious life could never properly flourish under Ignatius's régime, and that it would have to be sought elsewhere. The entry continues: 'A great number of trials & changes thro' this noviciate. Wanting to go & to take life vows alternately. He is a [illegible] & [illegible] & a fairly young novice; & so I think he will with GOD's grace hold his ground.' This last remark, especially, sounds suspiciously like wishful thinking.

That year three young men were recorded as having entered the community. The first was 22-year-old Frederick William Gold (Brother Bede), received as a postulant on 19 May 1873 at Feltham and clothed as a novice on 24 June at Llanthony. Four months later Ignatius reports in the Register that he '[r]an away from the Abbey, after having given many signs of an unsound mind...while I was absent begging'.[294]

Next came a person who certainly possessed that desirable and elusive quality of 'rank': Richard Alfred Todd, born at 51 Wimpole Street on 31 July 1856, so not quite seventeen when admitted as a postulant at Feltham on 9 June, and whose promotion to the noviciate was rushed through on 14 July. The difficulty was that as well as being socially superior his parents were articulate, angry at the apparent kidnapping of their son and knew how to set about getting him back. Calder-Marshall[295] relates how they had the Court of Chancery declare the boy a ward of court, how a writ was issued for his safe return, and how after less than two months in his care Ignatius was forced to yield him up. In the Register he notes the 'very fearful commotion – throughout the country' which the case provoked, and that when he showed up at court he was 'attacked by the mob', scandalised by this assault on the inherent sanctity of the English family. However, in Ignatius's scheme of things there could be no doubt that Brother Aelred's vocation came direct from God, and so trumped his duty to his parents. By opposing it they showed that they belonged to 'the world', and their legal rights were of no consequence.

---

[294] His birth was registered in Brixton in the third quarter of 1851. He appears in two censuses: 1861 as the third of five children of Henry Gold (Tea Dealer employing five men) & Susanna (née Jupp) living in Loughborough Road, Lambeth; 1891 living in two rooms in Leader Street, Chelsea; single; employed as a General Porter.

[295] Enthusiast pp209ff

Todd's father John was a merchant trading with Russia and the Baltic, and had married his wife (born Frances Hill) at the British church in Riga in 1834. Richard was the tenth of their eleven children, and attended Queen Elizabeth School, Ipswich; before this brief monastic interlude he had started work in his father's counting house. It seems that on his return he settled back into the business, and by 1881 is himself listed as a Russian Merchant. Over the years the family had various addresses in the new commuter belts around London. Richard himself never married; he died in Wiltshire on 21 September 1932.[296]

The third was Herbert Lansdown Gamble (Brother Sebastian), who was received as a postulant at Feltham on 11 December at the age of seventeen. His clothing as a novice followed on 25 February 1874 at Llanthony, but there is no indication of how long he stayed.[297] In the 1871 census his occupation had been given as 'Merchant's Clerk' and he was living with his family in Spurstowe Road, Hackney; his father is listed as a Retired Master Mariner.

Some time after his sojourn at Llanthony he emigrated to the USA and was ordained in the Episcopal Church (deacon 1882, priest 1888). In May 1889 he moved from the diocese of Nebraska to that of Iowa, where he was appointed Rector of Grace Church, Lyons (a suburb of the city of Clinton). Evidently this failed to work out, and

---

[296] Bertouch (p487) says that 'he finally posed in life as an Advocate at the Scottish Bar' — a curious way of describing his change of career. If he indeed became a Scottish lawyer he must have done so after the 1901 census, when he was listed as a Grain Merchant living with his 84-year-old widowed mother and younger sister in Walton-on-Thames. I was unable to find his name (in England or in Scotland) in that of 1911.

[297] Some light on the circumstances of his departure is shed by an undated note addressed by 'Sebastian' to 'Rev. Father Sup[erio]r', tucked into the Bible preserved at Ss Julius & Aaron, Newport. It opens with the admission that he felt he could never tell Ignatius 'the whole truth about [a named individual, not a member of the community], & therefore...could not be sincere in the life'. He asks permission to write home at once for clothes and money, of which he had neither.

the following year he moved again, to New York. When Ignatius and his travelling companions were there in the spring of 1891 he met up with them, and enjoyed a walk in Central Park with Fr Michael, chronicler of the tour.[298] Full career details of American clergy at this period are hard to come by, but I am told he is listed in the 1897 *Living Church Quarterly* as serving at Trinity Church, Boston, Massachusetts.[299]

UNWELCOME VISITORS

As THE NEW MONASTERY took shape the number of sightseers increased, among them sightseeing journalists. In the first year Francis Kilvert had satisfied his curiosity by paying three visits in the space of six months, but his impressions were confided to his secret diary. He would be followed by a host of lesser *littérateurs*, of whom many published accounts of their visits in newspapers and magazines.

An early example was printed in the *Birmingham Daily Post* of 26 December 1873. The anonymous author was on a walking tour with a group of friends, and the party were evidently in a jocular frame of mind. Here is the central section:

> We found the buildings to consist of an old farm-house and stabling, temporarily occupied by the fraternity; a long narrow edifice, recently erected, which appeared as if intended for a dormitory; and a commencement of what is apparently intended to become an abbey of stately dimensions.
>
> On approaching the entrance to the premises, we came across a board.... On this was painted, in conspicuous letters...an intimation that strangers could on no account be admitted until the guest house was erected.[300] Reading this, we made no attempt at entering by the

---

[298] FIIA pp253f

[299] Information from The Archives of the Episcopal Church and various internet sources.

[300] In due course this discouraging notice was removed. In July 1891 members of the Woolhope Naturalists' Field Club paid a visit and

doorway, but we pursued our way along a meadow which led up to the front of the new building. Here we encountered a hedge, which interfered with our going actually into the works, but one of the three or four masons who were at work came forward, and, in reply to our enquiries, implied that visitors sometime came over to see how they were getting on.

Encouraged by this observation, some of the party were looking for a convenient way over the hedge, when an apparition followed us through the gate by which we had entered the meadow. This was in the form of a member or servant of the brotherhood – a man clad in leather leggings, a billy-cock hat, and a black coat or robe, girded round the waist, and furnished with enormously wide and long sleeves, who peremptorily 'ordered us off'. In a stentorian voice he shouted out that we were trespassing on private property and were to take ourselves away at once.

We attempted to get up a parley with him, but, like a dog which barks at a stranger and retreats as he advances, the individual retired so expeditiously, as we approached, that I do not believe he heard a word that was addressed to him. Perhaps it is as well that he did not, for, among other irreverent observations, one of the party sought to inform him that we had come with the view of obtaining a pattern for a new scare-crow.

We withdrew from the meadow as we were directed, but not without remarking that the brotherhood, as represented by this individual, might possess many Christian virtues, though it certainly did not know how to give a graceful reception to strangers or wayfarers.... As we passed down the lane on our way back, we came upon him

reported that in contrast to Capel-y-ffin church the door of the abbey church was 'as it should be, always open'. 'A welcome is offered to the passer by, pilgrim in this world, and upon the entrance gates [to the monastery grounds] is offered an invitation to "Enter into His gates with thanksgiving, and into His courts with praise".' I am grateful to Dr Esther de Waal for providing me with the relevant extract from the Society's *Transactions*.

again. In front of the monastic building there is a kitchen garden – very neatly cultivated – running down to the lane. In this garden we found our friend at work with a four-pronged fork, and some of the party invited him to tell us the way to 'Buenos Ayres', or some such neighbouring place, but he went on with his work without looking round or appearing to take any notice of what was said.

Lower down the lane we met two boys, draped in the costume of the fraternity, and tried to learn from them who our peremptory acquaintance was,[301] but they answered that they were not allowed to speak about the monastery. We then offered the younger of the two a coin of the realm, but he said he was not permitted to receive money, which we – perhaps uncharitably – interpreted to signify that juvenile trousers of the monastic pattern were not provided with pockets.

As a final thrust, one of our number – a stately gentleman of mature years, with a fine white beard and aristocratic presence, who might have been taken for the Lord-Lieutenant of the county – button-holed one of the boys, and said he might tell the individual who was working in the garden, that he had come with the intention of presenting a piece of land to the monastery, but that he had met with a reception which rendered it impossible for him to carry out the purpose.

DUNSTAN TAKES FINAL VOWS

IN SPITE OF HIS ESCAPE ATTEMPT the previous year Brother Dunstan/ Thomas was made a 'Monk for Life' in the summer of 1874. On Wednesday 10 June ('Corpus Christi 1874 Eve of Octave') Ignatius made this puzzling entry against his name in the Register: 'Our LORD for a most special purpose took him from the Monastery 14 hours. Mount Moriah, Isaac, Theodore.'

On 4 August – perhaps on the strength of this mysterious experience – he admitted the young man to life vows. This provided

---

[301] The leggings and billy-cock hat suggest a 'secular'; the wide-sleeved garment a monk. Perhaps it was the penitent Serene, still at work in his garden?

an opportunity for a rather less unsympathetic press report than the one just cited, this time in the *Western Mail*.[302]

Apart from the details of the two-hour ceremony itself (for which one of the props was the mattress on which the candidate had to 'die to the world'; it was covered with a black and white pall and took up quite a lot of the available space) it is interesting to note that the 25-foot temporary chapel was divided into two by a curtained screen, and that apart from the visiting journalist ('Our Special Commissioner') the secular congregation consisted of 'some dozen men of the labouring class', whom he later identified as the builders supposedly working on the new church. With Ignatius was another clergyman, presumably to act as celebrant of the Mass. He was 'not a monk', and was distinguished by his 'long black hair, full beard and moustache, and spectacles'; perhaps it was Fr Cyril. They were assisted by 'boys in scarlet and white dresses' (number unstated), and a monk whose 'tall, swarthy, cadaverous' appearance (complete with a 'slight moustache' which 'shaded his upper lip') contrasted with the 'fair and almost girlish face' of the newly professed.[303]

After Brother Sebastian (Gamble)'s entry no admissions are recorded in the Register until 1878.[304] Either Ignatius was so disheartened by his defeat in the Todd case that he failed to note the names of those who arrived in the following few years, or the tide of public opinion had swung so far against him that the supply dried up entirely. It is difficult to tell how many occupants there

---

[302] Thursday 6 August 1874

[303] The writer estimated the age of this monk to be 'no more than twenty'. Apart from Serene (who by then would have been thirty, and may or may not have been in the community at the time) the likeliest candidates were Sebastian (Gamble) and Oswald (Powell) (after his penitential return in March).

[304] There is one entry between 1874 and 1878: that of John Lamond (Brother Walther) aged 27, but as apart from '1876' in the margin it shows no date of admission to postulancy or noviciate I suspect that if this individual actually arrived at the monastery he left very soon afterwards.

were in the house at any one time, but in the summer of 1879 there was only one monk, Dunstan (Thomas Bray), whose further history will be related in the next chapter, and a year later again only one (another Dunstan, William Magrath).

Picture 11: Abbey Church of Our Lady and St Dunstan, c1875. Note monks' entrance in centre of south wall.

Picture 12: The High Altar as first installed

CHAPTER 7

THE MONASTERY EXPANDS

AN IMPORTANT MILESTONE was reached in the spring of 1875, when the three easternmost bays of the proposed abbey church came into use, and the Reserved Sacrament was transferred to the new high altar from the temporary chapel in the west cloister. A report in the *Western Mail* of 3 April that year gives a full description of the interior, and names the builders as Jackson & Son of Cardiff. For the time being its furnishings were incomplete; another seven years would elapse before the arrival of proper stalls for the brethren and the erection of the 'grand organ' on the screen separating the monks' choir from the single bay accessible to 'seculars'.[305]

When these were installed in late 1882 the massive reredos would also be completed, its central pinnacle reaching over thirty feet above floor level.[306] At first it consisted solely of the lower stages of the central section (tabernacle and exposition throne), although a faded photograph pasted into Mother Cecilia's Bible suggests that the next level (up to the base of the exposition throne) was added some time before the final stages: this was probably where it had reached at the time of the appearance of the 'miraculous monstrance' in August 1880.

---

[305] For some information about the abbey organs see article 'The Lost Organs of Llanthony Abbey' by Cameron Luke, Father Ignatius Memorial Trust Newsletter No 38, Summer 2010 (but see Chapter 14 below for information not available to Mr Luke about the ultimate fate of the main instrument).

[306] Chronicle, quoted Attwater pp66f. Descriptions of the reredos were given in MT September 1883 and March 1884, where it was pointed out that if it seemed disproportionately large 'the dimensions were from the first arranged so that the whole should be viewed from 100 feet or thereabout by the general public'. The dates for the completion of the remaining domestic buildings are given in LMN April-June 1894.

This huge structure was conceived as a 'shrine of perpetual adoration', and was the focal point of the whole monastic enterprise. In the *Western Mail* report of the 1880 Ascension Day pilgrimage there is an extended quotation from the pilgrims' manual of devotions which explains the reason for this, and the rationale for the pilgrimage itself:

> At the Reformation, 1,500 years after the establishment of Christianity, a few men began to deny that the Adorable Sacrament was what our Lord declared it to be, viz, His very Body and Blood.... Day by day, in the English Benedictine Order, from six a.m. till six p.m., the adoration is continued, before the Blessed Sacrament, to offer to God, on behalf of the Church of England, acts of repentance and reparation for the sins of the Reformation and its miserable consequences in our beloved land. The shrine, then, is one of peculiar sanctity and interest to all who love the Lord Jesus and are faithful members of the despoiled English Church. Here, once a year, on the feast of our Lord's Ascension, the monks invite Christians from the outer world to come on a pilgrimage of reparation to the most holy sacrament in its own 'shrine of perpetual adoration'.

In the photographs mentioned above one can see that instead of a frontal there was a large picture resting on the floor under the altar. This is described in an anonymous account of a visit to the monastery made in the late summer of 1891:[307]

---

[307] I am grateful to the Reverend Norman Hulme of Spalding for a copy of this ms of thirty-two foolscap pages, entitled *Llanthony Monastery: a Pilgrimage*. It was received by him with other material from the Reverend Harold Moxon, an associate of H.B. Ventham (for whom see Chapter 11), and describes in minute detail and with numerous digressions the writer's journey on foot from Llanfihangel station and a fair amount about the layout and routine of the monastery. It will be referred to hereafter as '1891 ms'.

Behind these [the two central columns supporting the mensa of the altar] is a fresco [in fact a framed oil painting on canvas] representing Eucharistic Adoration on Earth & in Heaven. In the centre is set an altar upon which is a golden monstrance surrounded by clouds, at the foot of which kneel a Benedictine Monk & Nun in the attitude of adoration & prayer. A golden censer stands upon the grass between them, from which issues tiny pale grey circlets of perfume to the sky. The outer panels show the Church militant ['triumphant' is meant] in adoration, accompanied by their various symbols – S. John, in camel's hair, S. Agnes with her lamb, S. Catherine with her wheel, S. Paul bearing his sword, & pope, bishop, cardinal & warriors clad in mail. In the canopy of the clouds above are choirs of angels with harps & palms & thuribles.[308]

Picture 13: Completed 'Shrine of Perpetual Adoration'

---

[308] 1891 ms p30. The picture has for many years been kept at the church of Holy Trinity, Abergavenny, but is not currently on view.

As mentioned in an earlier chapter, the reredos was designed by the former Brother Brannock of Elm Hill (Harry Incledon Webber).[309] It was constructed by Messrs Mayer of Munich at a cost of £2000 (more than three times that of building the entire west wing, but this was entirely consistent with Ignatius's scale of priorities), a significant proportion of which must have gone on transport. The brass facade of the massive tabernacle was decorated with enamelling and studded with jewels; above it towered the pinnacled exposition throne, on either side of which were gradines and ledges to accommodate a forest of candlesticks and flower vases. Amid the candles one could just make out the inscription *Ave in aeternum sanctissimum sacramentum* in raised letters; above this were carvings of angels in attitudes of adoration. Ignatius's focus on devotion to the Blessed Sacrament would have seemed strange not only to St Benedict and his early companions, but to the mediaeval 'monks and hermits' whose way of life Llanthony was intended to be a revival:

> Unspeakably awful was the sacred mountain shrine. The deep silence, the mystic light, the gorgeous altar, glittering among the shadows, which thirty or forty crimson lamps flung over it; a soft glow of holy fire seemed to wrap the choir, falling from the dark ruby glasses of the lamps, swinging in the air, high up above the Exalted Presence.... And all this wondrous machinery of supernatural holiness and devotion, actually existed amid the faithlessness and ignorance of the poor, miserable nineteenth century, among those silent mountains in the lonely valley of old Ewyas. Ah! surely, ye saintly monks and hermits, who, in the ages of love and praise, peopled this lovely valley, ye must rejoice exceedingly to see those sacred times reviving 'in the midst of the years' of sin and unbelief; to hear the echoes of your own fond faith, resounding with their notes of almighty power,

---

[309] Ignatius (MT March 1884) names the designer as 'Mr H.F. Webber'; Bertouch (p461) says the reredos was carved 'from a design executed by one of the Monks'.

among the selfsame rocks and dells that once of yore re-echoed with your holy songs....[310]

They would, however, have well understood its underlying spiritual rationale, recalled by Bertie Cannell when revisiting the dilapidated monastic church four decades after his two-year sojourn:

> As I stood in front of that Altar, the other Sunday, I could not help thinking of the ceaseless prayer that went up, with the incense, to Almighty God for the thousands that have not time to think about Him. This was his [Ignatius's] idea of the Monastic Life: one long intercession for those who had given themselves entirely to the pomps and pleasures of the world.[311]

UNTIL 1878 THE HOUSEHOLD remained squashed into the cramped west cloister. In that year the domestic accommodation was increased by the completion of the north and east cloisters, to be followed in 1882-3 by that on the south side. A note in the December 1884 issue of the *Monastic Times* revealed that between £11,000 and £12,000 had been contributed towards these projects by Ignatius's friend Douglas Boutflower, who had died two years earlier at his brother's vicarage at Dundry, near Bristol. An earlier report[312] named him as 'the beloved Founder of our Abbey Church', and mentioned his last visit at Ascensiontide 1882, which had been distinguished by him 'saying daily the Latin Mass at Our Ladye's altar'.

---

[310] *Leonard Morris* pp276f. Ignatius's introduction of perpetual adoration has been criticised as unBenedictine, but there was a precedent of which he would almost certainly have been aware. Perpetual adoration was practised by nuns of the Roman Catholic Benedictine convent which had been in existence at Atherstone, Leicestershire, since 1859, and where his friend Edward Husband was curate of the Anglican parish a few years after their arrival. In *Call* p422 Peter Anson notes that perpetual adoration was practised at this convent, but he may not have been aware of Ignatius's indirect connection.

[311] *Abergavenny Chronicle*, 28 October 1932

[312] MT June 1884

The upper storeys of the southern and eastern wings were divided by matchboard partitions into individual cubicles, open at the top; those on the eastern corridor for the community, and those on the south for guests. A few years later Cannell described his introduction to the monastic sleeping quarters thus:

> After Compline I followed the others to the dormitory. The sleeping cells were in darkness, save for a solitary red lamp in the passage outside. By the subdued light from this I saw a small iron bedstead with a straw mattress, two blankets, and a red counterpane, marked with a great white cross. A strip of coconut matting, a chair, and a crucifix on the wall relieved the bareness.[313]

A visitor described his cell in the south wing as

> sufficiently if sparsely furnished. An iron bedstead well supplied with bedding, a Turkey red coverlet having a large white linen cross extending down its full length occupied one corner, a Windsor chair, a crucifix, a statuette of the Holy Mother and the Divine Infant, on the floor an imitation Persian rug and a few well executed texts on the walls was the modest schedule of its contents. A couple of cells reserved for visiting Priests alone have washstands, all other visitors wash in the Lavatory.[314]

The ground floor of the south wing was the nearest the new monastery came to possessing a traditional 'cloister'. It was a single room some sixty feet long by twelve feet wide, with no fireplace or other means of heating, and glazed doors opening on to the central garth. Contemporary photographs[315] show it furnished with

---

[313] FMTB p33

[314] 1891 ms p16

[315] e.g. that opposite Bertouch p453

various articles of *bondieuserie* and peopled by habited monks and youths in carefully contrived poses, apparently engaged in Bible study. The small room at its junction with the west wing was the guests' refectory, and the one above it (the 'Prophets' Chamber') their sitting room, approached by an outside staircase.

When these new additions came into use one of the upstairs rooms in the west wing was designated as a library, though its few books were kept under lock and key and distributed at the Superior's discretion. Serious study was not encouraged: books were primarily to provide fare for the daily hour of 'pious reading'.[316]

On the lower floor of the east wing were two large rooms, the 'community room' and sacristy. From the lobby at the north end of this block a narrow passage and stairway gave access to the monks' entrance to the church – a little door on the south side of the building, in the middle of the stalls. A smaller room at the south end of this wing (now a kitchen) was Ignatius's private sitting room, although he probably spent more time in the oriel-windowed 'Abbot's Cell' at the diametrically opposite corner of the building. In May 1883 he gave this downstairs room over to his friend and physician George Hanson, who became seriously ill and died there. In a moving and detailed account of the Doctor's last days[317] reference is made to its 'huge stone fireplace',[318] 'large Gothic window' and 'broad window sill' and to the 'private door' between it and the community room; also to the fact that because it opened on to the

---

[316] In Dom Cyprian Alston's copy of Bertouch at Downside Abbey a pencilled note in his hand against a reference to the 'library' (p521) asks 'Where is it?'

[317] MT September 29, 1883. The account includes the information that (the former) Brother Brannock sat up two nights running with the dying Doctor, which suggests he was staying in the monastery at the time.

[318] Said to have been copied from a surviving mediaeval model in the gatehouse at old Llanthony. A fireplace of this type can be seen high on the wall between the two portions of this building, and would have served an upper storey whose floor has long since disappeared.

recently completed but as yet 'unenclosed' south cloister it was possible to allow the dying man's wife and daughter to be with him in his last hours.

Picture 14: Aerial view c1980 of the monastery and ruined church. The west cloister (on the right) was the first part to be built; the south cloister, with double doors opening into the garth, the last. The jagged edge at the NE corner (since tidied up) is all that remains of the L-shaped passageway leading from the north cloister to the monks' entrance on the south side of the church.

THE DAILY ROUTINE

A FEW HORARIA SURVIVE, all written out in Ignatius's hand. The earliest date from the first years at Llanthony and occupy seven pages in the main Register; two loose double sheets dating from the 1880s are in the Abergavenny collection.[319] All follow the same basic pattern. In summer (Easter to All Saints' Day) Matins interrupted the night's rest at 2.0am, followed by Lauds at daybreak and a further hour and

---

[319] Museum refs A.1997.15.10 and .11

three-quarters' optional rest (later given up, according to Fr Alston) before 'wash' at 5.15am and Prime at 5.30; in winter the 'night office' seems to have been anticipated at 8.0pm, and the brethren had the whole night in bed (9.0pm to 4.45am). The other offices took place at intervals through the day, interspersed with devotional exercises. These included an hour of corporate 'pious reading' ('no writing', underlined twice) and an hour's 'watch' before the Blessed Sacrament for each brother and a separate 'visit' thereto, and a 'prayer of pious union' after the office of Nones. Bible reading is mentioned in a couple of the schedules, and a lengthy addendum to Compline (Office of the Dead, Litany of the Blessed Virgin and other prayers) extended it to a full hour.

In theory Mass ('or H. Communion') followed Terce at 7.20am, but as the presence of a priest was the exception rather than the rule a celebration of the Eucharist was rarely possible, and when Ignatius was away the brethren would have to forgo even Communion from the Reserved Sacrament. The optional 'pittance' of dry bread and coffee which took the place of breakfast preceded rather than followed this service, so those who wished to communicate went without food altogether until dinner at 12.30 (2.0 in winter). In summer the evening meal (variously designated 'tea' and 'supper'; the former better conveys its content) occupied the half hour between 5.0 and 5.30; in winter it was an hour later and called 'pittance', with only fifteen minutes allowed for it. An hour was devoted to Recreation, in summer after Vespers and in winter before 2.0pm dinner; it began with a prayer.

Most of the surviving timetables incorporate the duties of particular officials – the sacristan, kitchen or serving brother, 'house monk' and so on. The sacristan was responsible for ringing bells throughout the day to summon the community to offices, meals and everything else on the timetable, from 'Ring 5 minutes peal' to get his brethren out of bed for Matins at 2.0am to 'Ring 5 for dormitory' nineteen hours later. He was also responsible for lighting the altar candles for each service (two, four or six according to the relative solemnity of the occasion), and calling the boys in time for Prime (one of them being deputed to ring the bell for that office) and making sure they washed before they had their apology for breakfast.

The kitchen brother had to attend to the cooking fire as soon as he got up, and in the main morning work period (9.0am till 11) to 'get dinner' and sweep and tidy the refectory. As the hour and a half between the end of that period and the meal would be spent elsewhere (an hour of 'Pious Reading' and 'Observances' in the community room, followed by half an hour in church taking part in Sext and a 'meditation', which in practice often took the form of a sermon from the Superior) it seems likely that the two dishes of vegetables of which the meal chiefly consisted would have been rather less appetising than if he had had the opportunity of cooking them nearer the time they were served.[320]

Like the sacristan the kitchen brother was given some juvenile help, especially when there were visitors in the house and special meals had to be laid on for them. 'A boy' took in their supper just before Compline and cleared it away afterwards; perhaps they would have left a few morsels for him to help fill the gap between 5.0 tea and the morning pittance. Then there were Ignatius's own meals to prepare, although the only reference to these in the documents we have is the instruction 'Thomas [one of the boys?] to see to my tea' in one of the schedules from the 1880s.

'Observances' were explained by Bertie Cannell in his reminiscences from the following decade:

---

[320] The palatability of monastery meals varied according to the expertise or lack of it of the current kitchen brother. In his 'Reminiscences of Llanthony' in the December 1913 issue of *Pax* Fr Cyprian Alston recalled: 'Occasionally there were one or two brothers who had some idea of the culinary art, and so we would fare pretty well for one week, only to have to put up with fearful experiments the next. This was hardly conducive to good health or to economical housekeeping.'

You had plenty of rules to study, called 'observances'. You were given a book, and every day you were supposed to study them, and write down in the book any you had broken.

He mentions the penances imposed for two such infractions:

If you broke Simple Silence, you recited five Psalms. Solemn Silence – the whole Psalter – in your recreation time too![321]

but claimed to have forgotten the 'trivial' and 'ridiculous' penalties awarded for other breaches of the rules. Fr Alston recalled them without difficulty:

The penance for looking at seculars was to sit in the middle of the choir at the next office, blindfolded and facing the outer church; and for speaking to a secular to wear visibly some article of secular clothing for three days. I remember one brother performing this penance by wearing an ordinary high silk hat in addition to his habit, and another going about with a secular collar and coloured necktie!

He also remembered having had on one occasion to spend the duration of the *Magnificat* at Vespers kneeling in church with a piece of meat on a fork in one hand and an open copy of the Rule in the other; this was for having served to the community some meat left over after the departure of a group of visitors. However, he had the last laugh:

I may add that Fr Ignatius had to sing most of the Magnificat that evening as a solo.

---

[321] FMTB p35

BROTHER DUNSTAN RETURNS TO THE WORLD

After his life profession in August 1874 Dunstan/Thomas (Bray) survived Llanthony for a further five years. In July 1877 it fell to him to break the news to Ignatius of his mother's death. Later he published an emotional account of his bereavement, which included the following:

> At 6.30 in the morning a brother [identified elsewhere in the same publication as Dunstan] came to my cell, and breaking the solemn silence, asked me if he could get me anything, and he looked very strangely at me. But I thought this was probably because I looked as ill as I felt. I replied 'Yes, I should like some milk.' This he brought me and when I had drank [sic] it he said, 'Dear Father, can you bear to hear some bad news?' I replied, 'Yes, I think I can bear anything.' He said at once, 'Dear Father, our Lord has taken Mrs Lyne.'[322]

In June 1879 Dunstan was alone at Llanthony for several weeks – probably not for the first time. Finding the solitude hard to bear he escaped to London, thereby leaving the monastery with no-one to keep up the recitation of the offices. Once in the capital he found his way to 'Mr Nugée's Priory' in Walworth, where Ignatius reports that he 'acted most disgracefully'. He certainly seems to have found it difficult to decide what to do next. While in Walworth he 'engaged himself to be Married to a girl', but returned to Llanthony before the end of July. The Superior, knowing 'nothing of the engagement' once more 'left him here trusting him', but 'he carried on his love affair from these very walls: deceived me thoroughly, ruined all the Monastery by his evil example while I was away begging'. Finally he 'went off before my return, turned protestant and Romanist in one fortnight. Then Married, Easter 1880, has been miserable ever since. Still writes to me.'

---

[322] MT June 1885

Bray's marriage to Susannah (or Susan) Downing, daughter of a local cab driver, took place on 18 April 1880 in the Southwark registration district; he gave his Christian names as Thomas Dunstan. They are listed at various London addresses (together with their only child Thomas Dunstan Leycester, born 1885) in all the censuses from the following four decades, with Thomas senior employed initially as a clerk and later as a commercial traveller. If after leaving Llanthony the former Brother Dunstan 'turned Romanist' he did not remain one: a letter of 1969 from Dom Anselm Hughes of Nashdom Abbey to Douglas Lyne includes the mention that 'Thomas Bray used to serve my Mass at Walworth in 1913.'[323]

Sister Mary Agnes mentions a brother who was

> a life-vowed monk, though only about twenty-one years of age. He ran away and came back so may times, that at last he said, 'To prevent myself from ever returning, I shall get married,' which he fulfilled by marrying an opera girl. I was told afterwards he became a billiard-marker.[324]

Very likely this was Bray, who could easily have worked as a 'billiard-marker' before becoming established as a clerk; Susannah may well have been an 'opera girl' (perhaps what would later be known as a 'chorus girl'; the term 'ballet girl' had similar connotations) when they met.

ONE BOY COMES AND ANOTHER GOES

THE PERSON WHO would take over Dunstan's role as Ignatius's personal attendant – and business manager, farm bailiff and much else – arrived at the monastery in 1876. William Pritchard, then

---

[323] Letter in Abergavenny collection, ref A1993.139.11.10). Fr Hughes was then curate of St Peter's, Walworth.

[324] NL p82

aged eleven,[325] was the third son of David and Elizabeth Pritchard (Ignatius has her name as Ann) of Ty'r-ywen or Tyrewen, a farm on the other side of the valley, a little over a mile away in the direction of old Llanthony. In later censuses he had no hesitation in giving Llanthony as his place of birth, although the account he wrote of his life with Ignatius[326] conveys the impression that he was unfamiliar with the area before he entered the monastery, and he claims not to have seen a monk's habit before that time.

The boy is said to have been adopted by Ignatius, although only in adult life (in February 1892, two months before his marriage) would he change his name to William Leycester Lyne. He tells us that he lived as one of the 'monastery boys' but with special duties and privileges: these included ('while still a boy') the task of accompanying the Abbot on missions.

When he was 'old enough to take responsibility' his 'secular dress was replaced by [the] monastic habit', although he did not shave his head (this is borne out by contemporary photographs, including the cover picture). The floral wreath with which Brother David was crowned on his clothing was preserved, although no record of the event was made in the Monastic Register.[327]

The position of young William (or 'Child David', as he was called by Ignatius) would always be ambiguous. As a 'monastery boy' and later as a novice he claims to have been subject to the same discipline and timetable as his fellows, but also that he spent much of his time with the Abbot in his cell, from 7.0am when

---

[325] Born 23 April 1865.

[326] Compiled in the 1930s, and with a heavy bias in favour of Ignatius and against those he perceived as opposed to him and his memory. It was an important source for Arthur Calder-Marshall in his research for The Enthusiast.

[327] Brother David says his first habit was given 'by the sister of Admiral Sturdee' (Frederick Charles Doveton Sturdee 1859-1925, victor of the Battle of the Falkland Islands in 1914); this would have been the future Admiral's younger sister Annie, born 1856.

he brought him his early morning tea[328] (of which some was left in the bottom of the cup for his own consumption) until late at night, when like Placidus and Dunstan/Thomas before him he had the job of massaging the insomniac Superior's hands. He also mentions having had a room of his own near that of Ignatius, and having accompanied him on afternoon walks and pastoral calls in the locality as well as on journeys around the country. The 1881 census suggests that the ambiguity didn't stop there, although this was taken the year before he assumed the habit: he appears not at the monastery (or travelling with Ignatius, who was on that occasion listed not only at Llanthony but in lodgings at 6 The Paragon, Bath), but at home with his family, occupation 'farmer's son'. He had probably been at Ty'r-ywen the preceding August and September, as in his narrative he admits to having been away from the monastery at the time of the Apparitions, and appears hazy about some of the details.

WE LAST ENCOUNTERED the Infant Oblate on Ascension Day 1872, when he was to have acted the part of John the Baptist, leading a tame lamb to represent the Lamb of God. The lamb quickly grew into a large and aggressive ram, and the 'angelic child' would soon become a far from angelic adolescent. Nothing comparable to Brother Cuthbert's account has come to light to give us an insight into that stage of his life, but not much imagination is required to appreciate what lay behind the note added to his Register entry in June 1876:

> Brother Ignatius at fourteen no vocation I have apprenticed him to sea.[329]

---

[328] So the Abbot stayed away from Prime as well as from the night office.

[329] For details of the former oblate's subsequent career the reader is directed to Appendix 2.

MORE NOVICES

AFTER AN APPARENT FOUR-YEAR LULL, the years 1878 to 1881 saw a revival in the supply of monastic aspirants. The Register lists thirteen admissions in this period, after which there is another gap, also of four years. The new entrants were:

- Harry Frayton Fuller[330] (Brother Oswald), clothed as a novice on 3 March 1878. No other details are given, but he must have left before the clothing of the next Oswald the following year. An unattributable press cutting from 1878 reports that he acted as Thurifer at the Sarum rite midnight Mass at Easter that year.

- Alfred I. Rose (Brother Gregory), who was Oswald's junior in the noviciate by nine days. Nothing more is recorded about him in the Register – not even his age. Census records show one person of this name (born Warwickshire c1851) who would have been 27 at this time and another (born Middlesex c1864) who would have been fourteen. As he is reported to have acted as Subdeacon on the occasion mentioned above the first is the more likely candidate.

- Robert Lewin Howorth, admitted as a postulant on 24 April 1878 and as a novice (Brother Aelred) on 21 May. He was in priest's orders; details of his brief monastic career will be found in the following chapter, among the other 'abbey priests'.

- The next Brother Oswald – 'of the Crown of Thorns' – (Thomas Ebenezer Fairchild) was received as a postulant on 22 June 1879,

---

[330] Probably 'Frayton H. Fuller' whose birth is recorded in the first quarter of 1859 in the Ticehurst district; in the 1861 and 1871 censuses he is listed at home in Frant where his father Richard was a grocer and ironmonger. In 1891 he appears as a gardener with a wife and daughter living at Melbourne Place, Eastbourne.

a few weeks before the date he gave as his eighteenth birthday (29 July). He was clothed as a novice on 7 July, but according to the Register 'ran away in November from the shameful conduct of Father Dunstan [Bray] & others, while I was away'. Life 'in the world' failed to satisfy him, however; in May 1883 he returned, and if he is the same Brother Oswald mentioned in two issues of the Monastic Times[331] he stayed at least two years – maybe longer.[332]

• Meanwhile a new Brother Cuthbert (William Benjamin Chenoweth) had become a postulant on 28 April 1878, when he was also baptised, having been brought up a Baptist. Soon afterwards he 'went away ill', but after returning in August 1879 he was clothed as a novice on the 31st of that month. In December Ignatius tells us he expelled him 'for most terrible conduct – during my absence. He was a very bad person.' Later he 'came back from America to beg my forgiveness & to be received again, I refused his petition but freely forgave him.' This young man (born Newton Abbot on 30 November 1859, so eighteen on entry) appears to have returned to the USA, where he figures in several later censuses.

---

[331] September 1884 and March 1885.

[332] The birth of a 'Tom Ebenezer Fairchild' was registered in the South Stoneham district (Southampton) in the third quarter of 1863, making him – if they were one and the same person – not quite 16 rather than not quite 18 at the beginning of his postulancy. His father (also Ebenezer) was a sailor and not often at home; his occupation probably accounts for the family's move to the Liverpool area, where in the 1881 census (during the interval between his two spells at Llanthony) he was working as clerk to a Brazilian merchant. In 1891 and 1901 (now 37) he was still at home and still unmarried, and had been promoted to Book Keeper & Cashier. His daughter Mrs Annetta Reed was living in Southampton in June 1969: see letter in Museum file A1993.139.11.13. The dates she gives for her father's sojourn (1898-1904) are twenty years out, but her observation that he was often left in charge of the monastery during the Abbot's absences have a strong ring of truth.

- The next Brother Aelred (Henry Louis Frederick Daniel Wake), who was sixteen when he arrived in the summer of 1879: postulant 7 August; novice (with Cuthbert Chenoweth) 31 August. In December he 'ran away... after robbing my [Ignatius's] money box & smashing open a cupboard & breaking in at the window of [the] clothes cell' – perhaps understandably, if he was to find his train fare home and less eye-catching apparel for the journey.[333]

- Just before Wake's departure – on 25 November 1879 – Ignatius admitted 20-year-old William Moorhead Magrath. He was clothed as a novice the following St David's Day (1 March 1880), becoming the latest Brother Dunstan. Socially he was of a superior rank to many of those who had so far tried their vocations, coming from an Anglo-Scottish (and Presbyterian) family with medical and military connections in British India.[334] When William was a boy they had settled in Bath, where they seem to have moved in the evangelical circles prevalent in that city, and where he had first become acquainted with Ignatius at the age of twelve.[335] This Dunstan would be the recipient of the first of the Apparitions on 30 August 1880, which are discussed in a later chapter. By that time he was (apart from the Superior) the only occupant of the monastery who could

---

[333] Once on the train this would have been straightforward, as his family lived not far from the GWR terminus at Paddington. His father (also Henry) was a tutor, specialising in Classics and Mathematics; his mother (Louisa, with a brother named Louis) had been born in the Swiss canton of Vaud. In the 1881 census young Henry is living with his parents, employed like his father as a tutor.

[334] He and his five siblings had all been born there, and Magrath Road is still one of the principal thoroughfares in the city of Madras.

[335] Magrath's testimony as reported in accounts of his address at Ignatius's funeral. His introduction to the Superior would have been in or around 1871, when the latter spent several weeks in Bath, accompanied by Brother Cuthbert/John Spence (see above, Chapter 6).

reasonably be described as a monk,[336] a situation unchanged when the census came to be taken the following April. Some time after the Apparitions his health broke down; according to the Register he 'ran away, came back four times at last sent away', although no dates are given for these events. His failure to make the monastic grade didn't interrupt his association with Llanthony and its Abbot, to which we will return.

Two other novices were clothed with Magrath on St David's Day 1880:

- A priest named John William Compton (Brother Aidan), whose brief stay is described with the other 'abbey priests' in the next chapter.

- Clifford Underwood (another Brother Aelred), who was 26 and had arrived in early January. According to the Register he 'had to leave for very gross conduct' and was '[n]ot a moral person'.[337]

In the following year the first new entrant was

- William James Walker King (Brother Austin), who was admitted as a postulant on 17 May and clothed as a novice (with three others; see below) on 23 October. After an unusually long postulancy his noviciate turned out to be very short: 'Ran away

---

[336] This is confirmed by Sister Mary Agnes (Jane Povey), NL p171.

[337] A person of this name was born in Lexden (near Colchester) in the first quarter of 1854 and died in Thanet in the third quarter of 1909. He appears in censuses as follows: 1861 aged 7 in Brightlingsea, second of four children of John (oyster merchant) & Fanny Underwood. 1871 aged 17, boarding at an address in Harwich; occupation Clerk. 1881 aged 27 c/o his brother Ernest in Highbury: Merchant's Clerk. 1891 aged 37 again c/o Ernest, now in Greenwich: Colonial Merchant. 1901 aged 47 in same household: Australian Merchant. (He is listed as single in all entries.)

a month after [November 1881], because he said he could not face me on my return from Brighton on account of a sin he could not confess to me. Conceit & deceit were very strong in him.'[338]

• Between the departure and return of Brother Oswald (Fairchild) yet another entrant was given this name, eighteen-year-old Henry Carlyle Fairbairn ('Oswald Mary'), admitted as a postulant on 17 May 1881 and as a novice at the clothing on 23 October. In February 1883 he was 'sent away...for violence & temper, deceit & falsehood' – just in time for his predecessor as Brother Oswald (and near namesake) to resume his former identity.[339]

The 1881 intake was completed by two young boys:

• William George Whyley (George William, according to public records), who was given the name Maurus. The Register tells us he had been received at the Slapton convent (for which see Chapter 8) in December 1878 at the age of nine; he seems to have been a relation of Sister Mary Etheldreda (Agnes Huthwaite). His arrival at Llanthony on 14 September 1880 is mentioned in Chapter 9. He was clothed as a novice with the rest of this group on 23 October 1881; in the census earlier that year he had

---

[338] King's birth was recorded at St Germans in the first quarter of 1863; the Register has 'Walta' for 'Walker'. What seems to be his only appearance in a UK census was in 1871, when at age eight he was listed with his parents William W. (a Greenwich Pensioner aged 36) and Elizabeth in the Cornish village of Antony.

[339] An appeal for choirboys in MT December 1883 directs enquirers to 'Bro Oswald Mary', but this could have been a slip of the pen for 'Oswald of the Crown of Thorns'. In the 1881 census (just before his entry to the community) he is listed as an unemployed hotel porter staying at a household in Liverpool, and in 1891 as a bookbinder's clerk living with his widowed mother and sisters in Wandsworth. His death was registered in Lambeth in the first quarter of 1924, aged 50.

been listed at Llanthony as a 'choirboy'. Two years after that he was 'sent away'.[340]

• Enoch Holmes, who also figures in the 1881 census as a choirboy, and in the Register (as Brother Placidus) among those clothed on 23 October. As with the previous bearers of these names Ignatius obviously had hopes that these two child-monks would turn out to emulate their patrons, youthful followers of St Benedict, but in this case as in the others he was to be disappointed. The Register says he '[l]eft because he felt the rule too hard & he wished to go. He was a good honest boy, but was too severely treated by the brothers over him. He left when I took him to his parents at Sheffield April 1883.'[341]

WE KNOW FROM THEIR APPEARANCE in accounts of the Apparitions that there were two other young men at the monastery in the autumn of 1880 – an associate named George Swaine, who although referred to as 'Brother' was probably only a visitor, and Charles Rouse, who became a postulant on 20 September. He had arrived just six days earlier, and was reported in the Hereford Times of 18 September to be 'visiting the Abbey with the view of eventually becoming a

---

[340] On 4 June 1883; no reason given. The birth of William George Whyley was registered at Little Gonerby, near Grantham, in the first quarter of 1871, but in that year's census he is listed as aged two, the fifth child of Mary W. Whyley, a widow of that parish. This latter dating agrees with his entry in subsequent censuses, which list him successively as a basket maker and teacher of basket making – in 1891 as an unmarried lodger in Nottingham, and in 1901 and 1911 as a married householder in Birmingham, where he died aged 70 in the second quarter of 1939.

[341] Enoch Holmes was born in Sheffield in the summer of 1870, the fifth child of another Enoch (engine driver) and his wife Sarah Anne. In the 1871 census he is listed with his parents in the Brightside area of that city aged nine months; in 1901 aged 30 and single with his recently widowed mother and younger brother in Ecclesfield (occupation Rate Collector). By 1911 he had acquired a wife named Gertrude (they married in c1904) and had been promoted to Assistant Overseer in the same department; he died in late 1945 at Chapel-en-le-Frith.

Monk'. In the following week's issue (which described him as a 'lay deacon'; perhaps 'lay reader' was meant) we are given an account of his reception, which took place before First Vespers of St Matthew's Day and in the Ignatian use included a responsory drawn from the Song of Songs:

> Decani: 'Who is this?'
> Cantoris: 'Who is this?'
> Decani: 'Who is this?'
> Full: 'That cometh up from the wilderness, leaning upon her Beloved?'
> 'This is one who hath heard a voice upon the mountains saying unto him, Arise and come away!'

No record of Rouse's admission is given in the Register, but he seems to have survived at least until 25 December, when a letter from him (signed 'Brother Charles OSB') appeared in the *Hereford Times*.

CHAPTER 8

NUNS, PRIESTS &
MONASTERY BOYS

I N THE SUMMER OF 1868 Ignatius made a second attempt –
successful, this time – at establishing a convent of nuns. Its
chief work (when they settled at Llanthony, if not before) would
like that of the monks be 'perpetual adoration' of the sacramental
Presence, with the sisters taking turns of an hour at a time at the
watch. For this they would wear a 'large, flowing crimson veil' over
the ordinary black veil (or white veil, in the case of novices). This
colourful feature would not be visible to outsiders, however, as
the nuns were to be strictly enclosed. Ignatius took out a twenty-
one-year lease on a seventeenth-century farmhouse with suitably
discreet garden at Feltham, four miles across then rural Middlesex
from Laleham. As Prioress he appointed Harriet Emily Stewart, a
doctor's daughter from Plymouth, with whom he may have become
acquainted during his curacy there.[342]

Eight years his senior, Miss Stewart also had rather more
experience of the religious life. In Plymouth she had become
involved with Miss Sellon's sisterhood at the time of the 1849
cholera outbreak, and as an associate member was known as 'Sister
Ella'. In the 1861 census she is listed as one of the six 'Sisters of
Charity' residing at the linked establishment in Osnaburgh Street,
in the crowded quarter immediately east of Regent's Park. The
following year she transferred to Dr Neale's sisterhood at East

---

[342] Information from BUWP p89 and p92n, and from the *Church Times/
Norfolk Chronicle* report cited below

Grinstead, but in August 1866 returned to Osnaburgh Street, where she remained until receiving her call to Feltham.[343]

Anson describes her inauguration thus:

One day[344]...Sister Ella travelled from Waterloo to Staines, whence she either walked or was driven to Laleham. Having cast off the blue habit of Abbess Lydia's Sisters of Charity, she was clothed by Fr Ignatius with the black Benedictine tunic, veil, scapular, knotted cord girdle, rosary and sandals. He gave her the religious name of Hilda, because she was to be the superioress of the female section of the first Benedictine double-community established in Britain since Anglo-Saxon times.[345]

A few weeks later the Church Times printed an account of the clothing of a novice,[346] in the course of which it was mentioned that another member of the new community had already been professed (by taking the 'black veil'). The only female entries in the Professions Register are the very few dating from the 1890s, so the identity of these aspirants remains unknown and our account of who came and went must necessarily be very sketchy. We do, however, have the census record of the household at 2 High Street, Feltham, as it was three years after its inception, in April 1871. (Middle names and names in religion have been added where known.)

---

[343] Biographical information from T.J. Williams, op cit

[344] The website of the present-day successor community dates the foundation to 24 June. See http://www.curzonpark.org.uk/curzon02. htm (retrieved 10 December 2013).

[345] BUWP p87

[346] Reprinted in the Norfolk Chronicle of 12 September

Harriet Emily Stewart (Hilda)	42	b. Plymouth
Emma Rosina (or Rosanna) Beaumont (Dorothea)	31	b. Spitalfields
Florence Stanbridge (Werburgh)	20	b. Camden Town
Jane Mercy Povey (Mary Agnes)	18	b. City of London
Edith May Stanbridge	16	b. Bayswater
Elizabeth Orchard (later professed as Ursula)	21	b. Porthleven
Marianne Ling	36	b. Norwich
Rose L. Dick	26	b. Norwich
Agnes Olivia Donston Huthwaite (Etheldreda)	42	b. Leyton, Essex

All are listed as unmarried, and with two exceptions described as 'Nunns' [sic]. Elizabeth Orchard's occupation is given as General Servant (a few years later she would be promoted to 'sewing sister'); Agnes Huthwaite's as Associate Sister.

Some information about herself and others may be gleaned from Jane Povey/Sister Mary Agnes's *Nunnery Life in the Church of England, or Seventeen Years with Father Ignatius*, published in 1890, five years after her final departure from the community. Some of the dates in her record are inaccurate, and her polemical agenda seems sometimes to lead her to exaggerate less congenial features of community life. She came from a working class family in Cripplegate,[347] and recalls first

---

[347] The 1861 census listed the family under the name 'Pavey'. The father George was a cloth worker, and Jane the middle of three sisters; there was also a 2-year-old boy called Albert, who like the rest of the family

meeting the 'Feltham mother' at a Third Order meeting in Hunter Street 'early in 1868' (before the Feltham convent's foundation, but the future Mother Hilda may have been visiting from Osnaburgh Street). Having been 'mesmerised' by Ignatius and his teachings she went to Feltham for a trial visit in November 1868, when she thought she had been only fifteen.[348] As a result of moral pressure from Ignatius and Hilda and her own infatuation the visit led inexorably to her reception as a postulant the following February, and to her clothing as a novice three months later. By rights she should in due course have advanced from the noviciate to temporary profession, and thereafter if her vocation seemed secure to life vows, but because of her immaturity she was allowed to fall into the role of 'convent baby', a state of affairs which persisted until she was well into her thirties.

Admitted to the noviciate on the same occasion was Florence Stanbridge, Mary Agnes's senior by about a year. The two Stanbridge sisters came from a comfortable middle class family (their father gave his occupation in the census as 'merchant'); Edith probably arrived at Feltham rather later.

Marianne (or Marian) Ling and her brother Charles had been Third Order members in their native Norwich, where their father was a tailor and robemaker; it isn't known how long she stayed at Feltham. In the 1881 census she was listed as governess to a family in Putney, after which she moved to a modest address in Littlehampton, where she kept a shop selling sweets and toys. She died in 1904.

Rose Dick's birthplace is also given as Norwich, almost certainly erroneously; her census entries in 1901 and 1911 say she was born

---

reappeared as 'Povey' in later censuses.

[348] The Abergavenny collection has a copy of *Nunnery Life* annotated by the author (A1993.139.6.22), in which she amended this to fourteen (p 21). In fact her birth having been registered in the third quarter of 1852 she was at this time just sixteen, which would agree with her age as given in the 1871 census.

in Mauritius. By that time she was living in Sutherland Avenue, Paddington, with her slightly older brother; she died in 1917.[349]

Agnes Huthwaite belonged to an old Nottinghamshire family owning property near Worksop. She had been a member of the short-lived 'Oblates of Mount Calvary' in Norwich, and on joining the Feltham convent at its foundation was made Sub-Prioress,[350] although only an associate sister. Her obituary alludes to her popularity among the 'mountain people' at Llanthony, and the ease with which she conversed with French and German visitors in their own languages.[351]

Some time in the 1870s Georgina (or Georgiana) Martha Smith entered the community, taking the name Cecilia. She was born in November 1834 in Bedford, where her father was a shoemaker. After his death she and her mother went to live with two of her elder sisters who operated a small private school in Grantham, where in due course she became an assistant teacher. Later she moved to Hove, where she opened a similar establishment at 38 Brunswick Road. She was an accomplished keyboard player (hence her choice of patron), but a childhood accident had left her a cripple. At Llanthony she acted as organist, and contributed a couple of items to the little collection of *Hymn Tunes of St David's Monastery* published in 1890, as well as harmonies to those composed by Ignatius. Her family belonged to the Moravians, in which denomination her brother

---

[349] There is an undated letter in Abergavenny (A2005.186.2) from 'M. Benedetta OSB' to 'Revd & dear Mother'. The writer is evidently acting as companion to a 'Sister Mary' who lives not far from Mr and Miss Dick at 15 Chichester Road, Paddington – a house shown in the censuses to have been divided among several sets of short-term occupants, so it isn't possible to establish her identity. Sister Mary requires visits from a nurse but is able to attend church on weekdays at 7.0am, and is probably an Ignatian Tertiary. The previous day they had had two visitors: 'Mrs Mansfield, Sister Paula that was [another former novice?], and Miss Dick, the former having spent the day with the Dicks'.

[350] BUWP p87

[351] *Hereford Times*, 27 February 1886

was a minister;[352] Sister Mary Agnes alleges that she was never properly professed.[353]

An extern or associate named Sister Margaret 'attended to the Monks' clothes'. It was she who measured John Spence for his habit when in December 1871 he passed through Feltham *en route* for Llanthony.

Ignatius insisted on exercising personal control of the sisterhood, and would frequently descend on the convent, often staying overnight. Although Mary Agnes tells us he 'did not have very much to do with us there' it was enough to upset the smooth running of the establishment – one gets the impression that Mother Hilda had to draw on all her reserves of diplomacy to keep the household running on an even keel:

> The Mother, I think, used to let him know that she did not consider it a man's place to govern a number of women as entirely as he wished to do. Besides, he sometimes gave orders which she thought very indiscreet, from which great scandal might arise; and, being somewhat older than Father Ignatius, she took the liberty of representing to him, rather strongly, her views about his orders and doings. At times he would suddenly give orders...which would put the household arrangements out for the whole day, though he seemed to be in a great state of consternation when matters did not go forward smoothly in consequence of his orders. Sometimes, before breakfast, he would order that no one, not even the reverend Mother, should speak for a whole day, thus causing the utmost confusion, especially among the servants in the kitchen, who were included in the eccentric command. And yet if his own dinner was not properly cooked and served in time, he would show great displeasure.[354]

---

[352] MSO p421

[353] NL p65

[354] NL pp57f. There were also tensions between the individual sisters. A

SCHISM

AFTER TEN YEARS in this uneasy relationship Ignatius and Hilda finally parted company. According to Sister Mary Agnes matters came to a head when he

> boldly asserted that he was quite determined to have nothing but unconditional obedience. The Mother, and the majority of the nuns in the Feltham convent, refused to accept such an unconditional obedience, and so Father Ignatius said to those who refused: 'You no longer belong to the order of the Monk Ignatius of Llanthony in the nineteenth century.'[355]

Only four of them signed the declaration the Abbot imposed on his female subjects: Mothers Werburgh (Stanbridge) and Cecilia (Smith), and Sisters Mary Agnes (Povey) and Mary Etheldreda (Huthwaite). Having solemnly 'excommunicated' the rebellious majority, he installed the four loyalists in a rented house at Slapton, near Dartmouth. Appropriately it was named The Chantry, having been built on the site of a mediaeval college of clergy, fragments of which had been incorporated in the building.

The Baroness emphasises the speed with which it had been found and furnished – all within five days, at the end of which Ignatius met the sisters off the River Dart ferry and accompanied them to their new home, where food and freshly-made beds awaited them.[356] This suggests he may already have had contacts in the area. The local

---

pencilled note in an early copy of *Nunnery Life* recounts the experience of a friend of the book's owner, who had been there to stay for a few days' peace and quiet. In fact this was hard to find, as the sisters were said to have 'quarrelled like cats'.

[355] ibid p60. 1878 seems to have been an *annus horribilis* for Ignatius; it also marked the beginning of ten years of very public conflict with his ageing and increasingly cantankerous father, mad with grief since the death of his wife the previous summer.

[356] Bertouch pp540f

incumbent (the Reverend Richard Antram) appears to have been sympathetic, engaging the Abbot as locum tenens in his parish for two Sundays in September 1880 and celebrating a 'mass of thanksgiving' when Mother Cecilia was healed after applying a leaf from the 'holy bush';[357] perhaps they were already acquainted.[358]

We learn that in the Slapton convent Sister Mary Agnes was housekeeper, Mother Werburgh sacristan and Mother Cecilia 'scribe'; Sister Etheldreda's role wasn't specified. Mother Werburgh was (under Ignatius) in overall charge – a surprising appointment in view of the revelation in Nunnery Life that having broken her vows she spent six years 'in the world', marrying and having a baby. Mary Agnes reports that it was only after the deaths of both husband and child that she came back to the convent, only a short time before the split.[359] Perhaps she was the only one capable of taking responsibility.

In addition to its original four occupants, the 1881 census return for the convent lists the following:

Agnes Goodwin	27	b. Kentish Town
Maria Bough	64	b. Overton (Salop)
Ann Easley	59	b. London
Alfred Flook	10	b. Brighton.

---

[357] See Chapter 9

[358] Antram (1804-87) was Perpetual Curate of Slapton 1850-1884; his early years in the parish were clouded by financial and other troubles. To avoid arrest by County Court officials he locked himself into his house for several months, emerging only on Sundays, when they would not be working. His consequent failure to perform his proper duties resulted in three months' suspension by the Bishop of Exeter (Morning Chronicle, 4 November 1851). The following year the authorities succeeded in apprehending him, and he was tried and imprisoned for debt (Western Times, 10 April and 3 July 1852; Exeter & Plymouth Gazette 24 July 1852).

[359] NL pp60f. I can find no record of her alleged marriage. In the census returns of 1881-1901 inclusive she is listed under the name Stanbridge and her marital status given as single (but see below).

Agnes Goodwin and her younger brother Edgar had been orphaned some years earlier, and while he was a child she fed and clothed him out of her meagre earnings as a dressmaker; in 1871 they were listed as living in crowded conditions in one of the then mean streets off Bryanston Square. Soon after her arrival at the convent she felt she had done wrong to leave her brother on his own (he was then aged 19 or 20), and was given permission by Mother Werburgh to go back to London.[360] When Ignatius heard of this he wrote calling her a 'spiritual adulteress' and ordering her return, upon which for six weeks she was made to attend the choir offices sitting on the floor with a black mask over her face.[361]

Two years later (now at Llanthony) the dramatic ceremony of her life profession (as Mother Ermenild of the Sacred Heart) was reported in the *Hereford Times*. When she had had her hair cut off and been clothed in cowl and veil she took her vows and was given Communion from the tabernacle, after which

[a] stream of monks, nuns, sisters, acolytes, and layfolk from the congregation prostrated themselves before the newly-wedded Bride of Christ, kissing the border of her garment, while she placed her hands very lovingly on their lowered heads.

She was then laid on a bier, and covered with the thick black funeral pall borne into the 'Living Tomb' of the monastic enclosure.[362]

---

[360] He soon found a new life as a grocer's assistant in Ewell (1881 census).

[361] NL pp70ff

[362] At the time of writing the 1882 volume of the newspaper was not available, but the report is extensively quoted in BUWP pp117f. The combined population of convent and monastery would then have been at most fourteen or fifteen including children; perhaps the local 'layfolk' turned up in sufficient numbers to swell this trickle into a 'stream'. Sister Mary Agnes also gives a description of the ceremony (NL p71ff), and Mother Ermenild's confession to her that like her return from London her profession had been made under duress.

Maria Bough may have been an associate; as previously noted, Spence mentions a 'Sister Maria' as Sister Winifred's travelling companion on her visit to Llanthony in 1872. As for Winifred herself (Ann Easley), we know from the reference to her having been 'a Sister in our Order for over a quarter of a century'[363] that she was in the habit of spending 'half the year at Llanthony from April to November'; quite likely she had done the same at (Feltham and) Slapton before the nuns migrated to Wales.

Alfred Flook wasn't the first small boy to find a billet with the Slapton nuns.[364] He came from Brighton, where his coachbuilder father had died when he was five. Later his mother would marry a cab proprietor in Hove named Benham, who would provide employment for another of her sons and Alfred himself. He died there in 1955, having married in 1897 and produced at least two children of his own.

The Llanthony-published *Benedictine Calendar* for 1881 reported that Ermenild Goodwin's admission to (first?) vows had taken place the previous May:

> The Abbot spent Whitsuntide at the Priory, at Slapton, where the services were of a very joyous kind. The Senior Mother was solemnly appointed Prioress of the House and the Mistress of the Novices was also installed in her office. Sister Ermenild and Sister Faith were admitted to the vows. The Chaplain of the Priory said the Mass. The Priory seems to have become part and parcel of the village of Slapton.

It is interesting to note that although Mother Werburgh had been 'Senior Mother' since the move to Slapton it was only some eighteen months later that she was appointed Prioress; the wording suggests that Mother Cecilia, too, had been acting as novice mistress (i.e. as Mary

---

[363] LMN July-Sept 1894, article on 'The Monastery'

[364] William George Whyley had been there until the previous September: see Chapters 7 and 9.

Agnes's immediate superior) for some time before being confirmed in her post. The 'Chaplain of the Priory' would have been Mr Antram, who seems to have celebrated Mass in the convent as a regular thing.[365] With their strict rules on enclosure only Sister Etheldreda would have been seen outside the convent, so the comment about their being 'part and parcel of the village of Slapton' is probably based on their relationship with its incumbent (and maybe a few favoured visiting neighbours) rather than any involvement by them in life beyond their walls.

The identity of Sister Faith is unknown, but her unhappy experience in the noviciate is related by Sister Mary Agnes.[366] Having both money and portable possessions she was first required to part with her valuable gold watch, which she was 'content to give up for the time being'. Mother Werburgh then saw in her box 'some things she wanted for use in the convent', but having not yet committed herself to the community for life Sister Faith did not wish to put them into general circulation. Her lack of co-operation in this matter 'drew upon herself...displeasure and censure', which increased when she refused to hand over her money to fund the construction of a new cloister at Llanthony (this would have been the south cloister, completed in 1883), and led to her being 'packed off from Slapton as having no vocation'.[367]

Another inmate was a 'poor old woman' from Herefordshire who had sold her house in order to enter the convent, but had difficulty

---

[365] A letter from Ignatius to his sister Harriet dated 14 May 1879 (typed copy in Fr Ignatius collection; in file ref A2010.86.18) refers to the arrangements for Ascension Day the following week. 'The Vicar will celebrate in Convent Chapel at 8, at Church at 11. High Mass in Convent Chapel at 11, also at 7.' The 'High Mass' would probably have been Ante-Communion with exposition of the reserved Sacrament with Ignatius himself presiding, and the evening service Vespers from the monastic breviary.

[366] NL pp76ff

[367] A 'Dame Faith' of the community which settled at Milford Haven in 1911 (see below) died soon afterwards and was buried on Caldey Island (*Pax*, Spring 1919). She was said to have been 'connected' with Ignatius, so if Sister Faith of Slapton went on to join the Feltham convent they could conceivably have been one and the same individual.

learning nunlike deportment.[368] The strain of being continually corrected made her hysterical, and in the heat of the moment she seems to have lashed out at those around her. When she tried to run away she 'scandalized the nuns to the villagers', and because of her recently acquired reputation for violence the local policeman was called in. On Mother Werburgh's instructions he saw to it that she was 'conveyed away in the carrier's cart' and put on the train back to Hereford.

This 'old woman' (Mary Agnes says she was fifty; at the time she was in her late forties) was Janet Owens, for whom Ignatius then found a niche at Llanthony, where she would be one of the witnesses of the 1880 Apparitions. Before going to Slapton she been a teacher at the National School in Hay-on-Wye; in the earliest accounts of the phenomena she is referred to as a 'schoolmistress from Hay' rather than by name. Her father had been a doctor there, and she was born just over the Radnorshire border at Clyro.[369] Sister Mary Agnes describes her as 'certainly very eccentric and peculiar' and 'Fr Ignatius's devoted slave', although conceding that she 'had her good points'.[370] Either her eccentricity or her devotion to Ignatius might explain why she had previously been in the habit of walking from Hay to the monastery and back to perform her religious exercises before beginning her day's teaching – a feat comparable to that of

---

[368] ibid pp65ff

[369] In the 1881 census she was listed as an occupant of the monastery, described as 'housekeeper'. Her age was given as 43 and her birthplace as Hay. All other census entries confirm that she was in fact six or seven years older, and born in Clyro. In 1841 she was listed (as 'Jennett', aged 10) with her father David Price Owens (surgeon, aged 50), her mother Maria (30) and three siblings in Brook Street, Hay. In 1851 she was a 19-year-old 'house servant' at nearby Whitney Rectory, home of the Dew family, who two decades later would make frequent appearances in the pages of Kilvert's Diary. In 1861 and 1871 she was living with her widowed mother at addresses in Hay, aged respectively 29 and 39 and described as a schoolmistress. For the Apparitions see Chapter 9.

[370] NL p170. This is in the section of her book where she is discussing the Apparitions, and mentions Janet by name. The references to the anonymous 'poor old woman' describe her in very similar terms.

Kilvert a few years earlier, although even he didn't attempt the journey in the small hours of the morning, or all that often.

The information about Janet's early morning walk (could she *really* have done this, even only once or twice?) was given by an 'Abergavenny Correspondent' in the Hereford Times of 25 September 1880. The same writer mentions that she had passed 'some months' at Slapton, 'but left because the place did not agree with her health'. In later issues of the same paper there are suggestions that her physical health wasn't what was in question, and that she had 'had to be removed from Slapton in the interests of peace and personal comfort and...the safety of the inmates'. This significant detail emerged a few weeks later, when Ignatius and a low church antagonist named James Comley met head to head at a meeting in the Hereford Corn Exchange.[371]

Opposite the Slapton convent lived a large and rather bohemian family, the Wyatts.[372] One of the daughters, Lillie, was sixteen when the nuns arrived, and after seeing them walking peacefully in their

---

[371] Hereford Times 20 November 1880; the quotation is from Comley's reported words. Mention of her name provoked laughter in the audience, which led Ignatius to describe her in her defence as a 'good little body'. Comley wrote to the paper almost weekly around this time attacking Ignatius, his followers and the Apparitions. On the subject of Janet's alleged violence the 30 October issue had printed a letter in which Comley asked sarcastically whether her 'fluency of utterance was not incompatible with pugilistic fervency of action', and stated that she 'had...been an inmate at the Slapton "abode of love" before she so kindly showed one of the nuns a near cut over the banisters, and thus gained the promotion which landed her at Llanthony Abbey'. As this and the later reference to this incident seem to have gone unrefuted one must accept that there was some truth in the story.

[372] The children were named Minnie, Alphonso, Lillie, Alexandria, Percy, Conrad and Lotus; living with them was an elderly 'lunatic' named Charles Green. Their father John (whose occupation is given in the 1871 census as a 'general agent') died in June 1880 at the age of 44. Two years earlier he had been prosecuted by the local landowner for attempting to prove the right of residents to shoot wildfowl on the freshwater lagoon known as Slapton Ley, as on another occasion were Alexandria and their mother for fishing in the same waters (Western Times, 24 January 1878 and 8 May 1879).

garden and being invited to attend Sister Ermenild's profession (as a novice) she formed the notion that convent life must be 'heaven upon earth'. Her fantasies were rudely shattered when having followed the community to Llanthony she was 'given plenty of hard work...and taken no notice of', and took refuge in 'sighing and crying'. Sister Mary Agnes reported her unhappiness to Mother Werburgh, whose reaction was anything but sympathetic:

> Serve her right; she should not have pushed herself into a hornet's
> nest. If people will push themselves into a hornet's nest, they must
> expect to get stung.[373]

RELOCATION TO LLANTHONY

IGNATIUS'S ULTIMATE INTENTION had always been to bring the nuns to Llanthony. A site for the convent in the angle between the east cloister and the choir of the abbey church had already been levelled. There would have been room there for a permanent building on the same scale as the existing monastery, but money to build it would never be forthcoming. The Slapton house was taken for three years, at the end of which a single-storey structure of timber and corrugated iron was erected on the Llanthony site. This would be quite large enough for the loyal remnant and their few adherents, and was ready for them to move into in September 1881.

A few glimpses of life in the new convent are given in the *Monastic Times*. As a former dressmaker Dame Mary Ermenild (as she became after her final profession) was sufficiently neat-fingered to earn small sums for the community by selling 'Flowers from Llanthony,

---

[373] NL p106. Lest the reader be under the impression that the atmosphere of the Llanthony convent was uniquely bitchy or bullying, s/he is recommended to read Karen Armstrong's account of her seven years in a mainstream English Catholic community in the 1960s, *Through the Narrow Gate* (Macmillan 1981).

tastefully arranged on Cards' to their supporters, priced at a shilling per card (December 1883). The same issue reprints an account of a visit by 'Morien' of the *Western Mail*, who mentions the 'excellent tea' he had received from the 'kind hands' of Sister Etheldreda in the convent parlour. In June 1884 there were references to the 'puddings, broth, &c' supplied by the nuns to their needy neighbours, and to the 'black habits and long white veils' worn on Ash Wednesday by their resident pupils. These may have been Alice and Ada, the daughters (then aged respectively six and four) of a Hereford greengrocer named Frank Ulett, sent to live at the convent around this time.[374]

Picture 15: Nuns and/or Associate Sisters in the convent garden with 'Priory Girls'

That same number carried the first two 'Chapters from a Nun's Life', for the second instalment of which readers would have to wait a whole year. Although anonymous and presented as a work of fiction it was evidently the work the of Mother Cecilia, and its three surviving parts (the third appeared in the final issue of September 1885, with the tantalising but never-to-be-fulfilled promise at its

---

[374] Mr Ulett's little shop in Maylord Street was decidedly poky. Ignatius sometimes conducted services there for his local associates and supporters, causing the *Hereford Times* to describe it as 'the house of a gentleman resident in Hereford' and the room in which the service was held as 'an apartment fitted out as a domestic chapel' (issue of 30 October 1880). In the following week's paper (6 November) Ignatius's adversary James Comley pointed out that it was in fact 'a small greengrocer's cottage (eight feet wide) in a back street'.

foot 'To be continued') give a thinly disguised account of events from her first meeting with Ignatius (at one of his missions) to the eve of her entry into the convent. She seems mainly concerned with the reactions (predictable) of her family, friends and pupils to her impending change of career; like her real-life counterpart the central character is proprietress of a small girls' school in a fashionable watering place.

Between the first and second parts (in December 1884) she broke off her narrative to contribute (as Mother Cecilia) a sharply worded piece entitled 'Oh! how I should like to be a nun.' She reports that 'twice a year' – this would be in response to Ignatius's regular mission excursions – the monastery and convent are 'inundated' with letters from young men and women who want to join the community, but who have very little idea of the sacrifices involved. One or two get as far as being admitted as postulants, but almost always they fail to last even the six weeks officially devoted to this first step on the monastic ladder. Their romantic vision of a 'quiet, easy life, plenty of beautiful services, with music, and incense, and lovely vestments, and the Rev. Father Ignatius to preach' turns out to be very different from the hard reality, where they have to 'scrub floors, and clean candlesticks and such things'. She alludes to the particular case of a (recent?) female aspirant:

> Now this young lady evidently expected to be made much of by the Right Rev. Father and by the Nuns, for giving up her home, where by her own account, she had had very little happiness; to come into the Convent to find love, peace, quiet and uninterrupted service of and for God. She was terribly disappointed to find how real and self-denying the true Nun must be. Moreover, she had a chatty tongue, and the 'silence' tried her, although she was not allowed to keep this rule in its strictness. But to use her own words 'It was dreadful to see everyone going about their respective works and duties without talking.'

In the issue of December 1883 Ignatius reported that a young lady, the daughter of a clergyman, was considering entering the convent. We don't know whether she actually arrived (the date would fit the case just mentioned), but the fact that he draws attention to even a possible admission suggests it was a fairly rare event. Five nuns moved from Slapton to Llanthony in September 1881, of whom one (Mary Agnes) left and another (Etheldreda) died. When Henry George Alston arrived at the monastery in September 1887 the three survivors of this group (Werburgh, Cecilia and Ermenild) were the only nuns in residence,[375] and it was these same three who would finally give up the struggle four years later during Ignatius's absence in America.

A decade earlier John Spence had noted that both Sister Winifred (Ann Easley) and Mother Hilda were in love with Ignatius; it seems that in their different ways so too were both Werburgh and Mary Agnes. No doubt it was the resultant jealousy and frustration that were responsible for poisoning the atmosphere, and in particular why Mother Werburgh lost no opportunity to humiliate 'little' Sister Mary Agnes.

Three years after the move to Llanthony Mary Agnes could bear convent life no longer and decided to leave, going first for some months to her family, and then for a few more to Feltham. Here the absence of regular humiliations made her doubt the authenticity of Mother Hilda's regime, so in August 1885 she returned to Llanthony.

This was not a success. Probably at Werburgh's behest Ignatius himself turned against her, forbidding her to receive Communion on Christmas Day because he decided she wasn't 'converted'. Soon afterwards she left for the second and final time and was taken up by the militant protestants who oversaw the composition of her book, delighted to have another ex-nun to add to their propaganda pool.[376]

---

[375] Dom Cyprian Alston, 'Reminiscences of Llanthony' in *Pax*, Christmas 1913.

[376] In the censuses (1891, 1901 and 1911) she is listed at various addresses

The death of Sister Etheldreda (Huthwaite) was sudden, and occurred not long after the final departure of Sister Mary Agnes, on 14 February 1886. She was 57, and after a lengthy funeral in the abbey church her body was laid to rest in the cloister garth. It was her fellow resident associate Sister Annie (Mrs Grant) who had discovered her in a state of collapse in her room in the convent, having missed her from the 11.00 Sunday service, which the two of them used to attend with the lay congregation in the outer part of the abbey church.[377]

THE CONVENT DESERTED...

WHEN IGNATIUS LEFT FOR AMERICA in June 1890 the arrangements he made for the monks and nuns to receive the sacraments in his absence proved inadequate,[378] and after an unsuccessful appeal to the Bishop of St David's the three remaining nuns gave up the struggle. Mother Werburgh was the first to leave, in March 1891, followed in April by Mother Cecilia and in May by Mother Ermenild.[379]

All three became Roman Catholics, and found niches in stable and well-established communities — though not, as Peter Anson seems to suggest,[380] as professed nuns. The former Mother Werburgh (Stanbridge) went initially to Stanbrook Abbey in Worcestershire, where she was listed in that year's census as a visitor. Ten years later she had become a teacher at the school attached to another

---

in the north London suburbs, her occupation given in the first two as respectively 'nurse' and 'sick nurse' and in the last as 'sick nurse to [sic] old to get work'. Her death was registered in Hackney in the first quarter of 1935.

[377] Information from the Obituary previously cited. By the time of Eric Gill's arrival in 1924 the wooden cross marking her grave had all but rotted away, and was replaced by a stone memorial (Donald Attwater, *A Cell of Good Living*, Geoffrey Chapman 1969 p91).

[378] See Chapter 10.

[379] Dates from Dom Cyprian Alston's ms memoir

[380] BUWP p131 n45

Benedictine convent, St Mary's Priory, Princethorpe, near Rugby, her birthplace being given not as Camden Town but as Cape Town (in fact where her elder sister Emily had been born).

In 1901 ex-Mother Cecilia was also at Princethorpe, where she was listed as 'Mary Cecilia Smith' and her occupation given as 'Organist-Pianist'. In the next census she was still there, now named as 'Martha Smith' and her age given as 75 (in fact she was a year older). Florence Stanbridge doesn't figure in this list, or not under her own name; Miss Smith's fellow-boarder is identified 'Florence de Beverley', a widow whose age corresponds to that of former Prioress Stanbridge, and with the birthplace with which she had been credited in the last listing.[381]

Ermenild Goodwin found employment as a domestic servant at the Bartestree convent near Hereford, which operated a refuge for 'fallen women'. She was listed there in the censuses of both 1901 and 1911, and her death registered in Hereford in the final quarter of 1925.

...AND REPOPULATED

TWO YEARS AFTER HIS RETURN from America the Abbot received into the community 27-year-old Isabella Kennedy Stewart, daughter of a Lanarkshire industrialist, who had previously spent two years with the Sisterhood of St Margaret of Scotland in Aberdeen. Her details were recorded in the Register, as were those of the three other women who entered the convent in the same decade, though in a separate section from that devoted to the monks. When she took her novice

---

[381] In July 1913 the Princethorpe annals recorded the sudden death of 'Sister Cecily Smith, oblate, who had resided in the School quarters for many years' and was buried in the old cemetery there (information from Sister Mary Lucy, of the community formerly at Princethorpe). 'Mary F[lorence?] W[erburgh?] S[tanbridge?] de Beverley' died in Bicester on 19 March 1924. When three months later her will was proved her name was given as 'Margaret Mary de Beverley', probate being granted to her landlord (an ironmonger's assistant) and her net effects amounting to £33 8s 3d. The surname 'de Beverley' will be recognised by students of Sir Walter Scott as that of Marmion's mistress Constance, who was of course a 'spoiled nun'.

vows on Holy Cross Day (14 September) 1893 Miss Stewart was given the name Scholastica after St Benedict's sister. Her vows were renewed for a year on 2 October 1894 when she was made a 'professed novice' ('having been very ill', according to the Register), and were renewed again for two years on 26 September 1895. On this occasion the Abbot noted that he would have professed her for life 'but for two reasons: 1st, her bad health, although she is better; 2nd, her self will and impatience. She has tried to worry me into giving her the black veil.' Some time after this her bad health provided an excuse for her to be 'sent away', and in March 1897 she became a Roman Catholic.

She was probably still at Llanthony on 18 December 1895, when a second aspirant arrived. This was Violet de Pothonier, aged 19 (born 31 August 1876), one of the seven or more children of an evidently impoverished shipowner named Henry de Pothonier (he had died earlier that year leaving just £25 1s 6d); her admission as a postulant took place the following September. On St David's Day 1897 she took her novice vows as Sister Mary Helena of the Cross, renewing them on the same day the following year. At some point in the next two years she returned to the world, where in due course she would become a wife and mother (see Chapter 11).

Emily Angela Finn was 32 when she came to the convent a month after Violet de Pothonier, and was admitted as postulant and novice at the same time, taking the name Mary Nonna of St David. She also renewed her vows on St David's Day 1898, but was 'sent away 24 June 1899 because she seemed utterly unable to understand what monastic obedience was, after three years of patient teaching'.[382]

---

[382] Born Canterbury c1865. Her name is listed in the 1891 census as living in a flat or bedsitter in Willesden (occupation Cashier & Bookkeeper), and in 1901 at her brother's house in Lowestoft where she was acting as his housekeeper.

Picture 16: Mother Tudfil (Jeannie Dew)

Meanwhile on 15 February 1898 the person who was to have the distinction of being the last Llanthony nun entered the community. This was Jeannie (or Jessie) Dew from the Isle of Wight, also aged 32, whose father was a solicitor.[383] A week after her admission she was made a postulant, taking her first vows as a novice on 8 August of the same year, when she was renamed Sister Mary Tudfil of the Holy Name of JESUS. According to the Register it was only after a further three years (on 29 September 1901) that she renewed these vows ('until the time appointed for my Final Profession'), and over four years later (on 21 January 1906) that she made her 'Simple Profession'. I suspect that 'Final Profession' was actually meant.

The shortage of professed nuns at Llanthony was to some extent camouflaged by the presence in the convent of associate sisters, and in the mid-1880s by the little Ulett girls (and maybe others?) in their child-sized habits. On 13 April 1894 the *Western Mail* published an account by 'Our Lady Correspondent' of her visit to the convent at Easter, which that year had been on 25 March. Her article included the following details:

> The community consists, beside the nuns, of whom the visitors see and hear nothing at all, of several lay sisters, who come and go, who are under no vows, and who only wear the dress of an associate sister when they are 'in residence' at Llanthony, wearing, of course, their usual costume when they return home. The dress is [of] black serge, with white cap, collar and the scapular, a square of black serge with the Cross of St Benedict, and in church they wear a white veil.[384]
>
> Resident sisters are Sister Monica, the Guest Mistress; Sister Annie, who is so well known at every mission the reverend father holds, and

---

[383] Jeannie Dew was born in Reading in or around 1866, and her younger sister in Bromley, Kent; the Professions Register notes that she was baptised as an adult, on 25 July 1890 at Bonchurch, IOW. In the 1891 census the two sisters were listed with their parents as visitors c/o Miss Ann Bathe at 6 Altofts Villas, Newport Road, Ventnor. This house (also known as 'Sterlings') was in fact the Dew family home, and would be given as the former Mother Tudfil's last address when her will was proved in November 1960.

[384] The 1905 photograph of (associate) Sister Rose which appears later in this narrative shows her in the same habit as Mother Tudfil, as does that of four associates mentioned below.

through whose generosity the convent was built and furnished, and who lives in her own rooms there when not out on a mission. Another sister waits on the nuns; another, a niece of the Abbot's, is starting the outside delightful work of doing all she can for the poor of the district – a school for the children, and classes for the big lads, and in time her work will develop and grow into a blessing for the country around.

The reference to 'nuns' is puzzling, as only Sister Scholastica's name figures in the Register for this period; perhaps the fact that visitors could 'see and hear nothing at all' of them enabled the Guest Mistress to be a bit vague about their actual number. The absence at the time of proper nuns to receive her had necessitated Sisters Annie and Monica acting as 'matrons' at Sister Scholastica's clothing.[385]

This report is the only source we have for the information that Sister Annie funded the building of the convent in 1881, which was the year when she began her association with the community and its leader. According to Dom Cyprian Alston she was the widow of a Cheltenham tobacconist; later she would pay for the laying of turf and a 'good road' on the approach to the west door of the church,[386] as well as contributing 'a handsome mowing machine', 'a splendid heating apparatus' and 'a beautiful kneeler for the Father's cell'.[387]

Her main occupation was that of 'mission sister', accompanying Ignatius on his regular journeys around Britain as well as on the American tour of 1890-91. A Boston newspaper described her as clothed in black, with 'a peculiar bonnet, having a veil falling from its crown', and looking 'as if she had much determination, and intellectuality as well'.[388] She died on 28 June 1903.

---

[385] BUWP pp138f

[386] MT December 1883.

[387] LMN April – June 1894. The same issue includes a photograph of four 'Benedictine Associate Sisters'.

[388] FIIA p56

The 'niece of the Abbot's' was Francis Palmer's elder daughter Louisa Jane, then in her mid-twenties.[389] The schoolroom was the building at the foot of the monastery drive, afterwards converted to residential use. In the first issue of *Llanthony and Mission News* (January–March 1894) it was reported that six Salvation Army members from the barracks in Hay had paid a visit to the monastery, in the course of which they were 'taken down to the little room, where the valley children are daily taught by one of the sisters'.

FURTHER HISTORY OF THE FELTHAM SISTERS

IN COMPARISON WITH THE little group who stayed loyal to Ignatius, the 'rebel' community at Feltham grew and prospered.[390] Financially the first few years were hard going: the story is told of some ladies who complained that if the delicious meal to which they were treated in the visitors' quarters was any indication the convent couldn't be that badly off, little realising that meanwhile the sisters were dining off bread and cheese. In 1881 the census listed eleven nuns (all in their 20s or 30s apart from Mothers Hilda and Dorothea) and three other women, as well as five girl 'scholars' ranging in age between six and 13.[391] Ten years later (by which time the lease at Feltham had run out and they had found a temporary home in Twickenham, provided by the father of their chaplain the

---

[389] Not long afterwards she converted to Roman Catholicism and joined the Dominican convent at West Grinstead as Sister Mary Faith. She seems to have spent most of her religious life outside the convent caring for orphaned or other needy boys; the 1911 census listed her as a Maternity Nurse at a one-room flat in Bessborough Place SW which she was sharing with her three-year-old godson Albert Edward Fidelis Rabbetts and a single woman of 20 named Norah Kathleen Lackey, a noted Suffragette. The following year Miss Lackey would with fellow-protesters be sent to prison for four months for her part in a West End window-smashing campaign (*Dundee Courier* 27 March 1912).

[390] See *Call* pp324ff.

[391] The youngest of these was Helen M. Chawkley, younger sister of Joseph who was an acolyte at Llanthony and one of the 1880 visionaries.

Reverend Arthur Dale[392]) the number of sisters had risen to fifteen, and 'scholars' had given way to a mixture of 'patients', 'boarders' and 'domestic servants superannuated' (four adult and four juvenile).

From there they moved in 1893 to the surviving gatehouse of the pre-Reformation abbey at West Malling. This had been purchased the previous year by Charlotte Boyd, an associate of the community whose many philanthropic activities included founding and directing an orphanage in Kilburn.[393] A regular visitor at this time was the future Dom Aelred Carlyle, just then taking the first tentative steps to form the part-time brotherhood out of which would grow the Anglican Benedictine community on Caldey Island. He remembered Mother Hilda as a 'royal little figure with a great heart', from whom he received 'wise advice and motherly help'.[394] After Hilda's death in 1907 and the election of her successor (Abbess Scholastica Ewart, formerly Sister Mary Pauline of the All Saints' Sisterhood) the community began to increase in numbers, and like their brethren on Caldey to look increasingly Romewards. In 1911 they migrated to Milford Haven, and in March 1913 both communities were received into the Roman Catholic Church.[395] The buildings at West Malling were taken over by another group of Anglican nuns associated with Aelred Carlyle, whose successors remain in occupation today.[396]

---

[392] Their benefactor was the Reverend Pelham Dale, who had been imprisoned for infringing the Public Worship Regulation Act of 1874.

[393] For Charlotte Boyd see http://rosarymakeruk.blogspot.fr/2012/12/charlotte-boyd-some-notes-on-her-life.html#more, retrieved 10 December 2013. Soon after acquiring the property at West Malling she became a Roman Catholic; today she is best remembered for her purchase of the mediaeval Slipper Chapel at Walsingham, then in use as a farm building. Some years later it would be restored to religious use and become centrepiece of the Roman Catholic national shrine.

[394] Call p425

[395] See Chapter 12

[396] See Call pp462ff

One of those who stayed at Feltham after the break with Ignatius was Dame Werburgh's younger sister Edith Stanbridge, although she seems not to have persevered. In the 1901 census she is listed in lodgings not far from her sister in Princethorpe village, but further details of her history are hard to establish. Another was Sister Everilda, born Harriette Marion Ellis. She was, it will be recalled, the religiously-minded youngest daughter of Mrs Ellis of Bath, in whose house John Spence had stayed when accompanying the Abbot on his mission tour in Lent 1872. Later she and one or two others would break away, forming a tiny community known as the 'Benedictines of Ss Mary and Scholastica'.[397]

THE ABBEY PRIESTS

BETWEEN 1878 AND 1884 four clergymen were attached for varying periods to the monastery, each of whom would prove a disappointment. This is not surprising. While Ignatius had been hitting the headlines at Claydon and Norwich a more discreet beginning was being made by Richard Meux Benson at Cowley, where priests 'in good standing'

---

[397] Born Wiesbaden 1853. In the 1901 census she was listed at a house in Mary Tavy, near Tavistock, of which she described herself to the enumerator as the 'occupier' (amended by whoever checked his entry as 'head'); the next person on the list (Alice M. Steele, previously associated with the Knowle sisterhood in Bristol) was listed as her 'friend' (changed to 'visitor'). The rest of the household consisted of an elderly housekeeper and a boy of fifteen described as an 'orphan in care'. In 1911 she and another (former?) Feltham sister (Kate Louise Burdon, 39 to Harriette's 58) were living at Sandling, near Maidstone; both gave their occupation as 'Sister in Religion, English Catholic'. Peter Anson (Call p428n; BAL p183 and p326) mentions this little group's connection then or a little later with an *episcopus vagans* named Bernard Mary Williams, as well as the fact that one of their several temporary homes was in the famously ritualistic rural Suffolk parish of Kettlebaston, whose tradition was established by a nephew of Priscilla Lydia Sellon (see www. kettlebaston.suffolk.gov.uk/Tricker_s_Church_Guide_-_illustrated.pdf, which dates their sojourn there to 1920-24 and puts their membership at four). Harriette's death was registered in 1933 at West Malling, which suggests she may in old age have been living with the community which had moved there in 1916.

with a vocation to the religious life were able to test their vocations with the Society of St John the Evangelist; by the end of the century the choice would be considerably wider.[398] Any clergyman seriously considering life at Llanthony was likely to be a misfit, if not in some sense 'on the run'. Ignatius always believed his geese were swans – until they surprised him by turning out to be geese after all, or birds of an even less attractive feather.

WILLIAMS AND HOWORTH

THE FIRST OF THESE 'ABBEY PRIESTS' was Hubert Brymer Williams, known as Brother Hubert (Ignatius says he was received as a postulant, but like Brother David, Charles Rouse and others there is no entry for him in the Register). When he came to Llanthony early in 1878 he was forty, and had for the preceding five years been incumbent of Charminster, near Dorchester. *Crockford* lists him as such until 1888, although he seems to have spent more time away from his benefice than in residence.[399]

Williams was a son of the parsonage, but had initially gone into the Navy; after Lichfield Theological College he served a curacy in Derby, then returned to sea as chaplain of HMS Hercules. Ignatius describes him as having lived 'a rather unclerical life in the outside world',[400] and suffering from 'unusual trials and temptations for a

---

[398] The Community of the Resurrection (Mirfield), the Society of the Sacred Mission (later at Kelham), the (Franciscan) Society of Divine Compassion, Aelred Carlyle's Benedictine community and the quasi-Benedictine Order of St Paul all came into being in the 1890s. By this time a number of short-lived foundations (including Nugée's) had come and gone.

[399] In the reports of his court appearance in January 1881 he is described as 'formerly' Vicar of Charminster. A few months after his institution to that benefice he was declared bankrupt (*Morning Post*, 22 Nov 1873); in 1875 he was acting curate of Kintbury (Oxon), where at the trial of an 18-year-old girl for allegedly stealing his watch it emerged that they had been 'improperly intimate', although he was married and the father of three children (*Sheffield & Rotherham Independent*, 2 March 1875).

[400] Unless otherwise stated all quotations in this section are from Ignatius's account of 'The Four Abbey Priests' in MT September 1885, p3.

clergyman' which he leaves discreetly unspecified. However, he was 'desirous of leading a new life, ...of gentlemanly and attractive manners', and Ignatius himself liked him. At first he was allowed neither to receive Communion nor to say Mass himself, but when he had given sufficient evidence that he was 'converted' and had 'come to JESUS' the prohibition was lifted, and for a while the community enjoyed the luxury of daily Mass at 6.0am.

A few weeks later Robert Lewin Howorth, also from a clerical family, was admitted and given the name Brother Aelred; as has already been noted his admission as postulant (24 April) and novice (21 May) is recorded in the Register. He was five years younger than Williams and a Cambridge MA, and after two curacies in the diocese of Norwich had had two spells as a schoolmaster either side of a five-year incumbency (South Kirkby, near Pontefract; 1870-75).

Ignatius reports that the two priests became friends. They took it in turns to celebrate the community Mass, and each had his area of responsibility – Hubert was guestmaster (an appointment Ignatius acknowledged to have been 'foolish'), while Aelred's experience as a teacher made him the obvious person to take charge of the monastery boys.

Here he came unstuck. Although more than competent at managing the motley group of youngsters and instructing them in ordinary school subjects, he seems to have been shy of talking to them about spiritual matters. One of them was said to have been sent to Llanthony by his father in the hope that he would develop a monastic vocation, but Ignatius tells us Aelred did his best to 'thwart the father's wish, and to give the boy's mind a secular turn' by concentrating on subjects which would 'prepare him for commercial pursuits'. In fact this may have been for the best, as the father's sudden death resulted in his family withdrawing him from the monastery and putting him to work in a shop.

In another account[401] it is said that 'when he observed rule and was humble and industrious, [he] was as bright and joyous as a school boy in the Monastery and his intense enjoyment of the cloister life broke out in the offices in choir almost overpoweringly'. But more often he was proud and cynical, 'saying to a novice that he far preferred Shakespeare to the Bible[,] and that as for St Benedict, he was an old fool' (being asked in return 'Why do you stay here and wear St Benedict's habit?').

We don't know how long in fact Aelred stayed. At some point he 'went away', claiming 'it was because he doubted the Real Presence'. Later he 'wrote from [his parents' house at] Maidstone asking to be received back. I had fears of his sincerity refused did not encourage him', although according to Ignatius's account it seems that he was readmitted, after which he was 'far worse than ever', and had to be 'very summarily dismissed, for violence'. After this he fixed himself up with a teaching post in Birmingham, but early in 1881 whatever inner demons had originally driven him to the monastery finally gained the upper hand, and the unfortunate man 'killed himself by poison'.

Meanwhile towards midsummer 1878 Brother Hubert began to complain of feeling ill, and thought he might have cancer. Ignatius despatched him to his 'kind friend Dr Sutton' in London,[402] where he remained for a month before rejoining the Superior, who was conducting a mission in Ramsgate. Here it became apparent that 'Brother Hubert was not temperate, and he was not a safe person to have about me.' Fortunately it was possible shortly after this to arrange for his admission to 'an Inebriates' Home, presided over by a clergyman in R------ [Ramsgate?]'.

---

[401] MT March 1885

[402] A physician of this name is mentioned in Williams op cit, p251 and p266. He was involved with Miss Sellon's cholera hospital in Spitalfields in 1866, where Philip and Alban (and possibly also Ignatius) helped with the nursing in that year's epidemic, and in 1878 (two years after her death) was co-opted on to a committee to support her community's convalescent hospital at Ascot.

Two years later the errant alcoholic received the Abbot's permission return to Llanthony – 'not as a Brother, but in retreat from the world and its temptations' – so he took the train to Llanfihangel Crucorney. Once on the valley road he was sidetracked by the comforts of the Queen's Head in Lower Cwmyoy, and decided he would be better off there than at the monastery. Unfortunately the bill for three weeks' accommodation exceeded his limited resources and he attempted to pass a dud cheque, for which he was committed to nine months' hard labour at Usk Gaol.[403]

Some time after his release he resumed his clerical career, serving a brief curacy in Shoreditch (1890-91) before spending the remaining ten years of his life in another, at Holy Trinity, Bethnal Green. The censuses of 1891 and 1901 describe him as married, although on neither occasion was his wife living with him. His death was registered in Kingston on Thames in the third quarter of 1901.

COMPTON

BEFORE WILLIAMS'S ATTEMPTED RETURN the third of the abbey priests had come and gone. John William Compton was clothed as Brother Aidan on 1 March 1880, alongside Dunstan (Magrath) and Aelred (Underwood). He gave his age as thirty (he was in fact 27), and since his ordination five years previously had served two curacies in the (then united) diocese of Gloucester and Bristol. In the first, at Rodborough, he had had the misfortune to lose his wife Jessie (née Cattanach), who was only 23. After a few months in the monastery he left quite suddenly ('having said the Holy Eucharist Service, as usual, in the morning, without giving us any warning, and after the warmest expressions only the day before of pretended reverence for the Superior and the work here'), but remained in the vicinity for some weeks, teaming up

---

[403] Proceedings of Glamorganshire Quarter Sessions, as reported in the *Hampshire Advertiser* of 15 January 1881. In the following April's census he is listed among the inmates of that institution under the name 'William H. Brymer', occupation 'Rector of Charminster'.

with an unnamed former female helper of Ignatius's,[404] 'circulating every kind of falsehood against us, and threatening to come and break every window in the Church for no reason whatever'. Eventually he 'disappeared, because officers of the law were in search of him in order to serve a writ upon him. We were told that this "priest" escaped to France.'[405] In the Register Ignatius summed him up as 'a most diabolical man, [who] ran away because he was tired of playing a game of deceit. Said to me when I found him at Jenkins' farm [Maes-y-ffin], "I've treated you dear father like a blackguard & now I shall go to the dogs."'

Compton's sojourn in France wasn't permanent. In 1891 he was lodging with a Dr J.H.A. Laing in Edinburgh, where he gives his occupation as 'Priest, Church of England' and was probably completing his medical studies. With him was his second wife Lucy Mary, whom he had married in London shortly after leaving Llanthony, but from whom he later became divorced. (A third marriage was contracted at Stroud in the autumn of 1897, perhaps to one of his former parishioners.) In 1892 he was appointed Surgeon-Lieutenant in the Royal Engineers (1st Hampshire Regiment), and in the 1901 census listed as a Doctor of Medicine (and by this time once again a widower) in Portsmouth, where he died in 1907.

Bertouch (without mentioning his name)[406] tells of his departure from the monastery, continued presence in the valley and sudden disappearance. She adds the information that several years later he turned up at one of Ignatius's 'seaside missions, threw himself on his knees, and begged [his] forgiveness', claiming to have had no peace since his departure from the monastery, upon which his former Abbot 'sent him away happy and forgiven'.

---

[404] This may have been Miss Mary Stuart Fife, who brought an unsuccessful action against Ignatius for expenses alleged to have been incurred while assisting him as a voluntary worker. The case was reported in the *Western Mail* of 15 January 1881.

[405] MT March 1885

[406] pp552f

MAISTER

THE FOURTH PRIEST mentioned in Ignatius's account was Reginald Henry Maister, who spent some time at Llanthony in 1883-84. Ten years earlier he had been one of the first students at Chancellor Benson's new theological college in Lincoln, after which he served three curacies: two in Lincoln diocese, and one to his father in the East Riding.

Picture 17: The community c1883: Fr Ignatius with abbey priest R.H. Maister, Brother David and 'Acolyte Alfred'

Although given the name 'Brother Dunstan' he seems neither to have used it himself nor worn the habit. There is no entry for him in the Register, but his doings are reported on several occasions in the *Monastic Times* – usually as the 'Priest in Charge' or 'Abbey Priest' – and as such he ministered to the dying Dr Hanson and officiated at various services, as well as paying pastoral visits in the neighbourhood. Like his predecessor Fr Howorth he also took charge of the monastery boys, and supported Ignatius by writing a pamphlet taking his part in the controversy with his father following the death of his mother.[407]

---

[407] Mentioned *Enthusiast* p219n

The December 1884 issue of the *Monastic Times* included the terse observation that he had left, believing 'that he is called to preach to the Masses'; in June 1885 it was reported that after two attempts to join Anglican missions he had become a Roman Catholic and was living in Kensington. In fact he continued to function as an Anglican clergyman for a further nineteen years, his *Crockford* entry listing three curacies in this period: one of seven years' duration in Nottinghamshire, another of five years in Yorkshire, and a third of three years in Hampshire.

By this time Maister seems to have moved away from orthodox Christianity, and to have found a new spiritual home with the Unitarians. In 1905 he became minister of the chapel of that denomination in Stockton-on-Tees, not far from his birthplace,[408] but had to retire in 1912 after a serious illness. His obituary in the Unitarian periodical *The Inquirer*[409] paints a picture of a gentle, self-effacing character, good with children, whom he enjoyed introducing to the delights of English Literature and nature study. He spent his final years living quietly in Manchester, 'rather lonely without work, but never idle'; always available to the 'many poor souls from rooms round about' who 'have taken their troubles to him'. This doesn't quite fit with Ignatius's assertion that he had had to be 'expelled for violently assaulting several persons and seriously hurting them',[410] but maybe at Llanthony he was under different pressures. He died in Manchester on 3 March 1929.

SHARPE

ANOTHER PRIEST WHO STAYED for a while (after the period dealt with in the *Monastic Times* account) was Charles Henry Sharpe (c1859-

---

[408] His mother was a Sutton of Elton Hall, where he had been born on 19 June 1851.

[409] Issue of 9 March 1929. I am grateful to The Inquirer Publishing Company (2004) for this information and permission to quote from it.

[410] MT March 1885

1932), who would start an evangelistically-oriented but short-lived community of 'Brothers of the Common Life' at More Hall, near Stroud, just before the first World War. In 1887 − between curacies − he is said to have 'spent some time with Father Ignatius and for the first time wore Eucharistic Vestments and celebrated Cranmer's version of the Mass' (the rite of 1549, perhaps).[411] By this time William Moorhead Magrath (Brother Dunstan) had migrated from the noviciate to theological college, and would soon be available as an occasional visiting celebrant, and for a while as resident chaplain.[412] Other clergy certainly came as guests, but no record has survived of any more who served as chaplain or 'abbey priest'.

BOYS

IGNATIUS WAS PROBABLY unaware of the warning of St Macarius, fourth century founder of the monastic colony of Scetis in the Egyptian desert:

> When you see a cell built near the Marsh [i.e. not in the desert proper], know that the desolation of Scetis is near: when you see trees, it is at the doors: but when you see boys, take up your mantles and withdraw.[413]

The danger of bringing boys into the monastery is not just the obvious one that the brethren might become emotionally involved with them, or worse − as we have seen, something of the sort had already happened at Elm Hill. St Benedict had defined the monastery as a 'school for the Lord's service',[414] but a school for

---

[411] Information from http://btsarnia.org/2014/06/01/the-oxford-movement-in-gloucestershire/ retrieved 27 June 2014 and quoted with permission. In 1894 Sharpe joined the staff of the theological college in Gloucester, where one of his students would have been the former Brother William Alston (see Chapter 10). He converted to Rome in 1917.

[412] See Chapter 10.

[413] Quoted in Derwas Chitty, The Desert a City, Blackwell 1966; p66

[414] Rule of St Benedict, Prologue

the training of the monks themselves rather than other people, the business of which could easily become a distraction. He did, however, allow for the reception of child oblates, and monastic schools were common in the middle ages, as they have been more recently. While 'monastery boys' – whether oblates or pupils – could be absorbed with relatively little disturbance into a large and stable institution, at Llanthony they were highly obtrusive, and with the rapid turnover of novices and other adherents their supervision and education posed a continuing problem.

This point is made by Dom Cyprian (formerly Fr Cadoc) Alston, by that time a monk of Downside. His 'Reminiscences of Llanthony' (as it was in the late 1880s and early 1890s) appeared in the Christmas 1913 issue of *Pax*, the Caldey quarterly.

The fact that we nearly always had a few boys in the monastery, living with the community, tended, I think, to lower the strictly monastic ideal amongst the brothers, besides being sometimes a cause of friction between them and their superior.

He tells us that these boys were generally

orphans or the children of poor parents, whom Fr Ignatius took and provided for *gratis*. His idea was that they would develop vocations and eventually join the community, but this hope was never realised. On the contrary, they often soon got dissatisfied with the severity of the rule and life, and were only too glad to leave when an opportunity arose; in fact, more than one ran away, despairing of any such legitimate opportunity occurring. They assisted in choir and helped in the housework, and they also had three or four hours a day at their lessons, being taught in a desultory sort of way by one of the brothers – often one who had neither aptitude nor ability to teach. It was a mistake, I think, to have had them, as it were, living with the community. They ought to have been in a separate school or alumnate. That, however, was impossible under the circumstances, and the result was, I am sure, good neither for them nor for the brothers.

No specific record was kept of the boys who passed through the monastery, but we do know a little about some of them. From the early years at Llanthony we have the names of the two acolytes or pupils listed in the 1871 census return: Eugene Manlius Davy (aged 14, born Paddington) and Edgar Reader (aged 15, born near Stroud). A boy named Eugene is mentioned by Spence, although it is not clear from the context whether he is describing a person who was there in his own time or one who had already moved on. He may have been the same individual as 'Manny', mentioned by Kilvert on the occasion of the picnic lunch in the dingle:

> ...a fine noble looking boy, a gentleman's son, with a sweet open face and fair clustering curly hair. He had been sent to the new monastery by his parents to learn to be a monk. The boy seemed to be devoted to Father Ignatius and came running up with a basket of mushrooms he had just brought to show them to the Father. His cowl was thrown back and his fair young head, bright face and sunny hair made a striking contrast with his black robe.... He shook hands with us all before he went off to the barn. His hand was small, soft and white as a girl's.[415]

---

[415] Kilvert vol 1 pp223f. Manlius Eugene Adams Davy was the eldest child of William Adams Davy (who gave his occupation as 'tutor') and his wife Eliza, of 13 Pembridge Gardens, Kensington. His birth was registered in the second quarter of 1856, and his marriage in Holborn in the second quarter of 1877. In the 1881 census he was listed in Louth (Lincs) as a Foreign Language Teacher (allegedly aged 27, actually 24 or 25), with his wife Madeleine and son aged 3. In 1891 he appeared as a schoolmaster aged 35 with his wife and three children, and in 1901 as a private tutor and County Court official aged 45 (now with five children); both in the suburbs of Birmingham. By 1911 when he was 55 he had been widowed, and was living with three daughters in Putney, where he was once again working as a schoolmaster. His death was registered in Richmond in the first quarter of 1918, when he was 62.

Edgar Reader (whom both Spence's copyist and the census official misname as 'Reade') survived until the day of Spence's arrival, when he was sent away (for 'gossiping in the valley') in the vehicle which had brought him and Ignatius from the station ('He made a dreadful howling'). His appearance sounds so similar to that of Kilvert's description of 'Manny' that one may wonder whether there has been some confusion between them – he was '…an excessively beautiful child, curly hair like a girl's and lovely delicate hands', although unfortunately also 'repulsively cruel in disposition'.[416]

Apart from the departing Edgar Reader ('E. Reade'), John Spence mentions by name only one other acolyte resident at Llanthony in his time, a boy called Charley. He was at Feltham when the new recruit arrived there on his way to Llanthony, and joined the party travelling to the monastery the following day. Although he had been sent 'for the choir' he was then and at Easter – and probably for the whole of the intervening three months – the only 'monastery boy'. A little later Spence tells us that there were 'two choristers or acolytes outdoor lodgers', of whom Charley may have been one, but he left with Ignatius when the latter went off to Feltham in May, 'very glad to get away' and thankful that his mother 'would have him back'. One wonders why he had had to leave home in the first place. Later in the summer when Cuthbert was sent to Llanfihangel with

---

[416] Edgar Alfred Reader (birth registered at Gloucester in the first quarter of 1856) was listed in the 1881 census as a draper, boarding with relations in Kentish Town. Four years later he entered St Paul's College, Burgh (Lincs), which specialised in preparing young men for missionary service in the Anglican Church overseas. According to Crockford he was ordained to the diaconate 1890 in Grahamstown (South Africa), where he served one curacy of four years, and to the priesthood to 1896 in Riverina (New South Wales), where he was Vicar of Menindie 1896-1900 and Rector of Coopernook (both in NSW) 1900-07. After a two-year period of furlough he went to Lincoln diocese as successively curate of South Kelsey (1909-12) and Rector of Irby (1912-14), then to Salisbury as curate of East Knoyle (1914-23) and Vicar of Bradpole (1923-27). Thereafter he retired to the clerical almshouses known as the Beauchamp Community at Newland, near Malvern, dying in 1947 at the age of 91.

Philip to collect a load of coal he was told that two new acolytes might be waiting to be picked up from the station. 'He [Ignatius] told me I was to kiss them and be kind to them as they would be afraid of Father Philip', but they failed to materialise. In the final months of his stay he tells us that the household was down to three people (Philip, Serene and himself), so even if these two boys arrived sometime later they can't have stayed long.

Only one 'monastery boy' has left us a record of what their life was like. In January 1898 a former acolyte named Edward Jones contributed a two-part article to the South Wales Echo under the nom de plume 'Tonsure' describing his experiences at Llanthony in the previous decade.

Edward arrived in the early autumn of 1884. He doesn't tell us how long he stayed, or anything about the monks or other boys, but is quite good on the daily routine. The timetable appears to have been a slightly modified version of the monks' daily horarium, although the boys didn't attend the Night Office; they were woken at 5.0am in time to attend the office of Prime.[417] They did, however, take turns at the daily 'watch' in the abbey church (but only for half an hour at a time), and this could be at any time of day or night. They also enjoyed a period after midday dinner playing in the 'Abbot's Meadow'. Here their scope for enjoyment was seriously inconvenienced by the requirement to genuflect every time they passed the shrine commemorating the apparitions witnessed by their predecessors in August and September 1880, 'even if we passed the spot a hundred times in the course of the afternoon'. Not surprisingly they 'voted [this rule] to be a decided hindrance to the success of a game'.

Sometimes there would be a ramble on the mountainside instead. When Ignatius was in the party this would include what Jones describes – apparently without irony – as 'a good old-fashioned prayer meeting'. As well as copies of his two articles we have a letter

---

[417] He uses the term 'a service' for this and each of the succeeding offices.

to the boy's elder brother William (addressed as 'Dear Rev Brother', so evidently a clergyman) from the current 'abbey priest' (R.H. Maister), who reported that he sometimes took his young charges 'for a run' on the mountains, as well as 'brambling and nutting'.

Edward defines the duties of an acolyte as 'to be in attendance upon the priest at the altar [about which he doesn't go into details], 'and to perform certain household work, such as washing floors, cleaning windows, &c'.[418] These domestic tasks occupied most of the time between Terce at 8.30 and Sext at 11; he tells us that the Abbot himself sometimes lent a hand. 'Pittance', the monastic apology for breakfast, followed immediately after Terce, unless the individual was being punished for late rising, in which case he went without. The final hour or so before dinner was spent in reading (for the boys as well as for the monks probably of the 'pious' variety). He doesn't mention lessons, but we know from the letter to his brother that he was learning Latin, Greek, History and Geography, and making a start on French.[419]

Five o'clock tea, the last meal of the day, was followed by Vespers, after which one of the brothers read aloud 'out of the "Lives of the Saints", &c.' Compline was at 8.0, then

> we would go straight to our cells..., and the brother-in-charge [Fr Maister?] would say prayers. After the long day most of us were glad to get into bed, although it was exceeding hard and with very little on it. The bed covering consisted of a brown blanket and a counterpane − the counterpane having a red cross on it.[420]

---

[418] The household chores included cleaning up after the Abbot's collection of tame birds − 'canaries, magpies, crows, &c' − which were a dominant feature of Llanthony life, as they had been in the community's previous homes.

[419] Photocopies of Maister's letter (30 September 1884) and Jones's newspaper articles are in the archives at Abergavenny (ref A1997.22.1-4).

[420] The counterpanes were red with a white cross, on which was emblazoned the text of 1 Corinthians 2.2; they were a feature of the monks' bedding

The life was certainly tough, and corporal punishment doubtless formed a part of it, even if Sister Mary Agnes' description can perhaps be taken with a pinch of salt –

I recollect how a poor orphan boy at Llanthony monastery was almost always in disgrace, and had to endure the 'discipline'. The lads, when doing penance, were stripped, then laid on a long table, their faces downwards, and lashed for such faults as talking in silence time, slamming doors, leaving dust about[421]

– although the notorious account of the caning 'for dear Jesus' sake' of the (fictional version of the) Infant Oblate from *Leonard Morris* bears the authentic stamp of Ignatius in all his pre-Freudian innocence.[422] He may not have been an obvious specimen of 'muscular Christianity', but the image of monastery boyhood he was keen to project was well expressed when he set the scene for his account of the 1880 apparitions:

In the evening...the choir-boys were in the meadow playing, as they do at recreation time, and were having a very noisy game. The children were very strong and healthy from the mountain air, and from their good, plain food. They were not withered, shrunk, imaginative, namby-pamby boys, fancying all kinds of nonsense, as has been suggested...[423]

A full account of these phenomena is given in the following chapter. The four boys who were living at the monastery at the time and witnessed them were:

---

as well as that of the boys. An example survives in the Abergavenny collection (ref A1993.138.13).

[421] NL p115. She made similar allegations about the treatment in the convent of Ada and Alice Ulett, but these may also be exaggerated.

[422] *Enthusiast* pp203f

[423] MSO p411: Ignatius's account of the Apparitions as given in an 'oration' at Westminster Town Hall five years after the events (see Chapter 9).

- Daniel Maguire, aged fifteen. He was a native of the valley,[424] and if the letter he wrote to Ignatius after the second apparition is anything to go by his gifts lay in a practical rather than a literary direction. Ignatius's critic James Comley suggested that he was a liar, if not very accomplished one,[425] but Brother David (who was almost exactly the same age as Daniel and would almost certainly have sat in the same classroom at old Llanthony, although he nowhere admits to this) would not have agreed. In old age he recalled:

After a time the eldest boy left the monastery, and in time married and became a well to do farmer abroad. Years passed by, and eventually he came over to see us. During a conversation one night in our house, I asked him to tell me his confirmed opinion of the apparition, and the following is what he told me:

'I never go to church now, for the reason that I am hundreds of miles away from a church, and another reason I had more than enough of churchgoing in the monastery attending seven times a day for years. 'Still as regarding the apparitions of the Blessed Virgin – I saw her – and when I go to my grave I should say the same, because it is the truth.'[426]

He was evidently still at the monastery at Christmas 1880,[427] although by the time the census was taken the following April he had moved on to work as a farm servant at 'Maesberrian' [Maes-y-beran] in Upper Cwmyoy. His name is missing from the 1891 census,

---

[424] Born Abergavenny district in the second quarter of 1865, third of the eight children of Michael (farm labourer/small farmer) and Mary, both born Co. Cork but settled in Cwmyoy parish: first at a house on the valley road named Sunny Bank, then at a farm called Loxidge (also spelt Loxedge or Loxhead) on the mountainside above Llanthony Priory.

[425] Letter in *Hereford Times* 9 October 1880

[426] MS notebook in Norfolk Record Office (ref MC 2133/2)

[427] An account of the services over Christmas 1880 in the *Hereford Times* of 1 January 1881 says there were five acolytes.

when presumably he was abroad, but by 1901 had returned to his old family home, where he was listed as a visitor (married, although his wife was not with him), and working as a gas stoker. In 1911 he was again at Loxidge, now living there with his widowed mother. This time his occupation was given as colliery stoker (much the same as 'gas stoker'), a job requiring more brawn than brain, and a bit of a comedown if he had really made his pile overseas. He was now 46 and had himself been widowed, although he had fathered six children of whom five were still living. In this census the household included a 43-year-old unmarried female visitor, Emily Margaret Tillyer, born in Northfleet and living on private means, who seems to have had some connection with the monastery if not with Daniel himself.[428]

• John Stewart, aged twelve and a half. He was still at Llanthony for the following year's census, in which his place of birth is given as Carlow, Ireland.[429] His home was in Sheffield, where he accompanied Ignatius on a visit in late October. Here it was reported that 'he would go about the streets to speak to other lads about their souls'.[430] A few weeks later he appeared with Ignatius and Brother Dunstan at a meeting in the Hereford Corn Exchange and 'related to the audience what he had seen'.[431] To

---

[428] Among the papers preserved at Prinknash Abbey of Ignatius's monastery from the period between his death and its final shut-down are records of payments in the year 1911 totalling £54 to Miss Tillyer. Unfortunately no clue survives as to why a house-guest of the former monastery boy's mother should have been paid this (for then) considerable amount − perhaps she had made a loan to the struggling community and this was the repayment, or part of it. Her name also occurs in the monastery Visitors' Book, recording a stay of nearly three weeks' duration in August 1901.

[429] This is confirmed by the Irish lists of births and baptisms, which give his date of birth as 3 January 1868, his full name as John Eveline Spenser Stewart (in other records his middle names are rendered 'Evelyn' and 'Spencer') and those of his parents as Robert Stewart and Margaret Murphy.

[430] Hereford Times 6 November 1880

[431] ibid 20 November 1880

be able to buttonhole his contemporaries on spiritual matters
and address a hostile adult audience he must have been more
than averagely confident and articulate; one of the journalists
describes him as 'an ingenuous, good-looking boy of far higher
culture than most boys of his age'.[432]

An unidentified press cutting dated 4 September 1931[433] includes
Ignatius's reported reminiscence of 'the boy who first saw the
apparition' and who had doubts about the 'actual bodily presence
of Christ' in the Eucharist:

> One night he dreamt that the figure of the Virgin, which had recently
> been set up in the church, left its position, and proceeding to the
> altar opened the casket in the shrine in which the sacramental vessels
> were kept [i.e. the tabernacle], and presented to the lad the bread
> used in the sacramental offering, which was full of minute living
> bleeding hearts. 'This,' said the image, 'is my son's love.' The doubts
> of the boy from that moment for ever fled.

• Thomas Foord, aged eleven. Twin brothers Thomas John and
  John Thomas Foord were born in Pevensey in April or early
  May 1869, and baptised there on 16 May. They were the eighth
  and ninth of eleven children born to a labourer named Stephen

---

[432] ibid 18 September 1880, report by 'An Occasional Correspondent'. From
1883 to 1885 (when he resigned through ill health) Stewart was a 'van boy'
at Sheffield on the Manchester, Sheffield and Lincolnshire Railway (UK
Railway Employment Records 1833-1963); a surprisingly lowly occupation
if he was as bright as these 1880 reports suggest, but perhaps he went
on to do better things. In his Westminster Town Hall address Ignatius
offered to furnish enquirers with the name and address of 'the chief boy',
who was said to be 'now employed in business' (the reference would
almost certainly be to Stewart); he is also noted as having returned (with
the former Brother Dunstan) for the Ascension Day pilgrimage in 1885
(MT June 1885). The death of a John E. Stewart aged 81 was registered
in the second quarter of 1950 in the Surrey North Eastern district.

[433] In Barclay Album

Foord (this spelling of the name is common in Sussex and Kent) and his wife Eliza Bumstead Plumley; before the births of the youngest two they had moved to Brighton. Following Stephen's death by suicide in 1876 the family broke up, and at some point Thomas was sent to Llanthony. In the 1881 census (when his twin brother John was listed at a boys' home in Brighton) he was still there, but probably moved elsewhere within a year or two.

Picture 18: Bertram Joseph Chawkley in middle age

• Joseph Chawkley, aged nine (born 22 July 1871). Bertram Joseph Chawkley (misspelt in many of the reports as 'Chalkley'; Christian names registered at birth as Joseph Albert) was also from a family broken up by the death of a parent, in this case that of his mother. He had been baptised on 18 August 1878 at St John the Divine, Kennington, at the age of seven; his three siblings had been baptised at the same church on two separate occasions two months earlier, two of them conditionally. The names of their parents were given as Joseph (occupation 'law writer') and Frances, and their address as 2 Pewterers' Place, Charterhouse Square, although their mother had died in March of that year:

his grandson suggests that it was to secure places for them in religious institutions that their baptisms were carried out (or regularised) at this point. When the 1881 census was taken Joseph junior was listed at Llanthony and his six-year-old sister Helen (usually known as Ellen) in the care of the Feltham nuns; their father was living in a crowded lodging house in Holborn.[434]

MENTION HAS BEEN MADE of the grandiosely titled *Church of England Catholic Chronicle and Monastic Times*, the quarterly news-sheet published from Llanthony for the two years September 1883 to September 1885. This provides a certain amount of information about contemporary occupants of the monastery both young and old, as well as news of some events. In the first issue there are mentions in one report[435] of both 'acolytes' and 'Priory girls' (the latter would almost certainly have been the two Ulett children), and in another[436] to the 'abbey children'. There is also this charming description of that summer's 'Monastic Holiday', even if the amusements sound a little tame by modern standards:

> On July 3rd the Monks and Acolytes had their annual treat. They left the Abbey soon after the solemn silence bell had rung at nine a.m.,

---

[434] On 4 March 1893 Joseph married Mary Emma Harris at South Shore, Blackpool. A son, Bertram George Alma Chawkley, was born on 18 July of that year and baptised at the local parish church on 8 August, when the new father gave his occupation as labourer. Baby Bertram died the following January, but further children were born in succeeding years. In Blackpool he was involved in the construction of that resort's famous Tower; at the time of his death at Skegness on 21 March 1931 he was Works Manager for the holiday camp entrepreneur Billy Butlin, having built amusement rides in many parts of this country and mainland Europe. (I am grateful to his grandson Baden Chawkley of Benfleet, Essex, for much of this information. His descendants knew that he had spent part of his childhood at Llanthony, but not that in his time there he had witnessed apparitions of the Blessed Virgin.)

[435] September 1883: report of the last days and death of the Abbot's friend Dr Hanson.

[436] Of the 'Apparitions Feast' on 30 August

and taking their homely fare with them, with a kettle, mugs, &c., they climbed the Black Mountains, and spent a very enjoyable day among rocks and waterfalls. The boys bathed in the river, the monks gathered ferns and wandered about conversing with each other or reading. Sext, Nones and Vespers, were sung by the river side. A fire was kindled and their milk boiled, and a good supper was eaten with a good sharp appetite. The monastic party returned to the Abbey in good time for Compline, by about eight o'clock, without encountering a single human being in their wanderings among these lovely solitudes. The Rev. Father this year was able to accompany the excursion.

The boys who participated in this outing would probably have been among those encountered by 'Morien' of the *Western Mail*, who paid the first of many visits to Llanthony on the feast of the Nativity of the Blessed Virgin (8 September) that year:

On some steps...stood a group of bare-footed lads, numbering seven or eight, dressed in the peculiar monkish habit with the hoods over their heads.... When I approached near enough I asked, 'Are you the monks?' One of the lads, with a merry twinkle of the eyes, said instantly, 'No, sir; we are the nuns.' The other 'monkeys' smiled, and looked at each other as if half doubting whether their young brother had transgressed the canons of the Father. I chatted with them, and in two or three minutes one of them said to another, 'Tom, you had better ring the bell'; and away the Monk Tom went, his gown opening against the wind like the wings of a bird....[437]

Seven or eight of these 'monkeys' suggests a temporary overlap between boys recently arrived and others about to leave; the normal complement was four. By December 'three having been lately sent out into the world' it was necessary to advertise for reinforcements,

---

[437] *Western Mail* 10 September 1883

and again the following March (1884). For a while there seems to have been just one boy in residence – 'Acolyte Alfred' (Alfred Flook, formerly at Slapton?). In June it was announced that '[t]he vacancies for Choir Boys at Llanthony are filled up'; this edition also carried a pious 'aspiration' in verse for the Ulett sisters, 'now [still?] at the Convent', reprinted from the *Hereford Times*. A note in the September issue sheds more light on the boy situation, as well as on the recurring need for someone to look after them:

THE MONASTERY BOYS. – The vacancies are now filled up. One boy is the son of a widow lady in great poverty and suffering, her husband having been an officer in the Army, but of very unsteady habits, died leaving her with several children and penniless, she being a clergyman's daughter. Our nuns are now offering her a temporary home, with her youngest child. We should be very grateful if any of our lady readers could find a suitable situation for this poor widow. Two more boys we have just received who have just lost their mother, and their father being a very bad man, their sister and elder brother and friends were glad of the home provided for them here. We are always thankful for help on behalf of our acolyte boys, and greatly need some one who, for love of Jesus, in return for a happy and holy home, with all needful things provided, will give himself up to the care of these children.

Our cover picture almost certainly includes the boys mentioned in this report, one of whom may have been Edward Jones. Another of them may have been the subject of this little anecdote entitled 'Our Monastery Pets', in the issue of March 1885:

The other day a nice bright Welsh acolyte boy saw a strange cat run into the Monastery, and tried to catch it to put it out; in trying to draw it out from under a stove the cat savagely bit him and hurt him. This boy, who speaks better British than Saxon, and knew that the

Saxons call [a bite by a bird] a 'peck', came to Brother Oswald with his injured hand, saying, 'See, that cat has pecked me!' The young Briton is often taunted laughingly by the Saxon 'Well, Tom, has a cat "pecked" you again?'

CHAPTER 9

SIGNS AND WONDERS

O N 30 AUGUST 1880 the first of the 'Llanthony Apparitions'
were reported. That morning – a Monday – the consecrated
Host was seen to materialise on the altar of the abbey church (in
the monstrance, in which it was reserved in the tabernacle) by
Brother Dunstan (Magrath) and then separately by Janet Owens. In
the evening a white-robed figure, after some hesitation identified
as the Blessed Virgin Mary, appeared to the four monastery boys
who were playing in the Abbot's Meadow.

Miss Owens ('Sister Janet'; see Chapter 8) slept at a nearby
farmhouse, but had a makeshift daytime base just inside the monastery
entrance.[438] The monastic household at this time consisted of Ignatius
himself (as usual participating only selectively in the daily routine);

---

[438] 'We were in a passage from which doors opened into different parts of the
monastery, and this draughty apartment I found had been improvised as
a room for Sister Janet to dwell in. There was no fireplace in it, but she
said she would have a paraffin stove there in the winter' (*Hereford Times*
18 September 1880; report by 'Our Abergavenny Correspondent'). This
was the lean-to passageway at the junction of the north and west wings,
whose roof slopes out below the oriel window of Fr Ignatius's cell, which
visitors from an earlier era will remember passing through on their way
from the main entrance to the former indoor chapel. A letter in the 30
October issue suggests that she had migrated to a room with a 'nice bright
and cosy fire': this would have been the room in the west wing proper
immediately adjacent to this passageway, and which has a door connecting
with it; it also served as the acolytes' playroom/schoolroom. Before the
opening of the abbey church this room and part of the adjacent refectory
had formed the 25-foot temporary oratory mentioned in an earlier chapter;
the downstairs rooms at the monastery have been united and divided in
various configurations both during and since its monastic phase. In view
of this evidence that she had rather more than a toehold in the monastery
building it is strange that Ignatius would maintain in connection with
the 15 September apparition that she had to undertake the evening watch
in the meadow, because she wasn't allowed into the porch (see below).

one novice, twenty-year-old Brother Dunstan, the only one of the three clothed on that year's feast of St David to have survived the summer; the four boys, and two visitors. These were George Swaine, an associate whose home was in Wisbech,[439] and a 'young railway clerk' mentioned by both the Abbot and ex-Sister Mary Agnes, who alleges that he faked the Marian apparitions by beaming pictures from a magic lantern.[440] In his 'oration' on the apparitions delivered at Westminster Town Hall in 1885 Ignatius confirmed that this person was present on the first day, when he 'witnessed the boys' excitement on the subject' of what they had seen, though not the apparition itself;[441] if he was there beyond that day (and he must have been, if the magic lantern theory was being applied to subsequent sightings) it is strange that he figures in none of the other accounts, and we are not told his name or anything else about him.

A few days after the first apparitions Ignatius left for a ten-day visit to the convent at Slapton, having arranged to do duty in the parish church there on the first two Sundays of September. He arrived back on the 14th of that month, bringing with him a fifth boy, 11-year-old William George (or George William) Whyley, who, as mentioned in an earlier chapter, was clothed as a novice that

---

[439] Most accounts misspell his name as 'Swain'. Born 1855 in Wisbech, where he figures in the censuses of 1861 and 1871, in the latter as a Teacher of Music (aged 16). His name is missing from the 1881 census, but in the following three he is married with one son and employed as a (stipendiary) Licensed Lay Reader in the Church of England: at Bramshott (Hants) in 1891; Tring (Herts) in 1901, and Dunstable (Beds) in 1911. He died in 1927.

[440] NL p167, p175. It is known that there was indeed such a machine at the monastery (MT March 1884; LMN Jan-March 1894), although it's hard to imagine how anyone could have performed this feat on several evenings without giving himself away. (The possibility of a hoax is dismissed by one of those present at the final apparition; his account is given later in this chapter.) Other physical explanations for the phenomena advanced by contemporary sceptics included glow-worms and 'Will-o'the-Wisp', or *ignis fatuus*.

[441] MSO p413

October. On the same day another visitor, Charles Rouse, arrived, to be admitted as a postulant the following week.

When news of these happenings reached the outside world the monastery began to attract a number of other visitors, including newspaper correspondents both professional and amateur. As well as the extra information they give us about the events themselves these journalists provide us with some interesting insights into daily life at New Llanthony and the people who lived there. Brother Dunstan, for instance, is described by an 'occasional correspondent' to the Hereford Times as 'a young man whose manner and speech indicate considerable cultivation', and in the following week's issue as 'a gentleman' (two ways of making the same significant point), and one in whom there was 'no trace of fanaticism'.[442] This last observation ties in with Ignatius's own slightly unflattering assessment of him as a 'hard-headed, unimaginative half Scotchman, half Irishman'[443] – in other words not the sort of person to 'see things'. (But as we shall see, Dom Cyprian Alston had reason to describe him as 'a most unreliable person'.)

Janet Owens was quite different. Another newspaperman asked her about any previous experiences she might have had of the paranormal, and it emerged that she had had two, both 'on the occasion of serious events in her family'. One of them involved the appearance of light similar to that surrounding the apparition of Our Lady, which by this time she had witnessed for herself.[444]

THE EVENTS

VARIOUS ACCOUNTS of the phenomena were published, of which the first to appear was the report Ignatius sent to the local press.[445]

---

[442] Hereford Times, issues of 18 and 25 September

[443] Address in Sheffield on 28 October 1880, reported the following day in the Sheffield & Rotherham Independent.

[444] Hereford Times 25 September 1880, report by W.H. Harrison (see below)

[445] ibid, 11 September 1880

Cast in the form of a letter to the Editor, it had been sent five days earlier from the priory at Slapton.

Picture 19: The 'Ladye Altar' in the north-west corner of the abbey church

It begins with a reminder of the monastery's purpose as a place of 'prayer, praise and labour', and that in the ten years since its foundation it had developed two particular 'intentions'. The first of these was 'continual reparation to our Lord Jesus Christ for the insults he has received in our Church and country since the Reformation, in the Holy Sacrament', and the second 'to make reparation to the mother of our Lord Jesus for the neglect and dislike which have been heaped upon her' in protestant Britain. Although Ignatius doesn't here make the connection in so many words – he would do so in his 1885 'oration' – the fact that he mentions these 'intentions' before describing praeternatural manifestations of the Eucharist and the Blessed Virgin suggests that he understood the events as divine approval for having promoted them. In later articles and addresses he would make the additional point that the miraculous nature of the apparitions helped to confirm faith in something more basic, the truth of the supernatural realm itself. As the later Victorian Church began to accommodate its thinking to the theories of Darwin and the 'higher critics' he became obsessed by the apparent loss of such faith, and lost no opportunity to denounce his distant cousin Dean Stanley, Canon (later Bishop) Gore and others who downplayed or denied altogether the miraculous element in Christianity.

MONDAY 30 AUGUST: APPEARANCE OF
THE 'MIRACULOUS MONSTRANCE'

HE THEN TURNS to the events of that morning. At 9.0 'the senior brother' (in later accounts identified as Dunstan) took up his position at the prayer-desk in the centre of the sanctuary for his one-hour watch, succeeding another (unnamed) member of the household – a boy, perhaps, or one of the visitors. About half way through the allotted period he became aware that the monstrance containing the Host was visible in front of the tabernacle door.[446] He wasn't

---

[446] The monstrance was given by Dr Pusey; a note in the York Herald of 14 January 1871 (copied from the Church Times) stated that 'a friend of the order [had] presented a most costly monstrance'. With its accompanying custodia (evidently not in use on this occasion) it is now at Prinknash Abbey; Dom Damian Sturdy of that community remembers as a teenage visitor seeing a similar model at Ascot Priory, presumably also provided by Pusey (personal conversation, 29 November 2011).

sure whether or not it was an 'optical delusion', although he could still see it when he left the building at 10 o'clock.

Dunstan was succeeded by 'an associate member of the order, a schoolmistress from Hay'. Again no name was given, although in later accounts we are told it was Janet Owens. As a 'secular' (and a woman) she had to kneel at a desk in the outer church, although with a view through the lattice-work choir gates to the altar beyond – on which she also saw the monstrance. It never occurred to her that she might be witnessing a miracle; instead, she thought the Blessed Sacrament had been exposed for adoration, and was 'astonished to find that the Host was exposed without the usual signs of reverence and devotion'.[447] When her watch came to an end at eleven o'clock she

went straight to the door of the monastery and begged to see the senior brother at once. On his going to the grate, at the porch door the schoolmistress in question asked him in considerable excitement and astonishment 'What is the matter? Why is this [the?] blessed Sacrament outside the tabernacle? I have had such a wonderful watch.' The brother, to use his own words, 'pricked up his ears' at the good sister's questions, for now he saw at once that his vision of the blessed Sacrament could have been no delusion, but a reality. He then told her what he had seen and how astonished he had been. So the matter rests, it is entirely inexplicable, for the tabernacle doors had not been opened, and the key was put away in my cell.

A few weeks later the Superior would explain why Janet had found the watch so wonderful:

Fr Ignatius said he ought not to touch upon Sister Janet's private troubles; but she was troubled, because the Sunday before she was not at the sacrament service; and on Monday she thought it was a

---

[447] MSO p413f

make-up to her for her loss on the Sunday that the Blessed Sacrament had been left out. So she had a most wonderful watch.[448]

MONDAY 30 AUGUST: FIRST MARIAN APPARITION

IN LATER ACCOUNTS Ignatius insisted that Dunstan and Janet had kept quiet about their experience, and that the boys had no idea that anything unusual had taken place that morning, but it's hard to believe that their antennae hadn't picked up just a hint of their excitement (or that of Ignatius himself). His report continues with the events of that evening:

Four of our boys[449] were playing in the Abbot's Meadow at recreation time, after Vespers.... The sun had set – it was just after eight – light enough to see an object distinctly, though the evening gloaming had fairly set in.... A few minutes after 8, Chalkley [sic] came running into the monastery seeking for me. In the community room he came up to me in great excitement, 'Dear Father, dear Father, we've just seen such a beautiful spirit in the Abbot's Meadow.' I replied, 'Oh, nonsense,' and went on with what I was about, thinking nothing more of it. When the rest came in, full of what had appeared to them, John Stewart affirmed that as he was playing, he suddenly saw the figure of a woman advancing towards him from the road in the meadow that led to the enclosure gates.[450] The figure was dressed in

---

[448] Report of public meeting referred to above in *Hereford Times* of 20 November 1880

[449] The only four. Ignatius had an understandable temptation to make his modest establishment sound bigger than it really was. Compare his references to Dunstan as 'the senior brother', with the implication that there were other monks (as opposed to choirboys and the occasional visiting associate) junior to him.

[450] It might be helpful to point out that in Ignatius's sketch-plan (see next page) the 'Abbot's Meadow' (which then included the areas now occupied by the stables and the pony trekkers' car park; it was in this part of the field that the Apparitions were seen) has been foreshortened so as not to take up too much of the newspaper column. It was bounded

a white alb, only the sleeves were wider than alb sleeves. The hands were both raised, and from head to feet a dazzling white light, oval shape, was shining round the body. The figure and the light glided slowly towards him, only it moved thus. I give you the lines of the apparition path through the meadow. The numbers show where the boys Stewart (No. 1), Foord (No.2), Maguire (no. 3) and Chalkley [sic] (no. 4) were. The dots represent the path the apparition took.

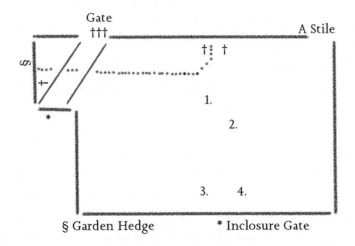

Stewart saw it before it got to the road. He called to Foord to look. Foord was very frightened, and caught up a large stick, and said if it came near him he would strike it. Then Maguire, hearing the cries of the other two boys, was attracted to look. The meadow is very large, and Maguire was a long distance off, but he saw the figure and the

---

for part of its southern (uphill) edge by the 'garden hedge' where the stables now stand; up the hill from this stood the dilapidated 'hut' or former farmhouse, surrounded by a small garden. Those arriving at the monastery had to pass through two gates; the one marked ††† (an ordinary field gate) where the drive left the lane leading on up the hill to the farmhouse, and an inner pair (the 'inclosure gate(s)') near the small stone building just past the stables (the former monastic laundry and bakehouse). These were probably the 'green gates' mentioned in the account of one of the later apparitions.

light enter the hedge and remain standing in it. Chalkley [sic] only saw the figure when it was in the hedge, and the light made the hedge seem all ablaze. The single † is where the figure first appeared. The two †† where it disappeared. Stewart stood close to the hedge, saw the figure vanish, but the bush[451] continued all in a dazzling glow for some moments after the figure had disappeared. The boys rushed round to the gate ††† to look for the figure in the road, but nothing was to be seen. The hedge is very thick and strong, and its great density would require great strength to effect a passage; and then, the marks of the violence needed would be manifest. It could not be climbed over by any possibility. It is quite nine feet high [a point later disputed; see below]. The boys could talk of nothing but the beautiful spirit they had seen. I forgot to mention that a long white veil hung over the back of the figure from the head.

Stewart was asked whether he was prepared to go before the Blessed Sacrament and swear on the crucifix to his statement. He answered, 'Yes, dear Father, to every part of it.' Ignatius warned him that 'no-one in Abergavenny or any of the towns round here' would believe his tale; 'they would say you were a young liar and deserved a good thrashing.' Considering his general readiness to accept the authenticity of strange phenomena it is questionable whether the warning was given with real severity, or that Ignatius *really* thought 'nothing more of' Chawkley's reported sighting of a 'beautiful spirit' (or even pretended to).

Accompanied by the four boys and 'some others' Ignatius went to examine the hedge, and concluded that it was too thick for a person to have passed through it, and found no signs of disturbance. The boys reasserted all they had said before.

---

[451] This is the first mention of the 'holy bush', a clump of wild rhubarb at ††. It quickly became the focal point of the cult.

ONE SIGNIFICANT DETAIL is missing from this account – Ignatius's institution of a daily 'watch' at the hour of the Apparition, starting the following evening. We don't know what form these first 'watches' took, but devotion to the Mother of God would certainly have been a prominent feature. Any question as to either the supernatural nature of the Apparition or its identity would have been hard to sustain as the cult of 'Our Ladye of Llanthony' began to take shape.

The influence of the Superior at this crucial point is suggested in the following fragment of oral tradition, preserved in Edward Jones's reminiscences of his time as a 'monastery boy' a few years later:

> Two boys were playing in the field at dusk one winter's evening, and they saw a strange object in the hedge. One of them said, 'What is that woman in the hedge?' The other answered, 'It is not a woman; it is a cow.' Looking more closely they saw what appeared to be a woman, and, as she was among the thicket, they thought it very strange, and they became frightened and ran to tell Father Ignatius. The Father came out, and he said at once, 'It is the Blessed Virgin, Our Lady of Llanthony.' Then all the inmates of the monastery were summoned, and the 'Ave Maria' was chanted.... The vision vanished, and the spot has ever since been regarded as holy ground. The Blessed Virgin appeared to be clad in white, and a light seemed to emanate from her, illuminating all around.

From his account of events on the Monday evening Ignatius jumps straight to the following Friday (3 September), when he had a visit from his 'kind legal friend Mr John Christie' ('of 18 Stanley Crescent, London W.'), who was staying in the neighbourhood and had come to discuss some point connected with the monastery title deeds: ownership had been transferred from Hilda Stewart to Ignatius in April of the previous year. When he mentioned the apparition Christie smiled a polite but incredulous smile. He said he should like to see the boys separately. I sent for them. John Stewart came in first, and the good lawyer commenced an examination of the boy –

who had now had three full days to think about what he had seen, and participated in three evening 'watches'. Not surprisingly he

gave precisely the same details as he had done before. Mr Christie said, 'What do you believe it was that you saw?' Stewart replied, 'I believe it was the blessed Virgin Mary, sir.' 'What makes you think so?' 'It was like I have seen her represented in pictures.'

This might have been conclusive, but according to Ignatius

[h]e said to me afterwards that the apparition was like the picture of our Lord walking on the sea, only the figure was a woman, and a white veil hung from her head –

so there was perhaps still an element of doubt in his mind. Mr Christie then questioned Foord and Maguire (and possibly also Chawkley, although his name isn't mentioned); 'all stuck to their first statements'. He then went to look at the hedge ('accompanied by the boys and some other persons who desired to see it'), before expressing his conclusion: 'It is extraordinary, but I feel satisfied that the boys believe what they are saying.'

A FURTHER DEVELOPMENT that Friday was the first recorded instance of a healing through the agency of a leaf from the 'holy bush', although there seems to have been some doubt at this stage as to what species of bush it was. 'A brother' (unidentified) who was suffering from 'weakness and great pain' went with another brother to pray at the bush:

All at once, as if by a sudden inspiration, the brother broke off a piece of a large dock leaf in the bush and put it on his forehead, saying 'If the blessed Virgin has touched this leaf it must do me good.' The moment the leaf touched his head the pain went, and the feeling of weakness also.... In the night (which is not to be wondered at and is no marvel) the brother who had been so relieved, and kept the leaf on his pillow under his head, saw in a dream the apparition of the Virgin, just as the boys had described it.

IN THE 1881 LLANTHONY *Benedictine Calendar* 30 August had already been appointed a feast with the rank of Greater Double ('Apparition of Our Lady at Llanthony and of the Most Holy Sacrament, AD 1880'), with the subsequent appearances being commemorated on the relevant dates. Elsewhere in this publication is an account of the events agreeing substantially with Ignatius's narrative, although with one or two differences of detail.[452] During Brother Dunstan's watch the monstrance appeared to be 'very shadowy at first', only 'gradually' becoming 'perfectly distinct'; and there is nothing in the narrative to prevent the reader assuming that Janet Owens was a nun, rather than a lay associate. In Ignatius's 1885 Oration the description of Dunstan's vision would be further refined:

The brother had been half an hour at his watch...when he raised his eyes and saw, in front of the Tabernacle, a kind of blue mist playing. As he looked at the mist he thought that his eyes must be affected, and he rubbed them, thinking it was an illusion; but as he still looked, the mist thickened and densified, until he saw the monstrance, or silver vessel which contained the Host, within the Tabernacle, glimmering in the mist, outside the massive door of the Tabernacle, which was locked.[453]

---

[452] This version is reproduced *verbatim* by the Baroness de Bertouch (pp546ff).

[453] MSO pp409f

The *Calendar* account also has John Stewart 'waiting for his turn to run in the game' when he first caught sight of the evening apparition, and the suggestion that it resembled 'pictures of the "Immaculate Conception"'. This version pointed out that Thomas Foord's violent reaction was the same as that displayed in similar circumstances by a boy of the same age three decades earlier at La Salette,[454] and mentions the institution of the watch.

SATURDAY 4 SEPTEMBER

ON THE FIFTH DAY, Saturday 4 September, when Ignatius had left for Slapton, the daily watch bore fruit. In the *Calendar* the account of this second Marian apparition continues in words said to be 'chiefly from the narration of Brother Dunstan':

> At a few minutes to eight I was up-stairs trimming the Choir lamp,[455] when I heard Daniel Maguire calling to me; I instantly went to him, when he exclaimed, 'Dear brother, the light is in the bush.' I looked and saw the bush, which was some hundreds of feet distant, full of bright light. We all went into the meadow; it was perfectly dark every where else. The Bush was all aglow with light, presenting a most mysterious appearance. We knelt opposite the bush, but some distance from it, and began to say prayers and sing hymns, but no figure appeared.
>
> Presently I suggested that, if it really was the Blessed Virgin, who had appeared to the boys on Monday, possibly if we sung the 'Ave Maria', she might again appear. So we began to sing the 'Ave', and on our doing so, we at once perceived the Form of a woman surrounded

---

[454] "O my God!" exclaimed Maximin's companion Melanie Mathieu, dropping the stick she was holding. The boy replied, "Keep your stick, do; I will take care of mine; if it does anything to us I will give it a good knock"' (W.B. Ullathorne, *The Holy Mountain of La Salette*, Richardson & Son 1854, p44).

[455] The 'night light' in the dormitory corridor. The same task was being carried out when the 8 September apparition began; see below.

by light at the top of the meadow by the gate. Slowly the Form and the light advanced towards the already illuminated Bush. Every now and then, as the Form advanced, we lost sight of it and then it reappeared, until at last it stood before us in the Bush, but sideways, the face and head covered with the veil as noticed by the boys on Monday.

On coming to the words in the 'Ave', 'Blessed is the Fruit of Thy womb, Jesus', the light in the Bush extended towards the right and in the light appeared the Form of a Man unclothed, save a cloth round the loins. His hands were stretched out towards the other Figure whose hands were folded on the breast. As the Forms met, both vanished. Frequently after this, for we remained two hours in the meadow, the Form of the Blessed Virgin – for we quite concluded that it was absolutely Our Lord's Mother – frequently appeared as we repeated the 'Ave Maria'.

Once, Daniel Maguire cried out for us to look, for a light hovered over his head, and I saw in the light the form of what I believed to have been an Angel, he did not see the form, but exclaimed, Something has touched my head and cured me of the pain. The boy was suffering much from headache, at the time.

The grass was wringing wet with a heavy dew, but we perceived that the ground in front of the Bush, where we knelt, was both dry and warm. We remained in the meadow till ten o'clock.

An earlier account of the 4 September appearance was printed in the following week's *Hereford Times*, immediately after Ignatius's narrative. It consisted chiefly of extracts from letters sent by four of the five witnesses to him at Slapton. The first was from 'the Senior Brother' (Dunstan):

I must say [that from] what every one of us saw on Saturday evening, September 4th, there is not a doubt left on my mind but that it is the Blessed Virgin, as the figure only appeared when we sang the 'Ave', and as we ended it, 'Blessed is the fruit of thy womb, Jesus', another figure appeared with hands held out towards our Ladye, and as they met they vanished. It was close on ten o'clock, and the grass was wringing wet in other places, but quite dry and warm where we knelt, and all about the hedge.

The next was from 'another brother', i.e. George Swaine. He emphasises that the figures appeared and disappeared, then reappeared when the appropriate words were sung: 'There were two figures twice seen by Brother Dunstan and me.' He also adds the detail that the figures were 'surrounded with wonderful light, and sometimes the meadow was quite bright with it', and that 'Brother Dunstan was quite nervous.'

John Stewart makes the point that there were differences in what the individual visionaries saw:

The two brothers [Dunstan and George] saw our Lord's figure and the Blessed Virgin's, and I saw our Ladye and our Lord, but not as Brother Dunstan saw them – I saw our Lord as if He were on the cross, with His arms stretched out, and our Blessed Ladye seemed as if she was coming towards Him. I also saw a light come down from the clouds, like the sunbeams coming through a window, and it rested exactly on the spot I pointed out to you [i.e. to Ignatius after the 30 August apparition]. I also saw a large star in the hedge which was so bright and beautiful, and spread light all round the top part of the meadow. Brother George and I are the only ones that saw a star which seemed to fall to the ground. Brother Dunstan kept on singing 'Aves' with us, and each time we sang an 'Ave' we saw either the figure of our Blessed Lady or some strange mysterious light, but when Brother George began to sing hymns [i.e. hymns not addressed to the Blessed Virgin; see reference to Fr Ignatius's 1885 Oration at the end of this section], we did not see anything.

Stewart's narrative certainly bears out his reputation for intelligence and articulateness. Daniel Maguire did not have these gifts, but he is quite clear about what he experienced:

[W]e were playing in the meadow (Saturday evening), and I saw a light appear in the hedge. Johnnie was close by me. I took Johnnie by the hand, and he saw it. Then Sister Janet saw it, and then the two brothers came out, and they saw figures, and so did I, and Johnnie too. We had said the Rosary after Vespers. I had a headache. We were kneeling down and I saw brightness over my head, and I felt something touch my head, and the headache left me.

Daniel's letter lists those who witnessed the 4 September apparition as himself and 'Johnnie', Janet Owens and the two brothers, Dunstan and George. The other two boys are not mentioned, although from a later account it seems they were there as well. This appeared in the 18 September *Hereford Times*, in the description of the visit by the 'Occasional Correspondent' to which we have already referred. He had taken statements from each of the witnesses, although he only includes those of the two brothers and John Stewart, and deals with the 30 August and 8 September apparitions as well as that of 4 September.

Dunstan's contribution to this article tells us a little more about what he and the others saw on the 4th than his description in the *Calendar*. He was 'in the Rev. Father's cell' when Daniel Maguire called to him from the bottom of the stairs. Leaving what he was doing he called Brother George and the other boys, and they all

went straight out into the Abbot's meadow. When we got to the green gates we decided on going to the centre of the meadow. It was very dark and we knelt down right opposite the light, which was in the hedge. We sang the 'Ave'. Then we waited a little time and saw nothing. On singing the 'Ave' for the third time Daniel Maguire looked and saw that the light pointed towards the gate leading out of the meadow. I looked and saw a white female figure just by the gate. It came slowly down by the hedge. Another figure (a male) met it. The male figure had its arms stretched out towards the other. The female figure had its hands crossed upon its breast. When the figures met, they vanished. The female figure was of medium height. The male figure was taller. The female figure was draped in white. The veil seemed to cover it in front, as well as behind. It stood sideways, and I could not discern the profile. The male figure was naked, except a cloth around the loins. I could not see the face. There was a pale, yellowish light round the figures. Between me and the light there appeared to be a mist, somewhat similar to that which we see before the sun when it is rising. The male figure reminded me of our Lord. The female figure resembled pictures I have seen of the Virgin Mary. The male figure was flat; the female rounded. Though the grass was wet elsewhere, it was quite dry round us.

George Swaine told the 'Occasional Correspondent' that when he heard the boys saying they had 'seen the light' he accompanied them and Brother Dunstan into the meadow, 'being very anxious to see the vision'. When they 'sang an "ave"' he also 'saw a light', which was 'very bright' and 'had a yellowish tinge'.

It seemed to fill the bush. There were several lights. Some burst in the middle of the hedge – some above it. The lights were oblong; a kind of vignette. They were very brilliant in the centre, and appeared to shade off. The light was so brilliant that I closed my eyes for a moment or two. I turned cold at the light. I could scarcely breathe. I saw two figures – male and female. The female figure was draped in white; the male had what appeared to be a cloth round the loins. The male figure held out its hands; the female figure had its hands crossed on its breast. I could not see the features of either. The male reminded me of the pictures of our Lord in His baptism; the female of drawings and paintings of the Blessed Virgin. The male figure advanced towards the female. As they met they vanished. Previously to the Saturday night of which I am speaking, I had been suffering almost incessantly from rheumatism. On that night it left me, and I have felt nothing of it since.

John Stewart's statement included the observation that the female figure was 'not so plain as before', and that (as he had already observed in his letter to Ignatius) the male one 'looked like Christ on the cross'.

In his 1885 Oration Ignatius reported that the 'junior brother' (George) arrived in the meadow before Dunstan, and began to 'say prayers and hymns'.

> The boys were indignant because he was saying collects and hymns that had no relation to what they considered the vision to be, and they said, 'Do not say those prayers, but say a "Hail, Mary", for we are certain it was the Blessed Virgin. If we do, our Lord will perhaps let the vision appear again.'

According to this later account it was during this discussion that Dunstan came on the scene, and agreed that they should sing an 'ave'.

> That instant the figure flashed again, in a cloud of light, in the same place where the first boy had seen it on the Monday.

WEDNESDAY 8 SEPTEMBER

IN REPLY TO THE LETTERS he had received after the 4 September apparition Ignatius 'wrote back that the following Wednesday, the 8th, being the Feast of the Nativity or Birth of the Blessed Virgin, it would please God, doubtless, again to vouchsafe the apparition to be seen,'[456] and this duly occurred. In his Sheffield address Ignatius reported that after Vespers that evening 'the sister-associate' was in the meadow and George Swaine standing at the porch door, while Daniel Maguire was in the Abbot's cell performing the regular evening chore of trimming the lamps.

---

[456] He made this admission in the address in Sheffield to which we have referred above.

All at once Bro Swain [sic] gave a great cry, and said the figure had appeared. All of them went on together, and saw the Blessed Virgin at the gate of the enclosure. Numbers of extraordinary lights were also floating about.

Brother Dunstan said that it was he who had been trimming the lamps on this occasion, and in his statement to the *Hereford Times* 'Occasional Correspondent' said that Brother George called to him up the stairs. This version of his account continues:

I kept him waiting about a minute. I then came running down the stairs. Brother George said, 'I have seen the figure distinctly, twice.' I said, 'Where?' He replied, 'There's an opening in the hedge and the figure is standing in the hedge, just by the tree by the green gates.' Sister Janet called out. I opened the porch door, and she said, 'Dear brother! I have seen the figure, too, distinctly, over the green gates.' I then looked and saw it in an exact line with where I had seen it on Saturday night. We knelt in about the same place as before. It was very dark. The hedge was completely dark. Every now and then, whilst we were singing, a bright star would twinkle in the hedge, and then fall to the ground. We continued singing 'Aves'. I saw shadowy figures passing to and fro in the hedge. The light was very pale; not bright at all. This kept on for a long time. It was just the same when we were not singing. The grass was lit up in front of me. I had a headache. Something touched my head, and the headache was gone. We stayed in the meadow till 10 o'clock, and then returned to the Monastery. As on Saturday night the grass was perfectly dry where we were, though wet everywhere else.

The stars, too, were reminiscent of the Saturday apparition, as was the cure of a headache. In the *Calendar* account Dunstan would mention Daniel Maguire, but in his testimony to the 'Occasional Correspondent' George Swaine implies that other boys were present:

On Wednesday night, the Nativity, I went to the meadow again with Brother Dunstan and the boys. The hedge seemed to open at the green gates. I saw a flash of light come right by me. Once I saw some very bright stars. They seemed to throw out light.

And John Stewart reported:

On Wednesday night, the Nativity, I saw the figure, after Brother George and Sister Janet. I saw it in the hedge. I also saw a male figure. The female figure was draped in white. The male figure seemed to have a cloth thrown around the loins.

When he came to compile his account for the *Calendar* Dunstan would omit the detail about his headache:

On Wednesday...the Vision of our Ladye reappeared, to Brother George (Mr Swaine), Daniel Maguire, and Sister Janet, closer by the enclosure gates. When I heard their cry I went to them, but although the light remained, the Form was gone. It reappeared as we all approached the light but very indistinctly, it flickered, as it were, in the light which moved before us to the now Holy Bush.

On each succeeding evening the watch was kept up. The 18 September report mentions Dunstan having

seen the light in the hedge on the following Saturday night [10 September], and Sister Janet having seen a flood of light in the meadow on the night following (Sunday),

but no further 'figures' were seen until the final apparition, on Wednesday 15 September.

INTERLUDE: A SPIRITUALIST VISITS
(Monday 13/Tuesday 14 September)

A DASH OF LOCAL COLOUR is provided by the account in the 25 September *Hereford Times* of a visit made by a correspondent named W.H. Harrison, who on the morning of Monday 13th had read in the Cardiff papers about 'the appearance of a spirit' at Llanthony. As a devotee of spiritualism he had a particular interest in such phenomena, and was keen to investigate the story for himself. He arrived at the monastery that evening after dark, having walked from Llanfihangel and been shown the way by a 'young agriculturalist'; this unnamed individual didn't believe in the visions because he considered the monks' 'doctrine [to be] dead against the Bible'.

Harrison watched in the meadow for half an hour,[457] then rang the front doorbell. There was no response, so he watched for another fifteen minutes before ringing again. This time

a light moved inside the monastery. Presently two boys, acolytes, put their heads out of a window, asking in a whisper – for the men in the monastery here ordinarily speak in a whisper – who I was and what I wanted. Afterwards the boys did some prolonged whispering between themselves, then brought the light of their candle to bear upon me, and made a close inspection. More whispering. Then they told me to push open the door and take a seat. I pushed open the door, and found a cold little passage or hall, with a candle burning on its tiled floor; two inner doors were furnished with minute iron gratings through which visitors might be inspected. I took my seat on a chair, near a table covered with devotional books, and wondered what was to come next.

After a long delay, Sister Janet, who had probably been sent for from a distance, put in an appearance from the haunted [!] meadow. She told me that she was an Associate Sister who had taken only the

---

[457] Presumably that evening's regular watch had by then already finished.

vow of obedience, and who did much of the exterior work of the Monastery. She had formerly been mistress at the National School at Hay. In the most obliging way she chatted about the apparition which had been seen by herself, as well as by others, and subsequently we entered the meadow and talked for some time by the side of the bush from which the apparition had come. It was a bush in a tall rough hedge, with a narrow lane deep down on the other side. She said that she had not believed the report of the boys, but supposed it to have been a mistake or a jest. Subsequently she saw the bush gloriously luminous; a Veiled Lady, whom she supposed to be the Blessed Virgin, came from it, and glided some yards towards her, nearly half-way from the hedge, then vanished instantly. The figure was a small one, about four feet high; she saw it for about two minutes. The light from it was so strong that it was reflected from the surface of her boots where they were polished, and she could see the mud upon them by it. Four persons had seen the apparition at the same time. The latter facts tend to show its objective nature, and that it was materialised. Under mesmeric or spiritual influence several persons cannot see by normal eyesight, but I do not know that reflection of light from a polished surface can be included in this category.[458]

Sister Janet cheerfully exerted herself in finding lodging for me at a farm-house, explaining that the 'Reverend Father' (Father Ignatius) was away and under that circumstance the 'Brothers' could not break through their rule, and give me the guest's chamber in the monastery. She whiled away the time occupied in our search, by giving very interesting information about the monastery, the principles believed in by Fr Ignatius, and her own happiness in doing even the humblest work connected with the establishment....

---

[458] Compare Janet's observation about the reflection of the light on her boots with Fr Asaph's report to Dr E. Hermitage Day that one of the witnesses (probably Dunstan) had told him that the light from the apparition had been 'so brilliant that "it made this rough stone" (laying his hand on the jamb of the doorway) "as translucent as alabaster"' (Enthusiast p236).

On my way yesterday afternoon[459] from the monastery to Llanthony Abbey [sic], I met Father Ignatius driving in the opposite direction. Special prayers had been offered during the day that he might see the apparition that night – prayers which I am afraid to say have not been granted, since concentration of mind upon a desired result is well known to be, by the action of some unexplained mesmeric law, an impediment to the materialisation of spirits. The apparition is far more likely to be seen when least thought about. Fr Ignatius expressed his regret at my connection with modern Spiritualism, the phenomena of which he believes to be diabolical, although he has spirits in his meadow, and is now waiting to see them himself....

The writer was impressed with the atmosphere of sincerity surrounding the events, but concluded:

I am in doubt whether the apparition was materialised, or whether seen by the synchronous clairvoyance of several individuals in spiritual rapport with each other from having held religious services together.... If the appearances at the monastery continue, votaries will flock there, and a town spring up....

TUESDAY 14 SEPTEMBER
When Harrison met him Ignatius was on his way back from Slapton, accompanied by the boy Whyley. On the same day Charles Rouse arrived, as did an unnamed 'gentleman from Hereford' and the 'Occasional Correspondent', whose report is brought to a climax in its account of that evening's events:

After the evidence given above I received a strange statement from a gentleman named Rouse from Yorkshire, who had come to this monastery only a few hours before. He said: I have been suffering

---

[459] i.e. Tuesday 14 September

from neuralgia very acutely. I was in great pain during part of the time that I was coming from Llanvihangel, and during the whole of the time since I arrived here – about half-past two o'clock. About five o'clock I thought, 'I will go to the bush, where the vision has been seen, and say a prayer there.' I did so. I prayed to Christ that He might manifest His glory. I then said an 'Ave'. Still suffering, I plucked a leaf. I applied it to my face. On my way back I was engaged in prayer. As I was going up the steps to the guest-room[460] the pain entirely left me. This gentleman, I was informed, is visiting the Abbey, with the view of eventually becoming a monk.

All this activity disrupted the normal timetable, and Vespers, which was scheduled for 6 o'clock, didn't start until seven. At this service '[t]he Rev. Father wore an alb, amice, and girdle' with the addition of a cope during the Magnificat. 'Brother Dunstan wore a cape, cassock, and hood; and Brother George wore a surplice and cassock. The monastery boys wore albs, amices and red skull caps. Some wore blue and some wore scarlet scapulars....'[461]

After Vespers the weather continued very heavy, although the rain had somewhat abated. The night was very dark. It was about five and twenty minutes past eight when, as I was standing in the porch, Brother Dunstan suddenly called out to me through the grill which separates the porch from the monastery, 'The Rev. Father says that Brother George has seen the light.' Upon this, I hastened out. Outside I found a gentleman from Hereford, who was visiting the monastery, and he and myself, accompanied by Mr Rouse (the gentleman from Yorkshire before referred to) proceeded at once to the Abbot's meadow. Here we looked most attentively, but could see nothing. We were

---

[460] The outside staircase at the south-west corner (now demolished)

[461] I think he means shoulder-capes, seen in a number of contemporary photographs.

presently joined by Sister Janet. She knelt down about the middle of the meadow, facing the hedge. Her example was shortly followed by Mr Rouse. The rest remained standing.

Presently, while we still waited, seeing nothing, we heard solemn chanting. This, we knew, issued from the Abbot and the other inmates of the monastery. Some considerable time elapsed, the chanting still continuing, when at length a procession of a weird and imposing character entered the meadow. It was headed by Fr Ignatius, who carried a large processional crucifix. He was followed by Brother Dunstan and Brother George, and by five lads — four who had seen the vision, and one whom the Abbot had that day brought from Slapton. They took up their station about the centre of the meadow opposite the hedge, the Father and the brothers standing, the boys kneeling in front of them. We were thus twelve in number, four having been in the meadow before, and eight having now entered. The Father, the brothers, and the boys continued singing 'Aves' with great vigour.... It was a strange sight. Nature, though heavy and gloomy, had yet a certain indescribable grandeur. The mountains rose, high and solemn, around us. The night was, however, bitterly cold, and rain fell drizzlingly, having commenced shortly after we entered the meadow.

A pause occurring in the singing, I told the Rev. Father I had seen nothing. He then told me that, from the monastery door, before the procession proceeded to the meadow, he had thought he had seen a light in the hut garden (the hut being a small lumber building adjoining the meadow). He also thought that he had seen a shadowy figure there. This, however, might be only a fancy. The others also believed that they saw something. They had, therefore, stopped at the monastery porch, singing, for some time, but seeing nothing more, had proceeded to the meadow. The singing then recommenced, and several of the party said that they saw a light in the hedge. I continued to see nothing.

At length the Rev. Father thought he saw something, but said afterwards that it might be the reflection of a lantern. He then sent

Brother George and Daniel Maguire out of the meadow by two different ways, that they might look down the road and see if they could see anything of a man with a lantern. They returned, saying that they could not. After more singing, the Abbot proposed that I (accompanied by the gentleman from Hereford) should proceed to the hut garden, to see if we could see anything there. His reason for sending us, he said, was because we were 'seculars', as it is termed. He and the others (as consecrated persons) must not go to seek for it. They must wait till it came to them.

Well, the gentleman from Hereford and I went through the hut garden, which was an uncanny looking place enough. We, however, saw nothing, and we returned with the information. We then all stood together in the meadow, 'Aves' being sung. Lights were then repeatedly seen according to the statement of the whole party, except myself and the gentleman from Hereford. Mr Rouse said that he saw, at one time, so bright a light that he was forced to start back. I continued steadfastly regarding the hedge, in which not the slightest change was visible to my sight. The Rev. Father addressed himself frequently to me. He said, 'Look there. Can't you see something now?' This question he repeated several times. Each time I replied simply 'I can see nothing.' He would say 'Ah! It may be only my fancy.' On one occasion when he said this, Brother Dunstan and Brother George said, in a tone which mocked at the idea of its being fancy, 'Well, dear Father, if it is fancy with you, it must be so with us, for we see the same things.' He then said, 'Well, I suppose I must see something.' He afterwards said to me, 'This shows it is not a trick. If it were you would see the same as we do.' This, of course, implies that the light was appearing only to the saints. None of them professed to see anything of a figure, save the shadowy one at the beginning, in the hut garden. It was a light always, sometimes red; sometimes paler. On one occasion the Rev. Father said to me, 'Perhaps you couldn't see it unless you had excellent eyesight.' I replied simply, 'My eyesight is excellent.'

Eventually the Abbot uttered a short prayer to Christ. He then said, 'Let us say the Lord's Prayer.' In this we all joined, and shortly after ten we left the meadow. We proceeded to the monastery, and had nearly reached it, when lo! some of the party said they saw something else. I looked to the place indicated. I could see nothing but the misty appearance which is so common when a wide gap occurs between the branches of a large tree. The tree was there in front of the hut and the hut garden. Very attentively I looked, for recent failures did not make me give up. In vain. While the others said they saw a light, the gentleman from Hereford and myself saw nothing. Fr Ignatius said once, 'It looks to me like the flickering of firelight on a wall.' Appeals to me were useless. The tantalising answer 'I can see nothing,' perforce followed. And ever, as I appealed to the gentleman from Hereford, his answer was the same as mine. At length we separated.

Upon what I have written, which is a simple statement of facts, I offer no commentary. There will doubtless be numerous commentators among your readers. I prefer leaving the matter with them, only adding that on the following day the Rev. Father told me that he felt sure what he imagined he saw was only fancy. I must, however, remark that as we were twelve in the party, and only two of us declared that we saw nothing, whole ten remained who said, from time to time, that they saw something, Fr Ignatius, if his were only fancies, is but one out of ten who might have been misled by their imaginations. I will not, as I said before, offer any theories of my own, but I never saw a hedge more barren of the supernatural than this (to so many of our party) mystic hedge appeared to my sight on Tuesday last. I never saw a gap between the branches of a tree more palpably a gap than that which we saw after we left the meadow was, to my eyes. Thus the 'watch' ended.

The *Calendar* account of that evening's watch is brief to the point of terseness, and seems to settle for Ignatius's experience (if not that of some others) having been a 'fancy' rather than a vision:

On Tuesday...the Reverend Father returned home. Nothing was seen on the night of his arrival, by himself or the persons he brought with him from Hereford. But some of us saw lights like stars in the Holy Bush.

WEDNESDAY 15 SEPTEMBER

THE NEXT DAY the correspondent revisited the monastery in daylight, and was shown the site of the earlier apparitions by John Stewart. He noted that the point at which the 'figures' had disappeared was marked by a bouquet of roses – and that just there the hedge was rather lower than previously reported: nearer five feet high than nine.[462]

In spite of my lack of vision on the previous evening, I was very courteously invited by the Rev. Father to remain for yet another night. This the claims of business forced me to decline, and I returned to Hereford considerably stiffer of limb than when I had left it. Indeed, I would advise any person who may be subject to violent colds and aching bones, to reflect seriously before he undertakes a 'watch' in the Abbot's meadow on such a night as that of which I have written....

The final apparition took place that evening. Ignatius's account of it was printed in the following week's Hereford Times (25 September), as part of an article by the same 'Occasional Correspondent'. It was (not counting the ambiguous event of the preceding evening) the only one of the 1880 apparitions he would witness himself.

About eight o'clock on Wednesday evening, the 15th instant, (after the last service of the [octave of the] Nativity of the Blessed Virgin) we all came to the porch door. With me were the brothers, Mr Rouse, and [a] gentleman from Oxford..., who had visited the monastery for the

---

[462] Although this would depend on which side of it he was looking at. At the relevant point ground level in the lane is between three and four feet below that in the meadow.

purpose of endeavouring to see the vision. The boys were kneeling in front of us. Sister Janet was kneeling in the meadow. It was a very wet night. We were singing the 'Aves'. We had sung three 'Aves' in honour of the Holy Trinity, and we had just finished a fourth to the Blessed Virgin, when, all of a sudden, when I was not expecting anything of the kind, I saw a tremendous outburst of light from the dark, heavy clouds over the farm buildings. It seemed to burst right upon the building. The light was all in bulging circles.

In the very centre of the light there appeared, coming down to us, a human form. It was a very commanding stately figure. I could only see it sideways. The face was turned towards the bush. I could only see it momentarily, as it were in the 'twinkling of an eye'. But in that moment it stood out so distinctly and startlingly that I am sure it was darker than the light. Had it been clothed in cloth of silver, or cloth of gold, it might have produced the same effect — the darkness against the light. There was an intense reality about the figure. It was momentary, as I before said, and yet it seemed that it might have been an hour's vision, so intensely real was it. In the majesty of the figure, and in its being dark against the light, it reminded me of Doré's picture 'The Triumph of Christianity over Paganism'. There were flashings of light about the figure. In a moment, as I looked, it vanished.

Before it vanished it had appeared as if it would have descended upon the church door or the church roof. I feel sure that it must have been the figure of the Blessed Virgin because, although I could not discern the dress it wore, I could see that it was fully draped; whereas in the visions which others have seen, when they have seen a male figure, it has always appeared with simply a cloth around the loins, as our Lord is represented in baptism, and at other times. I also feel sure that it was the Virgin, because the figure appeared immediately after we had sung the 'Ave' in her honour. The figure also had its face turned towards the bush, where our Ladye had first been seen. I have further confirmation in the fact that, about two or three minutes afterwards, the Blessed Virgin's figure was seen by the gentleman who was watching with us, and by one of the boys, nearer to the ground. We have seen nothing since, except a light at the hut on Thursday evening.

In his 1885 address Ignatius added two farmers to the group enumerated above, although they were at the back of the porch and failed to see anything out of the ordinary. The 'gentleman visitor' is said to have been 'an undergraduate of Keble College, Oxford, now in Holy Orders'; in the Calendar he is designated 'Mr E'.[463] Although when they saw the preliminary 'flashings of light' they 'all' expressed their 'amazement', or as the Calendar report put it 'in awed whispers commented on what we were seeing', the spectacular finale was over too quickly for them to be able to share their experiences of it while it was going on. Ignatius was at pains in his account to emphasise that he only told the others what he had seen when the two brothers and Sister Janet had given independent testimony. He also estimated the height of the Apparition when it first appeared as 'about sixty feet'. In another account (a statement he made to a representative of the Hereford Times, reprinted in the Bristol Mercury on 28 September) Ignatius suggested that the reason why not all those present in the porch saw the vision was that they were looking for it 'to appear, as on previous occasions, nearer to the ground' rather than from the sky.

The 25 September report continues with Brother Dunstan's account of the same episode. This includes the appearance to Chawkley and the 'gentleman from Oxford' of 'a female figure with long sleeves near the fir tree', the figure 'surrounded with light', and Sister Janet seeing a figure of indeterminate sex in a burst of light,

---

[463] A marginal note by Dom Cyprian Alston on p 549 of the Downside copy of Bertouch gives the name 'Egerton' opposite the mention of 'Mr E'. John Egerton (later Marjoribanks-Egerton) graduated in 1881, and served as Rector of Odd Rode in the Diocese of Chester before being received into the Roman Catholic Church in 1894.

at which 'a feeling of devout awe' came over her. This caused her to exclaim 'Oh, dear!' and to clasp her hands together.

The same issue contains an account by 'Another Occasional Correspondent'. He was identified by a later contributor as 'the gentleman from Oxford' ('Mr E'), who had arrived earlier that day:

The night was dark and stormy, rain falling heavily; the wind high. About 7.30 the brothers, with the Father Superior, came out to the Monastery door and, standing on the door steps with the Processional Crucifix, commenced singing 'aves'. Shortly after they came out the rain lessened, and, standing in the doorway behind the monks, I noticed that the sky looked much lighter. Before we had been there long the Father Superior exclaimed that he saw a burst of light high up in the sky, and others of the brothers corroborated this. I was looking down the approach towards the gateway, and in the direction of the field in which the apparition had appeared, and I saw nothing then; but shortly after the Father's exclamation I thought I perceived a faint light close to the gate, immediately to the right hand side of the Scotch fir which stands by the gate.

The light was very faint, oval shaped, and slightly raised from the ground. At times it grew stronger, waning again almost directly. Once when it appeared most clear I was just going to draw the attention of the others to it, as resembling a figure in flowing drapery, with loose sleeves and outstretched arms, when one of the boys (Chalkley [sic]) suddenly turned to me, saying, 'Oh! Did you see that?' I said, 'What?' He then, in almost the identical words that were on my lips, described what he said he had seen. I said nothing further then, as some of the brothers, thinking that they saw a light move towards the field, we went down there. I saw nothing in the field. In the morning I questioned Chalkley [sic] carefully about the figure he had spoken of, its height, attitude, dress, &c., and found all his answers exactly agree[d] with the description of the figure I thought I had seen. The coincidence is at least extraordinary.

I may add that we had put out all the lights in the Monastery which could possibly have deceived us, and the idea of a hoax having been played seems, considering the wild country and the state of the weather, absolutely untenable. Hitherto I have been unable to find any explanation of the circumstances.

AFTERMATH

AFTER THE APPARITIONS Ignatius sent leaves from the 'holy bush' to various friends and supporters, including the nuns at Slapton. Mother Cecilia applied one of them to her deformed leg, and reported an instant healing. 'When the wondrous miracle became known in the Village of Slapton, the people, of their own accord, rang a peal of joy on the Village Church Bells,' and the 'Rev. Chaplain' (identified elsewhere as the Vicar) celebrated a Mass of thanksgiving in the convent chapel.[464] As soon as the news reached Llanthony Ignatius wrote an explanatory letter to the Archbishop of Canterbury, and 'had an altar erected in the Abbot's Meadow, in front of the bush' consisting of 'a wooden Gothic shrine, draped with a crimson cloth' and on top of it a white one, trimmed with lace. On this he placed a 'statue of the Virgin, with sixteen lights' and vases of flowers; in addition, a 'crimson velvet carpet was laid down in front of the altar'. An impromptu service was held at this temporary outdoor shrine, attended by 'the inmates of the monastery, with some pilgrims from Abergavenny'.[465]

That evening (Tuesday 28 September) the correspondent who filed this report attended Matins of the feast of St Michael and All Angels, brought forward from the normal hour of 2.0am. At about 8.0 he came out for a breath of air, followed by Sister Janet who asked whether he could see 'a light at the hut'. He could: 'a faint light...like a sheet of light, of a somewhat pale colour'. They went closer, but it vanished.

---

[464] Benedictine Calendar for 1881
[465] Hereford Times, 2 October 1880

After Matins the watch bell rang, and we assembled at the door of the porch. The Rev. Father, with the brothers, Sister Janet and the boys, sang 'Aves'. Some of the party thought they saw lights. Suddenly, as they were still singing, Sister Janet stated that she saw a streak of pale light, which almost resembled a long, slim figure, descending upon my head. She suddenly started, and well-nigh fainted, clinging to the wall for support. After recovering a little, she told me of this light. She told me it was a glorious light. I, of course, saw nothing, the alleged light being above me. Having watched for about half an hour, we separated.

The same correspondent was still there (or had returned) the following Sunday, when he was present at the 'High Celebration' of the 'Offering of the Holy Sacrament', the deacon Ignatius's substitute for a proper High Mass.

After the sermon, and immediately after the singing of the final hymn, an incident occurred which produced considerable sensation in the church. As the final strains of the hymn rang out, the Rev. Father rose from his seat, and, coming to the grill which separates the inner sanctuary from the outer court in which the worshippers assemble, he told me that a light (which he believed to be supernatural) had appeared over the altar. I immediately quitted my seat (from whence it was impracticable to obtain a view of the light), and proceeded to the South side of the church, where I was able to secure a full view. The light which I saw was pale, and presented, on the stone coping above the throne upon the altar, a kind of oval shape, lying length-wise. I regarded it attentively, and I thought it might be the reflection from an arched window upon the North side of the building. The Rev. Father, however, told me he had seen it begin in a very small compass on the North side of the altar. All the congregation were eagerly straining their eyes; being grouped together, many of them in a kneeling position, while the Rev. Father was in a state of very considerable excitement. He said, 'It is a light similar to that which we have seen at the bush. Wait awhile, perhaps we may see the Blessed Virgin.' The congregation lingered, and as they did so the voices of those within the inclosure rang out in the solemn strains of the 'Ave' which have so often been sung of late in honour of the Virgin. But there was no further manifestation. The light was still visible. The sunbeams, behind which it was traceable, shone forth brightly. At length the sun drew in his rays, and then the light which had attracted so much attention was more plainly manifest than before. When, eventually, we quitted the church the light was still there. It was visible also on each occasion that I entered the church during the remainder of my visit, which lasted until Tuesday evening.[466]

Although this particular example would turn out to have a physical explanation,[467] Sister Janet continued to see strange lights. In the 30 October issue of the same paper a letter appeared over the signatures of four men who a few days earlier had ridden over the mountain from Hay to investigate the phenomena for themselves. After the 8.0pm service they were following Sister Janet out of the abbey church when she stopped in her tracks exclaiming,

'There is the light! Oh, the glorious light! Can you see it? I have seen it scores of time before!' She then fell on her knees and said, 'Blessed be the Lord for having sent it to convince you.' Then rising from her knees she ran into the monastery to inform Brother Dunstan that the light had appeared.

We saw the same light, which was in the direction of the hut – 'the hut' being the ruins of the old farmhouse. We were determined

---

[466] ibid, 9 October 1881

[467] In its issue of 23 October the *Hereford Times* printed a note from its 'Occasional Correspondent' relaying a message from Ignatius, who had discovered that when one of the windows to the side of the altar was covered up the light disappeared.

to fathom the mystery of the light if possible, and one of our party, being well acquainted with the locality, following the line whence the light proceeded found that it was nothing more or less than a tallow candle in the house[468] of Walter Williams, shepherd to Mr Price, Noyad Glasbury. This light could be seen from several positions. The shrine [at the site of the holy bush?] seemed fixed on purpose that it might be clearly seen through it. It could also be seen through the old passage of the hut. Strange to say, Sister Janet had to pass every night close under the window where the light came from to go to her lodging, so that it seems almost impossible for her [not?] to have known what light she was looking at when trying to persuade us that it was a supernatural one. When we pointed out to her where the light came from she said, 'Ah, if you had seen the glorious light I saw the other night, you would believe. Ten thousand thousand candles would not give such a light.' She was then reminded that she had shown this as the light.

READERS OF THE Hereford Times were also kept up to date with the various healings believed to have been wrought through the agency of leaves from the 'holy bush'. After initially identifying her only as 'a lady well known in the neighbourhood of Brighton' (issue of 2 October), the fact that Mother Cecilia was actually an 'inmate' of the Slapton convent was made public in that of 16 October. The same issue reported that someone called Sarah Parker in Cheltenham who had been suffering badly from insomnia had slept well for six nights running following receipt of 'holy leaves', and carried a reminder that George Swaine and Charles Rouse had been healed respectively of rheumatism and neuralgia, although the effectiveness of the leaves was not automatic. It was also stated that 'a sick child, living at Llanthony, who was said to be dying, has recently been

---

[468] Boxbush or Upper House, a quarter of a mile or so up the valley from the monastery

quite restored by the laying on of a monk's hands'. A letter from James Comley in the edition of 6 November drew attention to the clarification which 'Brother George' had recently published in the local paper serving Wisbech and district, following a report in its columns that he had visited Llanthony specifically 'to see the vision of the Virgin, and also that I was miraculously cured of rheumatism'.

> 1st, I did not go to Llanthony to see the apparitions; I happened to be staying there at the time. 2nd, I was not cured of rheumatism. I certainly did see the figures as seen by other persons who were present, but whether they were mechanical productions or not I am unable to say. All that I know of it is, that it was a very unusual sight.[469]

WHEN THE COMMUNITY began to celebrate the annual 'apparitions festival' the atmosphere could become a little feverish, perhaps in anticipation of further manifestations. By this time the nuns had moved to Llanthony, and Sister Mary Agnes remembered one such occasion:

> We were watching the procession of the Shrine, and its accompanying and subsequent rites, when suddenly the Reverend Mother [Werburgh] exclaimed: 'I see something; it's moving!' 'Where?' I asked, 'for I cannot see anything.' The Mother then pointed to the 'Abbot's Meadow'. There was something moving slowly, and I watched for a few moments, and then said, 'Why, it is the cow, with patches of white on her.' And so it was, as she was obliged to acknowledge.[470]

---

[469] George Swaine's letter was reproduced in the *Western Mail* of 2 November appended to one from a certain J. Hart of Wisbech, who stated that he had known him for fifteen years and had never heard him complain of suffering from rheumatism. He also doubted that his friend believed in 'such nonsense as the appearance of the Blessed Virgin or the curative properties said to be contained in the sacred bush'. Unfortunately the paper carrying Swaine's original letter cannot be traced, so I have not been able to check its files for possible further correspondence.

[470] NL p168

Perhaps as enclosed religious Ignatius's nuns didn't have the regular access to an optician we nowadays take for granted (or indeed to doctors or dentists).

In *The Graphic* of 3 September 1887 there is a description (by 'M.G.W.') of a visit to the monastery on what the author terms 'its *fête* day':

> In the grassy field outside, where the Virgin is said to have appeared, close to the hedge, some tawdry blue-painted railings enclose a small space of six or eight square yards. In it is set up a small altar, with a blue cloth on it, and a cross rising above, decked with flowers. As we looked, the [only] novice and another rather older man, bareheaded, and in black gowns, came jauntily down the field, smiling and passing remarks to each other the while, and carrying what resembled a large, gaudily-painted doll. It turned out to be an image of the Virgin which, with no great reverence, they deposited on the altar and left there, while pleasure-seekers joked, careless tourists smoked, and a general atmosphere of amused indifference pervaded the little assemblage around. We saw an attendant get into the enclosed space and tear up several handfuls of dock-leaves, which he presented to a devout lady, who carefully bore them away with her. They are reputed of sovereign value in cases of illness....

Among artefacts donated to the Father Ignatius Trust at its inception was a large oil painting of 'Our Lady of Llanthony'. It came into the collection via the Reverend F.H. Mountney, one of the original Trustees, having been acquired by the Reverend W.E. Fagan Dodd, Vicar of Ickford (Bucks), some time before 1960. Letters at this time from Fr Dodd to Fr Mountney mention a tradition that it was 'done by one of the monks who had seen the Vision' (Brother Dunstan, or perhaps George Swaine or Charles Rouse?), and convey the writer's impression that 'however clumsily or inartistically wrought' it was 'a very devout & honest attempt to convey what was very real and heaven-sent to the beholder', and had 'something other-worldly about it'[471]

Picture 21: "Our Lady of Llanthony, pray for us"

---

[471] Letters in Fr Ignatius collection, refs A2010.86.19.32-4

Later, two life-size statues of 'Our Ladye of Llanthony' were set up. The first, in plaster, formed the centrepiece of a new shrine in the already crowded public part of the abbey church. The other, carved from white Carrara marble, was installed in the enclosure mentioned by 'M.G.W.' in 1905, replacing an earlier, temporary, statue on the same spot. Ignatius also caused a cross to be erected on the summit of the mountain from which at its final appearance the Figure was seen to descend upon the Holy Bush. The cross itself quickly blew down, but the cairn still visible on the mountain top between the two converging valleys is said to mark the point where it stood.[472]

Henry Whitehead (Brother Dyfrig 1887-90),[473] who became a Roman Catholic after leaving the monastery, had this to say on the subject of the apparitions:

> A statue of our Lady surrounded by a railing stood just outside the monastic enclosure. Here it was alleged our Lady had appeared, and the fact was vouched for by five or six reliable witnesses. As far as I know she spoke no word and kept outside the enclosure, and went from it, as if to indicate that while she appreciated Fr Ignatius's devotion to her, she could not approach him nearer – he must follow her

into communion with the Holy See, presumably.

---

[472] The mountain-top memorial is mentioned in reports of pilgrimages in 1883 and 1884 in the *Western Mail*. In the former (10 September 1883) it is stated that the cross had already blown down.

[473] See Chapter 10. Quotation from his ms autobiography, courtesy of the Whitehead family.

CHAPTER 10

A PLACE OF PILGRIMAGE

IGNATIUS ANTICIPATED that devotion to 'Our Ladye of Llanthony' would increase the number of visitors coming to the monastery and requiring accommodation. Already in the spring of 1880 an appeal had been issued for £800 to build a guest house on the site of the old farmstead; among the signatories of the appeal letter were his friend Dr Hanson, and the lawyer John Christie. The fact that this project was never realised suggests that insufficient funds were forthcoming, but four years later it was announced that another of Ignatius's supporters, a Mrs Fawcett of Southsea, was planning to build a house in that vicinity for her own use, 'and so be able to attend our beautiful services'.[474] Actually 'Plas Genevieve' seems to have been used as much to accommodate female visitors to the monastery as its builder, although the house (but not the land on which it stood) remained in possession of Mrs Fawcett and her daughter until the death of the latter (associate Sister Mary Theodora), not long after that of Ignatius himself.[475]

The name of this house (now The Grange Pony Trekking Centre) has led people to assume that it was built for Ignatius's mother Louisa Genevieve Lyne, but by the time of this announcement she had been dead seven years. In fact it took its name not from its occupant but from the field in which it was situated ('St Genevieve's Meadow'), which in her lifetime had been let by Ignatius to his

---

[474] MT September 1884

[475] According to the schedule of 'real property' issued after Ignatius's death '[t]he deceased died possessed of this [Plas Genevieve] subject to the life enjoyment of Miss Mary Fawcett of the age of 60' (in Abergavenny collection: ref A1993.139.11).

mother. She may well have intended to build a house on it from which to keep a watchful eye on her son, but was prevented from doing so by her death.[476]

In July 1887 Ignatius's eldest brother Francis Palmer died at the age of fifty,[477] followed the next year by their father.[478] The third Lyne death in four years was that of Ignatius's youngest brother Clavering Mordaunt, on 27 August 1890. He had been ordained deacon in 1879 and priest in 1881 and served three curacies in the united diocese of Bristol and Gloucester before being overtaken by ill health; when he died he was only 41. In 1883 he had married a lady eleven years his senior, a Miss Emily Brooking. There were no children, but their shared passion for 'dumb creation' was reflected in his support for a Bristol dogs' home and his widow's eventual bequests to animal charities. She also left £1000 and all her 'live animals' to her coachman, who was ordered to dispose of them according to her written instructions.[479]

In September 1879 Harriet Jemima had married an up-and-coming young civil engineer named Paul Ewens. There were two children, both girls: Mary Hilda Leycester (always known as Hilda), born in the summer of 1880, and Irene Louisa Lyne, born early in 1882. Their first home was in Cheltenham, where most of the family seem to have lived off and on during the 1870s and 1880s. In December 1881 Clavering (at the time curate of nearby Leckhampton) and Augustus Adolphus put on a play at the spa town's Theatre Royal to raise funds for the new church being built by the latter at Westgate-

---

[476] The new house was included in the 1891 census, when its only occupants were the former 'monastery boy' Daniel Maguire's three sisters. Two of them (Dinah and Agnes) were the resident domestic servants; visiting them was their older sister, Mary Ann. On the relevant dates in both 1901 and 1911 it was unoccupied.

[477] His widow lived for some time in London; by 1901 she had moved to rural Middlesex, where her house in Heston was named 'Lyneville'.

[478] On 15 May 1888 at his home, 54 Montagu Square, aged 87

[479] *Gloucester Citizen*, 30 October 1905

on-Sea. *Theodosius, or the Christian Emperor* was written by Clavering, and the performance preceded by a lecture from Augustus on the subject of *Theatres, their uses and abuses, bringing forward a remedy*.[480] One wonder whether his brother's 'remedy' (whatever it was) would have been sufficient to entice the famously theatrophobic Ignatius actually to watch the play.

Picture 22: Ignatius's sister Harriet Ewens with daughters Hilda and Irene

---

[480] *Worcestershire Chronicle,* 10 December 1881.

According to that year's census their sister Louisa Jane (Mrs Drawbridge) was also living in the town, probably for the sake of her children's education.[481] In 1883 her husband returned from India, and they lived together in the various parishes he served until 1904, when they retired to 'Darjeeling', Castle Road, Camberley.[482] This was only a mile or so from the house in Chobham Road, Frimley, where Clavering had died and his widow Emily lived until her death in 1905; Ignatius himself would pass the final weeks of his life at their house in the autumn of 1908.

---

[481] The Drawbridges had four children:
(1) Cyprian Leycester (born 7 December 1868 in Darjeeling, died 23 January 1937 in Chislehurst) was a dayboy at Tonbridge School, from which he proceeded to Peterhouse College, Cambridge, and Gloucester Theological College. After three curacies he served for many years as Hon Secretary of the Christian Evidence Society, and published fourteen books, including *Training of the Twig* (on the education of children) and *The Religion of Scientists*. Until 1996 the Society organised an occasional (originally annual) Drawbridge Lecture in his memory, delivered by such distinguished figures as Bishop B.C. Butler OSB, Professor John Polkinghorne and Archbishop Desmond Tutu.
(2) William Hamilton (born Jabalpur 1870, died 31 January 1923 in London) followed his elder brother to Tonbridge and Cambridge (Corpus Christi), but between one and the other attended (King's) Lynn Grammar School, coinciding with his father's curacy there. He was ordained in the same diocese as Cyprian (Worcester) and served curacies there and in Surbiton, then like his father became a chaplain in India; his death occurred while at home on furlough.
(3) Wilfred Ralph Leycester (born Cheltenham 1878, died St Leonards-on-Sea 21 July 1951) qualified as a medical practitioner. In the 1911 census he was listed with his parents and younger brother at their house in Camberley; his death was announced in *The Times* (24 July 1951) as having occurred 'suddenly'.
(4) The 1911 census entry for Basil Hanmer (born Tonbridge January 1884; died Harrold (Beds) 1954) gives his occupation as 'nil'; ten years earlier he had been studying with a private tutor, which suggests academic weakness or disrupted schooling or both. His name occurs on the passenger list of a vessel returning from Canada in May 1904, when he is described as a farmer; in later life he became a bank official.

[482] Later renamed 'Pineleigh'; information for which I am indebted to Mr Simon Shreeve, Hon Editor of *The Old Roffensian*, the magazine for former pupils of King's School, Rochester, where Mr Drawbridge was educated. Mr Shreeve contributed an illustrated article about him to the issue of December 2014.

A few weeks after their father's death Louisa spent eleven days as Ignatius's guest at Plas Genevieve, on her departure presenting him with a handsome visitors' book. Above her own entry on the first page is the inscription in her brother's hand *Gorphwysfa Pererin Mynachdy Llanddewi Nant Honddu;*[483] it was just at this time that he began to develop an interest in all things Welsh, changing the dedication of the abbey church from Our Lady and St Dunstan to Our Lady and St David, inserting Welsh texts into the abbey church services alongside those in Latin and English, and bestowing the names of ancient Celtic saints on new entrants. This latest enthusiasm was noted by the *Western Mail* correspondent 'Morien' in his description of a visit two years later.[484] He tells us that the *Gorphwysfa Pererin* was a small cottage at the entrance to the monastery grounds; according to another visiting journalist it was a 'cool, inviting-looking summer-house'.[485] The visitors' book was in use (though with several gaps) until August 1914, well after the break-up of the community.

Among the twenty or so pilgrims who signed their names on the Apparitions Feast that summer was Thomasina Magrath from Bath, sister of the former Brother Dunstan, with the comment 'not her first visit'. The following June she returned with her brother, who had already been back for the Ascension Day pilgrimage in 1885,[486] and was just then nearing the end of his first curacy at Ewyas Harold just across the Herefordshire border.[487] From there he moved to London, where he served curacies successively at St

---

[483] 'Pilgrims' Rest, Llanthony Monastery'. The book is among the Llanthony memorabilia preserved at Prinknash Abbey.

[484] *Western Mail*, 3 March 1890

[485] 'Life at Llanthony'; article in the *Sheffield Daily Telegraph* of 17 October 1908.

[486] MT June 1885

[487] He was ordained deacon in 1888 and priest in 1889, having spent a year at the theological college at Chichester and another at the Scottish Episcopal college on the Isle of Cumbrae, where he would have been one of its final alumni.

Mary's, Primrose Hill (1890-92) and St Paul's, Paddington (1892-94), in spite of the distance continuing to maintain close contact with the monastery and its Superior.

In the pulpit he displayed evangelical zeal (and avoidance of the intellectual challenges of the day, another evangelical characteristic), but in the sanctuary displayed 'the more decorous and devout ceremonial of the higher Anglicanism'.[488] Like Ignatius he always preached *extempore*, and their resemblance both in appearance and manner would be noted at the time of the Abbot's death, when he officiated at his Requiem Mass and burial.[489]

After Paddington Magrath spent some time back at the monastery, although not as a monk; this was in the early years of his sister's marriage to Brother David (see below). When Francis Beverly Lawson entered the community in the summer of 1897 the household included 'Brother Dunstan (an Oblate Priest)', and it seems that around this time he regularly assisted Ignatius on his missions. A note in the abbatial Bible dated 2 June 1898 tells us that 'W.M. Magrath left here today after 3 ½ years chaplaincy', and the register of St David's, Llanthony, records one baptism at which he officiated during this period and two more in August 1899: he seems to have remained in the locality, the 1901 census listing him at a house in Pandy, a hamlet in the parish of Llanfihangel Crucorney.[490] There are some

---

[488] Copies of two newspaper reviews of his preaching from his time in Paddington from which these observations are taken are in my possession.

[489] The [South Wales?] Echo, 23 October 1908.

[490] For Lawson see below. The reference to 'Brother Dunstan' is in a letter Lawson wrote to Dom Dyfrig Rushton of Prinknash Abbey on 18 March 1958 (copy in Prinknash archives). Magrath's involvement in Ignatius's missions is attested by ex-Sister Mary Agnes: in her annotated copy of Nunnery Life (Museum ref A1993.139.6.22) she noted against the reference to him on p 171 'name Revd Magrath/the tall gentleman who takes the services at the Mission' (no date is given for her ms annotations), and his frequent presence at Llanthony by the report in LMN January-March 1894 that he took part in the monastery 'harvest festival' the preceding autumn, while still curate in Paddington.

discrepancies between his Crockford record and the account of his career printed in the *Abergavenny Chronicle* at the time of his death,[491] but after this intermission he spent some nine years (1904-13) as curate of the picturesque village of Coberley, near Cheltenham, and when he died (at the age of fifty on 21 December 1915, from heart failure) he was six months into a curacy at the church of All Saints in the centre of Hereford.

ABBEY BAPTISMS

THE 'BEAUTIFUL SERVICES' in the abbey church attracted local people as well as visitors from afar. Among them were members or connections of the Lewis and Watkins families (both still represented in the valley); at least a dozen of the latter were baptised in the abbey church, despite their longstanding association with the local Baptist chapel. One of them, John Gorst (son of the former Phoebe Watkins, born 1 July 1879), was baptised by Ignatius on 29 May 1887 and in the next decade would for a time be one of the 'monastery boys'.[492]

All three Ulett children were also christened there: Ada and Alice respectively in 1878 and 1880, and their baby brother Frank Ethelbert Dunstan Bede in 1883 (it may have been his arrival that prompted their parents to send them to live at the convent). So were Brother David (at the age of 16 in 1881), and in the following decade his own two children. A complete list of those baptised in the abbey church at Llanthony and earlier at Elm Hill and Laleham will be found in Appendix 1.

NEW ENTRANTS

AFTER RECORDING the admission of thirteen individuals between 1878 and 1881 (all of whom quite quickly melted away, as we have seen),

---

[491] Issue of 31 December 1915

[492] Later he went to work as a groom for the Marquis of Abergavenny, and like many of his generation lost his life in the 1914-18 War (information received from his granddaughter Amanda Price, November 2011).

the Register shows no new arrivals until 1886-7, when there were six.[493] The first of these was 20-year-old William Marriott Dodson,[494] who came to the monastery on 29 August 1886 and was clothed as a novice on 30 November of that year with the name Michael Mary of the Advent. On Christmas Day 1887 he was promoted to 'professed novice', and on 1 March 1890 made his life profession. Soon afterwards he would accompany Ignatius on his thirteen-month American tour, chronicling it as *Father Ignatius in America*.

Admitted to the noviciate at the same time was Claude Butler Newman Reader (Brother Iltud Mary), who had twice visited the monastery earlier that year but seems not to have formally entered until the autumn. He was eighteen or nineteen, the son of a grocer in the Dorset town of Bridport, and according to his later *curriculum vitæ* had attended various dissenting academies, though whether before or after his sojourn at Llanthony is not specified. The Register dismisses him with a crisp 'Sent away'[495]—at the end of his noviciate year, if not before.

In the following decade he moved to Canada, where he was ordained by the *episcopus vagans* Joseph René Vilatte (see next chapter),

---

[493] This is not to say that there were in fact no admissions. (1) One of the *horaria* mentioned in Chapter 7 dates from the winter of 1884-85 and was issued to the current 'kitchen brother', named as 'Br Placidus'. The last bearer of that name to be listed in the Register had been Enoch Holmes, who left in April 1883; the next would not arrive until ten years after that. (2) A letter dated 23 November 1892 (Museum ref A2005.348.6) from Ignatius to Brother David's wife Thomasina makes passing reference to (another?) Brother Placidus.

[494] Born 25 July 1866 at Smeeton Westerby near Market Harborough, the home of his mother's father, a surgeon, as was his younger sister Gwendoline. His early life would have been disturbed first by the unsuccessful attempt of his father (listed in the 1871 census as having 'no profession', and described elsewhere as a 'gentleman') to divorce his mother for adultery (Divorce Court File No 2063), and later by his bankruptcy (*Leamington Spa Courier*, 30 June 1877). His mother died the year before William entered the monastery.

[495] There are numerous discrepancies between the ages given for Reader in censuses and other records. In the 1891 census when he was listed as lodging at an address in St Pancras his occupation was given as 'Student of Divinity'.

assisting him in parishes there and in the US state of Wisconsin; at this period he was known as 'Fr Basil'. In a letter to the *Church Times* following Vilatte's bestowal of the priesthood on Ignatius in 1898[496] Bishop Grafton of Fond du Lac suggested that there was a connection between Reader's move to the New World and British police interest in his 'criminal conduct with boys'. Later he was reordained in the (Anglican) Episcopal Church; it may be significant that he took this step only after Grafton's death. Among the various posts he held was a curacy at the church of the Transfiguration, New York, under Dr Randolph Ray, who believed him to be 'the son of an aristocratic English family' and understood him to have trained as an actor; he was also impressed by his 'dramatic style at the altar' and 'excellent voice'. Reader died in 1948.[497]

The following year (1887) two more young men arrived who would make their final profession alongside Brother Michael, but who would in time both join Roman Catholic communities. Henry Edward Whitehead (Brother Dyfrig) was twenty, and after his mother's death had been brought up by his grandmother and aunt in the Bedfordshire countryside. Like many of his contemporaries he had become an enthusiastic Ritualist, joining a brotherhood working in a London slum parish. As this group (which has not so far been identified) could only be certain of retaining its position with the goodwill of a sympathetic incumbent, he decided to transfer to Llanthony.[498] No date is given in the Register for either his arrival or admission as a postulant, but his clothing as a novice is noted

---

[496] Quoted in BAL pp117f

[497] Information from UK census returns, various internet 'Free Catholic' sources, Dr Ray's memoir (*My Little Church around the Corner*, New York: Simon & Schuster 1957) and Research Archivist Sara Dana at The Archives of the Episcopal Church, P.O. Box 2247, Austin, TX 78768.

[498] Information about his life before, during and after his time at Llanthony from census records, Ignatius's Register and the Whitehead family, who kindly allowed me to read the ms autobiographical essay he wrote for his daughter in his late fifties.

as having taken place on 21 November 1887, which suggests he had arrived at the monastery in the late summer or early autumn.

Picture 23: Henry Edward Whitehead

Henry George Alston (Brother Cadoc) belonged to a well-known Suffolk family, many of whose members had over the generations served as lawyers and clergymen. His father (Edward Graham Alston) was a Cambridge-educated barrister who had emigrated to British Columbia, where he became Attorney General of what was then known as 'Vancouver's Island'; it was here that Henry George (known as George) and his younger brother William were born. Soon after William's birth he took up the post of Queen's Advocate of Sierra Leone, but almost immediately died of 'African Fever'.[499]

---

[499] The two boys (born respectively 25 September 1869 and 31 July 1872) were the children of E.G. Alston's second wife, Anna Maria Tuzo.

In middle age, as Dom Cyprian Alston of Downside Abbey, the former Brother Cadoc compiled an account of his career to date.[500] He tells us that after schooling at Merchant Taylors' he continued to live at home in the London suburbs, working for three or four years as a clerk in various city companies. He sang in the choir of his local church as well as contributing to parish life as a server and Sunday School teacher, and like Henry Whitehead developed an enthusiasm for High Church ways. He also came under the influence of Ignatius, attending his mission services at the Westminster Town Hall and elsewhere, and began to feel a call to the religious life. This was opposed by both his family and his parish priest, who judged that he 'was only smitten by the romantic and ritualistic side of the question', but after suppressing it for the better part of a year he 'decided to delay no longer'.

> [W]ithout telling anybody of my intentions, I left London on May 17th 1888, first going to Holy Communion at the church of the Transfiguration, Lewisham. I travelled that day as far as Hereford, where I stayed the night, and on the following day arrived at Llanthony, walking the eleven miles from Llanfihangel station. Fr Ignatius received me kindly and I stayed a week in the visitors' rooms as a guest.

On 27 May he was admitted as a postulant, and on 8 July 'took vows as a Novice for a year', renewing them for a further year in July 1889.

Two others entered the community before Ignatius left for America. Fifteen-year-old Oscar Heinrich Köhler arrived on 21 December 1887, and after an untypically long postulancy – perhaps because of his tender age – was clothed as a novice on 3 March

---

[500] This was added to at intervals during the remaining three decades of his life, and is preserved in the monastic library at Downside, to whose then Abbot and community I am indebted for their kindness in allowing me to consult both the document itself and Dom Cyprian Alston's personal copies of the Baroness de Bertouch's life of Fr Ignatius and From Monk to Busman.

1889. He was given the name Dewi Fair (David Mary) of the Blessed Sacrament.[501] Taliesin Griffith Davies came to the monastery on 8 July 1889 when he had just turned 21. After admission as a postulant on 4 August he took his novice's vows on 8 September of the same year, becoming Brother Taliesin Fair (Taliesin Mary) of the Incarnation.[502]

THE AMERICAN TRIP was intended as a sabbatical for Ignatius, who had for more than two decades continued to try and combine his responsibilities at Llanthony with intensive activity on the mission platform. In fact he was kept as busy on his travels around Canada and the United States as at any time on his home turf, his mission posters advertising him as the 'Evangelistic Monk of the British Church'. Funds for the transatlantic voyage were subscribed by his 'Kensington congregation', those who had attended a three-week mission there in April and May.[503] In addition to Fr Michael as secretary and scribe he was accompanied by three associates who regularly assisted with his preaching tours in Britain: the now 25-year-old Brother David, Sister Annie (Mrs Grant) and Brother Henry (Henry Fitzhardinge Berkeley) – evidence if any were wanted that he had other things on his mind than rest.

One consequence of having moved the nuns to Llanthony was that in his absence Ignatius was able to depute a measure of oversight of the monastery to Mother Werburgh, rather than to whichever of his partly formed monks happened to be the least junior. Brother Taliesin (Davies) was 'sent away by Revd Mother' when he was away 'on a Mission' (an earlier absence, perhaps), and Brother Dewi

---

[501] Oscar was fifth of the eight children of Thomas Köhler, a portrait painter and photographer living in south London.

[502] The birth of a Griffith Taliesin Davies was registered in Wandsworth in the second quarter of 1868. He appears in the 1881 census as the fourth of five children of 63-year-old Philip Davies, who combined the humdrum occupation of Commercial Clerk with the exotic-sounding one of Sword Maker and lived with his family in Clapham.

[503] FIIA p1

(Köhler) when he was in America.[504] According to Fr Alston those left behind at Llanthony numbered three brothers, two novices, three boys and three nuns. In the first two categories there is an apparent discrepancy with the details given in the Register, Alston and Whitehead being the only two professed brothers (apart from Dodson, absent in America). The third was probably Köhler, whose promotion to 'professed novice' would have been due in March 1890; perhaps Ignatius forgot to write this down, as well as the names of the two other novices.

Alston says that 'all the other monks and boys left for various reasons' in the two months following Ignatius's departure. Brother Dyfrig (Whitehead)'s decision to leave was bound up with his rapidly diminishing faith in the Anglican position:

> One day, while Fr Ignatius was away, I rang for the Abbess [sic] to come to the turn,[505] and told her that I had made up my mind to join the Roman Church. She was not at all surprised. I think she said 'I have been expecting this, and have kept the money you brought with you (a few hundred pounds) in readiness for such a decision. You can take it at any time.'

From Llanthony he went 'straight to the nearest Catholic Benedictine House' (Belmont, or perhaps the Ampleforth-run parish in Abergavenny), but was advised that before he could join a religious community in the Roman Church he would need 'first [to] get admitted into [that] Church and then remain in the world for some time till [his] mind was at rest, and free from all

---

[504] After leaving the monastery Köhler worked as a builder's clerk, marrying in 1900 and again after his first wife's death in 1915. He died in 1956 at Redhill, by which time he had changed his name to Oscar Henry Coler. I have been unable to trace further details of Taliesin Davies's career.

[505] The device by which items were passed in and out of the convent enclosure without the nuns being brought into direct contact with the outside world (or with the monks in the adjoining building).

the delusions and experiences of [his] Anglican life'. The Catholic priest at home in Bedford seemed in no hurry to receive him, so Whitehead went to stay in Ireland with someone who had been with him at Llanthony – possibly Köhler, whose grandfather had been a tailor in Dublin – and who was interested in taking the same step. A sympathetic Irish Jesuit carried out his reception, and directed him to the 'apostolic school' run by his French confreres in Littlehampton.

Four years later he joined the novitiate of the Jesuit mission in South India, writing to Ignatius, 'I should never have left Llanthony had you been at home.' (This is quoted opposite his entry in the Register, with the comment 'A very religious and true soul'; Cyprian Alston characterised him as '[t]he best, I believe, that ever went to Llanthony'.) Another few years of Jesuit formation brought him to the realisation that his true vocation lay in marriage and secular employment rather than the priesthood, so after obtaining release from his vows he became involved in various business projects in the field of engineering, living in and around Calcutta. His first wife died young, but he married again and had a family. In old age he returned to England, dying in Sheffield in August 1948.

GOINGS AND COMINGS

BY THE MIDDLE OF AUGUST Fr Cadoc (Alston) was on his own. His brother William, who had just passed his nineteenth birthday, had left Merchant Taylors' two years earlier and was apparently at a loose end, so he invited him to come and stay with him; the Register shows that he had been admitted as an associate the previous year. The work of keeping the house and church in order, not to mention the onerous daily round of services, must have been as much as the two young men could manage, or more – unfortunately his account fails to go into any detail of the little remnant's daily life.

The news-sheet circulating just then among Ignatius's supporters (the *West London Church Chronicle*) has descriptions of some of the festival observances, when (just as Brother Brannock had done 25 years earlier) Fr Cadoc presided in a cope at 'solemn' celebrations of the principal offices – on one occasion also reading the Communion service, although it is not clear exactly what this actually involved.[506] It was claimed that during Ignatius's absence 'all arrangements [had] been made for the safety and prosperity of the little community at Llanthony'[507] – doubtless including visits by a priest to say Mass – but this particular arrangement seems to have fallen through. The priest in question would almost certainly have been ex-Brother Dunstan (Magrath), and it was probably his failure to fulfil the engagement that prompted the former Fr Cadoc to describe him as 'a most unreliable person'.[508]

As recounted in an earlier chapter, it was while Ignatius was in America – in fact not long before his return – that the hitherto 'faithful remnant' of three nuns abandoned their corrugated iron quarters at Llanthony and moved elsewhere. The mother of George and William then came to live in the empty convent (did she perhaps cook nourishing meals for her sons, and help with the never-ending task of cleaning and polishing the vast expanses of tiled floor in church and monastery?), although we aren't told whether she stayed until or beyond the return of the American party on 30 July 1891.

---

[506] Undated cutting in album, Museum ref A1993.137.3. Not many years later (while still a layman) Aelred Carlyle found himself in a similar situation and exposed the Blessed Sacrament for his own and his brethren's adoration, although he stopped short of actually administering it (BUWP 169). One wonders how far if at all Cadoc went beyond merely reading the text of (part of?) the service.

[507] FIIA p1

[508] Against the reference to him on p545 of his personal copy of Bertouch. Magrath had no difficulty in getting to Llanthony to celebrate Mass for the returning travellers (FIIA p365), but this may have been during his annual holiday.

A NEW FOCUS BEGAN to develop in Ignatius's life when Brother David married the former Brother Dunstan's sister Thomasina on 27 April 1892, and the young couple set up house at nearby Maes-y-ffin.[509] That February he had changed his name from William Pritchard to William Leycester Lyne; the following January they produced their first child, Leycester William Dewi, and in November 1897 Josephine Mary Thomasina Lucy Gwendoline.

In the Baptism Register 'Willie' is styled 'Steward of Llanthony Abbey', which sounds rather grand. Henry Whitehead recalled that he had been running the farm before his marriage, and describes him as

> a laybrother [who] was really a local layman, and in love with a girl above his station whom he had met at one of the missions. He wore a plain cassock in the monastery and was Fr Ignatius's bodyguard on the missions. I heard afterwards that a decent sum of money had been given him for his faithful service which enabled him to marry the girl.

Cyprian Alston didn't think much of his stewardship:

> Money collected by Fr Ignatius, ostensibly for the benefit and support of the Monastery, was expended on behalf of an outsider and his family (William Pritchard, alias Lyne – 'Brother David') who really had no claim upon the monastery funds. The farm property of the Monastery, which was supposed to be a kind of endowment or source

---

[509] They were married by the bride's brother at St Mark's Church, Lyncombe, on the outskirts of Bath. Two letters in the Abergavenny collection (A 2005.348.4 and 348.2) indicate that there had been a last-minute hitch. The first (dated 23 April 1892, four days before the wedding) is from Ignatius to Thomasina (addressed by her familiar diminutive of 'Sena'), and expresses shock and grief at some moral lapse by 'Willie', said to be of a sort to be expected in a young man; it had taken place four years previously but had only come to light recently through gossip in the valley. The second (dated 'The Monastery – Monday', i.e. 25 April) is from 'Willie' to 'Sena', in which he confesses to feeling 'dreadful' about what has come to light but assures her of his trust in her love.

of income, was being so mismanaged by 'Brother David' that its maintenance became a heavy annual expense.[510]

Picture 24: Monks and associates, c1892. Fr Michael (Dodson) seated centre, with Fr Cadoc (Alston) standing second from right and his brother William in associate's scapular on the left. On the right stands Brother David, settling into his new role as 'Steward of Llanthony Abbey'.

ASSOCIATE BROTHERS

IF NOT VERY MANY were willing to commit themselves to the full rigours of monastic life under the Ignatian regime, there was never any shortage of (mostly young) men happy to become 'part-time' monks under one label or another. The network of Third

---

[510] Ignatius seems to have made no distinction between his own finances and those of the monastery, which he anyway regarded as his personal property. In his one surviving diary fragment (1 Jan to 4 March 1908) he recorded a payment of £25 for Lessie's school fees – presumably a regular expense, though one which surely ceased with his death.

Order branches seems to have fallen apart around the time of the move to Llanthony, giving place to the 'Associate Brothers of the Blessed Scapular' (twenty-eight admissions between 1869 and 1875) or just plain 'Associates' (eight admissions were recorded in 1888 and subsequent years, but there were probably many more). The completion in 1883 of the guest wing with its authentic monastic-style cubicles (ten in all) meant there was always room for associates to spend their holidays at the monastery, where they often wore cassocks. One such regular visitor was a young man named Alfred Field; pictures 24 and 25 are among several from his albums used in this book.[511] The author of the '1891 ms' may well be one of the young men in the first of these; among the little details he gives us are that Fr Michael was in charge of the kitchen garden, and Fr Cadoc as well as acting as organist, sacristan and cellarer had responsibility for the monastery hens.[512]

FURTHER ADMISSIONS AND DEPARTURES

A FEW WEEKS AFTER the Steward's wedding – three years since the last recorded admission, and ten months since Ignatius's return from America – a new aspirant arrived. This was Bertram George Aubrey (Bertie) Cannell, at the time not quite sixteen.[513] In *From Monk to Busman* he tells how he had been sent there by his widowed father (a doctor, according to the author himself; an unqualified 'quack', in the opinion of Cyprian Alston), and was initially 'classed with the monastery boys'.[514] A new group of juveniles had doubtless materialised by this time (John Gorst would have been one of them), and Cannell remembered that

---

[511] Museum refs for the two albums are A1993.137.5 and .6. Field was born in 1874 and probably first stayed at the monastery as early as 1891 or 1892.

[512] 1891 ms p32

[513] Born Tunbridge Wells 29 July 1876

[514] FMTB p33

they had the benefit of 'an excellent tutor, an MA of Oxford', who succeeded in teaching him more than he had ever learned before. This person (unfortunately unidentifiable) 'lived in the visitors' quarters of the Monastery, and only came to Church at noon and Vespers'.[515] After two months (on 19 July) Bertie was made a postulant; this was about the same time William Alston departed for Gloucester Theological College.[516]

Picture 25: A 'monastic holiday', c1893. Brother Gildas (Cannell) second left and Fr Cadoc (Alston) fourth left with two other monks (Maurus Closs and Placidus Sadley?), two boys and three lay associates. Alfred Field is on the extreme right.

In the following year (1893) there were two more admissions and one departure. The new recruits (named respectively Maurus and

---

[515] ibid p34

[516] This according to his brother's chronology, although Crockford gives the year he started at the college as 1894. Following ordination in Gloucester (deacon 1896, priest 1897) he served a curacy in that city before emigrating to South Africa, where he served as Priest-in-charge of St Luke, Maritzburg from 1911 until his death in 1949 and was made a canon of Maritzburg Cathedral.

Placidus, so for a while Benedictine patrons were being preferred to Celtic) were George Percy Closs, a carpenter's son from Gloucester who arrived on 17 February, a fortnight after his 21st birthday, and was admitted as a postulant on 21 May; and 18-year-old Charles William Sadley, received on 13 May and made a postulant on 12 July. On 17 August the two of them were clothed as novices, together with Cannell (Brother Gildas). Brother Placidus (Sadley) would not stay the course to become a 'professed novice' with Gildas and Maurus in August 1894, as he '[h]ad to be sent away as unmanageable' in May of that year.[517]

The departure was that of Fr Michael (William Dodson), who '[b]roke his vows & left [the] Abbey Nov[embe]r 1893, while I [Ignatius] was away'.[518] His account of the American trip had been published earlier that year and there must have been a compelling reason for his going, the circumstances of which are now lost in obscurity. The news snippets in the April to June 1894 Llanthony & Mission News (a new quarterly which seems to have lasted only a year) included the comment of an unidentified priest 'You do not know how I felt Fr Michael's cowardly behaviour', which was probably related to his departure.

THE SAME ISSUE OF Llanthony & Mission News included the information that the Night Office had been resumed at the beginning of 1894 after a lapse of three years 'owing to the smallness of the community'. It would almost certainly have been suspended again before the beginning of the next year, an outbreak of critical spirit among the

---

[517] In the 1881 census Sadley had been listed at the age of five with his widowed mother, a 27-year-old unemployed umbrella warehousewoman, at an address in Birmingham. In 1901 he appears at a lodging-house in the same city where his occupation is given as Factor's Clerk, and in 1911 with a wife to whom he had been married five years and sons aged respectively three years and one month at a house in suburban Washwood Heath, by which time he had become a Teacher of Music (pianoforte). He died in Birmingham in 1950.

[518] In the Register the name of the month is abbreviated and only partly legible, but November seems most probable.

monks that autumn resulting in all of them being expelled, and the male part of establishment being once again reduced to the Abbot and (perhaps) a handful of 'monastery boys'. Exactly what happened and when is hard to determine, but there seems to have been longstanding resentment at the existence of one law for the Abbot and another for everyone else − or rather no law at all for the Abbot, compared with extremely harsh ones for his subjects. There was also a discrepancy between what was said in public about the government of the monastery and how in fact it was run. In his memoir Fr Alston quotes from an interview Ignatius had given to an Isle of Wight newspaper in 1889 in which he claimed that the affairs of the monastery were managed democratically by the Abbot and Chapter, and its finances directed by one of the monks designated 'procurator'. Although when he was away Ignatius deputed day to day business to the 'senior brother' the responsibilities of this individual were strictly limited, and all decisions financial and otherwise were made 'by the Abbot's will alone'. When he requested that these and other matters might be looked into and discussed he was given a dusty answer:

> [Fr Ignatius] peremptorily and emphatically refused any discussion whatsoever and said that I must either leave the monastery forthwith, or be content to submit absolutely to him in everything, adding that as the monastery was his 'private establishment' those who lived in it could not be allowed to differ from him in any matter....

The inequality between Abbot and community hit Gildas Cannell particularly hard. One afternoon Ignatius favoured him with the privilege of a *tête-à-tête* walk, on which he told him that his father had been gravely ill and was now dead. The boy asked leave to go home on a visit, but was told that by doing so he would be breaking his vows. He doesn't actually mention it, but the contrast with the Abbot's practice of making an annual pilgrimage to his mother's grave in Margate would have made the prohibition particularly hard to accept.

Things came to a head at the regular 'Chapter of Faults', when each brother was supposed to own up to breaches of the Rule. When it came to his turn, Brother Gildas volunteered, 'Dear Father, perhaps it would be easier if you asked me the Rules I kept. As the Abbot does not keep any strict Rules, how can he expect us to?' The others then voiced similar complaints, and the meeting broke up. That evening after Compline the monks were ordered to kneel on the altar steps and divest themselves of their scapulars as a sign that by questioning Ignatius's authority they had broken their vows of obedience. When no-one made a move he went from brother to brother pulling them off himself. He then escorted them to the visitors' wing and dismissed them with a chilly 'Now, you gentlemen, you can make your arrangements to leave as soon as possible.'

No hint of this dramatic event is given in Ignatius's records or by the Baroness, although Cannell published two versions of the event.[519] Fr Cadoc (Alston) is said to have 'left us in Sep Dec[embe]r 1894', following the comment 'A good man but quite unable to get on in my absences' – in fact he had, as we have seen, survived rather well during Ignatius's thirteen-month American sabbatical. After Llanthony he spent three years with the Cowley Fathers, but his underlying difficulties being with the Anglican claim to catholicity he submitted to Rome in 1898 and became a monk of Downside. For many years he worked in parishes served by that community, dying on 11 January 1945.

The entry for Brother Maurus (Closs) concludes with the comment 'Sent away for constantly quarrelling', but no date is given. He became associated with Fr Hopkins's quasi-Benedictine Order of

---

[519] In an article in the *Sunday Express* of 16 March 1924, where he describes himself as having been 'senior brother' at the time (improbable, if Cadoc Alston was still in the community), and in FMTB pp53ff. Against the description of the scene in the abbey church the Downside copy of the latter has the pencilled comment 'Quite true' in Alston's hand.

St Paul, being listed in the 1901 census as 'missioner' at their house in Greenwich, 'The Priory', 38 Hyde Vale, which served as a hostel for unemployed sailors.[520]

Brother Gildas tells us that when the others had left Ignatius tried to offer him a second chance, suggesting that he had been 'led astray'; this is also the verdict Ignatius recorded in the Register. As ringleader of the rebellion he knew this to be untrue, and refused the offer – as he would its renewal four years later, when a holiday visit to the monastery coincided with that of 'Mar Timotheus' (Vilatte) and his bestowal of the priesthood on Ignatius: Cannell was also offered ordination if he would return to the cloister (which he wouldn't, as he was preparing to marry).[521]

The account in Cannell's memoir gives the impression of a community numbering rather more than the three recorded for that period in the Register, but he may have been emulating his erstwhile Superior in his tendency to inflate its numbers. However, once again there may have been others whose names weren't listed. For some years in the 1890s and early 1900s a strange character named Thomas Anthony Taylor occupied a cottage on Gaer Hill, Lower Cwmyoy, where he gave out that he was 'Fr Aloysius OSB', a former inmate of the monastery now living as a hermit, and

---

[520] For the OSP see BUWP Chapters IX and XII. In 1911 Closs was listed as a Ship's Steward lodging at an address in Sunderland. He married in 1918, and passed his declining years at Weston-super-Mare, where he died in 1944.

[521] FMTB pp59f; for Ignatius's priestly ordination see the following chapter. Cannell became a London bus conductor, publishing his reminiscences in 1935. His meeting with Mar Timotheus was not his only encounter with an *episcopus vagans*; according to John Kersey (*Joseph René Vilatte (1854-1929): Some Aspects of his life, Work and Succession*, European-American University Press 2011 p121n), between February 1949 and April 1950 he received Mar Georgius of the Catholicate of the West (Hugh George de Willmot Newman) and his wife into his home in Twickenham, serving that prelate's daily Mass. (Kersey confuses Cannell with another, later, Brother Gildas, but the Gildas who lived in Twickenham was indeed Cannell.) He died in 1957.

enjoyed a notably stormy relationship with his neighbours.[522] He was the son of a racehorse trainer in Newmarket (born 1860), and as a young man had studied with a country parson in Suffolk before travelling to America in the hope of being ordained, evidently without success.

Another person who was there for a few weeks in the autumn of 1894 (though he seems to have departed before the mass expulsion) was a notorious *poseur* who gave his name as Edward Rufane Donkin and was then aged 23. He claimed to have aristocratic blood and great wealth as well as to have been ordained by the Bishop of Bath and Wells, and had already tried his luck at Downside and a French community then domiciled at Glastonbury; history doesn't relate whether 'Brother Benedict' attempted to say Mass during his stay.

> [T]he unsuspecting Fr Ignatius - delighted at the prospect of priestly support - admitted him as a postulant of the Benedictine Order.... Ignatius was promised the gift of a fine house in Leamington and must have been very pleased with his new postulant until the end

---

[522] In the 1911 census Taylor was listed as sole occupant of Dower House, Partricio, and his death was registered in the Hay district in the second quarter of 1914. Among papers relating to him in the Fr Ignatius collection (Museum refs A1993.139.11.5 and 11.6) are

(1) a letter from J.C. Warrington Rogers, Rector of Blakenham, Suffolk, dated 19 Oct 1881 and addressed 'To any bishop or priest of the American Church: Mr T. Taylor was in my house as a boarder-pupil for some time before he left England for America.... From what I knew of him generally and of his good moral character I believe he could make a zealous and active clergyman....';

(2) this semi-literate note evidently circulated by one of his neighbours on Gaer Hill: 'THERE, IS, A, MONK, ON, THE, GARE, THE, PICTURE, OF, HELL, A, WOUND, ON, HIS, ASS, THAT, WILL, NEVER, GET, WELL';

(3) the report in the *Abergavenny Chronicle* (29 November 1901) of a Police Court hearing involving a dispute between Taylor and his neighbour Thomas Harris. Former Fr Ignatius Trustee the late Will Jackson told the author that when they were children his mother and aunt lived not far from Taylor and understood that he received an occasional allowance. When it arrived he would 'go on the binge', which inevitably led to trouble with those living nearby (personal conversation, 12 October 2010).

of October when discreet enquiries led to his unmasking. Donkin once more moved on and Ignatius was left to put warnings in *The Times*, *The Guardian* and *The Swansea Journal*.[523]

THE MONASTERY REPOPULATED

IT WASN'T LONG before Ignatius received further recruits, although the monastery was never filled to capacity. Within a few weeks of the rebellion (on 5 January 1895) he admitted 21-year-old Arthur Charles Cobb, making him a postulant on 18 April and a novice on 2 July. He was given the name Iltud Mary (appropriately 'of the Epiphany', considering his arrival on the eve of that feast). A year later he was made a 'professed novice', and on 1 March 1898 took his final vows.[524]

Cobb's arrival was followed on 13 April (Holy Saturday) by that of Richard de Mattos, aged 18, whose estranged parents Sidney and Katherine were minor figures in London literary circles – she was a cousin of Robert Louis Stevenson, and the dedicatee of *The Strange Case of Dr Jekyll and Mr Hyde*. On 12 June he was made a postulant, being clothed as a novice on 2 July alongside Brother Iltud with the name Gildas. He lasted barely six months, being '[s]ent away as being very strange in his fancies and mind' (a Stevenson trait, perhaps?) in September.

---

[523] Article in the 1987 *Glastonbury Bulletin* by Abba Seraphim, 'The Vilatte Succession in England 1898-1906', reproduced by kind permission of the author. The warning in the *Guardian* (a weekly Church paper, not to be confused with the then Manchester-published daily) appeared in the issue of 7 November 1894, and had been sent in by '"Cadoc, OSB, Monk", writing from 68 Middle Street, Brighton'. According to the 1891 and 1901 censuses this was the address of a private club, but Ignatius may have been staying there with Cadoc (Alston) on his regular travels. More about Donkin (who was later ordained priest by the *episcopus vagans* J.R. Vilatte and may also have received episcopal consecration) in BAL pp141f.

[524] Cobb was born in Hammersmith on 7 August 1873 and baptised at St Matthew's, West Kensington on 31 August. His father's occupation was given as 'writing clerk'.

His slightly younger cousin Ursula Wyllie Roberts (better known as the poet 'Susan Miles') recounted the former novice's next step:

> He stayed with Fr Ignatius's adopted son, Mr Lyne of Maes-y-ffin, Llanthony, while his tonsure was growing, or rather disappearing. The Father didn't like his sometime monks to go into the world with a tonsure. Mrs Lyne was much interested when I was at Llanthony years later to hear that I was a cousin of Richard's. She gave a realistic description of him taking large alternate bites of bread-and-butter and cake; a mild and respectable indulgence compared to some of those practised by the Father's monks. [525]

Soon after leaving Llanthony de Mattos became a Roman Catholic, spending seven years at a monastery in France.[526] His cousin continues:

> His Roman Catholic Superior was less considerate than Fr Ignatius. Richard was told...that he had no vocation and was sent out into the world with his tonsure and in his habit. He was given his ticket home but no money. When he arrived at his mother's house only a maid was there and she refused him admittance until he returned with a friend of the family to vouch for him.

Having already completed the necessary studies in the French monastery he was ordained priest soon afterwards by the Bishop of Nottingham, and served in that diocese until compelled by ill health to take early retirement. He died in 1950.

---

[525] From a brief family memoir published online at www.wyllie.org.nz/ documents/memoirs_of_a_soldiers_daughter.doc (retrieved 4 December 2013). Unfortunately no explanation is given for the statement about monastic indulgences.

[526] His cousin said it was a Franciscan house, but according to his obituary in the 1951 Nottingham Diocesan Directory he 'tried his vocation with the Carthusians'.

The next person to be admitted – and to receive the evidently unpropitious name of Gildas (there would be one more) – was 24-year-old Charles George Griffin. The son of a South London solicitor's clerk (and later a solicitor's clerk himself), he arrived on 24 May 1897 and was made a postulant on 2 July and a novice on 7 August. On 10 September of the following year he became a 'professed novice', but was dismissed in June 1899 for 'falsehood and disobedience'.[527]

Clothed as a novice on the same occasion with the name Dyfrig was Francis Beverly Lawson, who had previously visited the monastery in 1895 and 1896; he arrived 'to stay' on 7 July 1897 when not quite 18, and was made a postulant the following day. The fact that he had previous visits to his credit may explain this rapid promotion, as well as his advancement to the status of 'professed novice' a month earlier than that of Charles Griffin, on 8 August 1898. He only outlasted him by a few weeks, being '[s]ent away for repeated rudeness to a boy in the Monastery' in September 1899.

Lawson came from Nottingham, where his father was a lace merchant and he had attended the local art college; his mother, who was an American and had borne six or more children, died when he was three. After Llanthony he worked for a short time in the family business before spending three years with Aelred Carlyle's community,[528] then at Painsthorpe in Yorkshire. At his clothing there on 23 July 1902 he was given the name Bernard, which he continued to use in later life and also bestowed on his son. He was a skilled worker in metal: at Painsthorpe he and another monk helped to boost the monastery finances through arts and crafts, and as late as 1950 he made a reliquary for the successor community at Prinknash.

---

[527] Griffin appears with his parents and younger sister in the censuses of 1881 and 1901; in the first at Fulham, where he was born, and in the second at Deptford. In 1911 he was listed with his wife of nine years and 9-year-old daughter at an address in Lewisham. He died at Lewisham Hospital in 1945.

[528] See Chapter 11

In the autumn of 1904 he acted as *socius* to Aelred on his journey to America to receive the diaconate and priesthood from Bishop Grafton of Fond du Lac,[529] and was himself ordained subdeacon. On leaving Painsthorpe he returned to America in connection with the family business and married Bertha Maude Young, stenographer in a New York law firm, both of them becoming Roman Catholics. He died in 1968.[530]

Henry Matthews was thirty (born 1 January 1868) when he came to the monastery on 20 May 1898. He had been baptised at Christ Church, West Bromwich, so had probably been brought up in that area.[531] After a week's postulancy he was clothed as a novice on 14 July, becoming Brother Cadoc; twelve months later (on 17 July 1899) he was made a 'professed novice'. Two months after this he

> [r]an away, to our great disgrace, ~~Wednesday~~ Tuesday Sept[embe]r 12 1899 in our Habit, during Rest hour before Nones. He had said Sext being Reader. He seemed all right at Pious Reading Time. He had no ostensible reason whatever. Wed Sept[embe]r 13[th] he wrote me Letter pinned on here (the Register? No longer there) to be received back. He arrived Friday Sept[embe]r 15 1899 during the Solemn Watch of Apparition at Porch.[532]
>
> Nov[embe]r 1899 Ran away again, stealing all the House money for the Month in Bro Teilo's new habit. He wrote to me first from Young Mens Xtian Assoc Strand London then from Mount Melleray Abbey, Ireland.

---

[529] BUWP p186

[530] Aelred Baker OSB, *The Flood-Gates of Memory* (Blurb nd) p108; P.F. Anson, *Abbot Extraordinary* p86 and Publisher's Note; information from Prinknash Abbey archives.

[531] Public records have yielded only the date and place of his death; details here are from the Register and Baker, op cit.

[532] This was of course the date of the final Apparition in 1880.

After two years at Mount Melleray (now using the Christian name Thomas) he also joined Aelred Carlyle's community, not long before it moved to Painsthorpe after its first temporary spell on Caldey; Peter Anson[533] believed he was acting as an *agent provocateur* for the (militantly protestant) Church Association. In his history of the Painsthorpe/Caldey/Prinknash community Fr Aelred Baker gives a synopsis of his career then and later:

Thomas Matthews...came from Mount Melleray in Ireland on 17th January 1902 and was clothed on 29th receiving the religious name Malachy. He was a calligrapher of considerable ability but with a wayward nature. He had apparently left Mount Melleray while a novice without giving any notice. Later on when the Community moved to Painsthorpe he absconded with articles belonging to the Community and the villagers. He was last seen standing on the platform at York Station. He was arrested by the police and spent nine months in prison. He was not the first or the last member of the Community to be found guilty of theft. But Malachy made good in the end. Aelred heard of his death in 1931 and noted in his diary 'old Malachy Matthews who was with us at Caldey and Painsthorpe is dead. And he died in the savour of good Catholic as journalist, artist in black and white at Cardiff. Of course he was a runaway novice to us at Caldey...and he ran away from us as a thief and got a jail sentence for stealing bicycles. But he died well respected aet. 64. Did a large amount for local [illegible] latterly specialising in portraiture. It is good to know he ended well. I have often wondered what became of him – a cadaverous looking genius he was.'[534]

---

[533] BUWP p182

[534] Baker op cit p94. A report of his death from an unidentified South Wales newspaper is preserved in the Barclay album. It says he was known as 'Harry' Matthews, and had lived in Cardiff for the last six years of his life, contributing cartoons to the *South Wales News*.

Four days before Matthews's clothing as a novice – on 10 July 1898 – the monastery received another young man from Birmingham, 22-year-old Alfred Harris. He was made a postulant on 29 July and a novice on 10 September as Brother Asaph, but would have to wait another three years for his promotion to the status of 'professed novice' (29 September 1901). After a further lengthy delay he made his 'simple' profession on 27 January 1906 (in fact this was his profession for life, as it was for Sister/Mother Tudfil who took the same step on the same day). Like Cadoc/Cyprian Alston he would indeed remain a monk for the rest of his life, and like him as a Roman Catholic rather than an Anglican.

One more novice was admitted before the end of the century – John Eric Cospatrick Dunbar, who arrived on 2 August 1898 at the age of seventeen and a half. Both his father and elder brother were clergymen (and both named George); John was born on 10 February 1881 when his father was curate of Marske-by-the Sea in Yorkshire.

He was made a postulant on 12 September 1898 and a novice on 21 December of the same year, becoming Brother Teilo. He must still have been there in November 1899, when as related above Henry Matthews decamped in his (Brother Teilo's) new habit, but before he could be raised to the next level he '[l]eft by his own desire for a less strict Order, at Alton Hants' – i.e. Fr Hopkins's Order of St Paul.[535] By 1911 he had abandoned the monastic life and become a chicken farmer on the South London outskirts. A few days after that year's census he married a local girl in Eltham; the following May they sailed for a new life in Canada, under whose flag he served in the 1914-18 war.

A GLIMPSE INTO MONASTERY LIFE at this period is given in two letters Francis Lawson wrote in old age. In one (cited earlier in connection

---

[535] In the 1901 census he is listed as one of five 'aspirants' to the Order. Otherwise the Alton household consisted of five full members, including the Prior; a chaplain; an undergraduate visitor, and 28 'inmates', mostly retired or serving seamen.

with Brother Dunstan/William Magrath) he recalls that Asaph was 'absolutely tone deaf' and 'had no more idea of singing the office than our St Bernard dog Bruno; it was excruciating and ridiculous to listen to him particularly in Welsh (we sang Nones in Welsh in those days)'. (Whether the dog Bruno was his own at the time he was writing or the monastery dog when he was an inmate isn't made clear, but a St Bernard features prominently in Llanthony photographs from that era.) Asaph also figures in an incident recalled (with those that follow) in the other letter, to Aelred Carlyle on 26 June 1953. On this occasion they

> were singing Matins & we heard...mysterious weeping & the sisters in the gallery were so affected that I had to take their verses in the psalms or the night office would have broken down & the Lord Abbot would have put the whole world under an interdict!

Another uncanny experience was

> the night that Henry Matthews...saw me walk clean through the figure of the Black Monk standing in the Choir Door, when I went out to fix the incense for the office of Lauds about 3.30am.

He had two seasonal memories – how 'on Ash Wednesday... Ignatius just revelled in sitting on the Choir floor, pouring whole handfuls of ashes over his noggin', and the Christmas feast when 'old Farmer Evan Evans set his beard on fire with the flaming brandy'. An incident which surely contributed to his downfall was 'how I murdered the Father's pet dove when it flew into the rice pudding I was cooking in the kitchen. The gravestone erected in the Garth over its grave said it was killed by an act of violence & its companion never "cooed" again!!'[536]

---

[536] The full inscription (as reproduced by Dom Bede Camm OSB on p74

A final reminiscence is from the ordination of Fathers Ignatius and Iltud, which although properly belonging to the following chapter may appropriately be recounted here. The Bishop was at the north end of the altar but wanted his mitre, which was at the south end. He motioned Lawson to fetch it, whispering 'Go as ze crow fly' because the young monk had started to go down the sanctuary steps (eight in all), around the choir lectern and up the other side.

> It was one of the Abbot's ground rules that no one but a Priest must pass in front of the Tabernacle. If for example you were scrubbing the altar steps and had finished the north side you had to cart the bucket of soapy water a distance of 30 or 40 feet down around the choir lectern and back up the south side when you could easily have shoved the pail the distance of one foot and genuflected and knelt down and finished the south side.

ONE FURTHER NAME is listed in the Register among the 1898 admissions: that of six-year-old 'Brother Placidus' (Norton Emil Henry Rhys) on 8 August 1898.[537] He had already been at Llanthony for a year, and

---

of The Call of Caldey) was as follows: 'St Luke III, 22 / In memory / of / The Revd. Father's very tame / and affectionate little Dove / for many years flying in and / about our Monastery as a living / type to us of the Holy Ghost. / It was killed at last by / an act of violence on Sunday / August 20th, 1899 / Just before the Early Communion. / Its companion never cooed again / and died of a broken heart / 10 days after. / The grief of the Revd. Father / was very great. / The Loss is quite irreparable.'

[537] The deed of oblation is preserved at Prinknash among the surviving Profession Charts and is worded as follows. Apart from the signatures and date it is in Ignatius's handwriting.

'In the Name of the Father & of the SON & of the Holy Ghost. Amen. 'I Clara Rhys mother of Norton Emil Henry Rhys desire to place this Child in the Community of the Welsh Church Benedictines of Llanthony Abbey in Breconshire, to be trained for the service of GOD: &, in consideration for the expense & care they bestow upon him, I

seems to have been the only child to be received as an Infant Oblate (as distinct from a mere 'monastery boy') other than John Henry Docking thirty-four years earlier. As far as I can reconstruct it, his story is as follows. His father, Henry Percy Rhys, whose occupation is given in the 1891 census as 'translator', died in the summer of 1896 in south London, leaving a widow, Clara, and two children: Gwenllian, born 1 January 1888, and Norton, born late 1891. Like Mrs Docking, Clara Rhys may have been driven by economic necessity to part with the boy, as well as by the difficulty of combining paid work with care for a very young child.

When the 1901 census was taken Norton was still at Llanthony (his age given incorrectly as ten; he would in fact have been nine and a half), and his 13-year-old sister a 'visitor' with a clergyman and his wife in Dorset who had several girl pupils. Shortly before that date Clara had contracted a second marriage, with a German expatriate named William Eisen; they already had a child of two, and a second would be born six months later. The third witness on the deed of oblation, Elizabeth S. Rhys, was Norton's aunt, an older sister of his father's. For most of her adult life she ran various nursing homes and similar institutions in partnership with a certain Florence Norton; the fact that the boy had evidently been named for this lady suggests she was a relative or close family friend. Two of the institutions (their homes in 1881 and 1891) were in Margate, so there may have been a connection with Ignatius's brother Augustus Adolphus; the others were in Ealing, where Norton had been baptised (at the age of five) a few months before his arrival at the monastery.

Norton Rhys sailed to Montreal in 1907, and in 1918 signed on with the Canadian forces. His home was then in Regina where he

---

promise that I will in no way interfere with the Child's training or seek to remove him from their charge.

'Signed Clara Rhys
'Date   23rd August 1897
'Witnesses H. Evans Smith Alice Donaldson Elizabeth S. Rhys'

was employed as a clerk; as next of kin he gave his sister Gwenllian at their aunt's address in Ealing. He died in 1938, and was buried in the city of Edmonton.[538]

---

[538] As 'Brother Placidus' Norton Rhys makes a cameo appearance in Ignatius's account of 'The Monastery Children' (see Appendix 3). In 1908 Gwenllian's marriage to Alfred Sydney Killick was registered in the Brentford district, which included Ealing.

CHAPTER 11

IGNATIUS'S FINAL YEARS

BY THE FINAL DECADE OF THE CENTURY the liberal consensus had achieved theological respectability. By contrast Ignatius grew more dogged in his conservatism, and more vocal in opposing what he regarded as dangerous heresy. When Charles Gore was billed as one of the speakers at the 1893 Church Congress he hired a nearby hall to denounce him and his fellow 'higher critics', calling on them to resign their benefices and forfeit the stipends they received as teachers of the faith: that Gore held the office of Principal of Pusey House he found particularly galling, when in his view he 'taught a doctrine exactly opposite to Pusey's'.[539]

'A PRIEST FOR EVER...'

THIS MAY HELP TO EXPLAIN why he was prepared to accept priest's orders from outside the Church of England, and why his name was often mentioned in connection with a possible 'continuing' jurisdiction for Catholic-minded Anglicans seeking a refuge from doctrinal disorder. The bishop who ordained Ignatius was Joseph René Vilatte ('Mar Timotheus'), son of a Paris butcher and in a quite literal sense an *episcopus vagans*. When – with little warning – he arrived at the monastery in the middle of July 1898, Vilatte was in retreat from various problems of his own creation in America, where he had spent the first two decades of his adult life. In that time he had been successively Roman Catholic seminarian, freelance Presbyterian pastor, and priest in Old Catholic orders ministering under Anglican auspices to congregations of disgruntled ex-Catholic

---

[539] *Birmingham Daily Post*, 2 October 1893

Belgians and Poles. Six years earlier – in an attempt to form his little network of parishes into an 'Old Catholic Church of America' – he had been consecrated bishop. Not by Old Catholics of the Utrecht Union, who at the time saw no need for episcopal representation in the United States, but by Archbishop Antonio Alvarez (Mar Julius), leader of a non-Roman Latin-rite group in Ceylon who had received the episcopate from the Syrian Jacobite Church.

How did Vilatte know about Ignatius? He came with the recommendation of F.G. Lee, prelate of the Order of Corporate Reunion and Vicar of All Saints, Lambeth, but would certainly have heard of him and may even have heard him preach during the American tour of 1890-91, which included a foray into the Great Lakes region where he was based. Since then he had acquired as a collaborator the former Llanthony novice Claude Reader, whom he raised to the priesthood in 1896.[540]

The drama of Vilatte's arrival and subsequent events was chronicled in the margins of Ignatius's Churchman's Family Bible. At the time he was reading alternately from the minor prophets and St Matthew's Gospel, and the narrative begins with this note in the margin of the book of Hosea, dated Friday 22 July:

> Have been away – at Llandudno – got £27 on Sunday. Spoke at Eisteddfod at Blaenau Ffestiniog on Weds. Lord Carrington invited me to Gwydir Castle to meet the Duke of Cambridge &c. but I had to come as Archbishop Villayte [sic] Mar Timotheus was waiting to see me! He is willing to ordain me priest and Father Iltud too!

Iltud (Cobb) was then a couple of weeks short of his twenty-fifth birthday, and had taken his final vows the preceding St David's Day,

---

[540] For Reader see Chapter 10 above. A full account of Vilatte's life and wanderings across continents and between denominations will be found in BAL Chapter 4 (pp91-129), together with quotations from the letter of Bishop Grafton referred to below. See also Kersey, op cit.

having (as we have seen) entered the community three years before that ('a monk who has been in our Monastery for some years, and is noted for his gravity, piety and holiness of life', according to the press handout giving news of his and Ignatius's ordination[541]). With him ordained to the priesthood the monastery would now once more have a resident chaplain, able to provide sacramental ministrations when the Abbot was away.

The following Sunday Ignatius noted that 'Mar Timotheus...sang Mass in Latin, magnificently,' and observed that his connection with the patriarchate of Antioch would place the two ordinands 'in direct succession from St Peter'. There may have been a propaganda point here: to promoters of non-papal Catholicism the fact that the Apostle had presided over the church in Antioch before ever going to Rome gave that patriarchal see a precedence not often recognised in the west.

The next morning Iltud received the five minor orders, and on the Tuesday the diaconate. On Wednesday 27 July the two monks were ordained to the priesthood, the rite in the Roman pontifical being employed. Vilatte then continued on his travels, leaving the two new priests to celebrate their first Masses. Ignatius's took place on the Saturday, drawing from him the plea 'Help me O Lord' the day before and this comment on the day itself: 'Deo Gratias, I have said my First Mass today! So closely in union with Jesus: it is wonderful. I am 61!!' A week later he noted that 'Father Iltud sang Mass beautifully,' although by then they had probably each celebrated two or three times.

IGNATIUS TOOK PAINS to explain that he had accepted the priesthood solely for use within the monastery, but his action was condemned on all sides. One of the strongest criticisms came from Bishop Charles Grafton, whose diocese of Fond du Lac covered Vilatte's

---

[541] Quoted in *extenso* in Attwater p151

American stamping-ground, and who had inherited from his predecessor its curiously semi-detached relationship with that clergyman. As well as dwelling on his tortuous pedigree and numerous defects of character Grafton cast doubt on the validity of Vilatte's episcopal consecration, and therefore on that of Ignatius's ordination. Not unnaturally this was disturbing to the latter, who at once wrote to Archbishop Alvarez for his opinion.[542] The answer was reassuring: Vilatte had been consecrated 'canonically, legally and validly', and only after 'mature deliberation' and 'vehement investigation' (he had had to wait nine months for these processes to run their course after arriving in Ceylon). He believed Grafton's opposition to Vilatte to be the result of a 'private grudge', and felt it ridiculous for him as a 'Protestant bishop' to attempt to 'become a Pope of an Old Catholic Archbishop'. Alvarez also reminded Ignatius that the Old Catholic authorities in Utrecht had accepted the validity of Vilatte's consecration.

Nearer home Bishop Richard Lewis of Llandaff was asked by the *Western Mail* to comment on the Abbot's new status, and replied that when a clergyman sought 'ordination to the priesthood of another Church' he would be considered by so doing to have left the one to which he had hitherto belonged. Although the monastery was not in his diocese he felt able to add that Ignatius had rendered himself ineligible for advancement to the priesthood in the Church of England by failing to comply with its canons, and by holding 'services that made him regarded as a schismatic'.[543]

To Ignatius the matter was quite straightforward. If a Church of England bishop had offered him ordination to the priesthood he

---

[542] The correspondence was printed in the *Western Mail* of 7 January 1899. It comprised Ignatius's letter to Alvarez, dated 24 October 1898 and the Archbishop's reply dated 21 November, together with a brief covering letter from Ignatius to the Editor. Alvarez's letter is also reproduced in Kersey, op cit pp104-108.

[543] Issue of 3 August 1898

would have happily accepted it. But no bishop would do so without setting terms which seemed to him unreasonable, requiring him to give up wearing the habit, restrict himself and his monks to official Anglican forms of service and so forth. These were the same conditions by which he had felt unable to abide thirty years earlier, so he felt justified in accepting ordination from Vilatte. Later he would counter the suggestion that by undergoing ordination at the hands of a 'Syrian' bishop he was no longer a member of this country's national Church by citing the example of St David, who was consecrated bishop by the Patriarch of Jerusalem.[544]

A 'DIOCESE OF LLANTHONY'?

FOR THE LITTLE COMMUNITY at Llanthony the ordination of two of its members may have seemed like a gift from heaven, but Vilatte would scarcely have done it out of simple kindness of heart. The elevation of Ignatius to the priesthood was widely believed to be the first step in a definite plan to establish an Old Catholic[545] diocese in Britain, based on Llanthony and with him at its head.

It may have been Ignatius's ambivalence about this plan which five months later brought Vilatte back to these shores. On 23 December he conferred the priesthood on a London solicitor's clerk named Henry Bernard Ventham, having on the two preceding days admitted him to the minor orders and diaconate. Ventham (1873-1944) had

---

[544] *Hereford Times*, 12 August 1899. There was in fact an interesting precedent for such cross-denominational ordination, although it is unlikely that either Ignatius or his ordaining bishop was aware of it: the conferring of the priesthood on a Methodist lay preacher named John Jones by the Greek bishop Gerasimus in Amsterdam in 1763. See Kallistos Ware, 'The Fifth Earl of Guilford and his Conversion to the Orthodox Church' in Peter M. Doll (ed), *Anglicanism and Orthodoxy, 300 years after the 'Greek College' in Oxford* (Peter Lang 2006) p294.

[545] Or Orthodox diocese. To Vilatte (and perhaps to those to whom the plan was designed to appeal) the distinction between them mattered less than that between either of them and their Anglican and Roman counterparts.

been associated with George Nugée's Order of St Augustine and was a member of F.G. Lee's parish of All Saints, Lambeth, where he was conditionally baptised three weeks before his ordination. He was remembered by his friend and near contemporary Aelred Carlyle as a 'very eccentric and voluble young man'.[546]

Within weeks of this event Vilatte was reported to be in Rome and applying for reconciliation with the Holy See;[547] he spent the next year and a half enjoying the hospitality of various French and Italian monasteries while awaiting the Vatican's verdict. (Cynics maintained that he only applied for reconciliation so as to obtain recognition of his episcopal orders.) This apparent volte face clearly rattled Ignatius, who hinted that (like Grafton in the past and now the Roman authorities) he might now himself have doubts about Vilatte's sincerity. But he reassured himself and the public that if Mar Timotheos was as disturbed by the reductionist 'new Reformation' of Dean Fremantle[548] and his school as he had claimed to be (it had been 'the stand made by Llanthony for the Bible and the Faith of Christ' that he had given as his reason for bestowing the priesthood on its

---

[546] BAL p272. Nugée's community broke up following his death in 1893. Ventham is then thought to have joined the oblate group associated with Mother Hilda's sisterhood, of which Carlyle was also a member; in 1894 they went together to the site of the future Westminster Cathedral to witness the laying of the foundation stone by Cardinal Vaughan. He also had a long-standing interest in Llanthony, having as a boy set out to walk there from his home in Camberwell but failed to complete the journey. In a letter written in 1962 to Dom Michael Hanbury of Prinknash Abbey Peter Anson said that 'sometime in the 1890s' Ventham was a novice at Llanthony, but this is probably a misunderstanding based on his known presence there in the summer of 1899, for which see below. For information about Ventham (1873-1944) I am grateful to the Reverend Norman Hulme of Spalding, Lincs, whose friend Harold Moxon had at one time been a clerical colleague, and to Metropolitan Seraphim of the British Orthodox Church, who kindly furnished me with a copy of his article The Vilatte Succession in England 1898-1906.

[547] The report, together with Ignatius's lengthy comment, appeared in the Western Mail of 26 January 1899.

[548] W.H. Fremantle (1831-1916), Dean of Ripon and chief of Ignatius's liberal bêtes noirs

Abbot) he could not altogether be blamed if he sought refuge in the Church of Rome, whose adherence to orthodox fundamentals was beyond question. 'Sometimes, with the thought of Dean Fremantle's horrible infidelity patronised by our bishops, I have wished that I could [do the same].'

And from this cue he went on to berate 'our bishops' for their attempt to ban incense ('which God commands for the Christian Church by his prophet Malachi') and reservation of the eucharistic elements ('a practice common to all historic Christendom and ordered by the Church of England in Queen Elizabeth's Latin Prayer Book'). The combined effect of these restrictive measures and the bishops' condoning of modernist 'infidelity' might force the 'multitudes of Churchmen' who considered themselves 'Catholics but not Roman Catholics...to turn for help to the Old Catholic Hierarchy of other lands', a 'climax' he anticipated coming to pass 'in the near future'.

Meanwhile, so as to avoid being 'implicated in the awful treachery now rampant among the bishops and clergy against Our Lord Jesus Christ and the Church's creeds' he declared that he now regarded himself as being only in 'lay-communion' with the Church of England. This, he explained, meant that from now on he would refrain from performing ministerial acts in Anglican churches, 'even where the bishops may be willing that we[549] should do so'. In October (at the time of the annual Church Congress, meeting that year in London) he repeated this announcement, earning from the Daily Telegraph the observation that it was 'sadly discounted by the fact that it merely anticipates episcopal inhibition'.[550]

Further correspondence between Ignatius and Archbishop Alvarez was reproduced in the Western Mail of 20 July 1899, from which it appeared that of the two it was the Archbishop who was

---

[549] It is not clear who else he meant to include in the 'we'. Was he referring to Cobb and/or Ventham, neither of whom had (so far) acquired ministerial status in the Church of England?

[550] Quoted in the Hereford Times of 14 October 1899.

the more enthusiastic about establishing a British Orthodox diocese. As long as the Nicene Creed remained even nominally her standard of faith Ignatius would not desert his mother church, regardless of whether he could minister at her altars or preach from her pulpits. He repeated his point that the priesthood had been received strictly for use within the community, and ventured to ask whether it might also be granted the episcopate, which until Vilatte's recent 'fall' it had been hoping to receive from him, not necessarily in his own person. '[A]ncient provincial councils' had set many precedents for having bishops in monasteries, and although he couldn't yet see his way to founding a new denomination it would be useful to have a bishop in waiting in case the established Church actually apostasised. There would then be at Llanthony a ready-made 'fountain...for the supplying of the waters of salvation' to those thus deprived of reliable sacraments.

When this letter was written Ventham was staying at Llanthony, though on what terms and for how long is not clear. Ignatius found him 'a very sincere and devout young man' (an observation which suggests he had not previously been there as a novice), and appeared to be putting him forward as a suitable candidate for this putative bishopric; history fails to relate how Alvarez responded.

By October Ventham had left Llanthony for Barry, then a significant commercial port, where he was installed by Fr Hopkins of the Order of St Paul as chaplain to his seamen's hostel. When the census was taken eighteen months later he was listed at The Priory, Broad Street, as a 'visitor': a rather non-committal description if he was indeed acting as its chaplain. (The Bishop of Llandaff would have been horrified if he had known that he gave his occupation as 'priest, Church of England'.)

His duties at the hostel seem to have been very light. In May 1900 he travelled to Paris to visit Vilatte, who after his eighteen-month 'sabbatical' had settled there for the time being and begun once more to function as a bishop. The Archbishop clothed him in the monastic habit with the name of Columba Mary and authorised him to set up a mission in Liverpool, where according to a report in Le Temps[551] a 'large number of Roman Catholics' had requested his help and support.[552] The fact that for the previous five years Ventham had been married – to Sibella Mary Hicks, the daughter of an army officer and his senior by some four decades[553] – seems not to have been reckoned an impediment to his admission to the monastic state, but as he and his bride seem never to have lived together he probably kept this inconvenient fact to himself. Also involved in the Liverpool project was Richard O'Halloran, a Roman Catholic priest in Ealing who had fallen foul of the authorities of his Church;[554] there was one novice, a young man named Ambrose Thomas, who had earlier been dismissed from the novitiate at Erdington Abbey.[555]

---

[551] Issue of 2 June 1900

[552] It was reported in the Western Mail of 11 July 1900 that Vilatte had appointed Ventham (named as 'Father Bentham [sic] of Hay') as Prior of the OSP house at Barry Dock rather than to the Liverpool mission, and would shortly raise him to the episcopate. The first of these statements may have been the result of a misunderstanding, although it was certainly true (as the paper said) that on account of the extreme ritualism practised in the Barry Dock chapel the Church of England authorities would not license a priest to officiate there. In an earlier account (29 May 1900) the same paper reported that 'Father Bentham' had received a letter from Alvarez explaining that because of Vilatte's currently 'unsettled state' he could not be expected to proceed with establishing an Orthodox diocese either in England or America. However, both Alvarez himself and the Syrian Jacobite Patriarch of Antioch remained keenly interested in furthering this project.

[553] Shades of Charles Walker. When they married in July 1895 the new Mrs Ventham had given her age as 46 (she was in fact 59 or 60). The fact that for many years her husband seems to have survived without a regular job suggests that financial advantage may have been one of his motives for the marriage. Sibella Ventham died in 1907.

[554] For O'Halloran see René Kollar, The Return of the Benedictines to London, Burns & Oates 1989, especially Chapter 2.

[555] The Liverpool venture came to a speedy end when the bills for equipping its chapel could not be met. Thomas (1881-1959) took refuge for a while at Caldey, where Abbot Aelred Carlyle settled his debts; his name is listed there (as 'Benedictine Monk') in the 1901 census. Later in life he

Between early 1901 and the summer of 1903 Vilatte was in Canada. On his return to Europe he paid another visit to South Wales (though not, so far as we know, to Llanthony). On 14 June 1903 in the corrugated iron chapel of the Barry seamen's hostel he consecrated Henry Marsh-Edwards as 'Bishop of Caerleon', and on the following day with Vilatte's assistance Marsh-Edwards consecrated Ventham – who had given up the chaplaincy there the preceding January – as 'Bishop of Dorchester'.[556] Apart from surreptitiously reordaining Anglican clergymen (an activity he is said to have continued after joining their number) it is not known how Ventham discharged his new responsibilities, or how else he filled his time over the next couple of decades.[557] He was certainly a slippery character: it is alleged that at the time of his consecration he was acting as an Anglican lay reader in Somerset while posing elsewhere as a Roman

---

re-invented himself as 'Amand Edouard Ambroise Marie Louis Etienne Phillippe de Saint André de Tournay, Marquis d'Oisy', and enjoyed some distinction as a dress designer, decorator of furniture both domestic and ecclesiastical and director of elaborate theatricals in and around Thaxted in Essex, an area well supplied in the inter-war years with talented and eccentric personalities. I am grateful to Julian Litten for sharing his knowledge of this intriguing character and giving me sight in manuscript of the study he has since published as The Mystery of Marquis d'Oisy (Shaun Tyas in association with The Society of the Faith, 2015).

[556] Marsh-Edwards had previously served as an incumbent in the Diocese of Southwell, but not long before his consecration was forced to resign following allegations of immorality (Sheffield Daily Telegraph, 13 January 1904). 'Caerleon' and 'Dorchester' had been the territorial titles adopted by two of the three prelates in the Order of Corporate Reunion, J.T. Seccombe and F.G. Lee, both of whom were now dead.

[557] Ventham was still living in Barry when the next census was taken in 1911, at a terrace house in Trinity Street; this time he was listed as 'tutor'. As this was only a short walk from the Priory (which closed down the following year) he may have continued to officiate in its chapel. Living with him was a young railway clerk named Frederick Henry Ramsay Pursall; their names occur together in the Llanthony Visitors' Book in both June 1905 and May 1909, probably recording day visits. Earlier (on 19 July 1902) Ignatius had written to Ventham pleading shortage of monastic manpower for his inability to receive him just then as a guest (letter in private collection).

Catholic layman.[558] In 1922 he embarked on a two-year course of theological training at King's College, London, at the end of which he was reordained deacon and priest by Bishop Winnington-Ingram. His first post thereafter was a curacy at St Gabriel's, South Bromley, from which in 1927 he moved to become Vicar of South Creake, near Walsingham, remaining there until his death.[559]

No record has come to light of continuing negotiations between Ignatius and Archbishop Alvarez, but he was still pursuing the possibility of sending one or more of his monks to be ordained by an eastern bishop at the beginning of 1908, the year of his death. On 2 January he noted in his diary having an 'important talk' with Brother Gildas (Robert Clare Taylor, for whom see below; he was then a novice of less than six months' standing) 'about sending Fr Asaph to [the] Patriarch of Antioch to be ordained priest', adding that it had occurred to him 'to try to get them consecrated Bishops for the Monastery unless our dear Bishop of St Davids will ordain them priests'. The word 'them' suggests he was also putting Gildas forward as a candidate for the priesthood and possibly the episcopate.

Eight days later he recorded having written 'a very particular letter' to the Syrian Patriarch of Antioch, and on 4 February (in red ink) having 'sent The Appeal to Mardin' (headquarters of the Patriarchate). If this 'Appeal' was in response to a rejection of the

---

[558] H.R.T. Brandreth, *Episcopi Vagantes and the Anglican Church* (SPCK, 1st edn 1947) p 39n.

[559] Peter Anson points out that at this time St Gabriel's 'was unique in being staffed by three irregularly consecrated Old Catholic prelates, and some very irregular things went on there' (BAL p273). At South Creake Ventham devoted his energies to restoring the church to a fair approximation of its pre-Reformation appearance. His attitude to the rest of the Church of England was described as 'cynical indifference' (ibid), and on his deathbed he refused its Last Sacraments. A letter from Harold Moxon to W. D. Varney dated 1 Oct 1957 (Museum ref A1993.139.11.7) confirms Ventham's lifelong interest in Llanthony and mentions visits to Ty Cwm, the holiday home between old Llanthony and Capel-y-ffin he maintained until 1940 or thereabouts.

request in the 'particular letter' the international post must in those days have been extremely rapid, but there is no mention of a letter having come from Mardin in the meantime.

PRIESTHOOD IN THE MONASTERY (AND OUT OF IT)

A MONTH AFTER THE 'Llanthony Ordinations' the annual Apparitions Feast came round. According to the *Western Mail* report[560] the plan had been for it to be kept 'privately' that year – perhaps Ignatius wanted to avoid his newly acquired priesthood becoming an object of curiosity or an occasion of controversy. However, in spite of both this plan and the wet weather crowds of visitors turned up as usual, being treated to a 'grand mass' following the Prayer Book liturgy, with 'much intricate and ancient ritual'.[561]

The Llanthony 'use' had been shaped through thirty years in which more often than not there had been no priest to consecrate the sacrament. When Ignatius was at home he had been in the habit of administering Communion (in both kinds) from the tabernacle at eight o'clock on Sundays and feasts, followed at eleven by an observance he called 'Holy Oblation' or 'Offering of the Holy Sacrament'. In effect a combination of the Ante-Communion service and Benediction of the Blessed Sacrament, this was intended as a substitute for Solemn Mass without general Communion, in those days the normal mid-morning service in Anglo- and Roman Catholic churches.[562] When he was away or ill the community would sing the

---

[560] Issue of 3 September 1898

[561] Note in Ignatius's Bible against the concluding verse of St Matthew ch. 11: 'Apparition Day 1898. Very wet: no advertisements; no food for pilgrims, but crowds came – & the Holy Ghost was upon us!! The whole countryside kept Sabbath – and all the people in their Sunday clothes.' The day in question was a Tuesday.

[562] In devising this service Ignatius may have been aware of the Catholic Apostolic ('Irvingite') ceremony known as 'Proposition of the Reserved Sacrament', in which at the daily morning and evening services the prayers of intercession were conducted in the presence of the consecrated elements, laid on the altar 'before the Lord' (Rowland A.

office of Lauds instead of 'Oblation': the need to have a substantial public service in the middle of the morning seems to have been deeply ingrained.[563]

In the summer of 1901 Fr Iltud left the monastery, as we shall see. Ignatius was left as the sole priest, and the situation reverted to more or less how it had been before his ordination. For much of the year he was away, and the community would have to be content with non-eucharistic worship on Sundays and feasts. But when he was at home it would not be unusual for him to substitute Communion from the Reserved Sacrament and 'Holy Oblation' for the full eucharistic celebration, even when Iltud was still in the community.

A year after Mar Timotheus's visit the *Hereford Times* printed a lengthy account of how the community celebrated the feast of the Name of Jesus on 7 August.[564] This is interesting not just for the light it throws on the use (or lack of it) Ignatius was making of his priesthood, but for what it conveys of the devotional ethos at Llanthony, focused as it was almost entirely on the cult of the Presence in the sacramental elements. After Terce at 8.0am

the gratings of the monks' choir was [sic] slowly opened, and then such a sight presented itself.

Davenport, *Albury Apostles*, United Writers 1970, p289 and pp 326f).

[563] One wonders what happened to the 'little hours' of Prime and Terce on these occasions. The multiplicity of festivals resulted in 11.00 Lauds being quite a frequent occurrence; it may even have become daily routine. In his 1908 Diary Ignatius records taking a mid-morning walk on Monday 13 January (octave day of the Epiphany) 'while they [the other monks] were at Lauds'. On Tuesday 11 February the community celebrated the second day in the octave of St Scholastica with 'Solemn Lauds and Sermon' at 11.00 (the Abbot had been absent over the weekend conducting a mission in Hereford and had therefore missed the feast itself), and on Monday 2 March (St David's Day, transferred) he was 'too worn out for [the] 11 o'clock service; they waited in church till 11.45 then said Lauds'.

[564] Issue of 19 August 1899

THE MAGNIFICENT SHRINE
with its curtains, marble pillars, canopies, and statuary, adorned with
hundreds of candles, roses, lilies, flowers in brass and enamelled
and jewelled vases, burst upon our vision. Monks and boys in white
albs knelt upon the broad altar stairs, which was [sic] covered with
crimson velvet. Almost like a distant whisper of song rose the hymn –

> Jesus, let Thy presence breathe a sense of rest
> O'er our tired spirits by life's toils opprest....

Father Ignatius, as the hymn died away, rose from his knees, and amid
the tinkling of silver bells opened the Tabernacle and placed the holy
sacrament upon the altar[, t]he jewelled ciborium and the flagon being
veiled in richly jewelled coverings. These were removed, and a 'fair
linen cloth' placed over the vessels. Then, turning to the choir, he
commenced the address, 'Ye that do truly and earnestly repent you
of your sins'. Then followed the rest of the Communion service, with
the omission of the consecration, as all were to be communicated
from the 'Reserved Sacrament'. Just before the Communion of the
monks and nuns the hymn was very softly sung, 'Draw nigh to take
the body of the Lord, and drink the holy blood for thee outpoured'.
A long white linen cloth was held by the recipients under their chins,
and Father Ignatius and another priest monk, holding ciborium and
chalice [and] vested in albs and stoles, descended the steps, placing
the Host in the mouths of the communicants, and delivering the
chalice into their hands covered by the cloth.... The nuns were quite
invisible, and were communicated through a wicket in a very close
grating on the north side of the altar.

    The monks having made their communion, a strange ceremony
took place. The people in the outer church did not approach the altar,
or pass the choir gates; the priests prepared to bring the sacrament
in both kinds down to the outer church. The priests were attended
by [a] tonsured boy, carrying a light and the silvery bells. He held

up the light to the Sacrament, and rang the bells directly the priests began to move. The other monks had now received lighted tapers, and formed two lines; as the Host approached they lifted their tapers to it, and then as it passed fell prostrate on their faces in the profoundest adoration...

For the rest of the day the Host was 'solemnly exposed in a dazzling "Monstrance"', with 'incense continually ascending' before it; the occasion seems to have been (or the reporter interpreted it as) a kind of demonstration in favour of the two controversial usages of reservation and incense. It is strange that there was no 'grand mass' later that morning, or even a service of 'Holy Oblation' – unless there was and the correspondent failed to report it.

Ignatius may have claimed that his priesthood was intended solely for use within the monastery, but on at least one occasion he exercised it elsewhere. At the end of a three-week visit he paid to the house of his sister and brother-in-law Harriet and Paul Ewens at Foots Cray in January 1900 their daughter Hilda made this entry in her diary:

I must add here Uncle L[eycester] said Mass one day last week on our little prayer table, a real Altar now how glad I am.

No photographs appear to have been taken of 'Uncle Leycester' in eucharistic vestments, and only a few of him wearing a stole priest-wise (although a number of earlier ones portray him in deacon's stole, sometimes worn under a cope and with abbot's mitre and staff). A few of these seem to be making a deliberate point by showing Ignatius in surplice and priest's stole over his habit, with veiled chalice on a small table alongside. Was this his travelling Mass kit?

Picture 26: Ignatius the Priest

THE MONASTERY HOUSEHOLD

IGNATIUS WAS AT Foots Cray when the nineteenth century gave way to the twentieth; he had been absent from Llanthony since mid-November and would stay away for most of the winter, missions in London, Brighton and elsewhere alternating with visits to friends and relations. His departure from his sister's house was postponed by twenty-four hours after a sleepless night caused by receiving a letter from Fr Iltud, who told him he had 'broken down' and could no longer 'continue the hard life' at the monastery. This is how Hilda recorded it in her diary; she adds that 'Mother [Harriet] wrote to Father Eltud [sic] for Uncle L[eycester] telling him how his letter had upset [him] & saying nothing of an unpleasant nature was to be written to him while he was on his missions.'

What would have made the threat of Iltud's departure particularly inconvenient was the strain it would impose on Asaph, effectively the only other monk. For the time being he managed to hang on, just: a year later, on the feast of King Charles the Martyr (30 January) – a solemn day of prayer – Ignatius noted in his Bible that there had been '[n]o Exposition thro' Father Iltud', so perhaps he was causing further anxiety just then. When the census was taken at the end of March the household consisted of nine individuals:

Arthur C. Cobb (single, 27) (Iltud)	Monk & Priest	b. West Kensington
Alfred Harris (single, 25) (Asaph)	Monk	b. Birmingham
Cyril Gibbs (single, 13)		b. India
Norton Rhys (single, 10; actually 9½)	(Oblate Placidus)	b. Brixton
Jack Clark (single, 9)		b. London SW
James Gilbert (single, 55)	General Servant on Farm	b. Hereford
Jeannie L. Dew (single, 35) (Tudfil)	Nun	b. Reading
Alice R. Wheeler (single, 41)	Sister	b. Kentish Town NW
Rose A. Kidder (widow, 49; actually 62)	Sister	b. Brighton.[565]

---

[565] On Ascension Day that year the concourse of pilgrims included a party of students from the Calvinistic Methodist seminary at Trefecca. A brief report of the visit appeared in the Midsummer issue of their college

The Superior was listed on this occasion at a lodging house in Leamington with Brother David and Sister Annie, who regularly accompanied him on his missionary journeys. A day or two before the end of his turn-of-the-century visit to the Ewenses these two supporters had made their way from Wales to Kent so as to travel with him to his next engagement, a mission in Hastings.

Young Cyril Gibbs was also mentioned in Hilda's diary, because Harriet was considering offering him a home. Cyril (born 15 November 1887) and his brother Neville (born 15 October 1886) had started life overseas, their father (according to Hilda 'a big red faced man with an eye glass' and 'nicer than I thought he would be') having had a job with the Indian Railways.[566] Their mother was a cousin of Ignatius's,[567] but the marriage had ended in divorce. This may explain the negative reaction of her Ewens aunts[568] when Hilda mentioned her mother's proposal to them: '[I]t was quite amusing

---

magazine, whose author ('G.M.Ll') was nonplussed by the ceremonial but impressed by the evangelical tone of the Abbot's preaching. He notes that the establishment 'contains only about five monks, some of them boys' (probably the same five people heading the census return), and that 'the service was almost all choral, but, as there were only four or five singing, the effect cannot be described as winning, and the Father, as if conscious of the weakness thereof, at times assisted in a stentorian voice, which, though it gave power, did not improve the harmony. The tunes and chants were all Gregorian, sounding funereal and weird without possessing the pathos common to that form of music.....' (Museum ref A2010.86.113).

[566] In the 1901 census he was listed at Laverstock House Lunatic Asylum in Wiltshire, where he was employed as secretary. When two years later Ignatius recorded the baptism of his two sons in his Register his occupation was given as engineer. I am grateful to Neville Riddock and Margaret Haywood, grandchildren respectively of Neville and Cyril, for information about the two brothers, who both spent their adult lives in Australia. Cyril died in 1976, and Neville in 1969.

[567] Harriet Agnes Penelope (born Cornwall 1860), daughter of Decastro Lyne (Barrister & JP), who was a son of Prebendary Charles Lyne of Exeter and brother of the Charles Lyne mentioned in Chapters 1 and 3. She died in Suresens (Seine) on 16 Dec 1907.

[568] Elizabeth and Mary Ewens, spinster sisters of her father Paul; they lived at Stowfield House, Pit Farm Road, Guildford.

how excited they got about it, & how they were against it.' In the winter of 1903/04 the boy was at the monastery again, having been away in the interim boarding in another household; he and his brother were baptised in the abbey church on 27 December 1903, aged respectively seventeen and sixteen. In February 1904 Ignatius reported to Harriet that he

> had had to send Cyril away again. He troubled the brothers so with his temper. The thing he was sent away for was barricading his room door with his bed to prevent the brothers calling him for Prime and not leaving his room till 12, and then being in a temper all over nothing.[569]

Perhaps this tells us as much about Ignatius himself as about his teenage relation: he never did understand what made adolescents tick. Cyril was despatched to live with 'an old widow lady' (who Ignatius hoped might adopt him) and emigrated not long afterwards to Australia, after which Neville seems to have taken his place. The younger boy is mentioned in letters in 1905/06 from Ignatius to his cousin (Richard) Arundell Lyne ('Arley'),[570] Vicar of Hentland, near Ross-on-Wye, and his name is noted in the margin of his copy of *Hawker's Daily Portion* three times in the spring of 1905, when he seems to have joined the Evangelist Monk's travelling entourage. Picture 27 was taken in Folkestone, where both Rose and Neville were noted as having read from *Hawker* in the last week of May that year.[571]

The *Daily Portion* was compiled by Dr Robert Hawker, Vicar of Charles Church, Plymouth, and grandfather of his more famous namesake,

---

[569] One of a collection of transcribed letters in the Abergavenny collection (ref A2010.86.18)

[570] Son of Richard Stephens Lyne and his wife Mary Elizabeth (formerly Nicholas): born 5 May 1870, died 27 August 1955.

[571] The two Gibbs brothers appear in the group photograph in Bertouch opposite p594, aged perhaps ten and eleven, with Fathers Ignatius and Iltud, a small girl and an unidentifiable postulant.

the priest-poet of Morwenstow. For the last ten years of his life it was Ignatius's constant companion,[572] and he often noted where he had been in any particular year against each morning and evening's allotted reading. This not only helps us to reconstruct his movements; as he liked to get other people to read the passages for him and entered their names we also get an idea of who was with him, especially when he was on his travels. Brother David's name occurs most frequently, with his wife 'Sena' (Thomasina) doing the occasional turn and as he grew into his teens their son Lessie. After Sister Annie's death in January 1903 her place as 'mission sister' was taken by Sister Rose, whose name is found from time to time in the years 1904-06.

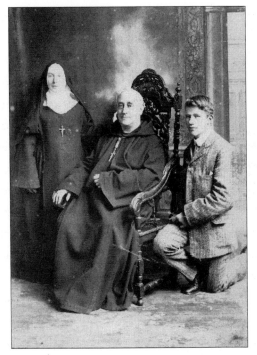

Picture 27: Fr Ignatius with Sister Rose Kidder and Neville Gibbs, Folkestone 1905

---

[572] Marginal notes only begin in March 1898, but Ignatius had evidently acquired the book many years earlier. In one of the *horaria* mentioned in Chapter 7 'Hawker' is timetabled as a community activity.

Another indication of how small the community was in its final decade is given in the handwritten list of those taking part in the Watch on the feast of Corpus Christi 1905.[573] The 'Revd Father' and Brother Cadoc (Davidson: see below) each filled one slot, as did Sister Rose; Sister Tudfil took two. Brother Asaph was down for one, with the possibility of a second if someone called Cornelius failed to show up – a guest, perhaps, or one of the diminishing number of enquirers. The two hours between three and five o'clock were the responsibility of the family at Maes-y-ffin: Brother David and Sena, and their friend Gwen Dodson, sister of the former Fr Michael.

An addition to the Llanthony household around this time was John Bates, then aged around forty. Someone who knew him in later life explained how he had come to be there:

Born somewhere in Radnorshire where his father was a forester on a large estate, as a lad he drifted into gamekeeping, but did not stay in any situation long. For a short time he was on the Enville Estate in Staffordshire as an underkeeper. He was a bachelor and became a roamer, drifting into the Wye Valley where for a time he was a water-keeper. Then off once again through Hay and up over the mountain landing down on the other side at Llanthony, in the valley of the Honddu. John found here sanctuary in the monastery of New Llanthony Abbey of Our Lady and St Dunstan which Father Ignatius had founded in 1870.

John was given the task of finding fresh food from the surrounding hills and fish from the river to sustain the small community at the monastery, and as rabbits were plentiful the task was comparatively easy. Father Ignatius had a tremendous effect upon him and John became a regular attendant at Chapel, and having a very retentive

---

[573] Tucked into the Bible belonging to Fr Ignatius preserved at Ss Julius & Aaron, Newport

memory he soon learnt most of the Prayer Book off by heart and years later he could quote most of it, even to the Thirty Nine Articles! He told us of days when housekeeping funds would be running low and bills unpaid, when he would drive Father Ignatius in pony trap to Abergavenny station where he would board the London train. Once in London, Father Ignatius would fulfil a series of preaching engagements and soirees. His impact on London was enormous and at the end of the series, ladies would take off their jewellery and other valuables and hand them to him for his work at the monastery. Having returned to Llanthony, John would drive him the next day into Abergavenny where at the jewellers he would exchange his valuables for cash, so allowing him to meet his creditors.[574]

Later he followed the Llanthony remnant to Caldey, where Donald Attwater became acquainted with him:

He had been imported from Capel-y-ffin to look after the game-birds on the island; he spoke broad Herefordshire English, and he spoke it to some purpose. His mind was shrewd and his tongue was caustic and irreverent; in those days it was nothing surprising that an unlettered man should have a good knowledge of the text of the Bible, but John knew his Shakespeare as well. He had worked for Father Ignatius of Llanthony, and told me a number of things that were useful when I came to write a biography of that 'Evangelist Monk of the British Church'.[575]

---

[574] From an account of his youthful friendship with Bates sent by Canon Keble Thomas to Douglas Lyne in 1988 (Museum ref A1997.19.10); his rabbiting activities suggest that the ban on flesh meat had been mitigated or done away with. More about Bates and how the future Canon Thomas came to know him in Chapter 13.

[575] From Donald Attwater, 'Et in Arcadia Ego' in *Pax*, Spring 1963. Bates's name is not included among those listed by Attwater in his book as having given help and information.

CHANGES IN THE COMMUNITY

EIGHTEEN MONTHS after his unsuccessful bid to leave the monastery of his own volition, Fr Iltud was dismissed for 'going into the Nuns enclosure'. A couple of years later he entered King's College, London, to study for the ministry. He was (re-)ordained deacon in 1906 and priest the following year by Bishop Winnington-Ingram, and over the next nine years served various curacies in London and Surrey. It seems likely that his departure from Llanthony was in some way connected with that of Violet de Pothonier, formerly Sister Mary Helena; they married in 1907 and had one child, Ronald Arthur Augustine (1909-1997). Fr Cobb retired from active ministry in 1915, probably through ill health, and died two years later at the age of 43.

Only three men joined the community in the first decade of the new century. The first was 19-year-old Samuel Davidson (Brother Cadoc Mary of the Ascension; born 16 January 1882 at Medomsley, Co Durham), who arrived on 26 June 1901. In that year's census he had been listed as resident servant to the Reverend Harold R. Jecks, assistant curate of Hanslope in Buckinghamshire. A few years earlier (1895-98) Jecks had been curate of Davidson's home parish, and he was a frequent visitor to Llanthony,[576] although whether the young man came to the monastery because his employer and former curate was a friend of the community or whether the clergyman stayed there because his erstwhile parishioner and servant was an inmate is impossible to determine. A year after his admission Brother Cadoc took vows as a novice (for an unspecified period – 'during the time appointed for my Noviciate by our Holy Father St Benedict'). He may then have gone away for a spell, which would expain why he apparently never advanced beyond that rank, but he seems to have returned in time to be included in the list of those taking part

---

[576] Against his entry in the Visitors' Book on 14 April 1904 he wrote '5th visit'; others were recorded for 1-4 March 1904 and 3-6 September 1910.

in the Corpus Christi watch in 1905. He also figures in the 1908 diary fragment, and remained at the monastery for some time after Ignatius's death.[577]

The second to be admitted was Charles Thomas Fullaway, although it was noted that he 'came to [the] Monastery' no fewer than three times (November 1902, August 1903 and May 1907), only being 'made a Novice' on the third occasion. At 51 (born in Stroud on 10 January 1856) he was rather older than the usual run of aspirants, which may explain why his admission to the noviciate was hurried through when he had been in the monastery just eleven days. As a young man the new Brother Iltud Mary of the Epiphany had been a music teacher, and more recently proprietor of a small private school in Brentford.

According to the Register he '[l]eft a month or so after taking his vows, & very odd conduct, on account of his health, so he said, but saying he would soon return & be professed! If I would allow it! He was here as a Spy we believe.' If he was two-timing with one of the protestant pressure groups his religious background was suitably ambiguous ('Baptised privately by Chas. Thomas Dissenting Minister and again conditionally by Roman Priest. Confirmed at Whiteshill Church Glosters by Bishop Ellicott'), as indeed was his marital status.[578]

---

[577] Davidson's profession chart (dated 29 June 1902) is in the Prinknash archives. See the following chapter for his presence at Llanthony in 1909 and 1910.

[578] In 1897 at Childe Okeford, Dorset, he had married a lady named Jane Georgina Keturah Goodridge, whose father was a naval doctor. The school of which he is listed as proprietor in the 1901 census had eight resident pupils, mostly from overseas; he was said to be single. Meanwhile his wife was living near her family in Dorset, where perhaps when not visiting monasteries he joined her in the holidays. In 1911 he seems to have avoided being listed, perhaps through absence abroad; meanwhile she was recorded at a farmhouse on the outskirts of Bath, with an agriculturalist lodger who may have actually farmed the land. When she died in 1919 she was described as a widow, although he himself survived until 1928.

The third was Robert Clare Taylor, son of a Bradford-on-Avon pawnbroker, who although baptised an Anglican had spent four years in Australia as a Baptist minister; he entered the community on 22 June 1907, a few weeks short of his thirtieth birthday. After an eight-week postulancy (from 27 July) he was clothed as a novice on 15 September with the name Gildas Mary of the Resurrection.

For some time in the middle of this decade the only monk at Llanthony apart from its Abbot (when he was at home) was Brother Asaph. This is confirmed in Aelred Carlyle's tribute to Ignatius in the December 1908 issue of *Pax*, his community's magazine; it may also be inferred from contemporary photographs such as those taken on the Wednesday in Easter Week (26 April) 1905, when the monastery received a visit from a party of boys and masters from Bellenden Road Higher Grade School, Peckham, who were enjoying an educational holiday in the district. Ignatius and Asaph are the only monks who appear with the visitors in the pictures taken on this occasion, one of which shows Asaph taking a serious interest in their elaborate photographic equipment.[579]

As we have seen, Asaph had been admitted as a postulant on 29 July 1898 (just two days after the priestly ordination of Ignatius and Iltud), having arrived at the monastery three weeks earlier. Born on 13 December 1875, he was the third of the nine children of Thomas Harris and his wife Harriett, whose address in the 1881 census was given as 'No 13, back of 68 Longmore Street' in the Birmingham district of Kings Norton. He evidently inherited something of the practical dexterity his father would have needed in his occupation as a bridle cutter as well as considerable ingenuity, if not the gift of a tuneful singing voice. In later life he would discover the suitability of

---

[579] Five years later he would spend the then considerable sum of £7 2s 6d on a 'tele[photo?] lens', which suggests that the interest was more than mere curiosity. This detail is from a cheque stub among the Prinknash Abbey papers, where a photograph album commemorating the Bellenden Road visit is also preserved.

the Prinknash clay for the pottery for which that community became well known in the 1950s and 1960s, and after the opening of its daughter house at Pluscarden in 1948 would initiate the manufacture of stained glass there and equip the premises with electric light. An earlier project in this latter field was carried out soon after his arrival at Llanthony, when he harnessed a mountain stream to create one of the first hydro-electric schemes in the country; contemporary photographs clearly show pendant light fittings in the refectory. It is said that he also tried with disastrous results to convert the abbey church organ to water power, but this may be just legend.

Picture 28: Fr Asaph and another monk helping with the haymaking. In the background the new Apparitions statue, installed in 1905.

In his obituary of Asaph Dom Bruno Webb pays tribute to his inventiveness, and to the 'childlike spirit of wonder' which accompanied it – a 'wonder...closely linked with the experience of God's presence', and which 'is itself prayer'. Canon Stanley Luff recalled a conversation with Asaph in his later years:

'Father Asaph – those miracles one hears so much about at Llanthony – what do you think of them?' He looked down a moment – Father Asaph was a very small man – then he looked up at me and said quite simply: 'All I can say is – I saw them.'

At the time Luff (then a layman living with the Pluscarden community) assumed that the monk was referring to the 1880 apparitions, but on reflection realised that these had taken place many years before Asaph came on the scene. The reply of this 'serious man of prayer' must have meant that 'he was aware of other marvellous happenings...in the subsequent history of the monastery', although as he was evidently a witness of them modesty would have prevented him from going into greater detail.[580]

IN THE EARLY YEARS of the new century Ignatius organised his supporters into the 'Scarlet Thread Company', whose newsletters kept them up to date with his missions and developments in the monastery.[581] In the May 1906 letter he wrote that he had been 'far too overworked to return to his home labours at Easter, and a Clergyman who had been a novice in the Monastery supplied his place in the Easter services'. He was also able to report that

---

[580] Information from Fr Asaph's obituary in Pax, Summer 1960; the quotation is from the sermon preached by Canon Stanley Luff at the Llanthony pilgrimage in August 1984.

[581] It took its name from the 'line of scarlet thread' in Joshua 2.18ff. Six copies from various dates between September 1905 and March 1907 are in the archives at Abergavenny: ref A1997.16.12; the January 1908 number is at Prinknash.

[a]pplications to the noviciate continue to be made, and two candidates may this month be admitted to the Cloister. The newly-admitted brother and sister continue in loyal observance of their Rule, and have made a most edifying Lent.

This time the 'Clergyman' is unlikely to have been ex-Brother Dunstan (Magrath), whose duties at Coberley would surely have ruled out a trip to Llanthony at a major festival. One of the 'two candidates' may have been Fullaway; the individuals mentioned in the final sentence were only 'newly-admitted' in the sense that they had recently taken their final vows; the reference is of course to Asaph and Tudfil.

Early in 1908 Ignatius had a significant conversation with a visitor named Albert Edward Thomas, who told him he was to be ordained deacon on Trinity Sunday.

I suggested appealing to our Vicar to give him a title to Capel-y-ffin that he should live here, get ordained priest & go on the Mission with me & say Masses here, he seemed delighted at the plan – what a blessing it would be. And he has money & could pay his own expenses.[582]

Once again he seems to have mistaken a goose for a swan. Two years later Thomas, then 26 years of age, appeared before Stroud Police Court on charges of obtaining credit by false pretences. It emerged that he had a history of bizarre behaviour which included ordering quantities of chocolate to stock a non-existent shop and posing as a detective; his spurious claim to be an ordinand had been quite in character. The case was withdrawn, but only on condition that his parents and friends would keep a watchful eye on him in the future.[583]

---

[582] Diary, 12 February 1908

[583] Gloucester Citizen, 9 February 1910; Cheltenham Chronicle, 12 February 1910

ENTER THE BARONESS

IN 1902, as a result of attending one of Ignatius's London missions, a lady with literary leanings offered her services to him as biographer. This was the Baroness de Bertouch, born Beatrice Caroline Elmslie and connected with the family of William Booth, founder of the Salvation Army. She was then 43, and after emerging from her unhappy marriage to a minor Danish aristocrat had made a name for herself as the author of The Outcast: a Monologue and a slim volume of verse entitled Passion Flowers, as well as contributions to the ladies' columns of various provincial papers. She wrote (and perhaps thought) in the arch and whimsical style then typical of many female writers, and like her subject had a weakness for picturesque turns of phrase: her magnum opus would employ this to the full.

The book was acknowledged to be the fruit of extensive collaboration between subject and author, who had passed lengthy sojourns for the purpose at Plas Genevieve. In a letter to his sister Harriet in February 1904[584] Ignatius reported that the 'wonderful, really wonderful Baroness' had been 'astounded and utterly overwhelmed' by 'the colossal and world-reaching character' of his life to date, and that 'all her literary powers [were] being exhausted in digesting and compressing' the material he was feeding her. It was nonetheless ready for publication by Messrs Methuen the following December. In spite of its indigestibility the book is essential reading for anyone with an interest in Fr Ignatius and his monastery.[585]

---

[584] One of the transcripts already referred to: Museum ref A2010.86.18

[585] In A New Medley of Memories (Edward Arnold 1922) Abbot David Hunter-Blair recalls meeting the Baroness's son, then an Oxford undergraduate, in the year of the book's publication. 'His mother, though a Catholic like himself, was a devotee of "Father Ignatius", and lived at Llanthony. She travelled about everywhere with the visionary "Monk of the Church of England", acting as pew-opener, money-taker, and general mistress of ceremonies at his lectures, and had published an extraordinary biography of him' (p11n).

THE CALDEY CONNECTION

THE LLANTHONY VENTURE WAS – and is – often held up as an example of how not to live the monastic life; Donald Attwater described it not altogether unfairly as a 'travesty' of authentic Benedictine observance.[586] Almost exactly thirty years after its beginnings at Claydon another young Anglican took the first step towards the foundation of an alternative Benedictine community. Benjamin Fearnley Carlyle was a nineteen-year-old medical student who in April 1893 joined a group of oblates initiated by the Reverend Arthur Dale, chaplain to Mother Hilda's community, at that time moving from its temporary home at Twickenham to Malling Abbey.

Carlyle felt drawn to a life of contemplation, but also to work in the East End. With two or three like-minded companions he lived for a couple of years in a makeshift priory on the Isle of Dogs, trying to stem the prevailing current of irreligion and immorality by keeping open house for local boys and young men and taking them on trips to the country. By the winter of 1897-8 it became clear that their attempts at social work were standing in the way of progress in the monastic life, so Brother Aelred (as he now styled himself) moved his nascent monastery to the empty vicarage at Lower Guiting, near Cheltenham.[587]

Various difficulties forced them to move on after only a few months, and several possible benefactors were approached in the search for a new home. One of these was Ignatius, whom Aelred visited sometime in the summer of 1898 – probably, in the view of his community's most recent historian, after leaving Lower Guiting

---

[586] Article quoted in Baker, op cit p62

[587] Otherwise known as Guiting Power. The house was made available by the incumbent, the Reverend John E. Green, who was also interested in combining monastic life with social work. Two letters written the following year by Fr Iltud (Cobb) in answer to Dr Green's enquiry about accommodation for himself and one or more boys from his parish, either under canvas or in the visitors' quarters at Llanthony, are preserved in the Fr Ignatius collection (ref A1993.139.11.4).

in July.[588] This makes it quite likely that he arrived at Llanthony hard on the heels of Archbishop Vilatte, and if he failed to receive help with housing his community he came away with at least one useful idea – the notion that monastic communities were *ipso facto* extra-diocesan, and that if they wished any of their members to be ordained they had the right to approach any bishop willing to do it for them. Aelred had too much sense to involve himself in the murky world of *episcopi vagantes*, but in 1904 he would bypass the normal Church of England requirements of formal theological training and a parochial 'title' by crossing the Atlantic to receive both diaconate and priesthood from Bishop Grafton of Fond du Lac.[589]

By this time he and his brethren were half way through a four-year sojourn at Painsthorpe Hall, Kirkby Underdale;[590] it was the loan of this substantial house (from the influential Anglo-Catholic layman Charles Lindley Wood, 2nd Viscount Halifax) that gave the new community space and stability to grow in this period from nine members to twenty-four. Aelred had already used his charm to receive endorsement from the Archbishop of Canterbury (Frederick Temple) for both his monastic profession and abbatial election; now he obtained approval from Archbishop Maclagan of York for his ordination, although he would have to accept the theoretical restrictions on his ministry which went with his status as a 'clergyman in colonial orders'.

In October 1906 the community settled on Caldey, an island off the Pembrokeshire coast with ancient monastic associations, and

---

[588] Baker, op cit p61

[589] The first clergyman in the post-Reformation Church of England to be ordained in a religious habit is said to have been H.E. Hardy ('Fr Andrew') of the Franciscan-inspired Society of Divine Compassion (deacon 1894 and priest 1895, by the Bishop of St Albans), but he was ordained to a curacy in the East End of London, and unlike Aelred had both obtained a university degree and attended a theological college.

[590] Where as we have already noted the community included for a time two former Llanthony novices.

where in 1901-02 they had already enjoyed a temporary perch before the move to Yorkshire. This would be their home for the next two decades, although by the time they left they would be in communion with Rome rather than Canterbury, and would have inherited both the remnant of the Llanthony community and its erstwhile monastery.

Aelred's vision of the Benedictine life was quite different from Ignatius's. Any idea of his monastery as a 'mission' had been discarded when he left the Isle of Dogs, and he made no attempt to introduce faux-mediaeval or 'Celtic fringe' observances into the life of his community. Its liturgy and daily routine were based on mainstream Roman Catholic models, with a bias towards the contemplative life.[591]

There was, nonetheless, some contact between the two foundations, and the two founder-abbots claimed to be good friends. In the spring of 1904 a journalist staying at Llanthony described being woken by the bell summoning the community to the Night Office. On this occasion they were 'augmented by visitors from the Anglican monastery at Painsthorpe, York, assembling outside the cells' – as visitors they would probably have been accommodated on the same corridor as the writer.

> Soon the procession moved forward, the monks chanting as they went. Very impressive did it sound through the dark night as the plain song of the primitive church rose and fell in ever decreasing volume....[592]

It could have been on this occasion that Ignatius lent Aelred a substantial sum of money. In one of his final diary entries[593] he

---

[591] There was, however, one antiquarian feature: the adoption of the white habit, believed to have been worn by the Tironian monks who occupied Caldey in the middle ages (Baker, op cit p125). It was Aelred's insistence on his community's right to adopt current Roman Catholic liturgical and devotional forms lock, stock and barrel which would lead to its eventual severance from the Church of England; see Baker Chapter 10.

[592] *Cheltenham Chronicle*, 7 May 1904

[593] 28 February 1908

notes receiving '£50 of what I lent him 4 years ago' from Aelred, together with 'such a nice letter'. The visit was reciprocated, Ignatius twice staying with the younger community in its Painsthorpe days; according to Aelred he 'liked to call himself "our Grandfather".'[594]

Picture 29: Visit of Abbot Aelred and his monks

THE NEW APPARITIONS SHRINE

AELRED AND THREE OF HIS BRETHREN (Leo Packer, Martin Vincent and extern brother Maurus Sutton) were back at Llanthony for a week in August/September 1905. Their visit on this occasion coincided with the twenty-fifth anniversary of the 1880 apparitions, when a new marble statue of the Mother of God was installed on the site of the 'holy bush', its foundation having been blessed on the Apparitions Feast the preceding year.[595] Originally the plan had been for the statue to incorporate a perpetually burning lamp held in its

---

[594] Baker, op cit p110f. The Painsthorpe visitors' book records a visit from Ignatius and Asaph from 7 to 12 July 1905.

[595] Portsmouth Evening News, 31 August 1904

right hand, perhaps based on the Statue of Liberty, by which the monastic voyagers had been impressed on their arrival in New York in June 1890;[596] happily this feature was abandoned in favour of the traditional *orans* pose with both hands outstretched and open, and a lamp in a separate holder nearby.

The dedication took place after a 'mission service' (at which '[t]here was no ceremonial') in the abbey church, attended by about three hundred 'Christians of all shades of belief'. At its close the congregation went in procession to the Abbot's Meadow singing a Latin hymn to the Virgin, and after the statue had been unveiled and appropriate prayers said the lamp was lit. It was reported that the statue was (like the abbey church reredos) the work of Messrs Mayer of Munich and London, and that the cost had been met from a fund of £200 collected by the purpose by the Baroness de Bertouch, part of which had been set aside for the maintenance of the lamp.[597]

'GRANDFATHER IGNATIUS'

IF IN A FIGURATIVE SENSE he regarded himself as 'grandfather' to Aelred Carlyle's community, Ignatius occupied that role more immediately towards the family down the valley at Maes-y-ffin. At first sight the newspaper article reproduced in Appendix 3 seems to suggest that Lessie spent part of his early childhood living as a 'monastery boy' alongside his near contemporary Jack Clark and the slightly older oblate Brother Placidus (Norton Rhys), although it is more likely that he was just a frequent visitor, perhaps occasionally staying the night. The 'forbidden strawberry' episode narrated in this extract was worked up from a brief account on the flyleaf of Ignatius's Bible, where it bears the date 20 July 1897, a whole year before the appearance of the newspaper story. When it took place the boy's

---

[596] FIIA p12

[597] The inauguration of the statue was reported in sundry regional papers; information here from the *Nottingham Evening Post* of 31 August and the *Wells Journal* of 7 September.

mother would have been pregnant with his younger sister Josephine, and may have been grateful for occasional periods of respite.

Picture 30: Maes-y-ffin family group, c1907

According to the account in the Bible the Maes-y-ffin children knew Ignatius by the pet name 'Ganfie', and Josephine certainly remembered him as a benign presence in her early childhood.[598] In the 1908 diary fragment they are mentioned several times,

---

[598] Conversation with the author (then a young teenager) on 18 June 1961

although a whole decade had now passed since the infant Lessie ate the unauthorised strawberry. That January he turned fifteen, and was preparing to be confirmed. Before he went back to school at Cheltenham Ignatius had a serious talk with him, asking the boy whether he thought he was 'converted':

> For once he was serious & attentive; he says he thinks he is converted because he likes Church so much better than he used to & he does witness on Christ['s] side[,] at least he has done so twice at College.[599]

IN THE EVENT Lessie's confirmation had to be deferred, as not long afterwards he went down with German measles. The strain on ex-Brother Dunstan's domestic economy of caring for an ailing adolescent led Ignatius to despatch a cheque for £5 to help with expenses (like the school fees presumably from monastery funds), and the ever-available 'Gwen' (Dodson) to help with the nursing.

She had lived with the young Leycester Lynes on and off since the children were small, and seems to have acted as nursemaid to both of them, although more as family friend than employee (the last of Josephine's five Christian names was Gwendoline). In middle age she would marry a man named Arthur Beckles and end her days in Brighton, but her brother would often be found at Maes-y-ffin, especially in his later years.

His adoptive family provided Ignatius with a focus in the periods he spent at Llanthony, even if these added up to a little over half the year. According to his (admittedly sporadic) annotations in the *Daily Portion*, in the last decade of his life he was away from his monastery for an average of around twenty weeks a year. He liked to be there for the great feasts of Christmas, Ascension and the Apparitions, but made a point of spending Lent elsewhere, and as we have seen did not always get back for Easter. A certain amount

---

[599] Diary, 9 January 1908

of time was passed 'resting' at the houses of family and friends, as well as some quite intensive activity 'on the mission': either three services with sermons on the Sundays (11, 3.30 and 7), or a series of weekday afternoon or evening meetings. The most frequently visited places for this purpose were London (the Portman Rooms, Baker Street), Brighton (Old Ship Assembly Rooms), Hastings/St Leonards,[600] Clifton (Bristol) and Southsea. Most of August 1906 was spent preaching to the holiday crowds at Llandudno, and August 1907 doing the same at Ilfracombe. Other mission destinations in this period included Cardiff, Penarth, Buxton, Leamington, Norwich, Torquay, Cheltenham and Tunbridge Wells, with the occasional foray to such northern watering places as Blackpool and Harrogate – the visits to Painsthorpe may have coincided with one or more of these.

'THREE-SCORE YEARS AND TEN'

IGNATIUS'S SEVENTIETH BIRTHDAY occurred on 23 November 1907. According to the Scarlet Thread letter dated January 1908 the occasion was marked by a 'Sale and Sacred Concert' in the hall attached to the fashionable Anglo-Catholic church of St Cuthbert, Philbeach Gardens, although according to his entry in Hawker he was in Southsea that day. As it had been arranged at rather short notice it turned out to be 'more of a family party for his London congregation than a public function', with stalls organised among others by the ever-faithful Baroness de Bertouch and Sister Rose; nevertheless, it succeeded in raising £50 for monastery funds.

From his diary entries for the first few weeks of 1908 it is clear that Ignatius was beginning to feel his age. Although he could still rouse himself to heights of activity – in late January and early February he conducted three missions in as many weeks, each involving the usual

---

[600] His visits to St Leonards included dental treatment at the hands of Mr William Meads, a devotee since the early 1870s and said to have been for a time an habitué of the Feltham establishment (*Hastings & St Leonards Observer*, 24 October 1908).

three Sunday services – he tired easily, and complained of various symptoms ('heart queer going back to bed' after a nocturnal visit to the 'cold lavatory' next to his cell; 'felt faint & had to lie down'; 'could not get warm'; 'blood to head and had to stop' trying to work at his desk), suggesting that his health was now in serious decline.[601]

In those weeks he kept mostly to his cell, the cosy bed-sitting room upstairs in the west wing, whose oriel window gave him a view of the Black Mountain weather in all its variety. In spite of 'sheets of ice' and 'fearful wind and snow' he would usually manage a little walk before the sun went off at lunchtime, his favourite destination being a field called The Dôl (meadow) which slopes down towards the river opposite the monastery lane. He may have had some sort of shelter, as he records happily sitting there in the middle of a rainstorm.

On 8 January he noted the death of his old friend Fr Husband, and on 5 February that of 'Our Darling old Sister Winifred our Foundress aged 88 Buried today so we believe'. On both occasions special services were held: 'Holy Oblation' with Funeral Sermon for the former, and 'Full Matins & Lauds' for the latter. On 15 January (the day after Lessie's 'Birth Day Feast' at Maes-y-ffin) they had a Requiem Mass to mark the first anniversary of the death of 'dear Mrs Magrath', mother of Sena and ex-Brother Dunstan, who officiated.[602]

---

[601] I am grateful to my friend and fellow-Trustee Dr Peter Davies for the following comment: 'This picture of intermittent symptoms would be consistent with a common heart condition known as paroxysmal atrial fibrillation, in which the patient has sporadic episodes of abnormally rapid heart rate with a simultaneous irregular and weak heart rhythm. The blood pressure can drop during these episodes because the heart is not beating effectively, and the patient may feel tired and faint. This condition also puts the patient at significantly increased risk of having a stroke – small clots can accumulate within the atrial ventricles during these episodes because blood is not being pumped through the heart properly. Nowadays this would be treated with an anticoagulant such as warfarin.'

[602] 'Bells tolled for Mass for Dead, & we had it at 11, of course in black.' 'Lessie took the incense, Brs Gildas & Cadoc served.'

One notable absentee was her son-in-law Brother David, who 'disappeared without a word to me', only showing up at the monastery the following morning. Reading between the lines one can detect a certain discomfort in his situation. While he had been lifted out of the poverty and narrow horizons which in those days went with the life of a small-time hill farmer and admitted by marriage and money to a higher social class, this was not without cost. We aren't told how in adult life he related to his natural family, or whether his privately-educated children were allowed to be on the same terms with them as with 'dear Mrs Magrath' and their grandfather-by-adoption; I rather suspect not. At times he must have felt himself a stranger in both camps, neither fully belonging to his wife's people nor any longer to his own, not to speak of the strain of continually having to be grateful. One can sense this unease in Ignatius's comment that 'we all wondered [at his absence], she was always so good to him'.

A surprising number of people crop up in its pages before the diary comes to an abrupt end on Wednesday 4 March. As well as his fellow-religious (Asaph, Gildas and Cadoc in the monastery; Mother Tudfil the only nun in the convent) and the Maes-y-ffin household there is John Bates out 'on the road' when he should have been busy spreading gravel from the pond on the level outside the church entrance (he did get on with it while Ignatius was away, however, much to his pleasure when he returned), and someone called Jack who 'disappears' along with Brother David on the day of his mother-in-law's Requiem. This may have been Jack Clark, a nine-year-old 'monastery boy' at the time of the 1901 census so now sixteen; he later migrated to Caldey, where he was employed on the abbey press.[603]

There were no acolytes or choirboys by this time, although a youngster named Willie Frewin was engaged as Ignatius's personal servant a few days before the Penarth mission in the middle of

---

[603] Pax, Spring 1982, p254. It is said that as a boy at Llanthony he was once made to kiss John Bates's feet for giving him cheek – a penance he was never allowed to forget! (Pax, Winter 1983, p193).

January. Evidently both he and Brother David were supposed to stay with him the whole time he was there (Saturday to Saturday, although apart from the usual Sunday engagements there was only one other meeting, arranged at the last minute for the Tuesday evening), but the boy took fright and ran away on the Monday. He may not have recovered from the ordeal on the first evening of having to find his way from Penarth to Llanthony and back for the 'Mission Box', inadvertently left behind.

Sister Rose doesn't seem to have been at the convent just then, as Ignatius reports receiving a 'long wailing letter' from her. The soi-disant ordinand Albert Thomas had brought with him a young Baptist named Howard Stanley, who surprised himself by his enjoyment of the ritualistic externals; when Thomas left ahead of him his fear of nocturnal 'apparitions' prompted Ignatius to send Brother Gildas to sleep in the adjacent cell. A Mrs Lowen from Seaford came to stay in the convent but was dismayed by the number of rats; another visitor was Ignatius's faithful disciple Alfred Field, who spent the week 6 to 13 January.

A few local people continued to attend services in the abbey church, and to receive pastoral visits. Sarah Lewis who lived with her brother at Ty Shorse battled her way across the river and up a steep stony track for early Mass on the feast of the Epiphany (she was then 56, and is still remembered by older residents); on another occasion Ignatius and Asaph called in to see the 'dear Prices' (probably the occupants of Chapel House by the bridge) and to 'chat and pray with them'. Someone called 'Charlie Clarke' arrived at the same time as the ex-novice Redhalls[604] on 15 February; he may have been the boy 'Charles Clarke, lately converted by the Grace of GOD' who had been confirmed by Mar Timotheus at the same time as the ordinations, and who had received his first Communion when Fr Iltud 'sang Mass beautifully' some days later.

---

[604] See Chapter 6

IN THE NIGHT OF 4/5 MARCH Ignatius suffered a stroke. Before going to bed he had filled in his diary; that day had been Ash Wednesday, and most of it had been spent in church:

> 10.30 Ashes, Holy Oblation, Commination, Sermon till 1.45.
> 3 Nones, Litany, 7 Penit[ential] Psalms, Hymns, sermon till 4.30.
> 5 Solemn Vespers, Hymns, Prayer till 6. Also prayers in Ashes.

To the running order of this religious tour de force he added the following comments (the sentence in bold type was written in red):

> But I did not fast. A very Holy Day, & great longings after GOD. I was very well. Snow. **Brothers kept Solemn FAST till 6pm.** Such spiritual blessing & GOD's Own Power working among us. Only we missed our Midday Communion because I felt I dare not fast.

The unstructured spontaneity of this entry suggests that he set down each thought just as it came to him. They may or may not have been his last written words, but they serve as a fitting coda to a life he had tried to live for 'Jesus Only'.

CHAPTER 12

POST MORTEM

After his stroke Ignatius lived on until 16 October, when he died at the Camberley home of his sister Louisa Jane. With the arrival of spring he had been moved from his abbatial cell to a cottage at Cropthorne, near Evesham. Later in the summer he spent some weeks on the Norfolk coast at Sheringham, before his final move in September to 'Darjeeling'. After 5 May (about the time he would have left Llanthony) there are only two entries in the *Daily Portion*, both at Cropthorne in June, but in the two months since his stroke the twice-daily extracts are noted as having been read on twenty-six occasions, in almost every case by a named individual. On sixteen of them this is 'Herbert', who first appears on 30 March; perhaps he was successor to the unsatisfactory page-boy Willie Frewin. 'FM' read on three occasions, one of which was Easter Sunday: this was William Marriott Dodson, the former Father Michael, who was evidently visiting his old monastery.

Another visitor in the weeks following Ignatius's stroke was a young priest named Richard Courtier-Forster, then serving a curacy at St Giles's, Cambridge. Like Brother Dunstan (Magrath) his first encounter with the Abbot had been as a boy in Bath, though several years later.[605] In a lecture delivered at Norwich in the 1930s he recalled his visits to Llanthony, including the occasion when from his hands the invalid monk 'received his last Communion in his Abbey cell with the Brothers gathered round his bed, while a heavenly radiance

---

[605] Richard Courtier-Forster (born 2 July 1875) was the son of a brewer at Freshford, near Bath. After attending (but not graduating at) University College, Durham, he served two curacies in the diocese of Carlisle before his third in Cambridge.

shone from his head'. He says that after this Ignatius 'recovered a little', and was well enough to be moved from the monastery.

Courtier-Forster was unable to take time off from his parish to participate in Ignatius's funeral, although at Asaph's request he had advised the brethren about 'arranging the services at the lying-in-state and the night watches by the coffin'. He mentions that 'a special Act of Parliament' had been passed to permit burials in the cloister garth and abbey church, presumably in connection with Sister Etheldreda's interment in 1886. Ignatius's grave had been prepared well in advance, earlier photographs showing what appears to be an iron grating in the floor of the monks' choir in the place where his remains would be laid.

Four days after his death the body was conveyed from Camberley to Llanfihangel by train. From the newspaper accounts we learn that the coffin had a glass panel over the occupant's face,[606] and that in attendance were his adopted son Brother David and the former Brother Dunstan (Magrath), together with 'Mr Dodson of Bettws-y-coed', who if only occasionally present while Ignatius remained at Llanthony had been his 'constant companion and friend' during the months that followed. The party was completed by 'a young lad who used to attend upon him at the Monastery' (Herbert, perhaps) and Chief Inspector Thomas of Paddington, paying tribute to a longstanding patron of 'God's Wonderful Railway'. On the journey up the valley (Inspector Thomas having presumably returned to London) they were joined by Mrs Mathews of Llanfihangel Court, said to be one of his most fervent local admirers.[607]

From the evening of that day (Tuesday 20th) vigil was kept in the abbey church until the morning of Thursday 22nd, when at 6.30am Holy Communion was celebrated in Welsh by the Reverend James H.

---

[606] Information in this paragraph from the *Western Mail* of 21 and 22 October 1908.

[607] Florence Blakiston Attwood-Mathews, née Wilkinson (d 1923), daughter of a prominent Swedenborgian and an accomplished amateur artist

Jenkins of Taff's Well. Two further low Masses followed before the public Requiem at 11.00, celebrated by Magrath with Ernest Clarke and Arundell Lyne as Epistoler and Gospeller.

Picture 31: Fr Ignatius's funeral, 22 October 1908. From left the Reverend Ernest Clark; the Reverend Arundell Lyne; Fr Asaph Harris with unidentifiable monk behind him; the Reverend W.M. Magrath, formerly Brother Dunstan; Brother Gildas Taylor.

The grave was twelve feet deep, and the space above the coffin filled with solid masonry and cement.[608] In May 1910 the sum of £27 10s was paid to Royal Doulton Potteries of Lambeth for fixing a tiled cross bearing the symbols of the four evangelists and a brass plaque. This bore the legend HIC JACET IGNATIUS JESUS OSB HUIUS DOMUS CONDITOR PRIMUSQUE ABBAS ('Here lies Ignatius of Jesus OSB Builder of this House and First Abbot'); perhaps even then there was still hope that there might be a second.

---

[608] These details were noted in a letter from Aelred Carlyle to Harriet Ewens on 9 November 1915 (Prinknash archives).

Picture 32: The grave newly tiled, 1910

COMMUNITY LIFE CONTINUES

IGNATIUS HAD LEFT the monastic property jointly to Asaph and Tudfil, and for the time being Asaph assumed control. The number of brothers had now increased from three (Asaph, Cadoc and Gildas) to four, and would shortly reach five. On 24 May, after Ignatius's departure for Cropthorne, 21-year-old Richard Bucknall Jackson was clothed by Asaph as Brother Iltud; on 20 November he was joined in the noviciate by Maurice George Stannard (Brother Dyfrig).[609] Dyfrig

---

[609] Dates from Dom Aelred Baker OSB (letter to author, 15 March 2010); neither brother's name was entered in the Register. Jackson was born in Ambleside on 25 March 1887 and Stannard in Kings Lynn on 29 December 1886; in the 1901 census he was recorded as a 14-year-old solicitor's clerk living with his family in Wisbech.

was the same age as Iltud, and had evidently been interested in the monastic life for some time, having sent postcards from Painsthorpe in August 1905 and Llanthony in August 1907 to a friend in Wisbech, Miss C. Williams.[610]

Various letters survive from this period. One of them – from the 'Monastery Secretary' to an unnamed 'Revd Father' and undated – enclosed a relic in the shape of a portion of the late Abbot's 'sleeping habit'. It gave the information that the farm had been left to 'Mr W.L. Lyne' (Brother David) for his lifetime, and went on:

> We are much afraid when all is settled there will only be a very small endowment.... This will not dishearten us as the brothers are each going to learn a trade and if our friends will only rally round us for the next two years we hope by that time to be a strong flourishing community absolutely isolated from outside influence.[611]

Picture 33: The community after Ignatius's death. Asaph as acting Superior with Cadoc, Gildas, Iltud and two associates.

---

[610] Both in the Abergavenny collection, refs A1993.139.1.48 and A2010.86.85.
[611] Museum ref A1993.139.11.6

A cache of household bills and related items preserved at Prinknash Abbey throws some light on the community's daily life at this time. In the months following Ignatius's death Brother Gildas required medical attention on three occasions, as (once each) did John Bates and 'Brother Maurice' (Stannard). In the summer of 1909 nearly £50 was spent at Boundy's the Abergavenny ironmongers: just under half on repairs and improvements by the firm's hot water fitter to the abbey church heating system, and the rest on items required around the house and farm. These included rafters and floor boarding (for repairs?), as well as electric wire for Asaph's hydro-electric installation, for which a further £3 was spent on unspecified merchandise from the Universal Electrical Supply Company in Manchester. This new system was evidently putting a strain on the supply of water from the mountain springs, causing the Monastery Secretary to request Lord Hereford's permission through his agent for the excavation of a storage pond 'to increase the water pressure and enable it to be used upstairs, etc.'[612] By 'etc.' he presumably meant (but did not say) 'to generate electricity'.

That summer the brothers laid out 5s 6d on cabbage plants and turnip seed from a local nursery, and continued to order printed writing paper and other stationery. This included publicity photographs of the monastery and its occupants, such as the one here and the earlier picture of monks haymaking.

Picture 34: Milking the monastery cows outside the 'new' barn, now in ruins.

---

[612] Letters from Monastery Secretary to The Estate Agent to Lord Hereford, dated 10 and 16 September 1909: Museum refs A2010.86.166 and A2010.86.169.

A NEW ABBOT?

ASAPH WAS A MAN OF MANY TALENTS, but gifts of leadership were not among them. Some time after the funeral a Chapter meeting was held and the decision made to invite Fr Courtier-Forster to accept the position of abbot. His Norwich lecture included an account of this, which he modestly cast in the third person:

> After his [Ignatius's] death a Novena of prayer was made to God by the Monks and Nuns of Llanthony for the guidance of the Holy Spirit in choosing another Abbot. It was expected that the Abbot of another community in the English Church [i.e. Aelred Carlyle] would be selected for the great office, and the name was well known as a personal friend of Father Ignatius, but like the call of St Ambrose in other days the unanimous vote of the Benedictine Brothers and Sisters in free and open Chapter fell on a simple Priest of the Church of England[613] and by the whole Community he was elected second Abbot of Llanthony. The new Abbot resigned his parochial work and prepared for his solemn Profession and the rule of the Abbey Community.

A meeting took place between Abbot Aelred and his prospective opposite number at which 'the future of the two great Monasteries' was discussed. Fr Courtier-Forster applied to the Bishop of St David's for recognition both for the community itself and for his appointment as its superior, making 'Episcopal approval and blessing a condition of his acceptance of the high office to which he was called'.

However, these lengthy preliminaries proved too much for the patience of Asaph and the others, who had quite likely not received Communion since the day of Ignatius's burial. In the spring of 1909

---

[613] In fact Ambrose was not yet baptised, let alone ordained, when elected to succeed Auxentius as Bishop of Milan in 374.

he and Gildas travelled to Winnipeg, where the two of them were ordained deacon and priest by Archbishop Vilatte.[614]

Their attitude to ecclesiastical authority (certainly Asaph's) would have been heavily influenced by that of Ignatius, who while referring in his diary to his Diocesan as 'the dear Bishop of St Davids' had apparently taken no steps to regularise his position with him.[615] As we have seen, he believed that a monastic superior had the right to send candidates for ordination to any bishop willing to ordain them, so a blank having apparently been drawn with Antioch the bishop who had ordained Ignatius himself was the obvious choice.[616] It seems strange, however, that the two brothers omitted to consult their Abbot-elect before taking a month's leave from the monastery as well as laying out what must have been a considerable sum on the cost of the expedition – and that he was insufficiently in touch with Llanthony not to be aware of what was going on. His narrative continues:

> All was going forward smoothly when every hope was unexpectedly shattered by the action of two of the Brothers at Llanthony who without the knowledge or permission of the new Abbot took a journey to America and got themselves ordained Priests by an Old

---

[614] They sailed second class from Liverpool to New York (where they disembarked on 23 April) on the ill-fated Cunard liner *Lusitania*, and for the return journey boarded her sister ship *Mauretania* on 11 May. Brother David's typescript includes the opaque observation that the trip was 'partly for ecclesiastical and partly for secular purposes'.

[615] Although after his ordination by Mar Timotheus he had made a point of swearing allegiance to him in *absentia*. The bishop throughout this period was John Owen, who occupied the see from 1897 to 1927.

[616] Why didn't they approach Ventham, who lived rather nearer – and who with his friend Frederick Pursall signed the Visitors' Book at Llanthony just two weeks after their return from Canada? Two possible explanations come to mind: (1) Ventham's consecration hadn't been made public, so his episcopal status wouldn't have been known at Llanthony; (2) he and Ignatius had fallen out. Either of these possibilities would also explain why Ignatius hadn't invited him to ordain one or more of his monks instead of approaching Antioch.

Catholic Bishop whose orders were pronounced irregular. The Abbot immediately informed the Bishop of what had taken place, and His Lordship refused to accept the new Priests and insisted they should not exercise Priestly functions. The Priests refused to submit, and as they persisted in their obduracy, the Abbot resigned.

Having given up his job in Cambridge, Courtier-Forster went abroad, assisting for a while at the Anglican cathedral in Valetta before being licensed as British chaplain at Odessa (1910-19). Here his period of duty coincided with both the 1914-18 war and the Russian Revolution, and after his return to England he published *Memoirs of the Downfall of the Romanoff Empire* and toured the country addressing meetings on the evils of Communism. From 1927 to 1932 he was Vicar of St Giles, Norwich, dying in Nice twenty years after his retirement.

Picture 35: The Reverend Richard Courtier-Forster, elected second Abbot of Llanthony

The Abbot-elect's exchange of letters with Bishop Owen can't have taken long, and he had probably detached himself from Llanthony well before the Apparitions Feast came round at the end of August. No report of the festival that year (or the year following) appeared in the local press, and the Visitors' Book only recorded a handful of pilgrims on each occasion.[617] It was, however, advertised in the *Hereford Times*,[618] intending pilgrims being asked to notify a Mr F.T. More, care of the Abbey Secretary.

ABBOT AELRED TAKES CHARGE

COURTIER-FORSTER MENTIONED the general expectation that Aelred Carlyle would take Llanthony under his wing, an expectation reinforced by the Baroness's assertion that this was what Ignatius himself had planned.[619] In his 'Community Letter' written shortly after Ignatius's death[620] Aelred explained how this had come about. In the lean years when Llanthony had been down to two monks (Ignatius and Asaph, so effectively just one), the two abbots had discussed the possibility of their communities amalgamating at Llanthony; this was also the time when the Baroness was working on her book. In spite of their friendship and occasional visits between the two houses their very different interpretations of the Benedictine life prevented them reaching agreement, so Ignatius then tried to interest various Roman Catholic communities in taking over the property, with safeguards for his own position and that of any remaining monks.[621] For understandable reasons this idea, too, came to nothing.

---

[617] Entries on the same date in 1907 had also been few, however, despite the reported presence of 'scores of people' (*Gloucester Citizen*, 31 August 1907).

[618] Issue of 21 August 1909

[619] Bertouch p595

[620] *Pax*, December 1908

[621] According to Abbot Oswald Hunter-Blair ('The Three Llanthonies': *Pax*, Summer, Autumn & Winter 1918) he had entered into negotiations with 'the Carthusians, the English Benedictines, and others'.

Since then Aelred had acquired what was intended to be a permanent home for his foundation on Caldey, and as we have seen, Llanthony had experienced a modest revival. Although Aelred may have realised that ultimately it would fall to him to salvage what was left of Ignatius's community, Asaph and his companions were 'determined to do their best' to keep the life there going, so for the time being he was content to give encouragement from afar.

Without the income from Ignatius's missions or money-making enterprises of their own, however, the little group stood little chance of survival. A year later Abbot Aelred explained that they had now admitted defeat:

For a year after the Father's death Brother Asaph and four other Brethren struggled along in isolation and difficulty, but in September last they came to the conclusion that it was not possible for them to continue any longer as they were. All the Brothers felt that they needed regular training, and that the ecclesiastical position of Llanthony – whatever it might have been during the late Rev. Father's lifetime – was becoming more and more undesirable. Brother Asaph then wrote to me and asked me to go to Llanthony to conduct a retreat for the Brethren and to preside at a Chapter which was to be held after the retreat to discuss the future. At this Chapter the Sister in the convent, who felt quite as strongly as the Brethren that the position was impossible, handed me a statement to read to them, saying that as she very much wished the work at Llanthony to be carried on – and as she foresaw there would need to be drastic changes – she was willing to make over her share of her property to Brother Asaph, and she would herself cease to live at the convent. This wise and generous action on her part considerably simplified the situation, and it was decided that Brother Asaph and those of the Brethren who wished should be given every opportunity of testing their vocation with us at Caldey. Brother Asaph and three of the Brethren have now definitely joined our community as simple laymen and Llanthony Abbey itself is being made over to us.[622]

What exactly did this mean? The reason Mother Tudfil gave for surrendering her share in the inheritance was so that 'the work at Llanthony [could] be carried on', yet with her departure and that of four of the five monks it was to all intents and purposes being wound up. Iltud Jackson was received at Caldey on 24 November 1909, and Asaph Harris the next day. Gildas Taylor and Dyfrig Stannard (who was given the new name Basil, by which he was sometimes known in later life) followed them in December, on the 1st and the 12th respectively.[623]

In June 1910 Aelred reported that although Asaph had 'found his vocation' at Caldey the others had now left. Gildas did so 'as a secular' on 23 April, his passage into the outside world eased by the receipt of £52 from the Llanthony bank account (probably money he had deposited on arrival). A month later both Dyfrig/Basil and Iltud were dismissed.

According to Peter Anson[624] there was one other monk who transferred to Caldey at this point, a certain Ernest Odell Cope, but he left after just two weeks. There is no mention of Cope in either the Llanthony or Caldey records; perhaps he was an associate who just happened to be at the monastery when it was in the process of dissolution. He was a native of Burton on Trent (born 10 March 1884) and as a young man employed as a railway porter – in 1906 at Coalville, which as the nearest station to Mount St Bernard's Abbey may have brought him into contact with the Cistercian community there. At the time of the 1911 census he was living with his parents in

---

[622] *Pax*, December 1909

[623] These dates and details of the later monastic careers of Gildas and Iltud from Dom Aelred Baker's letter of 15 March 2010

[624] BAL p 393

Burton, giving his occupation as 'Colliery Labourer under Ground'; he married later in the same year. In the late 1940s he would reappear at Llanthony as an *episcopus vagans*; he died in his home town in 1957.

THE INTERIM COMMUNITY

ABBOT AELRED'S LETTER of June 1910 included the news that 'several of the former community' were back at Llanthony awaiting 'something definite', the implication being that some, at least, of the remnant intended somehow or other to continue monastic life there.[625] Surviving household accounts suggest that Brother Cadoc (Davidson) had stayed on at the monastery after the others left, and was there for much of 1910. In April of that year he had his boots repaired by an Abergavenny cobbler (being named on the invoice as 'Father Cradock OSB'; compare the earlier misspelling of Brannock as 'Bannock'), and in June bought a cassock (at a cost of £1 12s 6d) from the London church furnisher then known as Vanheems & Wheeler. At the same time (as 'Cadoc') he received two payments (of £1 and £5) from the monastery account. The bank book records four payments (£28 16s altogether) to him between November 1910 and March 1911 as 'Davidson'. Like the money paid to Gildas this may have been funds he had deposited on entering or returning to the community, and its repayment probably signalled his final departure. In September 1910 his friend and former employer Fr Jecks paid a visit (the last of six or more over several years); in the 1911 census they were listed together at an address near Tiverton in Devon.[626]

---

[625] On 31 August the *Gloucestershire Echo* reported that a few monks from Caldey were staying at Llanthony 'in order to keep up the uninterrupted recitation of the daily offices'. While noting that the preceding day had been the 'Festival of the Apparition of Our Ladye of Llanthony' the writer expressed doubt about the likelihood of its observance under the new regime.

[626] They were living in part of a farmhouse named Ivy House in the parish of Halberton, where Jecks was identified as Head and Davidson (aged 29, living on private means) as a visitor. According to *Crockford* Jecks was at this time curate of Little Mongeham with Sutton by Dover,

Iltud Jackson had also returned to Llanthony, and was either at the monastery itself or nearby for the latter part of 1910 and much of 1911. The first evidence in the Prinknash papers of his presence is an auctioneer's ticket from September 1910 recording the sale of a cow to 'Mr Jackson'; another in the name of 'Mr Johnson' may also refer to him. He was living at the monastery when the census was taken, although by the following September he had moved out but was still somewhere in the vicinity – probably staying with the Lewis family at Upper Henllan in Cwmyoy parish, from which address he wrote to John Bates about the sale of some sheep (the letter is undated).

His main interest now appeared to be farming, which he was beginning in a small way to engage in on his own account. Another letter, written to Abbot Aelred on 5 September 1911 from Llanthony by Brother Cadoc Blanchard (for whom see below), is rather disparaging about him. Blanchard alleges that 'Jackson' was claiming personal ownership of some of the sheep belonging to the monastery, and implies that he had been using its credit with local traders to his own advantage. An itemised bill from a men's outfitter in Abergavenny (dated November 1910) shows that he had indeed been patronising local shops ('Trousers 9/6; 2 collars @ 6d; tie 1/-; suit £2 2s 6d...'), although marked as having been paid by 'Rev Iltud, Llanthony'. On the letter someone has pencilled rejoinders to some of Blanchard's assertions, among them (to the accusation that Iltud had paid no attention to Asaph's orders) 'What is your ground for this statement?'

Asaph was evidently still in charge, in spite of his move and reduction in status to novice and (from 16 July 1911) brother in simple vows. Caldey records for this period are patchy, but in 1910 and 1911 he seems to have been at Llanthony quite frequently, and in the latter year completed the census return for the household

---

although he may in fact by then have left that post; the following year he emigrated to New Zealand. Samuel Davidson's death was registered in Camberwell in June 1922.

in his own hand. Listed with him were Iltud Jackson and a farm labourer: Asaph as Head and Iltud as 'member of community', both giving their occupation as 'Religious of the Church of England'.

Just before his submission to Caldey (on 4 November 1909) Asaph had opened a new account with the London County & Westminster Bank in Lombard Street. His name on the record book (from which we have extracted details of the payments noted above) is given as 'Revd Alfred Harris', and the opening balance of £258 6s 2d was transferred from an account previously held jointly by him and Mother Tudfil. From time to time this was topped up by small dividends from Ignatius's shares in the Home & Colonial Stores and Mexican National Railways and then by the sale of the shares themselves (credits of a little under £1200 altogether), and in the course of the next two years payments continued to be made to local tradesmen and other businesses, as well as to various individuals. The last credit was received on 14 October 1911 (£14 in loose change paid in by Sister Rose Kidder) and only one small amount debited later that month, leaving a balance of £46 12s 9d and no indication that it was transferred elsewhere (perhaps it's still there).

For the most part these payments were for items required in the house and on the farm, including coal and groceries – it may be significant that most of the latter were purchased in the summer and autumn, suggesting that occupation was a seasonal affair. Various people with monastic-sounding names or titles are mentioned in the bank book and on bills and cheque stubs; they may have been associates working on the farm and around the house, but might nevertheless have been reckoned as members of 'the former community...still at Llanthony'. In April and July 1910 respectively 'Mr F.T. More' and 'Mr Thos More' were supplied with boots by Cash & Co of Abergavenny; on the stub recording payment for the first pair is the note 'Bro Frank boots'—probably one and the same person, and the same one whose name had appeared in the 1909 pilgrimage announcement. In November 1909 the Queen's Head at

Cwmyoy issued an invoice for 10s for transporting a passenger to the monastery; the words 'Br Basils account' have been pencilled at the foot, but this is probably too early for it to have been Basil (olim Dyfrig) Stannard. In January 1910 cheques were made out to 'Ansgar' and 'Placidus' for £1 10s each,[627] and in the same month a cheque for 15s to 'B. Philip' was cancelled. In September 1911 a further cheque was made out to 'B. Placidus' for £3 5s; this was cashed at a bank in York and may have been a modest resettlement grant. The name of the resident farm labourer on the 1911 census return was William Bennett, aged 43 and born in Much Wenlock; he may or may not have been one of these otherwise unidentifiable individuals. Bates came and went between Caldey and Llanthony; when the census was taken he was boarding with a family on Caldey, but had just harvested the oat crop at Llanthony when Blanchard wrote to Aelred in September.

Two associate sisters were still living in the convent, at any rate during the summer months. Peter Anson remembered taking part in a three-week 'holiday' there with his fellow Caldey novices in August 1911 and is quite specific that 'two aged nuns' (in fact the associate sisters) were present,[628] although neither of them had been there at the time of the census.[629] A letter from Sister Rose to Ignatius's cousin Arundell (the date is indistinct and may be either 22 or 23 August, with no year shown) includes the following:

---

[627] A 'Brother Ansgar' of Thurø, Denmark, signed the Visitors' Book on 19 May 1909.

[628] Anson, The Benedictines of Caldey (Prinknash Abbey 1944) pp145ff. The Visitors' Book shows he was there again (as 'Br Richard') for a fortnight in February 1914.

[629] In the census Sister Rose was recorded with her brother and sister at their house in Forest Gate, East London, and Alice Wheeler (if she was the other associate) on her own at an address in Bampton (Oxon). The name 'Sister Margaret, Llanthony' appears on a bill for coal issued in September 1910, the receipt for which was sent to Asaph at Caldey.

I had the pleasure of spending last Sunday week at Maes-y-ffin [with Brother David and family], attending the parish church in the morning. We had nothing here, as Fr Asaph, and all the Caldey brothers, were at Caldey. Fr A has been away now for 3 Sundays. We are expecting his return daily.

Can he love this dear place, or Our Lord's Sacramental Presence, and dear Father's memory, to act like this? It is so very sad. Even the villagers make remarks, as even the ringing of the Angelus is stopped, whereas when he is here the bells are going night and day.[630]

This probably dates from 1910 or 1911, and the amount of time Asaph was spending at Llanthony (when she was there herself, at any rate) was sufficient for her to think of it as still his normal place of residence. Whoever was or wasn't living at the monastery, daily services were certainly being kept up in the summer of 1910, when on two occasions someone noted in the Visitors' Book that outsiders had been present. On Ascension Day (5 May) the comment 'One visitor (a lady) 11am service' has been added, and on 4 September (one of the days commemorating the 1880 apparitions, but that may be coincidental) 'All these and others, 24 in number, attended Lauds' against five names entered on that date. The wording ('11am service', and Lauds at an hour when outsiders might have been present) suggests an Ignatian, rather than an Aelredian, horarium, with Asaph (or Iltud?) officiating rather than visiting 'Caldey brothers'.

Was Asaph still saying Mass? Rose's letter seems to suggest that he was, at least while at Llanthony. When Aelred reported that he and the others had entered Caldey as 'simple laymen' he may have meant that they did so as 'seculars' (whether clerical or lay) rather than as monks transferring their stability. In his history of the Caldey community Fr Baker observes that it was (only?) after their conversion to Rome in 1913 that 'it was decided that he [Asaph]

---

[630] Museum ref A2010.86.133

could not celebrate Mass', by which time he had anyway come to regard his ordination as a mistake, even if quite possibly valid in Roman Catholic eyes.[631]

According to the 1910 Caldey *Chronicle* Asaph went to Llanthony with Abbot Aelred on 27 July 1910; Aelred returned home on the 30th, but Asaph may have remained behind. In 1911 Aelred proposed sending not only the novices but other members of his community there for a change of scene, originally making the suggestion in a letter written from Switzerland to his second-in-command Dom Wilfrid Upson on 28 March. Wilfrid was at Llanthony with the novices when Aelred wrote to him from Caldey on 13 September (perhaps Anson's visit had been in September rather than August, or for longer than three weeks), and again on the 20th.

NEW OCCUPANTS?

UNLIKE HER BRETHREN Mother Tudfil had chosen to return to the world rather than move to another convent, although she continued to live her monastic vows as a private individual.[632] She could almost have stayed, however, as according to his December 1909 letter Aelred was just then considering turning the premises over to a female community:

---

[631] The Flood-gates of Memory p133. There may also have been an element of expediency in Aelred's choice of words, as a public admission that he had received Asaph and Gildas as clergymen would have added to the difficulties he was having just then with the Anglican authorities.

[632] Information from Mother Hilary FSJM, who grew up on the island and remembered as a young girl meeting the former Mother Tudfil, then approaching old age (conversation with the author, 14 September 2006). When the census was taken in 1911 Jeannie Dew was apparently visiting friends in Cardiff. For the rest of her life she lived in her old family home in Ventnor, dying at the age of 94 on 9 August 1960. Her 'monastic' activities included the pious art of book illumination: a volume incorporating the text of the 1662 Communion office which she wrote and illustrated was acquired for the Abergavenny collection in 2011 (ref A2011.4).

For the present, we have not quite decided what can best be done with the Abbey of Llanthony, but as it would be impossible, for some years at all events, to send a community of monks from Caldey, we shall probably arrange for some Sisters belonging to our Congregation to go there, who will continue the observance of the Benedictine rule as it is kept by us at Caldey and at Malling: the Divine Office will be recited regularly, and we hope that with a good strong community, Llanthony will realise at last all the best aspirations of him who spent so much time and money there, and who loved it so well.

Initially he thought of resettling the Malling nuns there, but after sending his architect (John Coates Carter of Penarth) to inspect the buildings he reported that the monastery and thirty-year-old temporary convent (especially the latter) had been found to be 'in a sad state of disrepair' as well as inconveniently laid out and too small for a household of between thirty and forty women.[633] Next he considered it for the other, smaller, women's community under his direction, then at Baltonsborough, near Glastonbury. Mother Monica and the convent chaplain Fr Vasey went to look at it in August 1910 (accompanied by Dom George Chambers from Caldey, who remained there for several days), but they, too, decided it was unsuitable.[634]

A LEGAL CHALLENGE

LURKING BEHIND THESE PLANS was the spectre of Caldey's disputed title to the property – or rather Asaph's, as he remained legal owner of the monastery until its sale two decades later. Attached to Ignatius's will his executors had found this document, addressed to Asaph and Tudfil:

---

[633] *Pax*, June 1910

[634] Caldey Chronicle, 14 August 1910. The Malling nuns moved to Milford Haven in 1911 and were received into the Roman Catholic Church at the same time as the majority of the Caldey monks; in 1916 the Baltonsborough community relocated to the vacant premises at Malling.

Whereas in my last Will and Testament I have devised the Monastery, Convent and Church at Llanthony, to you absolutely as joint tenants in full confidence that you will, as long as you can, carry on the work there according to the rules, customs and observances of the Order of St Benedict as I have done during the last 36 years. Now I declare it to be my most earnest and sincere wish that in the event of your being unable at any time after my decease to continue such work for any reason, you or the survivor of you should convey the premises so devised to you unto the Abbot for the time being of St Mary, at Buckfastleigh, in the county of Devon, for an estate of inheritance in fee simple for his own absolute personal use and benefit. This wish is expressed simply to guard our beloved Monastery from the 'Higher Criticism' supported as it is by the traitorous Bishops of our beloved and cruelly wronged English Church.[635]

This was evidently known to Dom Anscar Vonier, the dynamic young Abbot of Buckfast, who had visited Llanthony over a year before Ignatius's death, on 20 July 1907.[636] Buckfast was certainly one of the Catholic communities to which he had made overtures; it may have been on this occasion that the possibility of handing the monastery over to him but retaining safeguards for his own dwindling brotherhood was mooted and rejected, and this alternative suggested.

And it was probably to resist Buckfast's designs on Llanthony that Aelred took care to maintain at least a skeleton monastic observance there. Abbot Vonier was keen to acquire it, although for 'benefit' rather than 'use', as was made clear when on 28 April 1910 one of his monks wrote to a French abbess requesting prayers for the success of the claim. Dom Mellitus Hauler told Dame Marie Cronier of Dourgne in the French department of Tarn that the Buckfast monks

---

[635] Quoted Attwater p214
[636] Visitors' Book entry

weren't planning to occupy the monastery themselves but to sell it on to another community: 'the Fathers of Kergonan in Brittany, now in Belgium' were said to be interested in buying it from them.[637]

In a further letter of 26 May he reported that his community's 'chances of success [did] not appear as certain as [they had] believed at first', and on 7 December, having seen Llanthony for himself, he wrote:

> The site is magnificent but the buildings are not worth much. It would do for an Alumnate. The High Altar is worth about £500. It is situated in complete solitude, surrounded by mountains on all sides.... The lawsuit has started, but really it is difficult to say what the verdict will be. It is necessary to pray hard that we win. The property is worth about £3000.

The case 'Vonier v. Harris and Dew' was heard in the Court of Chancery before Mr Justice Joyce on 13 June 1911. According to the report in the following day's *Times* Abbot Vonier claimed that Asaph and Tudfil had been told of Ignatius's wishes and had undertaken to carry them out, but they denied this. Since this assertion could not be proved the Judge dismissed the case, the plaintiff being liable for costs.[638]

OTHER POSSIBILITIES?

HAVING SECURED OWNERSHIP of the property Aelred no longer needed to maintain a monastic presence there, and that autumn proposed

---

[637] Translations of the relevant extracts of this and Hauler's two further letters from Prinknash archives. The monks of Kergonan were forced into exile by the French law of associations in 1901 and only returned in 1920.

[638] Asaph spent the nights before and after the hearing at the suitably monastic-sounding Charterhouse Hotel. The receipted bill (slightly crumpled) has been preserved at Prinknash: the total cost of two nights' dinner, bed and breakfast (the dinner each evening accompanied by a sixpenny glass of beer) was eighteen shillings. Aelred had drawn attention to 'legal difficulties connected with the will of Father Ignatius, and his wishes as to the disposal of the property' in *Pax* of June 1910.

developing it as a retreat centre and house of studies for clergy.[639] Although in fact this idea never got off the ground it was partly to set it in motion that he sent an oblate brother to act as caretaker. This was Cadoc (John Charles) Blanchard,[640] for whom he declared himself 'sure [that] the solitary life [was] the best & possibly the only suitable rule'; like Fr Philip whom Ignatius had exiled there forty years earlier he may have been a 'difficult' character. In his letter of 20 September Aelred tells Wilfrid Upson to 'talk quite straight & forcibly (if you can) to Cadoc. I cant leave him at Llanthony if there are going to be fusses & quarrels & tales in the Valley' – these no doubt in response to Cadoc's accusations against Iltud Jackson. Wilfrid is to '[g]et him settled right up' before returning to Caldey the following week, and 'make Asaph act as if he were never going there again' – so Asaph had been there with Wilfrid and the novices, and Cadoc was now supposed to be taking over his responsibilities.

Aelred himself spent some time there in October with another group from Caldey, writing to Wilfrid (by then back on the island) on the 10th:

> The weather is quite beautiful, & these days at Llanthony are just what some of us wanted. On Sunday we go to the village church for Evensong, & I have already been to several houses in the neighbourhood to try and undo a little of Lyne's mischief. We are having the sheep, cow etc put up to auction next week, and there is quite a rush for the land to be let. Bates will drive down to Caldey next week. Please be sure to tell Longhurst not to buy another cob as I am bringing the Llanthony mare & cart down with Bates. It will do very well for the slip work, & is no use here. I hope to leave everything well settled & comfortable next week. Br Cadoc is thoroughly in his element & is making himself most useful.

---

[639] Pax, September 1911

[640] Cadoc arrived at the monastery on 25 August, on which date he signed the Visitors' Book.

The disposal of the animals marked the end of monastic farming at Llanthony, where the sheep had been identified with the branded letters 'OSB'.

Exactly what mischief 'Lyne' (Brother David) had been spreading in the neighbourhood wasn't recorded, but his emotional bond with Ignatius being as strong as it was the late Abbot's 'wish' would have had for him the force of divine law, and he was still fuming about the result of the case when he wrote his memoirs twenty years later. To him Asaph and Tudfil had been 'traitors' for letting the 'dear old Monastery' fall into what would shortly become Roman Catholic hands, despite Buckfast itself being a Roman Catholic institution. What upset him by that time wasn't just the change of ecclesiastical allegiance (although he would have viewed the 'Caldey conversions' as part and parcel of the same act of treachery), but the fact that a 'holy place' was now occupied by 'seculars'.

As that summer drew to a close the two sisters in the convent would also be leaving, perhaps for the last time. In his 20 September letter Aelred expressed the hope that they were 'taking all their things with them this time – they probably won't be able to go to Llanthony again in the same way'.[641]

Another request in Brother Cadoc's letter had been for a set of altar cards.[642] This was in case a priest from Caldey came to stay; he

---

[641] Rose Kidder lived another twenty years. The following cutting from an unidentified newspaper was pasted on to the flyleaf of a leather-bound Sarum Missal which she had given to H.B. Ventham in 1923: 'KIDDER – on Jan 29th 1931 at the residence of her cousin, Ashdene, St Davids Road, Laindon Hills, passed away Sister Rose Mary OSB late of Llanthony Abbey, S. Wales. Funeral at Extra Mural Cemetery, Brighton on Wednesday at 1.30. Jesus Only. R.I.P.' (information from the Reverend Norman Hulme, 17 January 2011). Alice Rebecca Wheeler (Sister Margaret?) died in Hitchin in 1942.

[642] Framed texts resting against the tabernacle or altar cross and the two outermost candlesticks, containing parts of the Liturgy more conveniently read from them than from the missal. These were *de rigeur* in the pre-Vatican 2 Roman Church, but were not in general use in the Church of England.

was half expecting a Brother Anthony – a Caldey oblate, perhaps, or a Caldey priest-novice. Although in itself an item of small importance, the request is symbolic of a significant change of focus. Llanthony would no longer be associated with Ignatius's romantic mediaevalism and Celtic revivalism but with Aelred's aggressive Anglo-Papalism, and from this it would be a small step to its rebirth as an outpost of actual Roman Catholicism.

MEANWHILE THERE WAS one more attempt to find a new use for the old monastery. At a Chapter meeting on 26 May 1912 Aelred announced that he had recently visited both Llanthony and a property the community had acquired at Pershore.[643] He told the brethren that he proposed spending £200 on repairs to each of them, and that he was hoping to let Llanthony for £200 *per annum* to a certain Ernest Newland Smith.[644] However, like his earlier idea of a retreat house or house of studies this failed to come to pass, and in October he reported that the building had been 'well repaired' and the water supply successfully reinstated (the previous September Cadoc complained that unnamed neighbours had been interfering

---

[643] The Victorian 'Abbey House', where after the 'conversions' two former members of the Caldey community would initiate the Anglican Benedictine fraternity which later became Nashdom Abbey. See Peta Dunstan, *The Labour of Obedience*, Norwich: Canterbury Press 2009.

[644] [George] Ernest Newland Smith (later known as 'Newlandsmith') (1875-c1957) combined musicianship and musicology with religious idealism. In 1906 he established the Laresol Society (*la re sol*, sol-fa equivalents of the initials of its motto *Ad Deum gloriam*) with the object of so infusing music and art with the love of truth and of God as to raise the human spirit into union with the Divine. In its early years a centre for the propagation of the Society's aims existed at various locations in Sussex and Devon; probably he planned to use Llanthony for the same purpose. Later, Newland Smith travelled the country as a 'minstrel friar', giving recitals and talks in churches and public halls. His most enduring achievement was his extended collaboration with Dr Rageb Mouftah (1898-2001) travelling through Egypt to collect and record the traditional music of the Coptic Church, to which he devoted the months of October to April each year from 1928 to 1936, gathering the results into sixteen folio volumes.

with it). Brother Cadoc had 'two good men to help in the work', and all was 'going well & happily'. 'The men' had been mentioned in Cadoc's letter, when he had asked Aelred to send supplies of tobacco – a pound of Oriental Mixture for himself and some single ounce packets of shag for the others. They weren't paid, but probably had board and lodging as well as this small luxury.

Ralph Pomeroy the Caldey Island steward spent two nights at the monastery in April 1912, and Mr Bryant the Clerk of Works was there a few weeks later. Members of the community continued to pay occasional visits; probably rather more than the five who wrote their names in the book between Cadoc's arrival and the 'conversions' eighteen months later.

GILDAS IN AMERICA

AS WE HAVE SEEN, Gildas Taylor left Caldey in April 1910. An undated statement in his hand says that he had 'abandoned the protestant jurisdiction' of Aelred's monastery and 'returned to the Orthodox Catholic Church' under Archbishop Vilatte.[645] In July he sailed from Liverpool to New Orleans, giving his last place of residence in this country as Bristol; he had lived there for a while before going to Australia seven or more years earlier and may still have had friends in the city.[646] His move coincided with the Archbishop's latest venture, the acquisition of a 50,000-acre plot in the Mexican province of Chihuahua, where he planned to establish a 'back to the soil' settlement for European expatriates to be known as Vilatteville. Taylor (who retained the name Gildas, sometimes hyphenating it with his surname as 'The Rev. R.C. Gildas-Taylor'[647]) evidently played

---

[645] Museum ref A1993.139.11.13

[646] In the 1901 census he was listed in lodgings in King Square, his occupation given as 'General Secretary & [illegible]'.

[647] 'Museum Musings' in The Big Band Sentinel (Marfa, Texas) of 24 December 1991 reprinted its 1914 report of the laying of the foundation stone of a new Masonic temple in that town, when alongside clergy of other

a significant part in this enterprise, but the intervention of the Mexican Revolution and consequent redistribution of land brought it to an untimely end.[648]

Gildas remained in Chihuahua until May 1912, collaborating with a group of schismatic clergy which Vilatte was attempting to organise into a 'national church'. He then crossed the border to Texas,[649] where he seems to have been accepted as a clergyman of the Protestant Episcopal Church. The 1913-14 Annual Report of its Board of Mission included the following, together with the information that he had been granted the sum of $43.75 from the Board's central funds:

St Paul's, Marfa and St James's, Alpine, in Texas, with their four accompanying missions at Sanderson, Langtry, Fort Stockton and Fort Davis, have been revived through the appointment in June of the Rev. Gildas Taylor as missionary-in-charge. By train, bicycle, horseback and buggy, Mr Taylor has succeeded in reaching all these places with some regularity, and the response to his ministrations has been remarkable. When it is considered that this particular section of Texas, embracing some 25,000 square miles, has been without a clergyman of our Church for nearly two years, and all mission work seemingly abandoned, the restoration to zealous Church life, with large and enthusiastic congregations, eager to co-operate in Church extension, seems gratifying. Improvements to our church edifice in Marfa have been made at a cost of about $400, defrayed by the congregation. Plans for a combination chapel and mission-hall have been prepared and funds collected for this object are now sufficient to proceed with its erection.

---

denominations 'The Revd R.C. Gildas-Taylor' had performed the 'Invocation'.

[648] Information in this section from http://www.guidinglight.com/ encyclopedia/R/René_Vilatte/, retrieved 9 January 2015.

[649] It is recorded that 'Robert Clare Gildas Taylor' crossed the border at El Paso on 30 May 1912.

However outwardly successful Gildas's ministry in Texas, he was back in Britain by early 1915 – perhaps the Protestant Episcopal authorities had discovered the irregular source of his orders.

DYFRIG

DYFRIG (OR BASIL) Stannard's whereabouts immediately after his dismissal from Caldey haven't been recorded. The Llanthony bank book shows payments to him of £10 in June 1910 and £2 in October, as with Cadoc and Gildas probably money he had deposited on arrival at the monastery. His name seems to have escaped inclusion in the 1911 census, although he was certainly in England not long after it was taken. In May of that year he was (re-)baptised and confirmed by an *episcopus vagans* named William Whitebrook and given the clerical tonsure and minor orders, and in June the remaining orders up to and including priesthood. On 7 April 1912 Whitebrook consecrated him to the episcopate.[650]

It is said that he served in the army during the 1914-18 War and demobbed with shell shock. In the 1918 London electors' list he was included as an 'absent voter' with the occupation of storekeeper for the British Red Cross Society; at the time his registered address was 112 Clapham Park Road. On 10 May that year he married his old friend Clara McNeile Griffith Williams at the nearby church of St James; it was to her that in 1905 and 1907 he had sent the postcards mentioned earlier. Records show that they went through the ceremony again on 8 April 1919 in Wisbech – perhaps for the benefit of their respective families.

---

[650] Information in this section from Metropolitan Seraphim of the British Orthodox Church (personal communication March 2015) and from BAL pp275f. Whitebrook and his brother (who also became an irregular bishop) had been servers at F.G. Lee's church of All Saints, Lambeth. Anson copied Mar Georgius' estimation of Stannard from the *Varied Reflections* of that prelate, who also brought out a cyclostyled pamphlet entitled *The Reluctant Bishop. Being the Story of the Right Reverend Mgr. Basil Maurice Stannard, Bishop of Walsingham.*

After the war the couple settled in Leicester, where for many years he worked as managing clerk at a firm of solicitors. Some time before his death (which took place there on 9 May 1953) Stannard was received into the Roman Catholic Church. Mar Georgius of Glastonbury (Hugh George de Willmott Newman) summed him up as 'learned, courteous and in every way respectable, but...quite content in the ultimate event to let his work die with him'. His daughter Margaret donated his collection of relics and liturgical paraphernalia to the headquarters of another 'Free Catholic' body, Steenoven Mission House in the North London suburb of Highbury. Among them were a cutting from the bush said to have provided the materials for the Crown of Thorns which had once belonged to Ignatius, as well as the late Abbot's 'old, ill-fitting and shabby cope'.[651]

---

[651] One Faith (cyclostyled newsletter put out by Bishop Geoffrey Paget King of Steenoven Mission House), issue no 1 of 1958; Museum ref A1997.16.11. The 'Christ Thorn' relic and the cope are also in the Abergavenny collection; refs A1993.138.6 and A1993.4. For many years in the 1970s and 1980s the cope was worn by the officiant at the annual Pilgrimage to Llanthony and Capel-y-ffin.

CHAPTER 13

CALDEY MONKS AND
CATHOLIC FAMILIES

O N 5 MARCH 1913 ABBOT AELRED and the majority of his monks submitted to Rome. Among them was Asaph, who unlike most of his fellow converts was exempted from the requirement of conditional baptism: no explanation has been given for this. Ignatius's monastery thus passed into Roman Catholic hands, as it would remain for the following seven decades.

Mass was first celebrated there by a Catholic priest on Sunday 13 July 1913, feast of the Patronage of St Benedict – or at least first celebrated officially and canonically, as Catholic clergy are known to have stayed at the monastery in Ignatius's lifetime, and would almost certainly have said Mass at its altars.[652] The celebrant was Dom Bede Camm of Erdington Abbey, who was acting as novice master to the newly converted Caldey brothers. He was himself a convert of many years' standing; as a young man he had been associated with Mother Hilda's community a decade or so after its break with Ignatius. As the abbey church was said even then to be 'fast falling into ruins'[653] a temporary chapel was rigged up in the community room in the east wing, conveniently adjacent to the sacristy; an altar stone was borrowed from Belmont. Among those present were 'a few Catholics from Old Llanthony', including the local postman and his 75-year-

---

[652] Forms for the admission of novices &c in Latin and English occupy several pages of the Professions Register. At the head of one section Ignatius has noted 'Copied here by a Roman priest, staying with us.'

[653] Dom Bede Camm, *The Call of Caldey* (Burns Oates & Washbourne 1937) p73; other information in this section from that and the preceding page.

old grandmother. The grandmother was Mary Maguire, mother of Daniel, eldest of the 1880 visionaries, and the grandson [Zacharias] John Powell, son of one of his sisters. They had signed the visitors' book on 29 June, a fortnight before Dom Bede's arrival, perhaps on an exploratory visit. It had probably been several years since Mrs Maguire had been able to attend a Catholic Mass, which she did on both the Sundays of his ten-day stay: Fr Bede says that on the second occasion she came fasting to make her Confession and Communion. It would have given her understandable pleasure that the priest was able to begin instructing her grandson, and to do the same for another (unnamed) young man, whom he conditionally baptised.

Other priests occasionally visited − Fr Cyprian (formerly Cadoc) Alston came from his current Downside parish for a few days in late August and early September, and in the June 1914 issue of *Pax* it was reported that Mass had been celebrated three times between mid-February and mid-May of that year. Otherwise Cadoc Blanchard and his unnamed assistant had to make the thirty-mile round trip by horse and cart to the nearest Catholic church in Abergavenny, as did any lay Catholics who came to stay.[654]

The community room chapel was known as the Lady Chapel, and a picture postcard of it was produced of which copies were offered for sale by Brother Cadoc. The altar was lavishly decorated with candles, flower vases and a statue of the Blessed Virgin, apparently transferred bodily from the main church, but was probably dismantled when the monastery was left empty a couple of years later. When Dom Joseph Woodford arrived in 1923 it was replaced by a less ornate arrangement in the long south cloister.

IN THE 1930s the now septuagenarian Brother David put together an account of Ignatius's life and that of his monastery, including

---

[654] Through the columns of *Pax* holiday accommodation for 'guests (gentlemen)' was offered at the rate of 5s per day or 30s per week, with the possible availability of 'tickets for fishing'.

his own part in its history, in which he continued the story for a few years beyond the Founder's death. He acknowledged a little grudgingly that there had been 'some intention by the Caldey Abbot of a partial continuance of community life at the dear old Monastery, but, ultimately, nothing eventuated'. Before his change of allegiance Abbot Aelred had, as we have seen, made some effort to interest other communities in taking over the 'dear old Monastery', and he can't be blamed for the fact that it was suitable neither for his own monks nor for either of the women's communities with which he was connected.

As a Catholic abbot he had access to a much wider circle of potential new occupants, and in that first year visitors from a number of orders made their way up the Vale of Ewyas. In September 1913 Dom Paul Seillour from the exiled Breton monastery of Caermaria at Llechryd, near Cardigan, spent a night at the monastery, and may have been interested in exploring its possibilities for his community.

Six months later a young monk of Belmont named Gregory Buisseret paid a brief visit. In 1917 he would take charge of a new alumnate at Belmont which ran for a few years before the community opened its school (itself now closed), but the impressions he confided to his diary suggests he found the place deficient – if indeed he was investigating its suitability for this project.

> Went on bicycle to New Llanthony.... Buildings tumbling down from want of proper building and from damp. Church most beautiful but literally dropping to pieces from want of decent care in building and damp.[655]

In May 1914 two nuns from the Cistercian abbey of Belval spent two days at Llanthony with their founder Abbé Hippolyte Trannoy and Dom John Chapman of Downside, acting Superior of Caldey

---

[655] Information about Dom Gregory and extract from his diary courtesy of Brenda Warde, Archivist of Belmont Abbey.

during the community's period of reorientation. Whether this convent fifty miles inland from Calais had any connection with the 'community of Trappistine Nuns from the South of France' about which Aelred wrote in that September's *Pax* is not known, but he felt able to announce that arrangements had been 'practically concluded' for this latter community to take possession of the premises the following spring, doubtless like the population at large expecting hostilities to be over in a matter of months. Until then he was putting the buildings 'in the charge of a [new?] caretaker', and had doubtless already found a use for the 'small sum' which had been agreed for their sale.

This particular plan having been overtaken by world events, on 5 March 1915 he wrote to Lady Mostyn, sister-in-law of the Bishop of Menevia, who had evidently been making enquiries about the monastery – possibly on behalf of the Benedictines of Termonde, taking refuge at the Mostyn family seat of Talacre after the destruction of their Belgian abbey the previous year. He gave a full description of the property and said he was prepared to sell it for £1000, suggesting that a further £700 to £1000 would be needed to put the buildings in order.

This was probably the last serious attempt to find monastic occupants for Llanthony. On Michaelmas Day that year the furniture and other household contents were sold by auction, together with the corrugated iron sheets and timber from which the temporary convent had been constructed. A fortnight later Plas Genevieve was sold to 'a local gentleman' for £760, and the adjacent farm (Boxbush, otherwise Trecae or Upper House) to its tenant John George.[656]

The monastery and church were now abandoned. The author of 'A Tramp in the Black Mountains' in the *Abergavenny Chronicle* of 4 February

---

[656] Auctioneer's poster in Prinknash archives; report in *Abergavenny Chronicle* of 15 October 1915. The new owner of Plas Genevieve was an Abergavenny businessman named Richard Tickle, who was probably the first inhabitant of Capel-y-ffin to own a car; I am grateful to Mr David Filsell for the information that in 1917 a Model T Ford was registered in his name at Plas Genevieve.

1916 observed that in the course of his walk he had found 'the sacred place deserted and in decay.... The once well-kept paths were overgrown with grass and weeds and the monks' quarters had been practically razed to the ground' (this probably referred to the recently-demolished convent). 'The beautiful "shrine" in the open field was still there', however.

News of the monastery's abandonment reached Ignatius's youngest sister Harriet, who wrote to Abbot Aelred asking whether it would be possible for her brother's body to be exhumed and reburied elsewhere. As noted in the previous chapter, Aelred explained in his reply that as the grave was twelve feet deep and filled with masonry and concrete, exhumation was not a practical possibility.

ILTUD & GILDAS

WE DON'T KNOW how long Iltud Jackson stayed in the Llanthony valley after Cadoc Blanchard's arrival, but by early 1912 he had followed Dyfrig Stannard into the shadowy world of *episcopi vagantes*. On 21 March of that year he was (re-)baptised by Bishop Whitebrook, and on 6 April confirmed and given the clerical tonsure and four minor orders. The next day (when Stannard received the episcopate) he was ordained subdeacon,[657] but there is no evidence to suggest he advanced beyond that rank. Were the two ex-novices perhaps trying to revive their old community in a new location?

Three years later Jackson found his way back to Caldey, at much the same time as Gildas Taylor, newly returned from America. Neither of them was destined to have an easy time in the community, or a particularly long one. Both were received into the Catholic Church that April (1915) and readmitted to the noviciate – Gildas on 23 May, and Illtyd (as his name was spelt at Caldey) on 17 October. The following year they were both simply professed: Gildas on 11 June and Illtyd on 18 October.

---

[657] Information from Metropolitan Seraphim of the British Orthodox Church (personal communication March 2015)

In August 1917 Illtyd Jackson was dismissed for pilfering, and left the island. As for Gildas, early in December of that year the acting Superior (Dom Wilfrid Upson) filled over four closely-written pages of his diary[658] with a detailed account of two interviews he had had with him about his 'particular friendships' with local seculars (one man and one woman in particular), which were causing tongues to wag in the village. A month later Gildas fell ill with appendicitis, and a further four pages of Fr Wilfrid's diary describe his rapid decline and death. The January storms made his removal by boat to the Tenby cottage hospital particularly hazardous; they also delayed the arrival there of the surgeon from Haverfordwest by some twenty-four hours. No doubt this hastened his demise, which occurred at three o'clock on the morning of 8 January 1918, when he was forty years of age. A party of monks crossed to Tenby the following day to collect his body, which was carried in procession to the harbour and returned to the monastery for burial – the first member of the twentieth century Caldey community to die and be buried on the island.

In December 1919 Jackson was allowed to return. The admission to the monastery in the interim of another Brother Illtyd meant that he had to take a different name, so he became Brother Ignatius, and on account of his lacklustre performance in two previous attempts at the noviciate was only allowed to enter as an oblate. Once again his behaviour gave cause for concern, and towards the end of 1920 he was dismissed. It seems, however, that he was allowed to remain on the island for some weeks as a secular, continuing to work on the abbey farm but living outside the monastery.[659]

After this he got another farm job in Sussex, where on 1 April 1927 he died of tetanus following an accident with a threshing machine. Like Gildas he died at the age of forty, although the local newspaper

[658] Preserved in the Prinknash archives

[659] Information about Jackson's monastic career from Dom Wilfrid Upson's diary.

thought he had been 38. First in the list of floral tributes at his funeral in the Catholic church in Bexhill was one bearing the inscription 'Jesus Only' from 'Mary Rose OSB and Bishop Maurice Stannard'. When his will was proved a few months later his name was given as 'Richard Illtyd Jackson', and his total effects valued at £166 9s.[660]

JOHN BATES

IGNATIUS'S OLD OUTDOOR SERVANT John Bates migrated, as we have seen, to Caldey, where as at Llanthony he became the monastery gamekeeper. A few glimpses of his life there are to be found in the columns of *Pax* and in Wilfrid Upson's diary. As Prior, Wilfrid found himself left in charge for increasingly lengthy periods when Abbot Aelred was away (the problems with Gildas and his illness and death had occurred during one of them), as well as acting Superior for several years after Aelred's resignation in 1921. Financial and other problems made this a particularly burdensome assignment, from which he found relief in occasional expeditions such as the following, on 11 December 1920:

> Went out with John Bates from 10.30 – 12 with a gun, & we brought down a pheasant each. I am afraid I am getting rather fond of this sort of thing, but I started it, because it seemed right that I should go, as some shooting had to be done – & now I go on with it because it's such a real recreation & takes one's mind entirely off everything else.

On the same day one of the junior monks admitted the serious offence of shooting a pheasant on the ground and was in dread of Bates finding out, as perhaps was Wilfrid himself.

Bates's gun had been put to use on 11 November 1918, when *Pax* reported that in answer to the official Armistice gunfire from Tenby

---

[660] Information about Jackson's death and funeral from the *Sussex Express* of 8 April 1927. I assume 'Mary Rose OSB' was Mrs Stannard.

'old John Bates' had let off a fusillade of cartridges on the island. Not many could be spared, however, as '[e]ach report meant so much ammunition less for his rabbits and birds.'

A year later Bates married Miss Lily Eden. She was some years his junior, and had come to the island at the same time as a priest-aspirant whose housekeeper she had been in his former parish; since then she had been helping in the guesthouse. After a year of marriage she gave birth to a dead child, and Wilfrid records how deeply Bates felt the loss and how grateful he was for his sympathy. Difficulties between the gamekeeper and his wife may have influenced his readiness to join Fr Joseph Woodford and others in the re-occupation of Llanthony in November 1923, although it is not known whether the plan had been for him to remain there in the long term – in the event he was sent back to Caldey after a little over a week, an attack of 'melancholy' rendering him unfit for work.

Three years after this he was admitted to the Joint Counties Mental Hospital at Llanllwch, just outside Carmarthen. Here he was befriended by the local Vicar and his son Keble Thomas (1909-92), then at Lampeter studying for ordination, and from whose account of Bates's life we have already quoted. The future Canon Thomas learned that his marital problems ('The marriage was not an easy one, and was a battle between the Book of Common Prayer and the Latin Mass') had been the cause of his admission to the hospital, 'he apparently having boxed [her] ears', but he quickly proved a model patient and was granted an increasing measure of liberty. He was allowed to keep a dog and a ferret in a shed in the hospital grounds and a gun at the Vicarage, and with these made regular foraging expeditions over the neighbouring countryside, often taking the young ordinand with him and giving him the benefit of his knowledge of wildlife and experience of country ways. On Sundays he 'used to walk the two miles to my father's church, sitting in the far corner following the Welsh service in his English Prayer Book', and towards the end of his life he accompanied the Vicar and his son on a sentimental journey to Llanthony:

From Abergavenny up the narrow valley he kept up a running commentary, he was in his seventh heaven. We got to the old Abbey, partaking of refreshments in the farm-cum-inn, then further up the valley to the monastery that Ignatius had founded; it was then a private dwelling owned by the late sculptor, Eric Gill. We walked to the ruined, roofless chapel and cleared away some rubbish from the flat stone in the church which marked the grave of Father Ignatius. John stood there cap in hand, head bowed with tears running down his gaunt cheeks. We got back to the car and drove home in silence more in respect for John's feelings than for the sad spectacle of Father Ignatius's chapel now in ruins.

John Bates died at the age of 85 in the summer of 1951, still a patient in the Carmarthen hospital.

THE MONASTERY REOCCUPIED

In November 1923 Dom Joseph Woodford of Caldey came to live at the monastery. A chronic sufferer from TB, his condition had been exacerbated by the damp sea air, and it was hoped the Black Mountain climate would provide relief.

Fr Joseph was at Capel-y-ffin for a little under five years, from time to time recording events in his diary, a single hard-covered notebook covering the years 1923 to 1929 now in the Prinknash archives. When he arrived in the valley on 16 October he noted that it was the fifteenth anniversary of Ignatius's death: 'I hope this augurs well that the Monastery may again flourish,' he wrote. This suggests that there was some idea of re-establishing proper conventual life at Llanthony, albeit on a small scale: a document in Woodford's hand listing 'Our Benefactors' refers to 'a fresh start' having been made there when he and a small group of companions took up residence.

For the first month he stayed at the Abbey Hotel at old Llanthony, while various more able-bodied helpers came and went between the hotel and Capel-y-ffin to prepare the building for occupation.

Among these were Prior Wilfrid Upson and Dom Jerome Holmes[661] from Caldey, who stayed on for a few days after Dom Joseph moved in on 17 November. He himself slept in Fr Ignatius's old cell; that night Dom Wilfrid and Dom Jerome occupied the big room next to it, and John Bates (who had come from Caldey the preceding day with fencing tools) the 'Prophet's Chamber'. According to the diary all four slept badly – perhaps because they were sleeping on beds made by Wilfrid and Jerome, most likely from oddments of timber and without springs.[662]

JOSEPH WOODFORD'S CLOSEST COMPANION in the first two years of his stay was 'Brother Davies', otherwise Michael Davies, like Woodford himself a convert to Catholicism then in his early thirties. He had arrived at Caldey as a postulant in 1920, but in common with other entrants in this period was unable to proceed to the noviciate until the summer of 1926, the Roman authorities having suspended professions and ordinations on account of the community's financial and other difficulties. During the war he had served in the Friends Ambulance Unit, and in later years (as Dom Raphael) would act as Infirmarian at Prinknash, so was the ideal companion for the semi-invalid Dom Joseph – as well as for a certain Brother Augustine, who was sent with them because only Davies could provide the attention he required.[663]

Also in residence was Donald Attwater – on and off during the first few months, then full time from March 1924 when he brought

---

[661] 'A tough Caldey monk who enjoyed cutting down trees' according to Robert Speaight (The Life of Eric Gill (Methuen 1966) p164), although on p153 he suggests that the far from robust Dom Joseph enjoyed the same pastime.

[662] Fr Joseph's diary entry for Thursday 15 November: 'Spent day at Monastery with Fr Prior & D. Jerome they have made some splendid beds & tables.'

[663] This detail is mentioned in Dom Raphael's obituary in Pax, Autumn/ Winter 1979. According to Dom Joseph's diary Brother Augustine was at Capel for almost exactly a year, from 12 July 1924 until 7 July 1925. His name does not figure in the list of brethren in Fr Baker's All Those Years in Exile.

his wife Dorothy and their young children to live in the west wing, together with her widowed father, the splendidly-named Jebus Bickle. It may have been their arrival which prompted Fr Woodford to move for the summer months into what he calls the 'tin shelter', according to Attwater 'a sort of hermitage constructed near the south wall of the ruined church'.[664] Attwater was much of an age with Fr Woodford and Brother Davies, and like them a convert to Catholicism; after active service in the 1914-18 war he had been living on Caldey and managing the village shop while beginning to make his way as a writer. He and his wife came to Capel to help run the house: Dorothy did the cooking, and Donald taught himself the art of lead glazing so as to repair the many damaged and defective windows. In January 1924 they were joined by eighteen-year-old Ampleforth-educated René Hague, who had 'recently escaped, rather precipitately, from the Jesuit noviciate', and made himself useful among other things by teaching Latin and Greek to Brother Davies.[665]

As noted earlier, Bates was sent back to Caldey after ten days, but by a stroke of good fortune a new helper arrived as soon as he left. This was Charles Baker (otherwise Charlie Stones), a carpenter originally from Lancashire who was working in the neighbourhood as an itinerant labourer. Over the next few years he became an

---

[664] Donald Attwater, *A Cell of Good Living* (Geoffrey Chapman 1969) p131. Fr Woodford also mentions living for a time in a building he calls Cae Melyn ('yellow field'), but to judge from the insurance documents current at the time of the sale of the property to Mary Gill in 1931 (now at the West Sussex Record Office, ref Raper Mss 490) this was a name used to denote the monastery itself rather than any of its ancillary buildings.

[665] Speaight op cit p156. As Davies had all but completed his undergraduate career (at St John's, Oxford) when war broke out in 1914 and Hague had hardly begun his own it seems strange that things were being done that way round; maybe it was more a case of 'brushing up' than of teaching from scratch. In *René Hague, a Personal Memoir* (Upton, Cheshire: The Aylesford Press 1989, p44) Barbara Wall quotes a 1975 letter from him in which he says he 'last read Lucretius with Dom Raphael at Capel, Christ [knows] how many years ago'.

indispensable member of the household, as much for serving as 'guide, philosopher and tactful but sometimes very candid friend'[666] as for his skill in repairing the buildings and adapting them to secular use. He remained at the monastery as caretaker until his death in 1935.[667]

IN FR JOSEPH'S LIST the principal benefactors for the new venture were identified as Mr and Mrs Dixon-Davies, Brother Davies's parents: 'By [their] kindness we were able to repair the roofs etc and make the place habitable.' (For some reason the material chosen for the reroofing of the north cloister was heavy clay tiles, whose weight would cause problems later on.) Although not Catholics[668] they were people of means, and one of their benefactions was an old Daimler car, nicknamed 'Dorothy Daimler'. The others he mentioned were Mr Paul Cadbury (of the Quaker chocolate dynasty; a friend of Brother Davies's from his time with the ambulance unit), Captain G.D.W. Rooke, who provided a newly bound altar missal, and Miss H.F. Cann.

Miss Cann's name was coupled with that of Captain Reginald Watson, a deceased relative, and it was explained that her generous support was partly in his memory. She was another Catholic convert, then in her mid-fifties and living in Bath; her father had been an Anglican incumbent in the city of Exeter. Her chief act of generosity seems to have been the purchase on behalf of the little monastic household of Plas Genevieve, which they renamed The Grange. When Fr Woodford arrived it was occupied by a Mrs Rawlins, to whose husband (who was living elsewhere) it had been sold by its 1915 purchaser Mr Tickle. The sale to Miss Cann was concluded

---

[666] Attwater op cit p95

[667] He is commemorated by a carved stone on the north wall of the monastery, and buried in Capel-y-ffin churchyard.

[668] Mrs Dixon-Davies was received into the Catholic Church in 1929, and became involved in setting up the Catholic Study Circle for Animal Welfare.

in the summer of 1924, in time for the Caldey brothers to move across to it and leave the monastery itself vacant for Eric Gill and his companions.[669]

THE GILLS

WHEN IT WAS DECIDED TO send Fr Woodford to Capel-y-ffin there was no suggestion that it would involve him in pastoral responsibilities – still less that he would find himself acting as chaplain to a settlement of colourful and independent-minded Catholics, of whose leader's now notorious sexual activities he cannot have been completely unaware. Gill's first biographer suggests that this 'quiet and simple' monk was 'rather bewildered' to find himself thus employed,[670] but no hint of this comes across in his diary. (This is, however, for the most part a severely factual record of people's comings and goings and changes in the weather the writer's state of health, the only possible exceptions having been removed by his own hand.[671])

Gill had heard about the disused monastery when Donald Attwater visited him at Ditchling Common in April 1923,[672] six months before Fr Woodford took up residence at Capel, but didn't go to look at it

---

[669] A minor hiccup occurred as they began to move in. On 8 August Fr Joseph wrote in his diary that '[a]bout 12 noon Mr Lyne [William Leycester Lyne of Maes-y-ffin, otherwise Brother David] came up with a telegram from Mr Rawlins asking for the key of Plas G[enevieve] to be retained as Miss Cann's cheque had not passed. I refused to move out & wrote to Mr R. explaining the circumstances.' Evidently the matter was quickly put right, as he made no further mention of it.

[670] Speaight op cit p158

[671] Two pages were removed in 1924 (in June and September respectively), and a group of three in 1928 (mid-January to mid-March). The entry preceding this gap reads as follows: 'The last few days I have been rather unwell & in bed. Departing from [my] usual custom of [not] recording very personal matters I wrote the following in case of necessity.' Whatever he had written on the missing pages he had removed both them and the blank leaves to which they were attached before reaching the place from which the latter had been taken a few weeks later.

[672] Attwater op cit p 84f

until the following January. The idea of moving somewhere really remote appealed to him, although at that stage he wasn't certain whether this would involve just him and his family, or the whole Ditchling Guild. There was talk of relocating the whole enterprise either to Caldey (possibly after an interim period at Capel) or to one of a number of other places – one suggestion had been the island of Crappa off the coast of Galway.

The Guild had evolved over the preceding ten years as a collective of like-minded Catholic artists and craftsmen. At the centre both geographically and spiritually was its chapel, and a major influence was the Dominican friar Vincent McNabb, who encouraged Gill and his fellows to enrol in his Third Order. Fr McNabb was an enthusiastic protagonist of Distributism, and lost no opportunity to promote the community as a model for Catholics wanting to go 'back to the land'.

Gill himself was scarcely backward when it came to publicity, but found it hard to accept the attention resulting from it. 'Ditchling' had become a buzzword among earnest seekers as well as the merely curious, and the place was just a little too accessible for his comfort.

Another problem was his deteriorating relationship with Hilary (Douglas) Pepler, friend and collaborator for the better part of two decades, and the other dominant Ditchling personality. Partly this was to do with business matters, but there were personal factors as well, particularly Gill's unhappiness at the growing closeness between his eldest daughter Betty and Pepler's son David. In the end he decided to separate from the Guild, and in August 1924 brought his family to Capel, where they became tenants of the Caldey community.

Accompanying them were an Irish farmworker named Dan Brennan and his family, and the wood engraver Philip Hagreen with his wife Aileen and their children, who had arrived at Ditchling the previous year. Neither stayed long. In May 1925 the Hagreens went to live in Lourdes and eventually returned to Ditchling; Philip couldn't cope with the cold, and Eric couldn't cope with Aileen, who in his words was suffering from 'the strain of motherhood on top of the strain of a university education'.[673] Gill's disciple and long-time collaborator Joseph Cribb 'came and went because his wife could not stand the climate',[674] although his brother Laurie (in Fiona MacCarthy's opinion 'perhaps the finest British letter cutter' of the twentieth century[675]) did settle at Capel, and his marriage to Teslin O'Donnell took place on the same occasion as Betty Gill's to David Pepler (3 June 1927, in Brecon), to which her father had in the end given his consent.

Picture 36: Gill family picnic, c1927. Eric in centre; Betty, Mary and Joan on left with Teslin Cribb in front of them. On right Petra and Gordian with David Jones; identity of three males on left and woman in centre not known.

[673] Letter from Gill to Fr Austin Barker, quoted in Fiona MacCarthy, Eric Gill (Faber & Faber 1989) p201

[674] Speaight op cit p183

[675] MacCarthy op cit p199

THE NEW OCCUPANTS arrived on 14 August, eve of the Assumption, as noted by Fr Joseph:

> A very heavy rainy day with clouds hanging about the tops of the mountains. Large's lorry arrived about 5pm bringing the Gill family, Hagreen & Brennan with 2 goats and various live stock, so begins today the new settlement from Ditchling.

Over the next few days he observed the arrival of their furniture, conveyed in relays from the nearest point to which the delivery lorry had been able to bring it. In early September the Brennans joined him and his fellow residents at The Grange, leaving the monastery to the Gills, the Hagreens and the Attwaters. The only bathroom (and operative lavatory) was in the Attwaters' part of the house, next to the former Abbot's cell.[676]

The gap left by the departure of the Hagreens was soon filled by Gill's sophisticated and cosmopolitan secretary (and mistress and model) Elizabeth Bill, whose presence Fr Woodford first noted in June 1925, followed a couple of months later by the delivery of her collection of antique furniture. Her illegitimate teenage son René (Ansted, after his father, but always named by Woodford as René Bill) was also there from time to time, and briefly apprenticed to Gill.

Another occasional resident was the artist and poet David Jones,[677] who had come to Ditchling in 1921 after war service as a private in the trenches and a few terms at a London art school. His introduction to

---

[676] According to Brother David the monks' lavatories had been stripped out and sold in the 1915 auction.

[677] In *Dai Greatcoat* (Faber & Faber 1980), his compilation of David Jones's life through his letters, René Hague gives Jones's periods of residence at Capel as December 1924 to March 1925, when he paid his first visit to Caldey Island (pp32f), then 'during the Summer of 1925' and for 'a good deal of 1926' (p40). In the same paragraph Hague lists other places where he stayed during the years the Gills lived at the monastery, and asserts that his parents' house in Brockley remained his 'base' throughout this time.

the Gill *ménage* gave him a much needed sense of direction, in life as well as in art. For a while he was engaged to the middle daughter Petra, and although never a member of the Guild followed the others into the Dominican Third Order. The valley scenery remained a significant inspiration in his work long after his stay, as did Petra Gill; he also left two tangible relics, both now sadly decomposing. When the new chapel came into use (see below) its iron tabernacle door was decorated by Jones with an *Agnus Dei* superimposed on a *chi-rho* cross, and in the south cloister – by this time Eric's workshop – he painted a Crucifixion on the side wall. Oral tradition has it that he dashed this off on an impulse using borrowed watercolours, and that an overflow in a washbasin installed immediately overhead washed much of it away.

Picture 37: Howard Coster's photograph of Eric Gill in his south cloister workroom, with Joseph Thorp, author of an early study of his work.

Myths and half-truths about Eric Gill and his household abound. His unconventional dress — belted homespun smock, with the addition when working of a folded paper cap — has been interpreted by some as his individual version of cassock and biretta, but the earthy and unclerical Gill chose them not for their ecclesiastical overtones so much as for their practicality. He maintained that a smock or tunic (whether ankle-length for the leisured or knee-length or shorter for artisans and children) was more becoming than jacket and trousers ('tubes', as he dubbed the latter), as well as being rather easier to make; the paper cap was to keep the stone chips out of his hair.

Gill had an ambivalent relationship with modern conveniences, and some saw the move to Capel as a deliberate flight from the corrupting influence of mains electricity and shop-bought comestibles. In fact he didn't make the move to avoid these things on principle (or claimed not to have done; inconsistency was one of his most enduring traits), but having settled in a place where they couldn't be obtained he and his family were happy to manage without them. 'We *had* to do our transport by pony and pony cart. We *had* to bake our own bread — we couldn't possible have bought enough loaves and got them from the shop. And all our neighbours were doing the same.'[678] However, the same passage in his Autobiography acknowledges that this way of life was now nearing its end: in the 1920s the Llanthony valley was a 'dying land', whose sons were 'wandering unemployed in the Rhondda' whither they had gone in search of work because 'the city of London found it more profitable to foster Australian Capitalist sheep farming than to preserve the thousand-year traditions of the South Wales mountains'. And he admits that their life there was only possible because his wife Mary Ethel and their three daughters did all the cooking and cleaning, as well as looking after 'the animals and the farm'.

---

[678] Eric Gill, *Autobiography* (Jonathan Cape 1940) p228

Picture 38: David Jones: *Mr Gill's Hay Harvest* (1926)

CHURCH AND CHAPEL[679]

AT FIRST GILL HOPED TO put the abbey church back into a useable state,[680] but although Joseph Cribb suggested that he and his brother could achieve this by the radical step of lowering the roof it was

[679] Information in this section mostly from Fr Woodford's diary.

[680] Letter of 14 September 1924 to Desmond Chute (Eric Gill, *Letters* (Jonathan Cape 1947) pp181f)

decided in the end to abandon the building altogether. Aesthetically the old church was at the opposite pole to the simple clean lines favoured by Gill and the liturgically-minded priests with whom he associated, and its gargantuan reredos and multiple tiled steps had been designed for worship as a spectacle – 'our beautiful services', as Ignatius liked to think of them – rather than as an activity in which the lay congregation had its proper part to play.[681]

Picture 39: The new chapel, c1925

At Easter 1925 the daily Mass and other services were transferred from the *ad hoc* chapel in the south cloister to a permanent one in the lower northern block. The various partitions with which its upper floor had been divided were removed and a simple stone altar erected; a few months later this was graced with a set of wooden candlesticks made by Laurie Cribb and René Hague. The Archbishop of Cardiff (at the time in temporary charge of Menevia as well as

---

[681] This of course was four decades before Vatican II and the ensuing liturgical revolution in the western Church, but the underlying principles had already been set out by Lambert Beauduin, Odo Casel and other continental scholars, and were being disseminated in England especially through the more enlightened religious orders.

of his own diocese) had given permission the preceding December for reservation of the Blessed Sacrament, so the household was able to complete its Sunday observance with the popular service of Benediction. On Sundays and special feasts the Mass was sung: complete with chanted propers, when monks from Caldey were there to perform the intricate music from the *Graduale*. Among special observances Fr Joseph mentions the blessing of candles on Candlemas Day and of palms on Palm Sunday, as well as processions of the Blessed Sacrament on the feast of Corpus Christi and the following Sunday, although fluctuations in numbers and his own bouts of illness sometimes caused these to be curtailed. The proper liturgies of Good Friday and Holy Saturday seem never to have been attempted, and from time to time even the Sunday Mass fell victim to his poor health. In February 1927 he recorded saying Mass for the first time in 'our temporary chapel upstairs', to which 'we have been obliged to move on account of the damp'; this may have been at Plas Genevieve rather than in the monastery.

A few weeks before the Gills' arrival Compline was sung in the old church two days running, on one of them with organ accompaniment; this was during a visit by the Prior and Dom Asaph. By the summer of 1926 the need to make a decision about the building had become urgent, and 'Mr Hill a Catholic builder of Abergavenny' was asked to report on its condition. He condemned it out of hand, describing it as 'a disgraceful piece of building' and saying that 'if it was his own he wouldn't spend a farthing on it'; he thought it might fall down at any time. Not long afterwards a Mr Pawson ('a friend of the Lynes') also came to look at the church, saying it would be 'a big business to restore it'. On Ascension Day 1927 a Mr Brown-Davies came to visit Fr Ignatius's grave and suggested a letter to *The Times* appealing for funds to pay for the necessary work, although in the event none seems to have been published.

Mr Hill – a partner in Foster & Hill, presumably the same firm which had built the first phase of the monastery half a century earlier[682] – had recently completed a large neo-Gothic church for the Catholic parish in Ebbw Vale, and wondered whether the high altar and reredos could be made use of there. Soon afterwards the priest from Ebbw Vale came to have a look, and as he paid a second visit two weeks later he presumably liked what he saw. It was left to the builder to 'go into the matter', but this is the last we hear of it in Fr Woodford's diary.

NEIGHBOURS & VISITORS

ACROSS THE FIELDS at Maes-y-ffin Brother David maintained a proprietary interest in his old monastic home, and in spite of his disappointment at how things there had turned out was in frequent contact with its new occupants. He made his first appearance (at the monastery and in the diary, where he is always referred to respectfully as 'Mr Lyne') as soon as Fr Joseph and company moved in. A few weeks later he was on hand with other neighbours when a heavy ladder needed setting up against the outside wall of the Abbot's cell, three storeys above ground level. This was for the removal of the mass of ivy originally propagated by Ignatius from the growth on his parents' elaborate memorial in Margate cemetery – an adornment beloved by the Victorians, but one which would have done neither structure any good if left unchecked.

His son Lessie was much the same age as Fr Joseph and his companions, and often at home. He was an officer in the Gloucestershire Regiment (usually referred to in the diary as 'Capt[ain] Lyne') and had recently returned from a spell of duty in Africa; on several occasions he gave the priest lifts up and down the valley. The favour was returned one day in May 1924 when Dom Joseph's friend Fr McLaughlin was spending a few weeks' holiday at the monastery. He also had a car, and the Captain's vehicle having broken down he towed it all the way to Abergavenny.

---

[682] But not the church

A few days later the two priests were invited to tea by Brother David's wife Thomasina, who according to Donald Attwater was a semi-invalid and housebound, as well as consistently hostile towards the 'secular' occupants of the monastery.[683] There would always be a clash between Gill's rumbustious 'music and laughter and good red wine' Catholicism[684] and the intense and sometimes lugubrious spirituality of Ignatius's devotees; it is perhaps significant that Mrs Lyne's one social effort towards the household took place before his arrival.

It was also in these first few months that Dom Joseph received visits from three men with strongly Ignatian associations. In January 1924 Henry Ventham was nearing the end of his two-year course at King's College, London. He was walking towards Capel-y-ffin from his holiday home a couple of miles down the valley when he was picked up by Brother Davies and the others returning from the 11 o'clock Mass in Abergavenny – it was a Sunday, and one when Fr Joseph was prevented by illness from saying Mass himself. As it was nearly 3 o'clock when they reached the monastery and they hadn't had lunch he was given 'a short reception' and only 'saw round a little'. In the diary he is referred to simply as 'Ventham' with neither Christian name nor title, suggesting disapproval; there is no further mention of him in its pages.

Two months later Dom Joseph recorded the visit of 'a man named Dorian Herbert, who knew Gildas Taylor well & used to come to Llanthony in the old days'. Herbert was one of the small company who had signed the Visitors' Book on the 1909 Apparitions Feast, but although a fervent admirer of Ignatius and a firm believer in the phenomena he was only a Christian in a tangential sense.

The third visitor was Taylor's predecessor as Brother Gildas, the monk turned bus conductor Bertie Cannell. According to his own

---

[683] Attwater op cit p96

[684] Hilaire Belloc: 'Where'er the Catholic sun doth shine, / There's music and laughter and good red wine. / At least I've always found it so, / Benedicamus Domino!'

narrative[685] Cannell spent a few days that spring at Cwmyoy, from where he accompanied Brother David (not named, but identifiable from the context) on a visit to the monastery. Here he was welcomed by 'the monks' and shown around, noting that the 'long cloister' had been turned into a chapel (still the south cloister, at this date) and that 'all our beautiful things had gone'. He had come to the valley by arrangement with the local Vicar, the Reverend Thomas Williams, but on discovering that this cleric combined his Anglican priesthood with belief in spiritualism Cannell decided to sleep not at the Vicarage but in a neighbouring cottage.

THE FIRST ANNIVERSARY of the Gills' arrival was celebrated on 15 August 1925, the feast of the Assumption. It was a Saturday, and both Prior Upson and Gill's friend the Reverend Dr McQuillan were staying. Fr Prior sang Mass in the morning; then

> [a]t 6pm Eric had invited all the valley as far down as New House to come to tea, quite a large number came. Tea was followed by hymn, sermon by Dr McQuillan, hymn, Benediction, hymn. Afterwards the people returned to the Refectory for songs & music.

The style may have been rather different, but although firmly protestant by birth and upbringing many of those present would have both heard about and in some cases practised devotion to the Mother of the Lord and to his sacramental Presence when Ignatius lived in their midst. We aren't told who was there, but quite early on Fr Woodford had struck up a friendship with the current Watkins of Talsarn (probably William, another contemporary: he had been baptised in the abbey church at three years old in 1891 with the additional names Illtyd Dewi), and a few days after the party he

---

[685] FMTB pp95-99. Strangely no mention of his visit is made in Fr Joseph's diary.

went to tea with Miss Lewis at Ty Shores, who had (as it will be recalled) battled through the river to one of Ignatius's last Masses at Epiphany 1908.

THE MONKS

BROTHER MICHAEL DAVIES lived at Capel until the restoration of the Caldey noviciate in the summer of 1926, with Brother Augustine also there for much of that time. Other members of the community came and went, the most frequent visitor being Prior Wilfrid Upson, who after helping to prepare the house in October/November 1923 returned no fewer than fifteen times over the ensuing four years. Sometimes he stayed just one or two nights, using this convenient *pied à terre* as a staging post on his way elsewhere; more often his visits would last three or four days or occasionally as long as a week, and would give him a welcome break from the worries at home on Caldey.

Picture 40: Surviving 'Caldey converts' at Prinknash, 1933. Aidan Angle standing; seated from left Joseph Woodford, Leo Packer, Asaph Harris, Norbert Cowin, Dunstan Whitsed.

Jerome Holmes and Norbert Cowin had also been present at the start. Jerome returned for a nine-month stay between September 1924 and June 1925 (perhaps it was then that he exercised his passion for felling trees; newly exposed stumps appear alongside standing trees in several of David Jones's Capel-y-ffin pictures), and Norbert stayed twice each in 1924 and 1925, on at least one Sunday saying Mass for the household when Fr Joseph was away. Dom Asaph came back to his old monastery for a week in May 1924, and for six weeks in November and December of the same year. He had acquired considerable skill in the stained glass workshop at Caldey, and on the latter occasion came 'to do the glass'; it may have been under his tutelage that Donald Attwater learned how to repair the leaded windows. In July 1925 Asaph returned for a fortnight's holiday, in the course of which 'he tried the "Wireless" and we got Daventry perfectly on a crystal set', and must have done so again that autumn as his name appears on the following year's voters' list (at 'Cae Melyn').

Gilbert Thomas stayed for almost the whole of January 1926, and Theodore Baily paid two visits in 1924 and two more in 1925. These lasted respectively for five weeks and nearly seven, and are significant for what he left behind him. Fr Theodore had recently spent time in Paris studying under Maurice Denis, and his distinctive neo-Byzantine style is to be seen in stained glass windows at Caldey and elsewhere. On one of his stays he painted a wooden crucifix to hang above the altar, and on another a mural of St Peter in the passage leading to the new chapel. He became a close friend of Gill, and Donald Attwater mentions conversations 'night after night' with him, David Jones and René Hague under Gill's 'sort of presidency', their 'sort of text book' being Jacques Maritain's Art et Scolastique.[686]

---

[686] Attwater op cit p97

Picture 41: Dom Theodore Baily: *Thou art Peter*.

Another half dozen or so monk visitors are mentioned by name in Fr Joseph's diary, including Benedict Steuart (who would succeed Wilfrid Upson as Superior at Prinknash) and 'Brother Richard'. This was Peter Anson, who had been in and out of the Caldey community more than once (as Brother Richard Whytinge, after the martyred last abbot of Glastonbury); the slightly breathless record of his comings and goings reflects his notorious lack of stability, as well as the change in his status ('Br Richard' in the earlier entries, 'Br Peter Anson' in the later ones):

(1924) June 27th Friday: Br Richard left this morning having decided to go to Italy next week to stay with Croft Fraser at Pracchia.
Nov 28th Friday: Br Richard left this morning for Liverpool, catching the 10.37 at the Junction.

419

(1926) Mar 30th Tuesday: Br Peter Anson arrived this evening. He is sleeping at the Grange & feeding at the Gills.

May 17th Monday: Br Peter Anson returned here from Caldey.

May 29th Saturday: Br Peter Anson left here this morning for Southampton, en route for France.

CRACKS IN THE FABRIC

FR WOODFORD HAD BEEN LIVING at Plas Genevieve/The Grange for scarcely six months when Miss Cann announced that the house would have to be sold, the purchase having exhausted her limited resources. This was at the beginning of March 1925. Two weeks later – after Montague Harris the Abergavenny auctioneer had been to look at the furniture and arrangements had been made for Dom Jerome and Brother Augustine to return to Caldey – the news came that their benefactress had died, followed after another few days by the revelation that she had committed suicide.[687] Montague Harris paid a second visit – this time to value the property for probate – and the monks reckoned they could stay put, at least for the time being. When her will was published in October they learned that Miss Cann had bequeathed the house to her godson Thomas Hayes, then studying for the priesthood at Osterley;[688] she had also left £1000 to Prior Upson. As Hayes wouldn't turn twenty-one until May 1926 his trustees agreed that until then the house could be rented in Gill's name with Fr Woodford and his companions continuing to live there, after which the young man would be at liberty to sell it.

---

[687] The cause of her death, which was reported in various newspapers, was the ingestion of concentrated lysol, although she had also cut her wrists and attempted to drown in the bath. At the inquest a verdict of suicide while of unsound mind was returned; it was stated that Miss Cann suffered from 'religious mania' and was under the illusion that she was too wicked to live. A note was discovered containing the message 'I cannot face the music.'

[688] Later a priest in the Diocese of Arundel & Brighton (d. 1975)

All this uncertainty was as nothing compared with that surrounding the future of Fr Joseph's parent monastery.[689] The lowest point had been in October 1924, when the Caldey community was in danger of being summarily disbanded. This was speedily followed by the offer of a new home at Prinknash Park in Gloucestershire, then by further uncertainty when in February 1926 their would-be benefactor Thomas Dyer Edwardes died before his deed of gift had been put into effect. Fortunately his grandson and heir Lord Leslie (like Thomas Hayes at the time still under age) was willing to honour Dyer Edwardes's intentions, but there must have been some tension in the air until the matter was finally resolved in November 1927 (the move was completed just over a year later).[690]

In July 1926 Thomas Hayes came to stay at The Grange, remaining for over a fortnight. Two days after his departure on 10 August Mr Lyne brought Vicar Williams from Cwmyoy to look over the house, the next day following the visit up with a note to say that Williams had paid a deposit and wished the name of the house to revert to Plas Genevieve. On Monday 30 August a further communication asked for vacant possession the following Friday; Fr Joseph countered this with 'a straight note in reply' and sat tight. Despite a 'passage of arms' between Gill and Lyne about their respective rights to the Plas Genevieve farm buildings and land, agreement was reached soon afterwards between the occupants and the new owner, Mr Lyne acting as his agent. Eric Gill would rent from him the buildings and the field known as The Dôl, and Donald Attwater become the official tenant of Plas Genevieve for the following twelve months.

---

[689] See Baker, *All Those Years in Exile*, Chapter 6.

[690] On 21 May 1926 Fr Joseph reported receiving '[t]he good news...from Caldey that Prinknash can go ahead'. This seems to have been only provisional, as it wasn't until 29 November 1927 that 'Fr B[enedict Steuart] brought the good news that Lord Rothays [sic: Rothes; Leslie had succeeded to the title on the death of his father] ha[d] offered Prinknash practically unconditionally.'

DISSOLUTION

BY THIS TIME the practical difficulties of living at Capel-y-ffin were beginning to catch up with the Gills. Elizabeth Bill had recently invested in a house at Salies de Béarn in the Pyrenees, intending that it should be a 'home from home' for the whole Gill/Bill ménage, including the elderly father of her son René (whom she had just got round to marrying), and the family decamped there for the winter of 1926/27.

The following summer, as we have seen, Betty Gill married David Pepler and went to live with him in Sussex.[691] As she had been responsible for the animals at Capel, her absence would have imposed an extra burden on her mother and sisters. Her father was away again for six months in the winter of 1927/28, having acquired a *pied à terre* in London. However dismissive he might have been about commerce and the commercial art world he came to depend on both of them to make a living, and needed to live within reach of, if not actually in, the capital; he also needed to be somewhere less inconvenient for transporting large blocks of stone.

It often happens that a short-term move provides a breathing-space between two distinct periods of a person's life, and this was certainly true for Gill at Capel. In later years he looked back on his time there as his 'spiritual puberty' – a necessary stage in his development, but one he had now passed through and needed to leave behind him. Two months after his return from London in March 1928 he and Mary started house-hunting, and in October they moved to Pigotts, near High Wycombe.

FR WOODFORD, TOO, was preparing to move on. Brother Davies's return to Caldey in the summer of 1926 deprived him of regular

---

[691] A few weeks after Gill's first exploratory visit Fr Woodford reported another by 'Mr Pepler and son', evidently interested in buying a farm in the vicinity (Woodford Diary, entries for 8-10 March 1924): 'Pepler is not very keen about Plas Genevieve but favours a start being made from Chapel Farm.' The owner of the latter (a Mr Powell) was prepared to sell, but in the event David (or his father) decided he would do better to stay in Sussex.

monastic company, and he began to look forward to rejoining his brethren when they relocated to Prinknash, which he visited for the first time soon after Davies's profession. In November of that year he returned to the 'tin shelter' to give the Attwaters more space at Plas Genevieve: not surprisingly he was ill for most of December, and struggled to celebrate one Mass at Christmas instead of the usual three (and none thereafter until Epiphany).

It would have been this spell of illness which precipitated his removal for the whole of March and April 1927 to More Hall, near Stroud, home of Charles Henry Sharpe. Forty years earlier Sharpe had briefly served as 'abbey priest' at Llanthony,[692] and shortly before the 1914 War (during which he became a Roman Catholic) had attempted to found a community of his own,[693] in which Fr Joseph had tried his vocation before going to Caldey. More Hall was only a couple of miles from the TB sanatorium at Standish, and he had at least one consultation with a doctor there during his visit.

On 12 June 1928 he noted the departure of Donald Attwater, 'having gone to join his family in Barmouth'. A month later he himself left – for a sanatorium in Switzerland, where he remained until well into the following year.

---

[692] See Chapter 8

[693] Call p219

CHAPTER 14

RECENT HISTORY

Aᶠᵗᵉʳ ᵗʰᵉ Gɪʟʟˢ' ᴅᵉᵖᵃʳᵗᵘʳᵉ Brother David (his assumed surname now often hyphenated as 'Leycester-Lyne') and the Reverend Thomas Williams, now living in retirement at Plas Genevieve, conceived the idea of buying back the monastery.[694] Their plan was to run it as an Anglican retreat house dedicated to the memory of Fr Ignatius. They talked about forming a committee to raise the necessary funds, and approached Prior Benedict Steuart of Prinknash.

The feeling in his community was that it ought if possible to be occupied by Catholic religious, Fr Asaph reminding his brethren that Ignatius had only made it over to him on the understanding that it would continue to be used for monastic purposes. They might perhaps have considered the proposal if confronted by hard cash, but as Lyne and Williams were evidently unable even to come up with a deposit their approach was rejected.

Tʜʀᴏᴜɢʜ 1930 ᴀɴᴅ 1931 Fr Benedict made overtures to various communities and others who might have been able to use the property for 'Catholic religious purposes', the formula agreed at a Chapter meeting in September 1930. In this he had no more success than Abbot Aelred had had before him.

In spite of having moved elsewhere, the Gills were still strongly attached to the place. In February 1931 Mary Gill's mother died. From her share of the estate she would be able to buy it as a holiday home for use by family and friends, and duly put in an offer of £400, the

---

[694] Information in this section from the Chapter Minutes at Prinknash, and from the archives of the Chichester solicitors Raper & Co, preserved at the West Sussex Record Office (Raper Mss 490).

valuation provided by the Prinknash agent and previously offered by Lyne and Williams.

The only other party showing serious interest was the Youth Hostels' Association, recently launched in this country on the model of a German original. They would only have been able to take the property on a lease, which was felt to be unsatisfactory – not least because it was feared that anti-Catholic bias on the part of some of its patrons might bring discredit on the community.

In September 1931 it was agreed to accept Mary Gill's offer. The monastery, together with the church and nine and a half acres of land, changed hands on 23 November, which by a happy chance was the ninety-fourth anniversary of Ignatius's birth.

From the several letters which passed between vendor, purchaser and the Chichester solicitor acting for them both, we learn that Prinknash were to retain ownership of the reredos, organ and stalls in the abbey church. They would have liked to remove the seats from the north cloister chapel and the pitchpine partitions from the two dormitory wings as well (the latter perhaps to be re-erected for the same purpose in their new home), but Mrs Gill wanted them to remain.[695]

For the next few years the Gills and their friends visited the monastery on and off, Charlie Stones remaining in occupation as caretaker until his death in 1935. In the 1933 electoral register he was listed there with Eric and Mary, who had perhaps been staying when it was compiled the previous autumn.

THE FAMILY CIRCLE increased as the two younger daughters married and produced children. René Hague had been attracted to Joanna (usually known as Joan) from the time he first spied her tumbling out of Large's lorry amid animals and furniture in August 1924. The

---

[695] When Betty Gill's daughter Helen and her husband and family settled at the monastery in the early 1960s they increased the size of the bedrooms by removing alternate partitions and fixing them across the top, thus forming an internal ceiling.

following year he moved to London to an ill-paid job in a Catholic secondhand bookshop, but it was only when he took up the craft of printing that Eric began to view him favourably as a possible suitor. The couple married in November 1930, René going into partnership with his father-in-law and producing some twenty of his later works, as well as books for leading London publishers; these included the first edition of David Jones's In Parenthesis.[696] Jones had, as we have seen, been engaged for a while to Petra; in the same year she married Denis Tegetmeier, a former pupil of Gill's who like Hague had dipped his toe into the religious life (in his case with the Trappists).[697]

THE ABBEY CHURCH DISMANTLED

AN ACCOUNT OF A VISIT soon after the Gills' move to Pigotts was given by a local clergyman, Ivor M. Haines, in his collection of essays The Ox's Byre (Mowbray 1941). Charlie Stones showed him round both monastery and church, which presented a sorry sight:

> Through the broken windows of the chapel the wind and rain beat in upon a sanctuary once glorious with the light and beauty of Catholic devotion. A statue, removed from its niche, still stood upon the high altar; beneath, the tabernacle stood, painfully vacant, and behind, huddled in inglorious confusion, still stood six brass candlesticks. The white carvings on the altar were turning green with damp and pieces of broken masonry strewed the floor of what was once a house of beauty of the Benedictine monks of Anglican Llanthony.

---

[696] The firm of Hague & Gill ran from 1930 until 1956, with a break during the war years. At first it operated in the workshops at Pigotts, then at premises in High Wycombe. In the early 1960s the Hagues moved to County Cork, where René was occupied by translating the works of Teilhard de Chardin and interpreting those of his lifelong friend David Jones. His last published book was Dai Greatcoat, published shortly before his own and Joan's deaths in 1980.

[697] Tegetmeier's career as a graphic artist included drawing out designs for Laurie Cribb. Like Jones he left evidence of his occupation at the monastery – in his case a humorous mural at the other end of the south cloister.

The chapel is closed now to all but the persistent visitor for fear of falling masonry. The glorious oak stalls still adorn the choir and add their charm to the pathetic beauty of its faded loveliness. But over all now brooded an almost eerie silence, rebuked only by a jar of primroses on the solitary tomb.

From that sanctuary where [Ignatius's] body lies, we passed at last out into the quiet garden that slopes down from the chapel. A lilac tree, a berberis, a japonica, still bravely held their own among the wild intruders of another day. Reluctantly we bade farewell to our kindly janitor and turned down the rough road Ignatius so often trod; but not quite farewell till we had passed the white statue of Our Lady at the gate.

In one of his letters to Mary Gill Fr Steuart mentioned that he was in correspondence with 'a clergyman' who was interested in buying the reredos. In fact it was sold soon afterwards to Ignatius's former disciple Alfred Field, who presented it to the newly completed church of Ss Julius & Aaron (otherwise St Julian) in Newport. In the summer of 1932 it was taken down stone by stone and re-erected at St Julian's by volunteer labour from the parish,[698] the rededication being performed by Bishop Timothy Rees of Llandaff on 23 September.

Other more portable items were disposed of piecemeal. In 1929 a number of them were acquired by Dorian Herbert, whose earlier visits to the monastery have been noted. A colourful character, originally from the St Julian's area of Newport, he was now living at Cae Kenfy Lodge, Abergavenny, and working as a freelance journalist; he also served for a time as a local councillor. In 1937 he was consecrated 'Bishop of Caerleon' by the *soi-disant* 'Primate of the Orthodox-Keltic

---

[698] All except for a couple of tiny pinnacles, which the roof of its new home was too low to accommodate. A small disc cut from one of them was used in 2013 by the sculptor Philip Chatfield to represent the host in a representation of the 'miraculous monstrance', one of a series of carvings at Pluscarden Abbey, Morayshire, commemorating that community's descent from Caldey and (through Asaph) New Llanthony.

Church of the British Commonwealth of Nations',[699] and from his Abergavenny home presided over a miniscule body to which he gave the name 'Jesuene' or 'Free Orthodox-Catholic' church. Emblazoned on his writing paper was its motto 'Agnostic': subscription to the articles of the Creed was optional, although a great deal was made of its claim to episcopal succession stretching back to St Peter.[700]

In his outhouse chapel pride of place was given to the three-foot high jewelled tabernacle and the life-size crucifix which had dominated the public portion of the abbey church. Favoured visitors were also able to view two of the massive high altar candlesticks complete with stubs of candles surviving from monastic days, together with a statue of St David with authentic 'Celtic' tonsure and part of the organ.[701] Towards the end of his life Herbert returned to his native Newport, telling Arthur Calder-Marshall and others that he had given orders for all his 'Ignatiana' to be shipped out into the Bristol Channel after his death and dumped overboard; in the event a number of the items were taken into storage by the local museum.[702]

Some – perhaps most – of the abbey church vestments had been sold off at the auction in 1915. On his 1924 visit Bertie Cannell learned that '[c]hasubles and copes had been sold to farmers who had cut

---

[699] BAL p294

[700] Abergavenny Chronicle, 6 August 1943: report headed 'Consecration of a Bishop/Picturesque Ceremony at Abergavenny'. As noted earlier, through Vilatte Ignatius had made the same claim.

[701] In a letter to the Reverend F.H. Mountney dated 16 July 1958 the then curate of Ss Julius & Aaron (the Reverend Donald Francis) reported having both seen and heard it when he paid a pastoral call on Herbert. He also passed on the news that 'the "Bishop"' had said he would be prepared to sell the tabernacle for £100, 'but I am hoping he will prove more generous'.

[702] Information from Abergavenny Chronicle, 1 May 1942 ('Ignatius Redivivus/ Llanthony Atmosphere at Abergavenny'), Enthusiast p288 and personal knowledge. Herbert died at Barnwood House, a private mental institution on the outskirts of Gloucester, on 17 December 1965.

them up and had been made into patchwork quilts for their beds'.[703] A few were taken to Caldey; a cope at Prinknash (recently remade) is said to incorporate the hood from one originally at Llanthony.

At that time the organ may have been 'rotting with water',[704] but this didn't prevent the Caldey community trying to find a buyer for it. On 23 September 1926 Fr Woodford noted in his diary that advertisements had been placed in the Western Mail and British Weekly and that so far there had been three expressions of interest, although none of them seems to have been followed up. After his community's move to Prinknash some of the timber pedal pipes were cut up to provide shelving in the scullery, and when they extended their domestic chapel into the adjacent Great Hall the monks brought a number of stalls from Llanthony to fill the additional space. These had been 'bolted to the organ', and their removal had caused 'damage to the organ but not to the stalls'. By this time (August 1933) its internal workings would have been so riddled with damp as to be beyond repair; two years earlier Fr Steuart had judged it 'past use', telling Mary Gill that he would gladly arrange for its disposal.[705]

Photographs taken in November 1935[706] show the church roof damaged but still largely in place. It must have been soon after this that the decision was made abandon it altogether and let nature take its course.

---

[703] FMTB p99

[704] ibid p98

[705] Letter dated 9 October 1931. Information about the reuse of the pedal pipes from the Prinknash archives, and about the salvage of the stalls from Baker op cit p67. In the ms draft of his memoir Brother David put it thus: 'Regarding the church all the beautiful oak stalls were taken away and the glorious organ simply torn to pieces, the pipes strewn in all directions,' but this information was omitted from his final typed version.

[706] In a newspaper cutting in the Barclay Album

'CAPEL-Y-FFIN BOARDING SCHOOL'

IN SEPTEMBER 1934 David Pepler died of cancer at the age of 28, leaving Betty with five children under seven years of age. At first they went to live with her parents at Pigotts, from where Betty attended a course at the Battersea School of Domestic Science; the next year they returned to her old home at Capel-y-ffin, unoccupied since Charlie Stones's death some months earlier.

With them went Mary (May) Reeves, a Lancashire schoolteacher in her middle forties: Eric had begun an affair with her while working on a sculpture in Morecambe in 1933 and brought her south to join the household at Pigotts. The Reeveses were an Irish Catholic family settled in Preston, where her father Joseph had also been a teacher; they became acquainted through her brother Fr John Baptist, one of Gill's many Dominican friends. May's two decades and more of teaching experience made her the obvious person to take the lead in the next attempt to find a use for the building: a Catholic school for girls, the older Pepler children providing a ready-made nucleus of pupils.

Miss Reeves was remembered by someone she had taught in Lancashire as having 'brought a breath of fresh air' into the classroom, introducing 'such...new subjects [as] art and design' and 'arranging memorable charabanc trips to Liverpool'.[707] She would certainly have been in sympathy with Gill's own educational theories, some of which were expressed in a letter to Denis Tegetmeier written a few months before the school opened its doors.[708] This was at the beginning of Gill's four-year collaboration with Neville Gorton, the unusually enlightened headmaster of Blundell's, a middle-ranking public school in Devon, culminating in the construction by the boys themselves of a freestanding stone altar with carved panels on all four vertical faces.[709]

---

[707] Account on internet at http://www.longridgenews.co.uk/news/local/the-sculptor-and-the-village-schoolmistress-1-1865075 accessed 23 October 2015.

[708] Dated 7 November 1934 (Eric Gill, Letters p 310f)

[709] The altar had the effect of bringing to life the school's rather pedestrian

In his letter Gill lamented that conventional schooling − of the '[i]ntellect,...trained almost entirely by books', and the '[w]ill,...trained almost entirely by games' − left little room for development in the world of 'things' and their making. This was regrettable because '[m]aking things is a large part of man's life − any man's', and 'reality [is only] knowable by experience of it'. The curriculum of the new school attempted to redress the balance, including as it did instruction in drawing, by Gill himself; spinning and weaving, by his daughter Petra; and church plainchant, by Fr Bernard McElligott, an Ampleforth monk and expert in the subject who at the time was acting as chaplain at Pigotts.[710]

A single-sheet prospectus issued in 1937 describes the buildings as 'admirably adapted to school use', having 'class rooms, recreation room, dining hall, library and domestic quarters on the ground floor, with dormitories and bathrooms on the first floor'. Girls were accepted from '5 years & upwards', although at ten or eleven they could be 'prepared for entrance examinations for senior schools if desired'. 'A few boys' could be also be accommodated up to that age.

The 'object' of the school was said to be to 'provide a good education and training for domestic and family life', and among the subjects taught were 'gardening and dairy work; cooking and all branches of housewifery, including the keeping of household accounts; simple arithmetic and geometry' and such practical skills

---

neo-Gothic chapel, in which the future Abbot Aelred Carlyle would have been a youthful worshipper when it was newly built in the 1880s. The introduction of the new altar caused outrage among conservative factions in the Blundell's establishment, who succeeded during the next headmastership in having it banished. It was taken to Coventry, of which city Gorton had become bishop, and installed in a home for unmarried mothers. When in the early 1990s this originally penitential institution was being converted into a 'family centre' the altar was sold back to the school for a five-figure sum and restored to its original position.

[710] Fiona MacCarthy took these details from the original illustrated prospectus, of which I also once saw a copy. Dr Peter Davies kindly gave me sight of the 1937 version.

as spinning, weaving, needlework and elementary first aid, with carpentry and 'stone work' for the boys. Handwriting and drawing were taught in connection with history, geography, 'nature-study' (in quotes) and what were rather vaguely referred to as 'other subjects'. Inclusive fees were £20 a term or £15 for weekly boarders, and because the food 'consist[ed] to a large extent of produce from the estate' and the pupils 'assist[ed] in its production' overheads were kept to a minimum. The chapel was mentioned, but there was not, by this time, any reference to the school having a Catholic affiliation: reading between the lines one has the impression that Miss Reeves and Mrs Pepler were fairly desperate to attract admissions.

Sadly 'Capel-y-ffin Boarding School' (by which name the monastery was listed in the 1937 electoral register) failed to survive beyond that year. May Reeves returned to Pigotts, where she lived in a caravan and operated an informal day school for the resident Gill grandchildren and others. Betty remained at the monastery, her children either following 'Auntie May' into her new enterprise or going to more conventional schools elsewhere.

SHRINES OLD AND NEW

AT A TIME WHEN relations between Anglicans and Roman Catholics are generally good, even if the measure of agreement required for intercommunion proves elusive, one has to remember that things were not ever thus. The papal condemnation of her orders in 1896 gave new impetus to Roman triumphalism vis-à-vis the Church of England and her overseas connections. Particular scorn was reserved for Anglo-Catholics (the term often surrounded by 'scare quotes' to emphasise their allegedly spurious claim to catholicity): the closer the approximation of their outward forms to that of the Roman Church, the greater the abhorrence in which they were held for peddling 'empty shams' in place of genuine Catholic sacraments. By the same token Anglo-Catholics were understandably defensive towards the claims of what some of them termed the 'Italian Mission'.

Catholic chauvinism may be one explanation for Gill's intolerance of Ignatian devotees wanting to visit the monastery; another, of course, was a wish for domestic peace and privacy.[711] One relic of monastic days whose removal must have given him particular satisfaction was the Apparitions statue, for which a new home was found at the church of All Saints, Hereford. The initiative for this – and for the erection of an alternative memorial, on 'neutral' ground the other side of the monastery lane – was taken by the Reverend John Windle, curate of All Saints between 1934 and 1941. Fr Windle had a great devotion to Ignatius, which may have been fuelled by local memories: the former Brother Dunstan (W.M. Magrath) had ended his days occupying the same post two decades earlier, and some years before that the Ulett family had lived only a stone's throw from the church.

At All Saints the statue was set up on the south side of the nave, its white marble surface relieved by overpainting in suitable colours. It seemed to have a power of its own: according to a report in the church's Parish Paper a blind visitor had had to turn away because the 'radiance' from it was causing him discomfort.[712]

The site for the new memorial at Capel-y-ffin was given by Thomas Williams of Plas Genevieve, and the memorial itself by Hilda and Irene Ewens, daughters of Ignatius's sister Harriet. A letter to Irene from William Leycester Lyne/Brother David (known to the two sisters as 'Uncle Dewi' although in fact their first cousin by adoption) was evidently written when Mr Williams first made his offer:

---

[711] 'Among the lettering jobs that Laurie Cribb did for me at Capel was the painting of a lot of notice boards – to warn off the hundreds of visitors who persisted in coming to see the monastery and Father Ignatius's grave in the big church. You can't imagine, unless you're one yourself, their impudence. They would walk in without asking and you would find them wandering in and out of your bedrooms. And when you asked them what...they were doing, they would say: Can we see a monk?' (Eric Gill, *Autobiography* p219).

[712] In Barclay album

Do write a nice little note by return if possible to thank old Williams for offering you the land: this is most essential. He is a queer old stick; but all right if taken the right way.... In my opinion: now old Williams has offered you the piece of land which belonged to the monastery: (just opposite the Holy Bush: only the lane between it [and the Bush]). It is the very ideal, and only, place to put it. It will be seen and admired by hundreds: and the one and only indication that your dear Uncle Leycester ever lived there or even owned the Monastery.[713]

The enclosure for the memorial was much the same size as the one formerly occupied by the Apparitions statue, separated from the surrounding farmland by iron railings, and approached from the lane by a flight of concrete steps let into the bank. It took the form of a wayside Calvary, with the inscription PEACE TO THE WAYFARER THROUGH THE BLOOD OF JESUS engraved on its canopy, and a photograph of Ignatius fixed at the rear. Below the corpus a small plaque acknowledged that it had been erected in his memory by his Ewens nieces, and at the foot of the steps the cryptic inscription THE BURNING BUSH OPPOSITE connected the memorial with the events of 1880, of which this was now the only indication.

The Calvary was dedicated by Fr Windle on 30 August 1936, which that year fell on a Sunday. A year earlier his parish had organised a modest pilgrimage, the first public observance of the Apparitions feast for nearly three decades, when about fifty people took part. However, the dedication service attracted some fifteen hundred, and there was a good turnout for a similar celebration in 1937, the centenary year of Fr Ignatius's birth. On the latter occasion the sermon was preached by Dom Augustine Morris of Nashdom Abbey, a community which originated with the little group of Caldey monks who remained Anglicans when the majority of their brethren converted to Rome. He

---

[713] Letter dated 'March 23' (year not stated) in Abergavenny collection, ref A1993.139.11.6. Other information in this section is either from contemporary issues of the Hereford Times or from the author's own recollections.

paid generous tribute to Ignatius as a 'pioneer of the Anglican monastic movement...by whose suffering and insecurity we, the monks of today, have obtained security and happiness within the body of the Church'.

Picture 42: Dedication of the memorial Calvary, 30 August 1936. Fr Windle on right in cope and biretta; the elderly Brother David in the background immediately behind the right-hand gatepost.

Further pilgrimages took place in 1938 and 1939, and although 'embellished with the fullest Anglo-Catholic ritual' their format was very simple. From Capel-y-ffin church the participants walked in procession to the Calvary, assembling in the field behind it. Three hymns were sung (the usual ones were *Firmly I believe and truly*, *Ye who own the faith of Jesus* and *Jesu, Lover of my soul*), interspersed with prayers and an address. Brother David attended in his cassock and the Ewens sisters in Salvation Army uniform: like their uncle Leycester they combined Anglo-Catholic sacramentalism with a taste for the evangelical hot Gospel. Irene (always the dominant sister) had attained the rank of Sergeant, and at each of the pre-war pilgrimages was accompanied by a party of fellow-Salvationists, the official service being followed by an informal evangelical one at which she presided from a portable harmonium.

With the outbreak of hostilities Fr Windle went off to serve as a naval chaplain, and organised pilgrimages were suspended for the duration. On his return to civilian life he was appointed to the parish of Llangrove, on the Herefordshire/Monmouthshire border a few miles north of Monmouth, and would spend the rest of his active life here and in the adjacent parish of Welsh Newton.

FR ASAPH

IN FR ASAPH'S FAMILY there was a history of mental instability. Entries in Wilfrid Upson's Caldey diaries suggest that he had had difficulties of this kind even before the move to Prinknash; in the 1930s he became progressively worse. When as legal owner of the Capel-y-ffin property he was asked to give his consent to the sale to Mary Gill he was said to be 'unwell' and 'unable to attend to business', so several days elapsed before he could be prevailed upon to sign the relevant document; it has been suggested that his subsequent deterioration was a direct result of having done so. To him the secularisation of the monastery was an act of sacrilege, and if he was aware of the fact it can't have helped that Brother David regarded him as a 'traitor' for letting it happen.

Eventually he was admitted to the local mental hospital. When Aelred Carlyle came back from Canada to visit his former community in 1937 he went to see him, his diary entry for 5 April that year including this report:

> I had one of the sadest [sic] experiences of my life today. Poor dear old Fr Asaph last monk of Llanthony has been gradually getting worse mentally & after doing all that was possible Fr Prior [Benedict Steuart] had to take him to the County Mental Hospital. There I saw him yesterday — in secular clothes — in abject misery & bewilderment of mind. It was heart-breaking to try to talk to him. Three of his family were lunatics

and his brother killed himself and sister drowned herself. So the poor thing must be shut up: & I can only pray God that his life of misery is not prolonged. He was in a pitiful state at seeing me, but resented Frs Prior & Raphael [Davies] going over. I could do nothing to make any impression on his poor distracted mind & I left him [at] the door sadly waving to me.

Happily his state of 'abject misery' didn't go on for too long. In 1947 he was one of a group from Prinknash sent to renew the mediaeval foundation at Pluscarden, near Elgin. Having entered the cloister at Llanthony forty-nine years earlier he had been a monk longer than any of his confreres, and at the age of 72 set to work to equip the house with electric light and initiate the manufacture of stained glass. His death on 24 February 1960 was the first in the new community, and his burial the first in its new cemetery.

THE GUEST HOUSE

IN THE SUMMER OF 1938 Betty Gill married Harley Williams, who had been working as a psychiatric nurse in Abergavenny, and over the next few years she had three more children. With the growing popularity of country holidays they decided to run the monastery as a guest house. An April 1940 letter from her father to his friend Desmond Chute[714] mentions her current pregnancy and reports that the new venture seemed 'able to keep going' despite wartime shortages, and that 'good numbers' were expected that summer.

The crucial factor in its success was Betty's skill in managing both kitchen and farmyard, together with Harley's labours in the vegetable garden below the now roofless church, laid out by Philip and Serene seventy years before. Milk, butter and eggs were never in short supply, and meat from their own pigs and chickens was an occasional extra; home-made wine also made a regular appearance (certainly for the family).

---

[714] Eric Gill, *Letters* pp446ff

Picture 43: Family group c1950. Betty (standing second left) and her second husband Harley Williams (standing right), with six of her eight children: Paul, Martin and Helen Pepler; Mary, Eric and Jessica Williams.

A vivid picture of the life is given in Jennifer Holloway's memoir of her husband Edgar, *Against the Odds*.[715] Then a young artist struggling to make his way in the world, Edgar paid his first visit at the beginning of 1943. The door was opened by 25-year-old Daisy Monica Hawkins, the last of Eric Gill's resident models, sent there by Mary Gill to help with the house and children in exchange for free board and lodging and occasional tips from guests. The two young people fell in love and were married that summer, spending much of their early married life in and around Capel.

---

[715] Bristol; Sansom and Company 2014. Edgar Holloway and Jennifer Boxall were married in 1984 after the deaths of Daisy Monica and her first husband Ronald.

It was the height of the season when they returned from honeymoon and she [Daisy Monica] was popular with guests, in particular the young Dominican postulants who regularly came for supervised holidays at the Monastery. She used to serve them drinks in the evening when they came back down to play cards after they were supposed to be in bed.... Sometimes the guesthouse was so full that there was no place for Edgar and Monica to sleep, and they had to go down to Chapel Farm; it had not been unknown for Daisy to sleep in a tent on the drying green.... Life was hit and miss, and everything was subservient to the guests. So, sometimes lunch was not forthcoming, especially when Betty had disappeared and forgotten everything, and evenings were one long washing-up session, in which Edgar was involved, after which supper was perhaps just a poached egg eaten at midnight.[716]

As well as the holiday visitors there were long-term residents. One of the later ones, George Thomas, had been traumatised by his war experiences and combined letter-cutting (which he taught himself) with work as the local rabbit catcher; the inscription LABORARE EST ORARE above the fireplace in Fr Ignatius's erstwhile sitting room is an example of his work. With his hospital experience Harley was able from time to time to offer accommodation and care to mental patients, which added to the already interesting mix of people passing through the house in these years.

After Eric Gill's death in November 1940 Dr Flood who had been chaplain at Pigotts spent some years at Capel. He was given the room at the north end of the west cloister (originally the sanctuary of Ignatius's temporary chapel, then variously acolytes' playroom and Sister Janet's monastery toehold; it had a door opening directly to the chapel entrance), and took his meals apart from the family

---

[716] Holloway op cit p64. I am grateful to Mrs Holloway and her publishers for permission to include this and the quotation below, and to Mary Griffiths and the late Helen Davies for sharing their memories of this period.

and paying guests in the adjacent sitting room. This was the larger part of the three-bay monastic refectory, the remainder having been added to the otherwise undersized kitchen.

Betty and Harley's daughter Mary Griffiths recalls how when her brothers or visiting cousins were detailed to serve the Doctor's daily Mass they had first to cajole him out of bed, his heavy slumbers having been induced as much by the bottle as by normal tiredness (doubtless to keep the cold at bay, although a primitive form of central heating had been installed before the school was begun, as well as additional toilet facilities). Eventually he moved to Australia, and his place was taken by a Fr Prince, whose poor health prevented him undertaking normal parish work.

In 1943 'Old Williams' (nicknamed 'Parson Billy' by his neighbours) turned eighty. He was a slightly sinister figure, dressed in black from top to toe and with shoulder-length silver hair. Soon after arriving in the valley during the 1914-18 War he had lost his much younger wife, and it was this which led to his involvement in the then fashionable cult of spiritualism. For some years in the 1930s he had as his companion at Plas Genevieve a lady named Emma Barclay, whose scrapbook of photographs and press cuttings has provided some of the information for this chapter; she died in 1941. His long-term housekeeper, Florence Price, also lived in the house, but when she moved away he was left on his own.

Mrs Griffiths has vivid memories of the bitter winter of 1947, when Plas Genevieve froze up and her parents sheltered the elderly clergyman at the monastery, where he joined Dr Flood for meals in the sitting room. When the thaw came instead of returning to Plas Genevieve he moved to another property he owned nearer the bright lights of Abergavenny, selling the house to Mary Gill; it was thus united once more with the monastery, and once more renamed The Grange.

The guest house was noted for its good and plentiful food, but the level of comfort was rather more basic. In 1949 Betty and Harley decided to resuscitate the idea of running it as a youth hostel. With overflow accommodation at The Grange they could take fifty visitors at a time; they also hoped that by getting their customers to do the domestic chores they would save the expense of hired help. Unfortunately the low profit margin left nothing for maintenance and repairs, so after two years it was turned back into a (relatively) conventional guest house.

CHANGES AT MAES-Y-FFIN

BROTHER DAVID DIED on 15 January 1941, the same day as his mother-in-law Mrs Magrath thirty-four years earlier. On one of his regular walks in the monastery lane he suffered a fatal heart attack, as Jennifer Holloway reports:

> Then there was the elderly member of Father Ignatius's community who collapsed in the lane on a freezing winter night. By the time he was found he was frozen stiff. The police were informed and they said he should be left in the snow until the undertakers could arrive. When they eventually came, they found it impossible to get the corpse into the coffin: as they settled the head in, the feet came shooting up; and when they pushed in the feet, the head sprang up.[717]

It was over a week before the ground unfroze sufficiently for a grave to be dug in the churchyard, so the ever-hospitable Betty made the north cloister chapel available for his lying in state.

His wife Thomasina survived him by barely three months. Their son Lessie was living in Bristol, and married later that year; he himself died in 1957 and was buried at Capel-y-ffin, his widow moving to

---

[717] ibid pp65f. One version of this story identifies the person in question as the 'Infant Samuel', i.e. John Henry Docking, but his death in America is well documented (see Appendix 2). The confusion between them doubtless stems from the fact that like him Brother David was a childhood protégé of Fr Ignatius.

Sussex and remarrying. In 1937 Josephine had married Harry York, who moved in with her at Maes-y-ffin. They had no children, but various relations and family friends shared the house with them. Among these were Sena's sister Lucy Magrath (died 1945) and her friend Jenefried Bain (died 1955), both of whom are also buried in the churchyard.

Another was the one-time Fr Michael OSB, William Marriott Dodson. As a little girl Mary Griffiths often encountered him walking in the lanes – a much more approachable figure than 'Parson Billy', who also took his exercise that way, and who had a profound dislike of children as well as a pathological hatred of soap and water. 'Mr Dodson' wore check plus-fours, had an interesting double-faced pocket-watch and a ready supply of mint humbugs which he was happy to share. After Ignatius's death he had lived in lodgings at Bettws-y-Coed and made a modest name for himself as a photographer; many of the publicity postcards from the Llanthony community's later years were his work.[718] He died in 1955 at Haverfordwest.

Josephine died in 1966. The house was sold, and the contents, much of which had come from the monastery, dispersed.

TWO BUNGALOWS

THE FORMER SCHOOLROOM at the foot of the lane ('The Bungalow') formed part of the Plas Genevieve property. For some time it served as an *ad hoc* village hall, but with the addition of extra rooms was converted to domestic use and over the years had various occupants. Edgar and Daisy Holloway lived there for a

---

[718] His photographs provided the illustrations for Emily Hewlett Edwards's *Castles and Strongholds of Pembrokeshire* (Tenby 1909). He may also have spent time in London: an undated picture postcard (probably from the 1920s: a whimsical composition showing a very small boy and a very large dog engaged in an unequal seesaw, probably his own work) apparently to Thomasina from 'W.M.D.' expresses pleasure at her impending visit to the capital with her husband, and hopes they will join him for lunch at 'Tussauds Café Baker St' (Abergavenny collection, ref A2010.86.23).

couple of years in the late 1940s; when the land on which it had been built was sold to the Georges at Boxbush it became home to Cliff George and his wife Violet (née Lewis), who for many years was a regular at the pilgrimage.[719]

The other bungalow, St David's, was built by the Ewens sisters half a mile up the valley from the monastery, just opposite the turning to the Watkins's farm Talsarn. Their main residence was in Brighton (Leycester Cottage, 13 Harrington Road), but when at Capel-y-ffin they were sometimes seen out and about in their Salvation Army bonnets.

After the war it was occupied by a group of would-be monastic restorers from the demi-monde of *episcopi vagantes* who had formed the idea that Mary Gill might be prepared to sell them the monastery, although it wasn't clear how they intended to pay for it. It is said that they were 'always trying to get a foot in the door', and that Harley once had to get police help to eject them. Among them was Ernest Odell Cope, the brewery worker from Burton on Trent who claimed to have been a monk at Llanthony at the time of its absorption by Caldey and later to have received episcopal orders; these he passed on to William Corke, the little group's leader, at a ceremony in the bungalow on 1 January 1948.

Corke spent much of his life in prison, so was never able to put his ambitions as a monastic founder into more than temporary effect.[720] For a short time the bungalow was run as an extremely small and probably unofficial youth hostel, either soon before or soon after the attempt to do the same at the monastery. The then occupant was a former schoolmaster named Turton, who is remembered for the noxious smell of his herbal tobacco and for the fact that he went about in a cassock, although not apparently a clergyman. Several years

---

[719] Violet died in April 2016, as this book was going to press.

[720] See BAL pp394-98 and *Enthusiast* pp288ff for fuller details of this monastic episode and Corke's later career.

later it was rented as a holiday retreat by the photographer Oswald (Ozzie) Jones, a member of the literary and artistic set with which Fr Brocard Sewell was involved at the time of his exile (see below). Among other local events he chronicled most of the pilgrimages in the 1970s and early 1980s, many of the photographs being preserved in the Abergavenny museum.

THE MONASTERY FOR SALE?[721]

BETTY WILLIAMS DIED in March 1956, at the age of fifty. Her second daughter Jane was then in her early twenties and had recently married Felix Cribb, son of Laurie, and for the next couple of years they kept the guest house going. When they moved away it was managed by Joyce Newport, remembered by Betty's grandchildren as a rather formidable figure preferring dogs and horses to human beings. She was an Anglican, a friend of Brother David's daughter Josephine, and like her a worshipper at little St Mary's church in Capel-y-ffin. It would have been in her time that the north cloister chapel was used for an Anglican Requiem Mass on 16 October 1958, the fiftieth anniversary of Fr Ignatius's death.

The celebrant was the Reverend F.H. Mountney, who had become Vicar of All Saints, Hereford (and therefore guardian of the Apparitions statue) two years earlier. He and his head server Mr Leonard Croker spent the preceding night in the former monastic cells, together with two prominent Anglo-Catholic laymen, Messrs Sam Gurney and Ivor Bulmer-Thomas. The local incumbent (the Reverend T.E. Williams, Rector of Llanigon) had given guarded approval and expressed interest in attending, although in the event he sent his apologies.

For the Roman Catholic authorities the celebration would have been gravely irregular, but they were unlikely to have been aware of it.

---

[721] Information here and in the following sections mainly from letters received by Fr Mountney from various correspondents (Abergavenny collection ref A2010.86.19)

There was, however, one mitigating circumstance. Since Betty's death the guest house had been losing support, and as most of her children were now settled elsewhere[722] their grandmother Mary Gill was now seriously considering selling the property. A letter in the Church Times[723] from Fr Mountney expressed the hope that an Anglican community would come forward and restore the monastery to its original use; at the same time he wrote individually to various religious superiors asking whether they would be prepared to take it on. As it happened none of them was able to do so – a similar situation to Abbot Aelred's unsuccessful attempt to find new occupants forty years earlier, and more recently to Prior Benedict Steuart's.

Fr Mountney also wrote to the local bishop (Glyn Simon, of Swansea and Brecon), who although sympathetic towards 'any practical scheme that [might] appear for preserving the site for the [Anglican] Church' could not see his way to involving his diocese financially. He might have been prepared to consider a joint effort with the neighbouring diocese of Monmouth, but its bishop (Edwin Morris) had declared himself 'dead against' such a project.

THE PILGRIMAGE RESUMED

WITH FR WINDLE'S RETURN from the war the annual pilgrimage was once again revived. For several years what was advertised as an 'Anglo-Catholic Pilgrimage' was organised on lines similar to those of the 1930s. The Hereford Times seems to have reported on the event only four times (in 1955, 1957, 1960 and 1961), although on the last occasion it was stated to have been the twentieth pilgrimage since 1935.

---

[722] Except for Mary (born 1939), the eldest of her children with Harley Williams. She married David (Dai) Griffiths, with whom for many years she ran The Grange as a pony trekking centre – as since his death in 2002 she has continued to do, in collaboration with her daughter Jessica.

[723] Issue of 3 May 1957. It prompted an enquiry as to the asking price from Hilda, the surviving Ewens sister, whose death lay just seven weeks ahead – was she thinking of buying it back?

Numbers were now significantly lower, with a reported attendance of around eighty in 1960 but (to judge from the accompanying photograph) rather fewer the following year, when the visiting preacher was Dr Glyn Simon, now Bishop of Llandaff. Many of the pilgrims came from All Saints, Hereford, Fr Mountney playing a major part in the organisation. In both 1957 and 1958 – and perhaps also in other years – the day began with High Mass at St David's Church, Llanthony. The celebrant was the Reverend Donald Francis, assistant priest of Ss Julius and Aaron, Newport, who also brought a coachload of parishioners; following strict Anglican practice Holy Communion was administered only to those who had given their names in advance, and who like Fr Francis would have been fasting from midnight. [724]

After Mass the able-bodied walked in procession to Capel-y-ffin, saying the Rosary; Fr Mountney's son Michael was ten years old in 1957, and remembers taking part in the walk. In the afternoon Vespers of Our Lady was sung in the little church at Capel-y-ffin (the Vicar had stipulated 'no incense', worried that low church nostrils might be offended if it hung in the air overnight), after which the pilgrims processed to the Abbot's Meadow for the customary short service and sermon. The preacher in 1955 was Canon E.P. Knight, Vicar of Monmouth; in 1957 it was Dom Boniface Nielsen of Nashdom Abbey, and in 1960 Fr Mountney's current curate, the Reverend Francis Hodges. After a final De Profundis at the Founder's grave the pilgrimage ended with a sit-down tea in the guest house refectory.

The pilgrimages in this era seem all to have been on a Saturday in early September, although Fr Windle always made a private visit to the scene of the Apparitions on the proper day, 30 August. In his younger days this was either by bicycle or by train from Hereford to Hay and thence on a hired horse; later in life, crippled by arthritis, he would make the journey by moped, his walking sticks strapped to the luggage carrier.

---

[724] A practice he kept up long after its abandonment by the majority of western Christians.

A FAMILY HOME

MARY GILL SURVIVED her daughter Betty by five years, dying in February 1961. The monastery having failed to sell she left it to her eldest granddaughter Helen, married since 1951 to Wilfred Davies, then serving with the Royal Air Force. On his retirement in 1962 they came to live in the east wing; Helen's brother Paul and his wife Marion were already established on the opposite side of the cloister garth.

Both couples had large families, and through the next two decades the gloomy pitchpine corridors echoed to the sounds of children at play, gradually giving way to those of adolescent enthusiasm for Bob Dylan and the Beatles. Not much change occurred when in 1968 Paul and Marion moved to their own house at Gilwern and the west wing was converted into two holiday flats: many of the visitors had children who joined those of the household for table tennis in the 'long room' (originally the Bible Cloister, more recently the guest house refectory) or badminton on the drying green, site of the old convent. In the holidays the former monks' cells were often filled to capacity with friends and relations. At such times the tables in the long living room (the one-time sacristy and community room, knocked into one) were placed end to end and chairs brought from upstairs, as many as twenty sitting down to meals. Home-made wine was a staple accompaniment as it had been in Betty's day, and Wilf (who had now embarked on a fruitful second career as Chief Warden in the local National Park) brewed beer in industrial quantities. And although home-reared cows and pigs were just a memory the kitchen garden under his care was as productive as ever.

In the early 1960s the weight of the tiles on the roof of the north cloister chapel caused it to collapse, and a new roof of corrugated asbestos was laid. Many of those who came to stay in the flats were practising Catholics, so in the holiday season Mass was celebrated most Sundays. Unless a priest was staying in the house this would be at the challenging hour (for the young) of 7.30am, Fr Healy from Hay-on-Wye making the double journey before his parish service later in the morning.

THE TRUST

THE PRIEST MOST OFTEN in residence at this time was the Carmelite friar Brocard (Michael) Sewell. His varied and interesting career had included a spell working for Hilary Pepler at the St Dominic's Press in the 1930s,[725] and he was a longstanding friend of the Pepler and Davies families. His longest continuous stay was from August 1968 to August 1969, in 'willing exile' from a house of his order in the Roman Catholic diocese of Southwark, its bishop having taken exception to his published views on the limits of papal authority.[726] He would return for weeks at a time each year through the following decade, during which he held academic posts in Canada.

In the wake of the Vatican Council relationships between the churches were growing more harmonious, and Fr Brocard was keen that Catholics and Anglicans should co-operate in the repair and maintenance of the ruined abbey church. As far back as 1960 (in a leaflet outlining the history of the monastery) he had mentioned it was hoped 'soon to restore' Ignatius's grave and its surroundings, and more recently he and Wilf Davies had been discussing with Fr Mountney the possibility of forming an ecumenical trust to own and maintain the ruins.

---

[725] A very few books from the middle of that decade bear the imprint 'Pepler & Sewell'.

[726] 'A Willing Exile' is the title of the relevant chapter of Fr Brocard's autobiography *The Habit of a Lifetime* (Tabb House 1992). On 6 August 1968 a letter had appeared over his signature in *The Times* suggesting that Paul VI might appropriately resign from the Roman see. The question at issue was the Church's teaching concerning the morality or otherwise of artificial means of birth control, on which the Pope had gone against the conclusions of the commission set up to advise him by restating in his encyclical *Humanae Vitae* the widely ignored prohibition of such practices. Fr Brocard devoted his enforced sabbatical to the composition of an elegant critique of papal authority as currently exercised, published in 1970 under the title *The Vatican Oracle*. An early visit had coincided with at least one of the pre-war pilgrimages: in the 1970s he recalled the presence of the 'dignified figure' at the service in the meadow of the elderly Brother David, as well as of the Ewens sisters in their Salvation Army uniform.

This came into being on 10 July 1967. The new body was named The Father Ignatius Memorial Trust, and its principal aim was to be the preservation of the Founder's tomb, together with that of the church as a 'place of religious worship'. At first there were just three Trustees, Fathers Sewell and Mountney and Wilfred Davies, who served as Secretary for the Trust's first twenty-five years of existence. The deed of foundation emphasised that the church was to be made available for pilgrimages and visits by 'Christians of all denominations', although an early Newsletter (no 2, dated November 1970) included the necessary qualification that the holding of services in it was 'at the discretion of the Trustees'.

Over the years the vaulted ceiling and masonry from the upper parts of the walls had fallen into the building, and saplings had rooted in both the resultant mounds of rubble and the remaining walls. Before the launch of the Trust Wilf Davies had had the worst of the debris cleared away by young offenders from a local approved school; through his work with the National Park he had contact with many institutions and public bodies, and then and later was able to call on junior soldiers from Crickhowell, Venture Scouts and other youth organisations to help keep the space clear for visitors and pilgrims.

Picture 44: The abbey church ruins in 1965

In April 1965 – again, before the Trust came into being – the Apparitions statue was brought back from Hereford and installed in a welcoming position on the 'Monks' Level', where it remains to this day. When this was suggested Fr Windle expressed concern that difficulties might arise if a future owner of the monastery should turn out to be unsympathetic to the memory of Fr Ignatius and of the Apparitions. This danger was averted by declaring the statue a possession of the Trust rather than of the Davies family; at the same time (early 1969) the Trust assumed responsibility for the Calvary, and Fr Windle – sole survivor of its original trustees – was co-opted to the new body. A few years later the Calvary was restored and set in a new stone base. The plaque on the front was still in position, although the photograph on the back had long since disappeared.

With the launch of the Trust came an appeal for funds. This had the backing of a number of distinguished individuals, including John Betjeman, Ignatius's biographers Donald Attwater and Arthur Calder-Marshall, and the Bishops of Llandaff (Glyn Simon) and Swansea and Brecon (J.J.A. Thomas), whose names were appended to a letter published in The Times and the Church Times. Donations amounting to £160 were received in response, and with the aid of an anonymous loan the Trustees were able to undertake the tasks of capping the walls with cement and enclosing the Founder's grave with protective railings. At the same time repairs were carried out to the tiled surface of the grave, and stone chippings laid on the floor.

The appeal letter also mentioned a plan to establish a collection of photographs, manuscripts and other memorabilia, to be housed in a room at the monastery and made available to visitors. The largest item to be received at this time was the 'miraculous tabernacle', passed on from Dorian Herbert's estate by way of the museum store in Newport. Sadly shorn of its jewels, it was placed on a pile of stones where the high altar had once stood, and would quickly lose its enamelled decoration and what was left of its sparkle to the depredations of the Black Mountain climate.

Picture 45: First service in the restored abbey church: Eucharist for the
Society of St David, Summer 1970

A significant boost to this project was given by the involvement
of Douglas Lyne, a distant relative of Fr Ignatius, who as a young
soldier had been present at the destruction of St Benedict's abbey of
Monte Cassino in 1944. Watching the defenders of western Christian
civilisation destroying one of its principal monuments had had a
profound effect on him, and in middle age he became devoted to the
quest for international and interreligious reconciliation, of which
he saw the Trust as a potentially significant agent. When in 1969 he
attended the commemoration of the 25th anniversary of the battle
in the restored abbey church at Cassino he presented its Abbot with
a symbolic gift on behalf of the Trustees. This was the decorative
centrepiece of the tiling on Fr Ignatius's tomb, whose shattered
remains had been painstakingly reassembled and mounted by the
boys of St Thomas More's School in Norwich.

Douglas was appointed Archivist to the Trust, and succeeded in
gathering numerous items for the collection. The 1969 Newsletter
singled out 'two substantial unpublished accounts of Fr Ignatius by
contemporaries, a complete set of his periodical *The Monastic Times*

[and] the allegedly "miraculous" crucifix',[727] as well as numerous books, pamphlets and photographs. At Douglas's behest a large portrait in oils of Fr Ignatius was restored and presented to the Trust by a prominent representative of British Jewry, Mr Edward A. Kanter, in recognition of Ignatius's enthusiastic support for the Zionist cause. Today it hangs in his former cell in the west wing, now the sitting room for one of the holiday flats, on loan with certain other items to the present owners of the monastery.

The ground floor room at the junction of the west and south wings (the guests' refectory, in monastic days) was given over to these new acquisitions, although apart from one large item (an example of the monastic bedspread, mentioned earlier; it was suspended from nails high up on one wall) it was found impossible to place any of the collection on permanent display. For some years a selection was arranged on screens and tables on the day of the annual pilgrimage: the exhibition had to share the adjacent 'long room' with tea, cake and often very damp pilgrims, which can't have done the more sensitive items much good.

At this time interest in Fr Ignatius seemed to be growing, stimulated to some extent by the publication in 1962 of The Enthusiast, Arthur Calder-Marshall's 'Enquiry into [Ignatius's] Life, Beliefs and Character', as its subtitle defined it. In October 1968 a group of Anglo-Catholics in Norwich organised a Requiem Mass to mark the sixtieth anniversary of his death. The sermon was preached by Fr Mountney, and an exhibition organised by Douglas Lyne: this included some of the material Calder-Marshall had assembled in the course of his research and which he had subsequently presented to the Norfolk Record Office, as well as items later added to the collection at the monastery. Both biographer and archivist were

---

[727] A photocopy John Spence/Brother Cuthbert's narrative made its appearance at the monastery at this time, but it is not known what other 'substantial account' the writer may have had in mind. All but one of the nine issues of MT were in a bound volume bearing the bookplate of Mr Ulett of Hereford and stamped with a presentation inscription by Mother Werburgh.

involved in the preparation of a television documentary on Ignatius entitled *No Ordinary Monk*, screened on BBC2 in May 1969, as in a small walk-on part was the present writer, whose association with the Trust began around this time.

CENTENARY CELEBRATIONS

THE FOCUS TOWARDS WHICH the work of the Trust was directed was the celebration of the centenary of Fr Ignatius's arrival at Capel-y-ffin, originally scheduled for the summer of 1970. For various reasons it was found more convenient to postpone this event until 5 August 1972, by a happy chance just a few days short of the centenary of the laying of the abbey church's foundation stone.

Picture 46: Pilgrims arriving for the Centenary celebrations, 5 August 1972. Fr Brocard Sewell in middle distance with two vested visitors; Wilfred Davies in right foreground looking out of the picture.

That afternoon, blessed by warm sunshine ('miraculously, in this dark summer', according to the report in the following week's *Tablet*), between three and four hundred people from several Christian denominations and none processed from Capel-y-ffin to the ruined abbey church for Solemn Evensong. Hymns both *en route* and in the abbey ruins were accompanied by the Abergavenny Borough Band, and halts made at the Calvary for the reading of a Gospel, and at the Apparitions statue for the chanting of the *Salve Regina*, led by monks from Belmont. The officiant was Fr Mountney, and the lessons read (from Brother David's Bible) by Douglas Lyne and Fr Windle. In the absence through sickness of the Bishop of Hereford the celebration was presided over by his assistant bishop, the Right Reverend W.A. Partridge, and the blessing given by Dom Augustine Morris, Abbot of Nashdom. He had, it will be recalled, as a young monk preached at the pilgrimage marking the centenary of Ignatius's birth in 1937. Accompanying him on this occasion was his aged *confrère* Dom Anselm Hughes, who as a young curate in 1913 had been served at Mass by the former Brother Dunstan (Thomas Bray), who had himself arrived at the monastery in the same year as the laying of the abbey church foundation stone.

Picture 47: Monastery Centenary, 5 August 1972: at the Calvary. Fr Mountney officiating, wearing Fr Ignatius's cope.

The service concluded with a sermon from Fr Brocard, who drew together a number of seemingly disparate strands in the monastery's history. Two men more different than Joseph Leycester Lyne and Eric Gill would be hard to imagine, but both in their different ways had laboured to create (in Gill's phrase) a 'cell of good living in the chaos of our world', and both had much to teach our present generation. Ecumenical sensitivities were respected by an absence of explicit reference to the Apparitions, although Marian hymns and prayers were included, and by the omission from the official programme of a celebration of the Eucharist. However, Mass that morning was said as usual in the north cloister chapel by Fr Brocard, who combined extreme political conservatism and loyalty to the unreformed Carmelite Rite with a liberal interpretation of certain aspects of his Church's doctrine and discipline – not only regarding contraception and the limits of papal authority, but also respecting admission of 'non-Catholics' to Holy Communion.

THE POPULAR RESPONSE to the centenary observance encouraged the Trustees to revive the pilgrimage as an annual event. Around seventy people came in 1973, and rather more in 1974 when Bishop Partridge returned as guest preacher. For the following year, 1975, three of the Trustees (Fr Brocard, Douglas Lyne and Hugh Allen) joined with others to organise an ecumenical celebration for the 800th anniversary of the Augustinian priory at old Llanthony. This took place on Saturday 30 August, when both officiant and preacher at Anglican Evensong in the ruined priory church were Roman Catholic Augustinian canons, Abbot Ambrose Whitehead and Prior Charles White of Bodmin Abbey. Around five hundred people attended the service, at which the Bishop of Monmouth (the Right Reverend Derrick Childs) presided and gave the Blessing, and the singing was led by the Newport Catholic Boys' Choir.

To preserve a link with Fr Ignatius and 'new' Llanthony the day began with an Anglican Eucharist at Capel-y-ffin, like Ignatius's 1872 Ascension Day celebration transferred on account of uncertain weather from an *ad hoc* outdoor altar to the little church by the bridge; fortunately the clouds had dispersed by the afternoon. This set a precedent for including such a service as a regular feature of the pilgrimage, which since 1976 has been done each year (with one exception) in St David's Church, Llanthony. Until 1992 it ran concurrently with a Catholic Mass in the monastery chapel, celebrated in the early years by Fr Brocard and later by Fr Stanley Luff.

For a few years in the late 1970s and early 1980s detailed arrangements for the pilgrimage were made by a committee of local clergy and others. Fr Francis was now Vicar of Llantilio Pertholey on the outskirts of Abergavenny and once again became involved with the pilgrimage, as did his neighbour the Reverend Peter Price, who as incumbent of Llanfihangel Crucorney and Cwmyoy was also responsible for the church at Llanthony, and the Reverend Hugh Broad who had succeeded Fr Mountney at All Saints, Hereford. The participation of local clergy helped to keep pilgrim numbers up, some of them bringing parties from their parishes which included choristers and servers. Attendance for several years hovered at around 80 to 100 in the afternoon, with 50 or 60 at the Eucharist in Llanthony and a dozen or so at the Mass in the monastery chapel.

CHANGE AND DECAY

IN THEIR 1975 NEWSLETTER (from the end of that decade an annual publication) the Trustees reported that the abbey church was 'now in good order as a place for open-air worship', although the sanctuary steps were in a poor state and it lacked a proper altar. The death that year of Fr Windle provided a suitable opportunity for this deficiency to be made good: in 1980, on the centenary of the first of the 1880 apparitions, a simple freestanding altar was consecrated in his memory by Bishop B.N.Y. Vaughan of Swansea and Brecon, the pilgrimage Eucharist that year taking place for the first and only time in the ruined church. To provide a level surface around it the uppermost three steps were removed, as were the many loose and broken tiles in the sanctuary and on the lower steps.

Picture 48: Apparitions Centenary, 30 August 1980: Bishop Vaughan of Swansea & Brecon flanked by Canon Ivor Davies and the Reverend Donald Francis. Clergy looking on from the right are the Reverend F.H. Mountney; the author, and the Reverend Hugh Broad of All Saints, Hereford. The server nearest the camera is Jeremy Dowding, later ordained and appointed a Trustee.

By this time it was becoming clear that maintaining the church in a useable state was going to involve the Trustees in a running battle with the forces of nature, which more often than not would have the upper hand. In the winter of 1976/77 masonry falls put it out of commission for the following summer, causing the relocation of the pilgrimage Evensong to Capel-y-ffin church. More masonry fell in 1983/84 and 1987/88, although on both these occasions the damage was repaired in time for the following summer's pilgrimage. By 1993 the Trustees had decided that the abbey ruin was too dangerous for public entry except by individuals doing so at their own risk. That year's Evensong took place on the level alongside the north cloister.

At every pilgrimage since then Capel-y-ffin church has been used, the procession to the monastery following on from it and prayers taking place at the Calvary, the Apparitions statue and at the door of the abbey church (or more recently inside it, the danger notwithstanding).

IN 1976 FR MOUNTNEY moved from Hereford to a continental chaplaincy. After a couple of years he returned to these shores, retiring from his trusteeship on relocating to far distant Norfolk in the early 1980s. By this time an additional clerical trustee had been appointed in the person of Canon Ivor Davies, who as Vicar of Hay-on-Wye with Llanigon also had responsibility for the church at Capel-y-ffin. While maintaining a critical stance towards Ignatius, the Apparitions and Anglo-Catholicism in general he had been a regular at the pilgrimage and supporter of the Trust since its earliest years. In the early 1990s it was decided that its business would be discharged more efficiently if one of its members were to serve as chairman for a term of years instead of rotating the office from one meeting to the next. Canon Davies served in this capacity from 1994 to 1999, conducting meetings with no-nonsense firmness laced with his characteristic dry wit, as well as contributing much unseen activity in the intervals between them.

Six decades of occupation by Eric Gill and his descendants came to an end in 1985 when Wilf and Helen Davies, their children now grown up and settled elsewhere, moved from the monastery to Abergavenny. The new owners were Stanley and Karol Knill, who with their son Andrew (himself a trustee since 1999, and Treasurer from the following year) have lived there ever since. Stanley was soon drawn into the affairs of the Trust. Elected a trustee in 1986, over the next 25 years his expertise in the field of building construction was to be tested in equal measure with his patience and perseverance, as schemes for restoring and reinforcing the walls of the ruined church were drawn up and submitted for approval to the relevant authorities, and grants to finance them applied for and obtained. It is sad that in spite of all this work the structure is still fundamentally insecure, and its future by no means clear.

Picture 49: Pilgrims at the Apparitions Statue, 20 August 2011

Wilf Davies continued to act as Trust secretary until 1992, and as a trustee and editor of the Newsletter until 2000. This had now grown from a single page of folded A4 to a publication three times that size, its appearance becoming more sophisticated under his successor in that role, local publisher Michael Woodward. From his retirement home in the house of his order at East Finchley Fr Brocard was no longer able to take an active part in the Trust affairs; however, co-incidentally with his withdrawal, the Reverend Stanley Luff, Catholic priest in Llandovery, began to be involved. Between his appointment as a trustee in 1986 and his sudden death six years later he made a number of significant contributions. These included the lengthy and carefully researched Newsletter articles to which allusion has already been made, as well as the organisation of a residential symposium at Belmont Abbey in 1991 and two study days at a country hotel owned by one of his parishioners.

On his move to Abergavenny Wilf Davies took most of the collection of archives and artefacts with him, initially storing them in his house in Park Street. In 1993 they were handed over to the local museum, its then curator Frank Olding being invited to join the Trustees. When in the early 2000s he moved to another job his successor Rachael Rogers took his place.

From half a dozen in the late 1970s and early 1980s membership of the Trust grew to ten in the 1990s and fifteen in 2015, since when two senior members have accepted 'emeritus' status. With the deaths of Stanley Luff (1992), Brocard Sewell (2000) and Ivor Davies (2005) it became so far as clerical representation was concerned exclusively Anglo-Catholic. The new generation of Trustees has been less reticent than their predecessors in promoting the cult of 'Our Lady of Llanthony', taking justifiable pride in the fact that although its following is not large (and is in fact not an exclusively Anglican event) theirs is the oldest Marian pilgrimage in the post-Reformation Anglican church.[728]

---

[728] Attestation of this was generously given in his sermon at the 1998 pilgrimage by Canon Peter Cobb, Master of the College of the Guardians of the Shrine of Our Lady of Walsingham, the post-Reformation history of which only began with the arrival of Alfred Hope Patten as incumbent of the parish in 1921.

APPENDIX 1

Baptisms at the Monastery

THE THIRD ORDER/ASSOCIATES' REGISTER[729] was also used to record baptisms administered in Ignatius's successive monastic houses. Sixty-two are listed altogether, of which the first twenty-three were in the chapel at Elm Hill; a number of the family names are recognisable from Third Order and other records.

The first baptisms took place within two months of the community's arrival. It is significant that they ceased abruptly when troubles began to engulf the establishment the following year, and perhaps also that the Superior signs himself 'Br' or 'Bro' Ignatius up to September 1864, and 'Father' Ignatius from the next entry two months later. By this time Gideon Ouseley was functioning as chaplain, and shared the duties with him.

Of the two males baptised at Laleham one was a postulant's brother and the other a postulant, as were a few of the early ones at Llanthony.

---

[729] Preserved at Prinknash Abbey

ELM HILL PRIORY, NORWICH

BIRTH	BAPTISM	NAME	PARENTS	SURNAME	OCCUPATION	ADDRESS	OFFIC: MINISTER
11 Feb 1864	26 March 1864	Eleanor	Charles & Eleanor	CROW	Upholsterer		Br Ignatius
5 Apr 1845	Do.	John Nathanael	Nathanael & Maria	WEEDING	Tailor		Do.
(age 20)	21 May 1864	Caroline Ellen	Stephen & Elizabeth	ARMES			Do.
(age 20)	Do.	Augusta	Mary Ann	LIDDELOW			Do.
(age 16)	Do.	Eliza	Edward & Sarah	CARTER			Do.
(age 12)	Do.	Charles	Chas & Rachael	SCOTT			Do.
13 Jan 1799	30 May 1864	Robert	Robt & Sarah	LIDDELOW	Farmer		Do.
27 Dec 1846	23 June 1864	Edward Alban	David & Mary	WYATT	Tailor		Do.
27 May 1864	24 June 1864	Albert Ignatius	William George & Ann Charlotte	GOLDSPINK	Accountant		Gideon J.R. Ouseley

BIRTH	BAPTISM	NAME	PARENTS	SURNAME	OCCUPATION	ADDRESS	OFFIC: MINISTER
(age 3½)	28 July 1864	Emily Miriam Elizabeth	William & Sophia Rachel	D'ALBERG	Artist		Bro Ignatius
9 Nov 1863	3 Aug 1864	Earnest [sic] Edmund	James & Naomi	PERRY	Weaver		Gideon J. Ouseley
1 Jan 1862	20 Aug 1864	John Henry Ignatius	Emily Sarah & Joel	DOCKING	Builder		Bro Ignatius
8 Sept 1848	26 Sept 1864	Mary Ann	Paul & Harriet(?)	ROWNDREE	Weaver		Bro Ignatius
9 Apr 1854	22 Nov 1864	Amelia	Frederick & Amelia	WOODARD	Shoemaker		Father Ignatius
29 Jan 1857	Do.	Elvira	Do.	Do.	Do.		Do.
27 Sept 1861	Do.	Emily	Do.	Do.	Do.		Do.
?	Do.	Frederick	Do.	Do.	Do.		Do.
6 Jan 1857	Do.	Esther	Benjamin & Mary Anne	DRUMMEE	Fishmonger		Do.
24 Feb 1848	22 Mar 1865	Anna	Benjamin	BALLS	Carpenter		Rev G. Ouseley
28 Dec 1847	Do.	Elizabeth	John	MASE	Warehouseman		Do.

Date of birth	Date of baptism	Name	Parents	Surname	Occupation	Address / Place	Minister
17 Oct 1851	15 April 1865	Mary Ann	John & Mary Ann	HARDY	Weaver		Do.
? Nov 1849	Do.	Eliza	Matthew & Elizabeth	JOHNSON	Shoemaker		Do.
25 Oct 184?	25 April 1865	Mary Henrietta	John Thos & Mary	CLARKE	Druggist	Norwich	Gideon J. Ouseley

LALEHAM PRIORY

Date of birth	Date of baptism	Name	Parents	Surname	Occupation	Address / Place	Minister
25 Mar 1868		Adeline Ethelburga		RICH (Independent)			Ignatius
26 Jan 1833	6 Jan 1869	Emily	Henry & Eve Lipman	PLATNAUER (Jewess)		73 Clarence Rd, Bow	Ignatius
5 Mar 1866	Ascension Day 1869	Alfred Augustin	William & ?	WICKING	Pianoforte Maker	98 Holly St, Dalston NE	Ignatius
6 July 1869		Alfred		GRIFFITHS (aged 16)			Ignatius

LLANTHONY ABBEY

BIRTH	BAPTISM	NAME	PARENTS	SURNAME	OCCUPATION	ADDRESS	OFFIC: MINISTER
	24 Dec 1871	John		SPENCE (Quaker)		Lendal, York	Ignatius
23 Sept 1875	6 Oct 1875	Daniel Michael	Henry & Winifred	WILLIAMS	Labour[er]	Wanderers	Ignatius
10 Apr 1865 at Saltry	2 Sept 1877	Mary	James & Sarah Ann	WATKINS		Maes-y-ffin	Ignatius OSB
(adult)	28 Apr 1878	William		CHENOWETH		(Torquay)	Do.
20 Aug 1878	25 Sept 1878	Myra Ann	Stephen & Alice	DAVIES	Haulier	Hay, Brecon	Do.
15 July 1878	28 Oct 1878	Ada Jane Agnes	Frank Thomas & Jane	ULETT	Market Gardener	Hereford	Do.
14 Feb 1880	2 Aug 1880	Alice Cecilia Etheldreda	Frank Thomas & Jane	ULETT	Greengrocer	Hereford	Do.

7 Aug 1848	4 June 1881	George Augustine	James & Mary	WATKINS	(Farmer)	Talsarn, Capel-y-ffin	Do.
23 Apr 1865 at Tyrewen	23 Oct 1881	William David	David & Ann	PRITCHARD	Farmer	Tyrewen, Cwmyoy Upper	Do.
??? at Tyrewen	8 March 1882	Priscilla Winifred	Do.	Do.	Do.	Do.	Do.
27 Feb 1882	9 July 1882	Lewis John	George Augustine & Amelia	WATKINS	(Farmer)	Talsarn, Capel-y-ffin	Do.
7 Feb 1876	24 Sept 1882	William Morgan	Edward & Mary	BOWEN		Do.	Do.
26 Aug 1882	11 Jan 1883	Frank Ethelbert Dunstan Bede	Frank Thos Albert & Jane	ULETT	Greengrocer	Hereford	Do.
16 May 1882	26 Aug 1883	Emma Blanche	Lewis & Mary	WATKINS	Farmer	Chapel House, Capel-y-ffin	Do.
Do.	7 July 1883	Lewis John	Do.	Do.	Do.	Do.	Do.

BIRTH	BAPTISM	NAME	PARENTS	SURNAME	OCCUPATION	ADDRESS	OFFIC: MINISTER
27 Sept 1870	30 Aug 1883	Edward James	Edward & Mary	BOWEN	Goods Guard	Neath	Do.
?	5 April 1885	David Cadoc		JONES			Do.
7 Jan 1884	27 Sept 1885	Cosmas James	George Augustine & Amelia	WATKINS		The Wain, Capel-y-ffin	Do.
25 April 1885	Do.	Damian Arthur Charles	Do.	Do.		Do.	Do.
19 Nov 1885	24 Oct 1886	David James	Mary & Lewis	WATKINS	Farmer	Chapel House, Capel-y-ffin	Do.
1 July 1879	29 May 1887	John Iltud	Phoebe & George	GORST		1 Church St, Hay	Do.
11 Feb 1881	Do.	Margaret Winifred	Do.	Do.		Victoria, Ebbw Vale	Do.
5 Feb 1860	9 Oct 1887	Phoebe Theonia	Jane James	WATKINS PRITCHARD		Tal-y-sarn	Do.

? Sept 1873	Do?	Elizabeth Gwladys	Sarah & Joseph	JONES		Blaen Bwch	Do.
15 Sept 1877	30 May 1889	Caradoc Ifor Daniel	John & Ellen	ROWLANDS		Tyn-lon-isaf, Pen-morfa, Tremadoc	Brother George, priest
6 Aug 1890	6 Sept 1890	Jemima Smith	Joseph & Miriam	BRIDGES		(Travelling)	Edward Hudson Edman, Rector of Thornton-le-Moss, Lincs
7 Feb 1888	8 Oct 1891	William Iltyd David	George & Amelia	WATKINS	Farmer	The Wain, Capel-y-ffin	Ignatius OSB
14 Jan 1893	2 April 1893	Leycester Dewi William	William David & Thomasina E.M.	Pritchard by birth; assumed name LYNE Feb 1892	Steward of Maes-y-ffin & Llanthony Abbey	Maes-y-ffin, Llanthony	Do.
24 Nov 1897	6 Jan 1898	Josephine Mary Thomasina Lucy Gwendoline	William David & Thomasina Eliza Mary	LYNE	Steward of Llanthony Abbey &c	Maes-y-ffin	Do.

BIRTH	BAPTISM	NAME	PARENTS	SURNAME	OCCUPATION	ADDRESS	OFFIC. MINISTER
24 Dec 1897	13 Feb 1898	Arthur James	Joseph Henry & Mary Jane	GIBBONS	Shepherd	Brychan, Capel-y-ffin	Do.
29 Apr 1898	29 May 1898	Thomas Reginald	John & Eliza Anne	PRITCHARD	Farmer	New House, Cwmyoy Upper	Do.
27 July 1865	?? 1902	John Patrick	John & Margaret	MACCULLUM	Plate Layer	Abersychan	Do.
15 Nov 1887	?? (same as following?)	Cyril Arundel Innes	Neville Alexander Innes & Agnes Harriett (Lyne)	GIBBS	Engineer	Mussoorie, Himalayas, India	Do.
15 Oct 1886	27 Dec 1903	Neville Ernest Innes	Do.	Do.	Do.	Do.	Do.
19 Nov 1859	21 July 1907	George David	John & Catherine	WARBURTON	Engine Driver	Plymouth	Do.

Later Life of the Infant Oblate

I N ADULT LIFE John Henry Docking would rewrite his early history, inventing a fictitious adoptive family and editing out any reference to Ignatius and his monastery. After his death in February 1947 a lengthy obituary was published in the daily newspaper serving the part of New York State where he had lived for some years – composed, it is said, by his much younger widow. Part of it runs as follows:

He was born in Norwich, England on January 1, 1862. At the age of two, while his father was in Australia his mother died and he was adopted by a neighbouring family and separated from his brothers and sisters. At a tender age he became determined to find his father who was a brick mason and a champion bicycle rider and see the world. He started out one day but was caught and taken back.

He was nine when his adopted parents apprenticed him on the ship 'The Ellora' which carried cargoes from the Indies, both East and West to England.... The round trip from England to India and the Indies required close to 18 months.

The sailors on these trips never knew the taste of bread or vegetables, the main part of their diet being salted horse meat and hard biscuits which at times were wormy. The fresh water allowance was three quarts daily for drinking, cooking and washing.... Ship coffee was minus milk and sugar.

The ship carried six apprentices divided between the first and second watches, attending the officer on duty and shortening or trimming sail as was necessary. They received lessons in navigation from the officers, and from the old time sailors learned obedience, fearlessness and respect for their elders.[730]

Details of shipboard life are doubtless authentic, though he would have first experienced them at fourteen rather than at nine. (Nautical coffee sounds very much like the variety served for the morning 'pittance' at Llanthony, so that detail at least goes back a bit further.) He claimed to have been present in Calcutta when the Prince of Wales (later Edward VII) arrived there early on his grand tour of India; as this was a clear six months before the beginning of his apprenticeship — Edward was welcomed to Calcutta with considerable displays of patriotic fervour on 23 December 1875 — he may in old age have got muddled up between things he had seen himself and things he had been told by senior shipmates.

The growing boy obviously felt the lack of father, family and 'normal' childhood, and the invented version was doubtless easier to explain than the extraordinary reality. The description of his father as a 'champion bicycle rider' may or may not have come from his imagination, but that source must have been responsible for at least some of the five shipwrecks he claimed to have suffered, as well as the visits to a plantation-owning relative in the 'interior of India':

On these visits he was in contact with old Indians who taught him the language and showed him many of the mysteries which proved useful to him while aboard. These people of India had implicit trust in the boy and he was not only able to calm their fears in a bad storm but listened to their complaints and often settled their disputes.

---

[730] *The Daily News*, Batavia NY: report dated 'Monday evening February 17, 1947'. For information about his life in the USA I am indebted to Bernie Wright (Docking's grandson by his third marriage) and his wife Debbie of Alexandria, VA.

Young Docking was certainly in India in April 1878, when Ignatius noted that he wrote 'very lovingly' from the Subcontinent. In the summer of 1882 (now aged 20) he came back to visit his erstwhile spiritual father, and the two of them seem to have gone on holiday together to an (unspecified) 'isolated part of the country', where with the aid of Lourdes water Ignatius effected the healing of a young Roman Catholic.[731] This brief idyll came to an unhappy end, however: in the Register the last we hear of the former Oblate is this laconic entry:

1882 Came home robbed me of £10 went back to Edinburgh got married.

The marriage was solemnised on 17 February 1882 at 4 North Elliot Street, South Leith, by the local Church of Scotland minister, the Reverend James Mitchell.[732] His bride was Margaret Ann Macintosh Macpherson McDougall, born on 15 December 1860 at Dingwall (Ross-shire) to a coachman named Alexander McDougall and his wife Janet (Jessie) McDonald. Eight days earlier Margaret (known as Maggie) had given birth to their first child, a girl they registered in the name of Jessie Elizabeth Genevieve – the last presumably (and slightly surprisingly) in memory of Fr Ignatius's mother.

All was not straightforward, however. The young husband and father gave his name not as John Henry Docking but as Harry Johnson, and those of his parents as Henry William Johnson and Elizabeth Lamb. A second child (Donald William John Henry, always known as Daniel) was born on 24 December 1883; even if for the time being the former Oblate was concealing his real name part of it was preserved in two of the child's Christian names.

---

[731] Bertouch p496

[732] At this date marriages in Scotland were routinely conducted in the family home. I am grateful to Colin Affleck for this detail, as well as for information about this first marriage and subsequent events.

On 26 May 1886 little Jessie died from the effects of measles. Earlier that month the records had been altered and 'Harry Johnson' resumed his true identity, following depositions (now lost) made by both John Henry and his father Joel, who seems to have re-entered his life at this point. His American obituary agrees that their reunion took place in Edinburgh, claiming that it was 'through a strange coincidence'. Soon after this the family crossed the Atlantic,[733] presumably to join Grandfather Joel and perhaps also John Henry's elder brother Richard, who like his father is known to have been working as a bricklayer in San Francisco in 1883 (he had been following the same trade in Oregon three years earlier).

Maggie and Daniel didn't stay long in America. Within a couple of years the marriage seems to have run into the sand, and mother and son returned to Edinburgh.[734] In the 1900 US census (to anticipate a little way) John Henry claims to have been married to his next wife (born Harriet Morgan) for ten years, which means he must have detached himself from Maggie and remarried (bigamously or otherwise) in 1890 or thereabouts. This is confirmed by that of 1930, where he claims to have been 28 at the time of his 'first' (in fact second) marriage.

When he signed his daughter's death certificate in May 1886 John Henry was still giving his occupation as 'Chief Mate, Merchant Service'. According to his obituary he also fitted in spells logging

---

[733] Mrs J.H. Docking and Master D. Docking are recorded as having arrived in New York on 5 July 1887 on a ship named the *Colon*. According to the Obituary Docking's 'last voyage' (from Swansea to San Francisco, but including an unscheduled rounding of the South African cape) took nearly six months and ended with him bringing the ship 'safely... through the Golden Gate and home to his Father'. Perhaps this happened before Maggie and Daniel were also on American soil for him to come home to?

[734] Daniel (who died in 1955 having fathered 13 children of whom nine survived into adulthood) knew that he had travelled from San Francisco to Edinburgh as a small boy. Maggie died on 11 September 1898 (four days before her 38th birthday); her death certificate describes her (incorrectly) as a widow.

in Canada, diamond trading in South Africa and gold prospecting in Alaska and South America as well as in the western parts of the USA; it was on one of these expeditions that a discovery was made which significantly altered the course of his life. A 75th birthday newspaper interview explains it as follows:

> While prospecting in New Mexico with two other men he discovered a peculiar walled-in place on a cliff. 'We opened it up,' he explained with a note of excitement in his voice, 'and found five mummies. They weren't Indian mummies either but had fine hair and light features. I later bought my partners' share and exhibited them throughout the country.' [735]

Ten years later the obituary gave a slightly different version, and identified them as of Aztec origin:

> Although Mr Docking discovered the mummies, he allowed his prospecting partners to share in them. His desire to own them was realized when his father bought out the partners and gave their interests to him. Together the father and son toured the country, displaying the collection of mummies.[736]

In 1887 Joel published a pamphlet with the impressive title *Naturally Mummified Aztecs. A Narrative of Their Wonderful Discovery, Together with an Historical Sketch of the Race* in which the discovery is credited to unnamed 'hardy prospectors', and the press carried suggestions that 'Professor' Joel Docking was thinking of presenting them to one of the great scientific institutions in Europe or America. History doesn't relate what eventually became of them, although the *Catalog*

---

[735] Unidentified press cutting hand-dated 'Jan 12, 1937', supplied by Bernie & Debbie Wright.

[736] Obituary previously cited.

of the Smithsonian Institution includes a 'Photograph of Ancient Aztec Mummy No. 3' said to have been created by Maggie Docking on 16 June of that year.[737]

This experience of travelling showmanship (carried on as his Obituary puts it 'in many large theaters and gaining much fame') stood him in good stead for his next career move. Some time before 1900 (perhaps as early as 1890, if the Obituary is to be believed) he had been taken on by the important theatrical impresario Sylvester Z. Poli as assistant manager of his establishment in New Haven, Connecticut. After a brief spell as its resident manager he moved to a similar job in Scranton, Pennsylvania, in 1907.

In New Haven John and Harriet Docking lived in the suburb of Allingtown, where he served as one of the three members of the local school committee. As middle age drew on he became an enthusiastic devotee of various Masonic and other benevolent organisations, attaining the 32nd degree of Masonry and an honoured position in the Benevolent and Protective Order of Elks.[738]

In 1915 John Henry retired on grounds of ill health. He and Harriet relocated to the small town of LeRoy in New York state, not far from her home town of Pavilion and famous as the birthplace of the popular American dessert 'Jell-O'. Here again he was a pillar of the community, joining the First Presbyterian Church and the Knights of Pythias as well as keeping up his membership of the Elks and Masons. After Harriet's death he married 27-year-old Edna Tutchell on 12 June 1919 (he was then 57), and fathered two children.

In LeRoy Docking was a member of the local (volunteer?) police force, and tried his hand at farming (did he remember his childhood encounter with the lamb?). In old age he took on the job of janitor at the village hall, where for some obscure reason he was known

---

[737] Probably a misprint for July, which is the date given for two other mummy photographs by Maggie held at Harvard University (Information from Colin Affleck).

[738] Details from Colin Affleck and from the Obituary previously cited

not as Docking but as Rocking.[739] He died at home on 11 February 1947 and was buried in the family plot at Machpelah Cemetery. The service was conducted by the Minister Emeritus of First Presbyterian, with assistance from various Elks and Masons.

---

[739] 1937 press cutting previously cited

APPENDIX 3

The Monastery Children

THIS EXTRACT FROM THE *Western Mail* of Monday 29 August 1898 provides an insight into the distinctive Llanthony piety, as well as shedding a little light on the boys who were in residence at the time (see Chapter 11). 'Little Brother Placidus' is Norton Rhys and 'Jack' almost certainly Jack Clark. The 'monk' in each of the anecdotes is doubtless Ignatius himself, and the unnamed child in the final two probably Lessie. An early version of the account of his disobedience over the strawberry was pencilled into one of the blank pages at the beginning of the abbatial *Churchman's Family Bible*, without the subsequent conversation over the washbasin but with the variation that it made 'our Lord Jesus sorry, and me too'. The date given for it there is 20 July 1897, when Lessie was just 4½.

CHILDREN OF LLANTHONY MONASTERY:
Their Views on the Moral Government of the World

Father Ignatius sends us the following interesting account of some of the young members of his little community at Llanthony:–

Last week there was a terrible thunderstorm in the Vales of Ewyas; the monks and monastery children were out in it. They were soaked through with the rain. The thunder was so terrific it seemed to shake the ground. A monk overheard the following:– Little Brother Placidus, an oblate child of seven years, in his white habit and tonsured head, said very solemnly, but calmly, to a bright, curly-headed little acolyte of five, 'Lessie, I think blessed Jesus is going to kill us.' 'I don't,' said Lessie, 'we are too good to Him in church.'

478

This same 'Lessie' had a word of consolation for another boy in the monastery named 'Jack', aged six, who had a sore finger, which a monk had tied up with wet rag and oilskin. He had knocked it, and was crying. 'Lessie' was soothing him – 'Don't cry, Jack; think how blessed Jesus had a nail right through His hand for us, and you'll be better.'

But some time ago this same Lessie was taken into the garden to pick strawberries for tea. He was told by the monk who took him that he might eat some. But when he had eaten enough the monk said, 'No more, Lessie,' but Lessie had a large, ripe one, just ready to put in his mouth; so Master Lessie said, 'Just this one,' and popped it in his mouth. So the monk said, 'Now, you've been disobedient; you must come in – you know what God says in the Bible about disobedience.' Quite lately there had been a Bible lesson about the disobedience of our first parents, and how by it they had brought the curse upon us all – the animals became savage and wild, the monstrosities of thorns came upon many plants – and evil grew everywhere, through the power of Satan. Nothing more was said till after tea, and when the monk took Lessie's hand to take him to the lavatory to 'tidy him up' for church, Lessie, who had been thinking of that last strawberry all tea-time evidently, said, looking up in the monk's face very seriously, 'Do you think that my taking that strawberry has made the wild beasts more savage?' 'No,' said the monk, 'but I am sure it made blessed Jesus sorry, and made Satan glad.'

Many most interesting anecdotes could be told of these children, showing how they take in and apply among themselves the Bible stories and stories from the lives of the saints which they hear.

One day one of the children had been careless in his manner on the altar steps when the Holy Sacrament was exposed at Benediction. Someone said to him, 'I wonder you are not afraid to behave so; you know what our Lord Jesus could do to you if he likes.' The five-year-old child answered, 'Oh, I'm not at all afraid of him; I know how he loves me.' 'Well, then,' was the answer, 'you ought to behave all the more reverently.'

We always sing Psalm cx at Vespers on Sunday. Some Sundays ago a little boy said to a monk, 'What are the places that Jesus will fill with the dead bodies?' and 'Why will He smite in sunder the heads over divers countries?' which led the monk to give the child an account of the coming battle of Armageddon, in which he was deeply interested. 'But I shall be caught up with the saints to meet the Lord in the air, shan't I?' said the same child!

PICTURE CREDITS

U NLESS OTHERWISE STATED photographs are from the Father Ignatius collection at Abergavenny Museum, reproduced by kind permission of the Curator. Pictures 46 and 47 from this collection are the work of the late Oswald Jones.

The picture on the front cover is reproduced by kind permission of Devon Archives and Local Studies Service (document reference PD058616), and Edgar Holloway's woodcut of the monastery by that of his widow, Mrs Jennifer Holloway.

Other illustrations have been provided by the following, whose kind permission is hereby acknowledged:

5	Bernie and Debbie Wright, grandson and granddaughter-in-law of the former Infant Oblate
21	Philip Chatfield, Consultant to the Father Ignatius Memorial Trust
18	Baden Chawkley, grandson of the subject
23	Paula Drinkall
36	Janet Cribb, whose mother is one of the subjects
37	National Portrait Gallery (ref x12007)
38	© The Estate of David Jones; image courtesy of Lund Humphries, publishers of *The Art of David Jones: Vision and Memory* (2015)
39 & 41	Dr Peter Davies
40	Rt Revd Fr Abbot OSB, Prinknash Abbey
43	Mary Pepler, whose father Stephen (Betty's eldest son) took the photograph.

Pictures 2, 7, 20 (photographic original of the diagram on p256), 44 and 49 were taken by the author, and 48 on his camera by a third party.

INDEX OF PERSONS & PLACES

Persons mentioned by name in the text and footnotes are listed below, with the following exceptions:

- Fr Ignatius (Rev Joseph Leycester Lyne);
- those listed in the acknowledgments sections at the beginning and end of the book;
- authors and sources cited in footnotes (except for those who have provided information directly to the author).

References to Ignatius's biographers (de Bertouch, Attwater and Calder-Marshall) are listed only when they figure in a personal capacity (eg Attwater as an occupant of the former monastery). No account has been taken of names occurring only in the record of Baptisms in Appendix 2.

Members of Ignatius's community are indexed by name in religion. Where a person's secular name is known this appears in brackets after the religious name; this is also given in the alphabetical sequence with a cross reference to the name in religion. Repeated instances of the bestowal of the same name are numbered consecutively (Cadoc 1, Cadoc 2; Placidus 1, Placidus 2 etc).

Associates (including the resident Abbey Priests) and members of the Third Order appear by secular name, where known, with a cross reference to the religious name. The letters TO after a religious name are used to distinguish members of the Third Order from those of the resident community.

Members of other monastic communities are identified by the inclusion of the names of their monasteries after their own names, eg

McElligott, Dom Bernard (Ampleforth).

All but the largest British towns and cities are listed with county names. As the greater part of this narrative is set in the period before the local government reorganization of 1974 the older county designations have been preferred.

'New Llanthony Abbey' was situated at Capel-y-ffin, some four miles from 'old' Llanthony; index references to 'Llanthony' are all to the latter. Occurrences of the name Capel-y-ffin (and its diminutive 'Capel') have not been listed.

A

H

Y